SCC

Taking Sides:
Clashing Views in
World History, Vol. 2, 4/e

**Helen Buss Mitchell**
**Joseph R. Mitchell**

http://create.mcgraw-hill.com

ISBN-10: 0078133254    ISBN-13: 9780078133251

# Contents

# Preface

In *Taking Sides: Clashing Views in World History*, we provide context and depth for understanding the issues that are typically covered in the study of world history, using scholarly and readable sources that argue these issues. We have chosen topics that reflect current historical scholarship, as well as the complex world of race, class, and gender in which historical events occur. Many issues can be related to other issues in various ways. A Topic Guide offers the instructor opportunities to compare/contrast issues with like/unlike content and explore relationships across time, geographic, and cultural boundaries. What are the roots of revolutions and genocides? How do ideologies and worldviews shape trade negotiations as well as decisions about war or peace? Our goal is to assist instructors and students in acquiring enhanced skills in critical thinking.

## Book Organization

This reader is arranged in three sections, each reflecting a time period in world history. Each issue begins with *Learning Outcomes* that preview the Issue Question for the student before moving into an *Introduction* that sets the stage for the debate as it is argued in the YES and NO selections that follow. Each issue concludes with *Exploring the Issue*. There are questions for *Critical Thinking and Reflection* that point the way to other considerations related to the issue and a section that asks: *Is There Common Ground?* In reading the issue and forming your own opinions, you should not feel confined to adopt one or the other of the positions presented. There are positions in between the given views or totally outside them, and the *Additional Resources* section that concludes each issue should help you find print, visual, Internet, and other sources to continue your study of the subject. At the end of each selection is a brief biography of the *Contributors* that will give you information on the historians and commentators whose views are debated here.

## Using the Book

**A word to the instructor** An *Instructor's Resource Guide with Test Questions* (multiple choice and essay) is available through the publisher for the instructor using *Taking Sides* in the classroom. A general guidebook, *Using Taking Sides in the Classroom*, which discusses methods and techniques for integrating the pro–con approach into any classroom setting, is also available. An online version of *Using Taking Sides in the Classroom* and a corresponding service for *Taking Sides* adopters can be found at www.mhhe.com/createcentral.

Helen Buss Mitchell
*Howard Community College*

Joseph R. Mitchell
*Howard Community College*

## Editors of This Volume

JOSEPH R. MITCHELL was a history instructor at Howard Community College in Columbia, Maryland, and is a popular, regional speaker. He coauthored a history of the planned city of Columbia, *New City upon a Hill* (The History Press, 2006). He received an MA in history from Loyola University in Maryland and an MA in African American history from Morgan State University, also in Maryland. He is the principal-coeditor of *The Holocaust: Readings and Interpretations* (McGraw-Hill, 2001) and *Taking Sides: Western Civilization* (McGraw-Hill, 2000).

HELEN BUSS MITCHELL is a professor of philosophy and the director of the Women's Studies Program at Howard Community College in Columbia, Maryland. She is the author of *Roots of Wisdom: A Tapestry of Philosophical Traditions*, 7th ed., and *Readings from the Roots of Wisdom*, 3rd edition (Wadsworth/Cengage). *Roots of Wisdom* has twice been translated into Spanish and is currently being translated into Mandarin Chinese. She is also creator, writer, and host of a philosophy telecourse, *For the Love of Wisdom*, distributed nationally by Dallas/Telelearning. She has earned numerous degrees, including a PhD from the University of Maryland, College Park.

## Acknowledgments

We would like to thank Larry Madaras of Howard Community College—fellow teacher, good friend, coeditor of *Taking Sides: Clashing Views in American History*—for his past and present assistance in making our work possible. Special acknowledgment also goes to David Stebenne of Ohio State University—friend, scholar, teacher, and author of *Arthur Larson: Modern Republican* (Indiana University Press, 2006)—for his suggestions and advice. Our thanks also goes to the library staffs of Howard County, Maryland, University of Maryland, College Park, University of Maryland, Baltimore County (UMBC), and Howard Community College, particularly Ela Ciborowska, Susan Kirker, and Chart Chalungsooth who mined databases and interlibrary loan.

At McGraw-Hill, a debt of gratitude is owed to Senior Developmental Editor Jill Meloy, who guided us through the process of publishing this book, offering advice, support, and encouragement when they were most needed, and to DeAnna Dausener, who went to extraordinary length to secure permissions in a rapidly changing environment.

We dedicate this book to Jason, our first and finest collaboration.

**A final word** We would appreciate any questions or comments that you may have on our work, especially which issues work best in your classroom and which issues you never use. Please contact us at joemitch@bigjar.com. We will use this feedback in shaping future editions.

## Academic Advisory Board Members

Members of the Academic Advisory Board are instrumental in the final selection of articles for each edition of TAKING SIDES. Their review of articles for content, level, and appropriateness provides critical direction to the editor and staff. We think that you will find their careful consideration well reflected in this volume.

**Rafis Abazov**
*Columbia University/Hunter College*

**Dawn A. Dennis**
*Los Angeles Community College District*

**Ellen Emerick**
*Georgetown College*

**Michael Flores**
*Cypress College*

**Christopher J. Fuhrmann**
*University Of North Texas*

**Delia C. Gillis**
*University of Central Missouri*

**Gina Hames**
*Pacific Lutheran University*

**Aimee Harris-Johnson**
*El Paso Community College*

**Amy C. Hudnall**
*Appalachian State University*

**Laura Kamoie**
*US Naval Academy*

**Mary Kinchen**
*Georgia Military College—Valdosta*

**Keith Knuuti**
*Leeward Community College*

**Jessica Kovler**
*John Jay College*

**Michael McMackin**
*Blue Ridge Community College*

**Teresa Mushik**
*Empire State College*

**David D. Peck**
*Brigham Young University*

**Gwendollyn Ulrich-Schlumbohm**
*Mt. San Jacinto College*

**Lavanya Vemsani**
*Shawnee State University*

# Correlation Guide

The Taking Sides series presents current issues in a debate-style format designed to stimulate student interest and develop critical thinking skills. Each issue is thoughtfully framed with an issue summary, learning outcomes, an issue introduction, and an "Exploring the Issue" section with critical thinking questions and additional resources. The pro and con essays—selected for their liveliness and substance—represent the arguments of leading scholars and commentators in their fields.

Taking Sides: Clashing Views in World History, Volume 2: The Modern Era to the Present, 4/e is an easy-to-use reader that presents issues on important topics such as rulers, diplomacy, economics, ideology, wars, and revolutions. For more information on *Taking Sides* and other *McGraw-Hill Contemporary Learning Series* titles, visit www.mhhe.com/cls.

This convenient guide matches the issues in **Taking Sides: Clashing Views in World History, Vol. 2, 4/e** with the corresponding chapters in two of our best-selling McGraw-Hill World History textbooks by Bentley/Ziegler and Bentley et al.

| TAKING SIDES: World History, Vol. 2, 4/e | Traditions & Encounters: A Global Perspective on the Past, 5/e by Bentley/Ziegler | Tradition & Encounters: A Brief History, 3/e by Bentley et al. |
|---|---|---|
| Did the Industrial Revolution Lead to a Sexual Revolution? | Chapter 29: The Making of Industrial Society | Chapter 26: The Making of Industrial Society |
| Was the French Revolution Worth Its Human Costs? | Chapter 28: Revolutions and National States in the Atlantic World | Chapter 25: Revolutions and National States in the Atlantic World |
| Does Napoleon Bonaparte Deserve His Historical Reputation as a Great General? | Chapter 28: Revolutions and National States in the Atlantic World | Chapter 25: Revolutions and National States in the Atlantic World |
| Did British Policy Decisions Cause the Mass Emigration and Land Reforms That Followed the Irish Potato Famine of the 1840s and 1850s? | Chapter 29: The Making of Industrial Society | Chapter 26: The Making of Industrial Society |
| Did the Meiji Restoration Constitute a Revolution in Nineteenth-Century Japan? | Chapter 29: The Making of Industrial Society | Chapter 26: The Making of Industrial Society |
| Was Popular Opinion a Significant Ingredient in Nineteenth-Century British Imperialism? | Chapter 32: The Building of Global Empires | Chapter 28: The Building of Global Empires |
| Was China's Boxer Rebellion Caused by Environmental Factors? | Chapter 32: The Building of Global Empires | Chapter 28: The Building of Global Empires |
| Did Prussian Militarism Provoke World War I? | Chapter 33: The Great War: The World in Upheaval | Chapter 29: The Great War: The World in Upheaval |
| Was the Treaty of Versailles Responsible for World War II? | Chapter 33: The Great War: The World in Upheaval Chapter 34: An Age of Anxiety | Chapter 29: The Great War: The World in Upheaval |
| Did the Bolshevik Revolution Improve the Lives of Soviet Women? | Chapter 33: The Great War: The World in Upheaval | Chapter 29: The Great War: The World in Upheaval |
| Was German "Eliminationist Anti-Semitism" Responsible for the Holocaust? | Chapter 36: New Conflagrations: World War II and the Cold War | Chapter 32: New Conflagrations: World War II |
| Was Stalin Responsible for the Korean War? | Chapter 36: New Conflagrations: World War II and the Cold War | Chapter 33: The Cold War and Decolonization |
| Are Chinese Confucianism and Western Capitalism Compatible? | Chapter 38: A World Without Borders | Chapter 34: A World Without Borders |
| Was Ethnic Hatred Primarily Responsible for the Rwandan Genocide of 1994? | Chapter 38: A World Without Borders | Chapter 34: A World Without Borders |
| Does Islamic Revivalism Challenge a Stable World Order? | Chapter 38: A World Without Borders | Chapter 34: A World Without Borders |
| Have Afghan Women Been Liberated from Oppression? | Chapter 38: A World Without Borders | Chapter 34: A World Without Borders |
| Is the Influence of the European Union in World Affairs Increasing? | Chapter 38: A World Without Borders | Chapter 34: A World Without Borders |
| Is India's Secular Democracy Severely Threatened by Religious Nationalism? | Chapter 38: A World Without Borders | Chapter 34: A World Without Borders |
| Will the So-Called Arab Spring Benefit the Region? | | Chapter 34: A World Without Borders |

# Topic Guide

This topic guide suggests how the selections in this book relate to the subjects in your course. You may want to use the topics listed on these pages to search the web more easily.

**All issues, and their articles, that relate to each topic are listed below the bold-faced term.**

## Economics

Did the Industrial Revolution Lead to a Sexual Revolution?
Did the Bolshevik Revolution Improve the Lives of Soviet Women?
Are Chinese Confucianism and Western Capitalism Compatible?
Is the Influence of the European Union in World Affairs Increasing?
Will the So-Called Arab Spring Benefit the Region?

## Diplomacy

Did Prussian Militarism Provoke World War I?
Was the Treaty of Versailles Responsible for World War II?

## Economic

Did the Industrial Revolution Lead to a Sexual Revolution?
Did British Policy Decisions Cause the Mass Emigration and Land Reforms That Followed the Irish Potato Famine of the 1840s and 1850s?
Is the Influence of the European Union in World Affairs Increasing?

## Environment

Was China's Boxer Rebellion Caused by Environmental Factors?

## Genocide

Was German "Eliminationist Anti-Semitism" Responsible for the Holocaust?
Was Ethnic Hatred Primarily Responsible for the Rwandan Genocide of 1994?

## Historical Leaders

Does Napoleon Bonaparte Deserve His Historical Reputation as a Great General?
Was Stalin Responsible for the Korean War?

## Ideology

Did the Industrial Revolution Lead to a Sexual Revolution?
Did British Policy Decisions Cause the Mass Emigration and Land Reforms That Followed the Irish Potato Famine of the 1840s and 1850s?
Did the Meiji Restoration Constitute a Revolution in Nineteenth-Century Japan?
Was Popular Opinion a Significant Ingredient in Nineteenth-Century British Imperialism?
Was China's Boxer Rebellion Caused by Environmental Factors?
Was German "Eliminationist Anti-Semitism" Responsible for the Holocaust?
Are Chinese Confucianism and Western Capitalism Compatible?
Was Ethnic Hatred Primarily Responsible for the Rwandan Genocide of 1994?
Does Islamic Revivalism Challenge a Stable World Order?
Is the Influence of the European Union in World Affairs Increasing?
Is India's Secular Democracy Severely Threatened by Religious Nationalism?
Will the So-Called Arab Spring Benefit the Region?

## Military

Does Napoleon Bonaparte Deserve His Historical Reputation as a Great General?
Did Prussian Militarism Provoke World War I?
Was the Treaty of Versailles Responsible for World War II?
Was Stalin Responsible for the Korean War?

## Political Issues

Was the French Revolution Worth Its Human Costs?
Does Napoleon Bonaparte Deserve His Historical Reputation as a Great General?
Did British Policy Decisions Cause the Mass Emigration and Land Reforms That Followed the Irish Potato Famine of the 1840s and 1850s?
Did the Meiji Restoration Constitute a Revolution in Nineteenth-Century Japan?
Was Popular Opinion a Significant Ingredient in Nineteenth-Century British Imperialism?
Is India's Secular Democracy Severely Threatened by Religious Nationalism?
Will the So-Called Arab Spring Benefit the Region?

## Religion

Was China's Boxer Rebellion Caused by Environmental Factors?
Are Chinese Confucianism and Western Capitalism Compatible?
Is India's Secular Democracy Severely Threatened by Religious Nationalism?

## Revolutions

Was the French Revolution Worth Its Human Costs?
Did the Meiji Restoration Constitute a Revolution in Nineteenth-Century Japan?
Was China's Boxer Rebellion Caused by Environmental Factors?
Did the Bolshevik Revolution Improve the Lives of Soviet Women?
Does Islamic Revivalism Challenge a Stable World Order?
Will the So-Called Arab Spring Benefit the Region?

## War

Was the French Revolution Worth Its Human Costs?
Does Napoleon Bonaparte Deserve His Historical Reputation as a Great General?
Did Prussian Militarism Provoke World War I?
Was the Treaty of Versailles Responsible for World War II?
Was Stalin Responsible for the Korean War?
Have Afghan Women Been Liberated from Oppression?

## Women's Issues

Did the Industrial Revolution Lead to a Sexual Revolution?
Did the Bolshevik Revolution Improve the Lives of Soviet Women?
Have Afghan Women Been Liberated from Oppression?

# Introduction

## What Is History?

History is a dialogue between the past and the present. As we respond to events in our own world, we bring the concerns of the present to our study of the past. What seems important to us, where we turn our attention, and how we approach a study of the past—all these are rooted in the present. It has been said that where you stand determines what you see. This is especially the case with history. If we stand within the Western tradition exclusively, we may be tempted to see its story as the only story or the only one worth telling. And whose perspective we take is also critical. From the point of view of the rich and powerful, the events of history take one shape; through the lens of the poor and powerless, the same events can appear quite different. If we take women, or non-Western cultures, or the ordinary person as our starting point, the story of the past may present us with a series of surprises.

## Tools of the Historian

Much of the raw material of history consists of written sources. Original sources—from a period contemporary with the events or ideas described—are called *primary sources*. These may include documents of all kinds, including official records as well as personal letters and diaries. The writings of historians reflecting on the past are called *secondary sources*. It is important to keep in mind that primary sources may not automatically be assumed to be free from bias. Each contains historical and personal perspectives. Their principal limitation, however, is that they record what people considered noteworthy about their own age and not necessarily what would most interest us today. As the concerns of the present evolve, the questions we bring to our study of the past will also change. Much of what you read in this book will reflect differences in focus between one historian and another. As Edward Hallett Carr points out, the historian constructs a working model that enables him or her to understand the past. It would be a great mistake to confuse this working model with a photocopy.

## Traditional History

Only recently has history considered itself a social science and striven for a kind of scientific accuracy in speaking about the past. For much of human history, until perhaps the late nineteenth century, history was considered a branch of literature rather than a kind of science. It was concerned first of all with narrative, with the telling of a compelling story, and its focus was on the fascinating characters whose lives shaped and defined the past.

Biography, the recounting of the life and times of a powerful man, was regarded as one of the most reliable windows on the past. The so-called great man was credited with shaping and defining his own time. As a result, an influential historical figure was long assumed to offer one of the most reliable keys to unlocking a specific historical time period.

And, traditional history looked relatively uncritically at the great men from the past. Military heroes, for example, were lauded for their conquests with little or no focus on the carnage that made those conquests possible. Another unspoken assumption was the dominance and superiority of the West as the creator and bearer of human civilization. Divine power was sometimes seen as directing or, at least, approving the actions of powerful nations and men.

The traditional areas of focus for the historian have been political, diplomatic, and constitutional: Political history considers how power has been organized and enforced by the state within human societies. Diplomatic history looks at what has influenced the power struggles between states as they continually struggled for dominance. Constitutional history examines the evolution of national states with special attention to who rules and who or what confers the right to rule.

A related domain of the traditional historian has been that of intellectual history or the history of ideas—in the fields of politics, economics, sociology, theology, and science. Probing the power of world religions, understanding the ideological aspects of conflicts, examining the influence of a worldview on a nation's commercial enterprises—all these are the province of intellectual history. Taking this approach to its widest scope, one might explore the intellectual climate of an entire age, such as the Age of Revolutions, Imperialism, or the period of World Wars. Which ideas shaped and defined each of these distinct historical periods? And, what marked the change from one to another?

## Revisionism

However, history is not a once-and-for-all enterprise. Each generation formulates its own questions and brings new tools to the study of the past resulting in a process called revisionism. Much of what you will read in this book is a product of revisionism as historians reinterpret the past in the light of the present. One generation values revolutions, the next focuses on their terrible costs. One generation assumes that great men shape the events of history, the next looks to the lives of ordinary people to illuminate the past. There is no final answer, but where we stand will determine which interpretation seems more compelling to us. Some issues introduce the tension between traditional and revisionist interpretations of influential figures in world history.

As new tools of analysis become available, our ability to understand the past improves. Bringing events into clearer focus can change the meaning we assign to them. Many of the selections in this book reflect new attitudes and new insights made possible by the tools that historians have borrowed from other social sciences. For instance, finding and deciphering long-hidden manuscripts can shed new light on religious belief systems. And, physical artifacts can help us decode elements of language and culture as we examine explanations for the artifacts and architectural elements cultures have left behind or even causes for the collapse of their civilizations.

## Presentism

While we stand in the present, we must be wary of what historians call presentism, that is, reading the values of the present back into the past. If we live in a culture that values individualism and prizes competition, we may be tempted to see these values as good even in a culture that preferred communalism and cooperation. And, we may miss a key component of an ancient civilization because it does not match what we currently consider worthwhile. In defining the overall context, can the West acknowledge the role of non-Europeans in shaping the modern world? We cannot and should not avoid our own questions and struggles. They will inform our study of the past; and yet, they must not warp our vision. Ideally, historians engage in a continual dialogue in which the concerns but not the values of the present are explored through a study of the past.

At the same time, though, we might bring the moral standards of the present to bear on the past. Cultural relativism, pioneered in the field of anthropology, made us sensitive to the many and varied ways in which civilizations define what is "normal" and what is "moral." So, we remain appropriately reluctant to judge individuals from other times and places by our standards since they were or are, in fact, behaving perfectly normally and morally by the standards of their own time and place. However, from the perspective of the present, we do not hesitate to condemn slaveholding, genocide, or even the zealotry that leads to what the modern world calls "ethnic cleansing."

## Changing Historiographical Focuses

All cultures are vulnerable to the narrow mindedness created by ethnocentrism—the belief that my culture is superior to all others. From inside a particular culture, certain practices may seem normative—that is, we may assume that all humans or all rational humans should behave the way we do or hold the attitudes we hold. When we meet a culture that sees the world differently from ourselves, we may be tempted to write it off as inferior or primitive. As an alternative to ethnocentrism, we might want to enter the worldview of another and see what we can learn from expanding our perspective. These issues will offer you many opportunities to try this thought experiment.

Stepping outside the Western tradition has allowed historians to take a more globocentric view of world events. Accusing their predecessors of Eurocentrism, some historians have adopted a multicultural view of world history that explores, for example, the responses of indigenous peoples to imperialism. Questions about how civilizations begin and end can be of great relevance to modern peoples. Within the Western tradition, women have challenged the male-dominated perspective that studied war but ignored family. Including additional perspectives complicates our interpretation of past events but permits a fuller picture to emerge. We must be wary of universalism—assuming, for example, that patriarchy has always existed or that being a woman was the same for every woman no matter what her historical circumstances are. If patriarchy or the nuclear family has a historical beginning, then there was a time when some other pattern existed. If cultures other than the West have been dominant or influential during the past, what did the world look like under those circumstances?

## Social History

Some historians have moved beyond political, diplomatic, military, and constitutional history to explore economics and demographics as well as to study social processes. Moving from a focus on nations and rulers to a close examination of forces and structures that can be studied analytically has opened up the realms of business and the family to the historian. Proponents of the so-called new social history rejected what they called history from the top down. Instead of the great man whose influence shaped his age, they looked to the lives of ordinary people and called what they were doing history from the bottom up. The previous generation of historians, they claimed, had sometimes acted as if only the influential had a role in shaping history. Social history assumes that all people are capable of acting as historical agents rather than being passive victims to whom history happens. With this shift in attitude, the lives of slaves, workers, women of all kinds, and children, too, become worthy subjects of historical investigation.

Because the poor and powerless seldom leave written records, other methods must be used to understand their lives. Applying the methods of social scientists to their own discipline, historians have broadened and deepened their field of study. Archaeological evidence, DNA analysis, the tools of paleoanthropology, computer crunching of demographic data—all these have allowed the voiceless to speak across centuries. Fossil evidence, for instance, and the analysis of mitochondrial DNA—the structures within cells we inherit only from our mothers—may each be employed, sometimes with strikingly different results, to trace the migrations of pre-literate peoples.

What historians call material culture reveals the everyday lives of people by analyzing what they discarded as well as the monuments and other material objects they intended to leave as markers of their civilizations. At certain points in human history, owning a plow made the difference between merely surviving and having some surplus food to barter or sell. What people leave to their heirs can tell us how much or how little they had to brighten their lives while they lived. As we continue to dig, we may find our assumptions confirmed or denied by the fossils of once living organisms. Evidence of sea life on the top of a mountain lets us know that vast geologic changes have taken place. And, in another example, our genetic material has information we are just now learning to decode and interpret that may settle important questions of origin and migration as we learn to read the data locked inside our DNA.

The high-speed comparative functions of computers have allowed the historian to analyze vast quantities of data and look at demographic trends. How old are people when they marry for the first time, have a child, or die? Only with the expanded life expectancy made possible by the modern world has it been possible for people to see their children's children—to become grandparents. Looking at the time between marriage and the birth of a first child can help us calculate the percentage of pregnant brides and gain some insight into how acceptable or unacceptable premarital sex may have been in the context of an expected future marriage. If we study weather patterns and learn that certain years were periods of drought or that the glacier receded during a particular time period, we will know a little more about whether the lives of people who lived during these times were relatively easier or more difficult than those of their historical neighbors in earlier or later periods.

## Race, Class, and Gender

The experience of being a historical subject is never monolithic. That is, each of us has a gender, a race, a social class, an ethnic identity, a religion (even if it is atheism or agnosticism), an age, and a variety of other markers that color our experiences. At times, the most important factor may be my gender and what happens may be more or less the same for all members of a particular gender. Under other circumstances, however, race may be predominant. Being a member of a racial minority or of a powerful racial majority may lead to very different experiences of the same event. At other times social class may determine how an event is experienced; the rich may have one story to tell, the poor another. And, other factors, such as religion or ethnic identity, even age, can become the most significant piece of a person's identity, especially if prejudice or favoritism is involved. Historians try always to take into account how race, class, and gender (as well as a host of other factors) intersect in the life of a historical subject.

## Issues Involved in Historical Interpretation

Often historians will agree on what happened but disagree about why or how something occurred. Sometimes the question is: Were internal or external causes more responsible? Both may have contributed to an event but one or the other may have played the more significant role.

Looking at differing evidence may lead historians to varying interpretations. Similarly, historians ponder whether an empire fell because of internal weaknesses or external pressures. A related question is: Was it the circumstances that changed or only the attitudes of those who experienced them? If we find less protest, for instance, can we conclude that things have gotten better or only that people have found a way to accommodate themselves to a situation beyond their control

## Periodization

Even more basically, the student of the past must wonder whether the turning points that shape the chapters in our history books are the same for all historical subjects. The process of marking turning points is known as periodization. It is the more or less artificial creation of periods that chunk history into manageable segments by identifying forks in the road that took people and events in a new direction. Using an expanded perspective, we may learn that the traditional turning points hold for men but not for women or reflect the experiences of one ethnic group but not another. And, if periodization schemes conflict, which one should we use? Several issues examine questions of periodization. If Britain was having one experience of imperialism and the "colonies" another, which one more accurately describes the time period? And, was there a distinct break at the periods we designate the Renaissance, the Scientific Revolution, and the Modern World? If so, did women and men experience these breaks identically?

It is also important to keep in mind that people living at a particular moment in history are not aware of labels that later historians will attach to their experience. People who lived during the Middle Ages were surely not aware of living in the middle of something. Only much after the fact were we able to call a later age, the Renaissance. To those who lived during what we call the Middle Ages or the Modern World, marriage, childbirth, work, weather, sickness, and death were the real concerns, just as they are for us. Our own age will certainly be characterized by future historians in ways that might surprise and shock us. As we study the past, it is helpful to keep in mind that some of our assumptions are rooted in a traditional periodization that is now being challenged.

## Continuity or Discontinuity?

A related question concerns the connection or lack of connection between one event or set of events and another. When we look at the historical past, we must ask ourselves whether we are seeing continuity or discontinuity. In other words, is the event we are studying part of a normal process of evolution or does it represent a break from a traditional pattern. Questions of continuity versus discontinuity are the fundamental ones on which the larger issue of periodization rests. Did the Industrial Revolution redefine the lives of workers? Were the periods we refer to as the Enlightenment or the Contemporary World really more discontinuous with the past than continuous with it? And, if some elements shift while others constitute a seamless web, which is the more significant element for the historian?

Sometimes events may appear continuous from the point of view of one group and discontinuous from the point of view of another. Suppose that factory owners found their world and worldview shifting dramatically, whereas the lives and perspectives of workers went on more or less as they had before. When this is the case, whose experience should we privilege? Is one group's experience more historically significant than another's—and how should we decide? Modern historians are struggling with these questions as the voices of indigenous peoples compete with those praising explorers.

## The Power of Ideas

Can ideas change the course of history? People have sometimes been willing to die for what they believe in and revolutions have certainly been fought, at least in part, over ideas? Some historians believe that studying the clash of ideas or the predominance of one idea or set of ideas offers the best key to understanding the past. How significant is a nation's worldview and view of itself? Could this factor be more significant than more practical considerations?

What do you think? Do ideas shape world events? Would devotion to a political or religious cause lead you to challenge the status quo? Or, would economic conditions be more likely to send you to the streets? Historians differ in ranking the importance of various factors in influencing the past. Do people challenge the power structure because they feel politically powerless, or because they are hungry, or because of the power of ideas?

## The Timeliness of Historical Issues

When we read the newspaper, log on to online sources, follow blogs or a Twitter feed, or listen to the evening news or comedy shows, there is a confusing array of present-day political, economic, religious, and military clashes that can be understood only by looking at their historical contexts. The perennial conflicts in the Middle East, China's, and India's emerging roles as economic superpowers, the threat posed by religious fundamentalism, the question of whether revolutions are ever worth their costs—these concerns of the global village have roots in the past. Understanding the origins of conflicts gives us the possibility of envisioning their solutions. The issues in this book will help you think through the problems facing our world and give you the tools to make an informed decision about what you think is the best course of action.

In a democracy, an informed citizenry is the bedrock on which a government stands. If we do not understand the past, the present will be a puzzle to us and the future may seem out of our control. Seeing how and why historians disagree can help us determine what the critical issues are and where informed interpreters part company. This offers a foundation for forming our own judgments and acting upon them. Looking critically at clashing views also hones our analytic skills and makes us thoughtful readers of all our textbooks as well as magazines, newspapers, and blogs.

## Why Study World History?

You may be wondering why this book deals with world history rather than exclusively with Western civilization. At times the West has felt its power and dominance in the world made only its own story worth studying. History, we are sometimes told, is written by the winners. For the Chinese, the Greeks, the Ottoman Turks, and many other victors of the past, the stories of other civilizations seemed irrelevant, unimportant, not nearly as valuable as their own triumphal saga. The Chinese considered their Middle Kingdom the center of the world; the Greeks labeled all others barbarians; and the Ottoman Turks expected never to lose their position of dominance. From our perspective in the present these stories form a tapestry. No one thread or pattern tells the tale and all seem to be equally necessary for a complete picture of the past to emerge.

Any single story—even that of a military and economic superpower—is insufficient to explain the scope of human history at a given moment in time. Our story is especially interesting to us, and you will find many issues specific to Western civilization in this book. However, as we are learning, our story achieves its fullest meaning only when it is told in concert with those of other civilizations that share an increasingly interconnected planet with us. As communications systems shrink the Earth into a global village, we may be ignoring the rest of the world at our own peril. At the very least the study of civilizations other than our own can alert us to events that may have worldwide implications. And, as we are beginning to learn, no story happens in isolation. The history of the West can perhaps be accurately told only within a global context that takes into account the actions and reactions of other civilizations as they share the world stage with the West. As you read the issues that concern non-Western civilizations, stay alert for what you can learn about your own.

Your textbook may take a global focus or it may be restricted to the study of Western civilization. In either case, the YES and NO selections will enrich your understanding of how the peoples of the world have understood themselves and their relationships with others. As we become a more clearly multicultural society, we have an additional reason for studying about other civilizations that have blended with our own through immigration. Perhaps the biggest challenge for an increasingly diverse United States is to understand its own role in world affairs and its relationship with other countries, which may have different histories, value systems, and goals.

# Unit 1

# UNIT

# The Modern World

**A**s European voyages of exploration in the fifteenth and sixteenth centuries carried adventurers to the ends of the earth, a unique Western worldview began to emerge. Shaped by events, ideas, and people, this worldview flowed from the development of capitalism and democracy and the impact of both on the modern world. Fueled by the rise of nationalism and the emergence of national states, Western civilization in the modern world confronted the changes, both positive and negative, that flowed from economic and political revolutions. The unique character of Western civilization included the skillful manipulation of economic systems, the articulation of humanistic and secular values, and a renewed valuing of the "common people" over the "Great Man"—even one as esteemed as Napoleon Bonaparte.

When Adam Smith, the great Scottish economist, set forth his theory that, if left alone by government (laissez-faire), the marketplace would be self-regulating and the invisible hand of market forces would regulate the economy, he laid the foundation on which the Industrial Revolution would be built. Although Smith's law of supply and demand has been modified by later conditions such as social welfare and the creation of large, multinational corporations, more powerful than governments, during this early period, industrialization radically changed the lives of ordinary people. What had been a household—where the entities we describe as "work" and "family life" both took place—was redefined as "home," after "work" became redefined as what one does for money in a place separate from "home." And, both women and children became "workers" to fill the need in an industrializing economy.

In France, centuries of control by clergy and nobles during the Ancien Regime, were replaced by a people's revolution. During the second phase of the revolution, however, the initial attempt to replace monarchy with democracy devolved into violence. Japan, by contrast, restored its monarchy and decided to modernize in an evolutionary, rather than a revolutionary, way. The Meiji Restoration happened from the top-down, rather than from the bottom-up. And, it introduced the telegraph, telephone, and wireless radio. Britain emerged as a major imperial power, and its decisions during the Irish potato famine, as well as the American Revolution and other unrest in the "colonies," are being re-examined by historians. Revolutions in many forms—economic, industrial, political, and ideological—defined this period.

Selected, Edited, and with Issue Framing Material by:
Helen Buss Mitchell, *Howard Community College*
and
Joseph R. Mitchell, *Howard Community College*

# ISSUE

## Did the Industrial Revolution Lead to a Sexual Revolution?

**YES: Edward Shorter,** "The Reason Why" from *The Making of the Modern Family* (Perseus, 1975)

**NO: Louise A. Tilly, Joan W. Scott, and Miriam Cohen,** from "Women's Work and European Fertility Patterns," *Journal of Interdisciplinary History* (vol. VI, no. 3, Winter 1976)

---

### Learning Outcomes

**After reading this issue, you should be able to:**

- Explain the impact of industrialization on the personal and working lives of young, European women.
- Understand how evidence may be interpreted in different ways by different historians.
- Explain what changed and what remained the same during this period in European history.
- Understand how "history from the bottom up" works and how it differs from the "great man" theory of history.

---

### ISSUE SUMMARY

**YES:** Historian Edward Shorter argues that employment opportunities outside the home that opened up with industrialization led to a rise in the illegitimacy rate, which he attributes to the sexual emancipation of unmarried working-class women.

**NO:** Historians Louise A. Tilly, Joan W. Scott, and Miriam Cohen argue that unmarried women worked to meet an economic need, not to gain personal freedom; and they attribute the rise in illegitimacy rates to broken marriage promises and the absence of traditional support from family, community, and church.

---

All these historians agree that between 1750 and 1850 the illegitimacy rate rose across Europe. In many of the European countries this time period coincides with industrialization. Did the arrival of capitalism change the living and working habits of unmarried women and introduce new attitudes that made them more interested in sex? When the outcome is agreed upon, what matters most is the evidence offered to explain the cause.

Edward Shorter boldly claimed a nineteenth-century sexual revolution that had its roots in industrial capitalism. In his view the market economy with its values of self-interest and competitiveness changed the value system of the proletarian subculture—the young men and women working for wages in industrializing countries. Earning their own money, in Shorter's view, gave these workers the means to live independently. Young women in particular, he argues, declared their independence from family control, struck out in pursuit of personal freedom, and began to enjoy sex as a way of finding individual self-fulfillment. The predictable result was the rise in illegitimacy rates.

Tilly, Scott, and Cohen fault Shorter for offering little or no hard evidence for his hypothesis. Citing the work of other historians, they assert that family interest rather than self-interest led women to work. Women moved very slowly into industrial work and, even by the end of the period (1850), most were employed in domestic service, dressmaking, laundering, and tailoring. Many earned far too little to permit them to live independently. Those who did probably kept the traditional assumption that premarital intercourse with an intended bridegroom would be followed by marriage. What changed, Tilly, Scott, and Cohen argue, was not the attitudes but the external context. In the absence of traditional pressures, young men moved on to other work or better opportunities, leaving pregnant women behind.

As you read these two conflicting interpretations, look for the explanation offered by each essay and, most importantly, at what evidence is offered to support the interpretation. It may seem logical to assume that an increase in rates of illegitimacy must be due to a sexual revolution. But, is that the only or the best explanation that existing information can support? There is a real temptation to use our "common sense" to fill in the gaps, but the historian insists on evidence.

For centuries history was written from the point of view of the rich, the powerful, and the literate. For some, understanding the "great man"—Alexander the Great, Julius Caesar, Napoleon Bonaparte—was the key to understanding his age. Calling this history "from the top down," many scholars of the past half-century have begun to uncover the lives of the poor, the powerless, and the illiterate—what some call history "from the bottom up." Borrowing the methods of the social sciences, such as archaeology, anthropology, sociology, and psychology, and using quantitative analysis of economic and demographic data, historians are trying to fill in the missing pieces of the past. The YES and NO selections take on the challenge of assessing the motives of people who left few, if any, written records. Since we cannot read their diaries and letters, we must use what evidence we do have about the lives they led and attempt to imagine how they might have seen the world.

In this issue, the chief question concerns continuity versus discontinuity. What changed? What remained the same? Did the attitudes of working women change as they entered the capitalist labor force, as Shorter claims, leading them to pursue personal pleasures like sex, which, in the absence of birth control, resulted in higher rates of illegitimacy? Or, did the attitudes stay the same (premarital sex, as usual, in the context of courtship and with the expectation of marriage), as Tilly, Scott, and Cohen argue, while the context changed, leaving women pregnant and with no expectation of marriage?

In the world of the "great man," women, people of color, and all the poor are nearly invisible. They appear as passive participants in the historical drama. It is as if history happens to them. Revisionist historians insist that even the apparently powerless have the potential to act as agents of historical change rather than passive victims. Both the essays you have just read assume that working-class, European women in the hundred years between 1750 and 1850 made decisions and acted upon them. For reasons that may never be completely clear, there was a rise in infertility rates, evidence that more babies than in the past were being born outside of marriage. What changed? A higher illegitimacy rate can mean more sexual activity is taking place and it can also mean fewer unmarried and pregnant women are marrying.

Lacking letters or diaries that might offer a window into the attitudes of the young women at the heart of this study, historians have made good use of marriage and birth records, typically recorded in village churches. Noting all the marriages and all the births of first children to those marriages permits historians to calculate how many months intervened. Fewer than 9 months between marriage and first birth suggest the possibility of a pregnant bride. Other historical evidence from the period has revealed the sanction for premarital sex under very specific conditions: the woman's partner would be her intended bridegroom and the sexual relationship was presumed to be a precursor to marriage.

In *The World We Have Lost* (Scribner, 1965), Peter Laslett describes the household as the center of production, a place where all residents both lived and worked. The chief effect of the Industrial Revolution was to separate work from home and to deprive the home of its traditional productive focus. Prior to industrialization the unit known as a household was the place where what we call "work" and what we now call "home" were both located. Families, along with other blood relatives and people hired to do the work of the unit, all lived and worked together. Everybody worked, and all the work was regarded as essential. Between sunrise and sunset, the work of the household took place. Households supported their own needs and bartered with neighbors for what they needed and did not produce.

Industrialization, accompanied by capitalism, changed all this. "Work" was redefined as something one did at an off-site location and for which one was paid. The factory determined the starting and stopping times for work, as well as when workers could eat, go to the bathroom, and rest. Perhaps most significantly, what remained in the household—now renamed "home"—was defined as "not work." Since work in the home was unpaid, it quickly became devalued. Women were encouraged to think of the work they did in the home as an act of love. Karl Marx believed that capitalism was inherently flawed. Only those tasks for which we are paid have value; and those who own what he called the "means of production" (i.e., the factory owner) grow rich from the labor of the workers who remain poor. For a Marxist interpretation, see Friedrich Engels, *The Origin of the Family, Private Property and the State* (International Publishers, 1972).

These major changes to the ways people lived and worked were the eventual effects of industrialization. This issue is concerned with the more immediate effects. When industrialization occurs, as it did in both Europe and North America, in a place where there is no existing workforce, the young are often the first recruited. As this issue suggests, the young women workers might have had a different experience than their young male counterparts did.

# YES ↵

**Edward Shorter**

## The Reason Why

Some of these trends in family history are not well documented, to say the least. And when our knowledge of even the basic narrative of maternal love or domesticity is so shaky, attempts to explain why such things happened must be speculative indeed. Now in fact, I am fairly confident that the evidence from local doctors, antiquarians, and bureaucrats presented in this book points to important historical changes. And I'm pretty sure as well that the reasons I'm about to suggest for the great transformation of sentiment strike close to the mark. But the reader has no assurance of this.

I can justify my speculations about the reason why on two grounds alone. For one thing, the professional scholar might be sufficiently enraged by my analysis to sally forth and perform the research necessary for refutation; this itself would be an advance, because discovering that Shorter is wrong about the causes of the revolution in sentiment is preferable to neglecting the question entirely. For another, the general reader, who is more interested in understanding where his or her own world comes from than in the intricacies of these scholarly debates, might seize from such a discussion some small added insight into what's happening to family life in the 1970s.

Market capitalism was probably of the root of the revolution in sentiment. At the same time that mentalities were undergoing the historic shift toward individualism and affection, the economic substructure of the world in which village people lived was in upheaval as well. It was most likely the replacement of this traditional "moral" economy with a modern marketplace economy that changed so thoroughly values and behavior.

Consider for a moment what "capitalism" entailed for traditional Europe. There was, first of all, the smelting of countless little economically self-sealed units into great nation- or region-wide marketplaces. During the eighteenth century, political economists everywhere urged that the flow of labor and goods from one place to the next be unimpeded by the customs barriers, dues, taxes, and local privileges that had so hampered long-distance commerce in the old regime. Formerly, of course, the local guilds had guaranteed that commodities produced elsewhere would not invade their towns. The complex system of grain-trade regulation saw to it as well that food produced locally would be sold locally. Finally, the price of most hired labor, from fieldhands to live-in servants, was regulated by administrative decree. So, in effect, each district would represent a hermetically sealed economic unit, transactions within which were run more by custom than bu the free workings of the law of supply and demand. And the trickle of outside foodstuffs or peddler-born commodities that managed to penetrate this seal nowhere near righted the balance. The traditional economy was a local economy, where moral notions about how much people were entitled to charge or earn in order to support a family replaced market transactions.

But the political economists' war on the guilds and the state administrators' anxiety about feeding such great, potentially turbulent, cities as Paris punctured these watertight seals. Far-flung markets in grain were opened up in France, for example, so that speculators could come into a grain-producing district and use the leverage their cash gave them to pry the local grain supply away for resale in some distant area of shortage. And the scholar-bureaucrats who ran Prussia or Austria were equally concerned to abolish the guilds' fairprice restrictions which were keeping output at a minimum. For them national power was tied closely to industrial production; so they stripped the coopers and tanners and locksmiths of their traditional police powers, and ensured that the law of supply and demand would coax upward the production of barrels and hides and door hinges. Finally, the administrators abandoned their efforts to enforce traditional master–servant regulations, and let employee wages and labor mobility be set by the free working of the economy. All these are often-told stories, and I wish merely to remind the reader that by 1830, most West Europeans would find themselves competing for wages or profits in a free market whose circumference was many times larger than those of the traditional economies in which their grandfathers had found themselves.

Secondly, "capitalism" carried the material standard of living upward. This rise began in England sometime in the second half of the eighteenth century, and on the continent at some point in the 1830–1850 period. Whether the early days of the factory system brought an absolute immiseration in the lives of industrial workers remains a moot point. But few would dispute that after the machine's enormous increases in productivity had begun, real wages climbed—and began to shift the fundamental material conditions of life. Outside the factory system similar changes took place, as agricultural capitalism boosted the productivity of the fields: new crop rotations, drainage, and fertilizing made available a better-balanced diet to the average person at less cost. Almost none of this happened on the continent before the 1840s, but thereafter the improvement was so quick as to be one of the great dramas of the social history of the popular classes. This story, too, is well known to specialists, and I merely remind the reader that most of the improvement stemmed from capitalist entrepreneurs' technological innovations.

A third consequence of "capitalism" was the recruitment of an industrial proletariat, clearly differentiated in cultural and material terms from the surrounding traditional populations. Economic historians are only now beginning to appreciate the rural origins of this development; for it was first in the countryside, as a result of cottage industry, that a modern industrial work force began to form. The great demand for cotton cloth, fashionable gloves, or lace doilies motivated urban entrepreneurs to buy up raw materials that would be sent to rural outworkers. Peasant women would spin raw cotton into yarn, and other peasants (or at least people who had formerly been peasants) would weave this yarn into cloth. The cloth would be turned into garments, probably in an urban sweatshop; tailors and seamstresses in some dismal loft would be hunched over their own small contribution to this far-flung industrial system coordinated by these capitalist entrepreneurs.

In textiles, small-scale ironmongery, wickerware, and a host of other popular consumer goods, the cottage-industrial system made giant strides during the late eighteenth and early nineteenth centuries. At a reasonable estimate, one in every three rural dwellers was caught up in it. Some were traditional peasants who, in the veillées or dreary winter days, would take advantage of these new earning opportunities. Others were landless laborers—or peasants who had made themselves landless by selling off their holdings—who were able to wrench themselves up from absolute misery through this form of domestic industrial work. Unlike the other two above-mentioned spearheads of capitalism, the "domestic system" still lies in darkness. We are only beginning to discover how widespread it was and what changes it effected in the lives of its work force. What is important for our purposes is that popular involvement with the market economy—rustic outworkers were subject to all the mercurial price fluctuations and competitiveness of the market system—commenced during the eighteenth century, even as the first of the great revolutions in sentiment was getting underway.

Is there a direct causal relationship between the two? May we argue that the illegitimacy explosion or the surge of sentiment in courting was propelled upward by these economic changes? Although any satisfactory explanation must ultimately be complex, and incorporate many different kinds of variables, I believe that laissez-faire marketplace organization, capitalist production, and the

beginnings of proletarianization among the work force were more important than any other factors in the spread of sentiment.

Analytically, the relationships are not complicated. So let's take up the argument. How did capitalism help cause that powerful thrust of sentiment among the unmarried that I have called the romance revolution? To what extent may sleeping around before marriage and choosing partners on the basis of personal attraction rather than wealth be associated with economic change? The principal link here is the increased participation of young unmarried people, especially women, in the free-market labor force. The logic of the marketplace positively demands individualism: the system will succeed only if each participant ruthlessly pursues his own self-interest, buying cheap, selling dear, and enhancing his own interests at the cost of his competitors (i.e., his fellow citizens). Only if this variety of economic egoism is internalized will the free market come up to the high expectations of its apologists, for if people let humanitarian or communitarian considerations influence their economic behavior, the market becomes inefficient; the weak cease to be weeded out. Thus, the free market engraves upon all who are caught up in it the attitude: "Look out for number one."

I am arguing that, among the common people whom the eighteenth century had forced into the marketplace, this egoistical economic mentality spread into various noneconomic domains of life, specifically into those ties that bind the individual to the surrounding community. Egoism that was learned in the marketplace became transferred to community obligations and standards, to ties to the family and lineage—in short, to the whole domain of cultural rules that regulated familial and sexual behavior. In this book I have suggested a "teeter-totter" relationship between community obligation and individual self-fulfillment. In traditional society, the balance was very heavily tilted toward the community, toward adhering to the rules and standards of those about you and away from pursuing your own desires and pleasures. Capitalism tilted this balance the other way. And once the rules of marketplace individualism had been learned, they easily took control of the whole arena of conscious attitudes. It is this *prise de pouvoir* that Fred Weinstein and Gerald M. Platt call "the wish to be free." My argument is that for young people in late eighteenth-century Europe, the sexual and emotional wish to be free came from the capitalist marketplace.

In the domain of men–women relations, the wish to be free emerges as romantic love. The desire to find personal happiness, to commence that long voyage of personality development and self-discovery that constitutes the Inner Search, rises to the conscious surface as romance: you look into another person's eyes in the hope that you'll find yourself. And even if we believe that these eighteenth-century lower-class young people were about eight pegs below this level of self-awareness (an assumption I'm not automatically willing to concede), there still remains the simple force of sexual desire. Sexual experience is part of all this self-fulfillment, and people cut loose by individualism from the mooring of community allegiance would quickly drift towards fooling around. So capitalism exerted its impact upon romantic love through involvement in the market labor force: economic individualism leads to cultural egoism; private gratification becomes more important than fitting into the common weal; the wish to be free produces the illegitimacy explosion.

This is an old argument—a favorite, in fact, of conservative nineteenth-century social theorists who never tired of calling the wish to be free *l'amour déréglé du plaisir.* Two modifications encourage me to bring it forth anew.

In the first place, we should note that this wish to be free affected women more than men. We can probably assume that men have always been avid for intercourse, that a male desire to get women into bed is probably a historical constant. But how do we explain this new, eighteenth-century willingness on the part of women to climb into the sack with them? How may we account for this historical reversal in the willingness of young, unmarried women to abandon traditional chastity and instead go out with different men, have sex before marriage, and preoccupy themselves generally with personal happiness? I believe it was the new access to paid employment. In 1803. Prefect Colchen of the Moselle department supplied a plausible explanation.

> As for women, they were never entirely strangers to hard work, but today they take on almost as much as the men, above all in the vineyards. The losses caused by the war have contributed to this. Moreover these rustic women have strong constitutions and are able to perform the hardest jobs. But this kind of life changes in them the modest bearing of their sex, and the habitual frequentation with the opposite sex it necessitates gives their morals a certain libertineness that causes the premature loss of their innocence.

Not only did paid work give young women an inclination to escape the sexual restrictions of their parents and the town fathers, it also gave the *possibility* of doing so. Economically independent women have greater liberty than economically dependent ones, for paid work makes it possible to ignore parental admonitions and to shrug off the parson's scolding. During the eighteenth century the industrial town of Annonay (Ardèche) saw illegitimacy increase much more rapidly than did the neighboring traditional *bourg* of Serignan. And while in Serignan only one fifth of the unwed mothers were economically independent (most of them servants), in Annonay fully one half were, a mixture of servants and workers. Alain Molinier concludes: ". . . having used the advantages of their job to escape the moral constraints of the family milieu, these mothers were able to adopt a freer style of life. More numerous in the cities, above all in the eighteenth cen-

tury, these women might have contributed to the increase in the illegitimacy ratio."

A second modification of the classic notion that economic individualism means sexual experimentation is that it seems to have happened mainly among the lower classes. The new proletarians of the eighteenth century were the vanguard of the sexual revolution because they were the first to be caught up in the market economy. Oh, to be sure, the upper bourgeoisie—the bearers of Max Weber's famous capitalist rationality and religious anxiety—were the class that gave these lower orders work. But the capitalists themselves escaped being caught in the sexual revolution because for them family values overrode everything else. The lower classes who labored in the laundries and sweatshops of the bourgeoisie, on the other hand, didn't have any property to preserve. They owned no great patrimonies to be transmitted, and so they were free to pursue individual rather than family objectives once the idea of doing so had occurred to them—which is to say, once they were able to shake free of *communal* controls upon their intimate lives. Although we don't normally think of things in this way—so firmly has our collective historical gaze been riveted on the upper orders—it was the lower classes who first were fully socialized in the ways of the market economy. The people whom the budding proletarian laborforce scooped up were marginal farmers, agricultural laborers, and the noninheriting or miserably-dowered daughters of propertied peasants.

Did these women seek out capitalism because the dawning wish to be free had aroused within them a desire for personal independence and sexual adventure? Or were they driven by hardship from their traditional nests into this uncongenial new economic setting, there to be sexually exploited? The former possibility seems more generally applicable. From one end of Europe to the other, young unmarried women in the nineteenth century were rejecting traditional occupations in favor of paid employment within a capitalist setting. The tailors of Bavaria's Wolfstein county, for example, complained that many girls, avoiding the "unpleasantness" of domestic service and wishing for themselves instead "a free and comfortable life," were becoming seamstresses. In France's Tarn department, children were repaying, by leaving home, the patriarchal fathers who "treat them as minors even after they reach adulthood, seeing in them mere field-hands to whom nothing is owed and who themselves own nothing. . . . One may admire this abnegation and devotion that gives a family so much solidarity, but it's unlikely this situation will be maintained without some protest." By the interwar years of the twentieth century, complaints were heard from all sides in France about young women who no longer wanted to marry peasants and were taking off for the city in droves.

Nor was England different. One observer explained the enormous migration of young people to late-nineteenth-century London as the result of "the contagion of numbers, the sense of something going on, the theaters and the music halls, the brightly lighted streets and busy crowds—all, in short, that makes the difference between the Mile End fair on a Saturday night and a dark muddy country lane, with no glimmer of gas and with nothing to do. Who could wonder that men are drawn into such a vortex, even were the penalty heavier that it is." And not only men, for J. A. Banks argues that young women in particular who left home to accept work in London were not so much responding to economic opportunity as to "a means of independence from the often severe restraints on behavior inherent in rural family life, dominated by the Victorian paterfamilias." Once in the city, these young women "copied the example of the young men, becoming

lodgers . . . or fending wholly for themselves where they did not marry early." Such testimony, unless entirely unrepresentative, points to a close interaction between capitalist work, escape from traditional controls, and the wish to be free. It is the argument of this book that these things came together late in the eighteenth century and that they made, for young women especially, "romantic love" a codeword for personal autonomy. . . .

---

**EDWARD SHORTER** directs the history of medicine program at the University of Toronto. He is the author of *From the Mind into the Body* (Free Press, 1996).

Louise A. Tilly, Joan W. Scott,
and Miriam Cohen

 **NO**

# Women's Work and European Fertility Patterns

According to [Edward] Shorter, a change in fertility rates can only mean a change in sexual practices, which has to mean a change in attitudes, particularly of women. The sequence must be linear and direct. As Shorter argues:

> It seems a plausible proposition that people assimilate in the marketplace an integrated, coherent set of values about social behavior and personal independence and that these values quickly inform the noneconomic realm of individual mentalities. If this logic holds true, we may identify exposure to the marketplace as a prime source of female emancipation.

This statement, as its language clearly reveals, is based on a claim of reasoning, not on evidence. Shorter offers nothing to prove that more women worked in the capitalist marketplace in this period. He merely assumes that they did. Similarly, he assumes that women at the end of the eighteenth century had different family roles and attitudes from their predecessors. And he assumes as well that changes in work opportunities immediately changed values. Ideas, in his opinion, instantly reflect one's current economic experience. Shorter employs a mechanistic notion of "value transfer" to explain the influence of changes in occupational structure on changes in collective mentalities: "In the eighteenth and early nineteenth centuries the market economy encroached steadily at the cost of the moral economy, and the values of individual self-interest and competitiveness that people learned in the market were soon transferred to other areas of life."

For Shorter, sexual behavior echoes market behavior at every point. "Emancipated" women gained a sense of autonomy at work that the subordinate and powerless women of pre-industrial society had lacked. That work, created by capitalist economic development, necessarily fostered values of individualism in those who participated in it, and individualism was expressed in part by a new desire for sexual gratification. Young women working outside the home, Shorter insists, were by definition rebelling against parental authority. Indeed, they sought work in order to gain the independence and individual fulfillment that could not be attained at home. It follows, in Shorter's logic, that sexual behavior, too, must have been defiant of parental restraint. As the market economy spread there arose a new, libertine, proletarian subculture "indulgent of eroticism." Once married, the independent young working women engaged in frequent intercourse because they and their husbands took greater pleasure in sex. Female "emancipation" thus began among the young and poor. In the absence of birth control, the sexual gratification of single working girls increased the illegitimate birthrate; that of married women (who worked or had worked) inflated the legitimate birthrate. In this fashion Shorter answers a central question of European historical demography. The fertility increase in the late eighteenth century was simply the result of the "emancipation," occupational and sexual, of working-class women. . . .

It is now time to examine the historical evidence that Shorter neglected on women's role in pre-industrial society; on the effects of industrialization on women's work and on their attitudes; and on the motives which sent young girls out into the "marketplace" at the end of the eighteenth and beginning of the nineteenth century. None of the evidence that we have found supports Shorter's argument in any way. Women were not powerless in "traditional" families; they played important economic roles which gave them a good deal of power within the family. Industrialization did not significantly modernize women's work in the period when fertility rates rose; in fact, the vast majority of working women did not work in factories, but at customary women's jobs. Women usually became wage earners during the early phases of industrialization not to rebel against their parents or declare independence from their husbands, but to augment family finances. Indeed, women in this period must be studied in their family settings, for the constraints of family membership greatly affected their opportunities for individual autonomy. No change in attitude, then, increased the numbers of children whom working women bore. Rather, old attitudes and customary behavior interacted with greatly changed circumstances—particularly in the composition of populations—and led to increased illegitimate fertility.

Women eventually shed many outdated priorities, and by the end of the nineteenth century some working women had clearly adopted "modern" lifestyles. But these changes involved a more gradual and complex adaptation than Shorter implies. The important point, however, is that the years around 1790 were not a watershed in the history of women's economic emancipation—despite the fact that the locus of women's work began to move outside the home. These *were* the crucial years for the increases in fertility in Europe. All of the evidence is not in, by any means; what we offer, however, indicates that in this period, women of the popular classes simply were not searching for freedom or experiencing emancipation. The explanation for changed fertility patterns lies elsewhere.

## Women's Place in "Traditional" Families

In the pre-industrial family, the household was organized as a family or domestic economy. Men, women, and children worked at tasks which were differentiated by age and sex, but the work of all was necessary for survival. Artisans' wives assisted their husbands in their work as weavers, bakers, shoemakers, or tailors. Certain work, like weaving, whether carried on in the city or the country, needed the cooperation of all family members. Children and women did the spinning and carding; men ran the looms. Wives also managed many aspects of the household, including family finances. In less prosperous urban families, women did paid work which was often an extension of their household chores: They sewed and made lace; they also took odd jobs as carters, laundresses, and street cleaners.

Unmarried women also became servants. Resourcefulness was characteristic of poor women: When they could not find work which would enable them to contribute to the family income, they begged, stole, or became prostitutes. Hufton's work on the Parisian poor in the eighteenth century and Forrest's work on Bordeaux both describe the crucial economic contribution of urban working-class women and the consequent central role which these women played in their families.

In the country, the landowning peasant's family was also the unit of productive activity. The members of the family worked together, again at sex-differentiated tasks. Children—boys and girls—were sent to other farms as servants when their help was not needed at home. Their activity, nonetheless, contributed to the well-being of the family. They sent their earnings home, or, if they were not paid wages, their absence at least relieved the family of the burden of feeding and boarding them. Women's responsibilities included care of the house, barnyard, and dairy. They managed to bring in small net profits from marketing of poultry and dairy products and from work in rural domestic industry. Management of the household and, particularly, of finances led to a central role for women in these families. An observer in rural Brittany during the nineteenth century reported that the wife and mother of the family made "the important decisions, buying a field, selling a cow, a lawsuit against a neighbor, choice of future son-in-law." For rural families who did not own land, women's work was even more vital: From agricultural work, spinning, or petty trading, they contributed their share to the family wage—the only economic resource of the landless family.

In city and country, among propertied and propertyless, women of the popular classes had a vital economic role which gave them a recognized and powerful position within the household. It is impossible to guess what sort of sexual relations were practiced under these circumstances. We *can* say, however, that women in these families were neither dependent nor powerless. Hence, it is impossible to accept Shorter's attempt to derive women's supposed sexual subordination from their place in the pre-industrial household.

## Why Women Worked

Shorter attributes the work of women outside the home after 1750, particularly that of young, single women, to a change in outlook: a new desire for independence from parental restraints. He argues that since seeking work was an individualistic rebellion against traditionalism, sexual behavior, too, reflected a defiance of parental authority. The facts are that daughters of the popular classes were most often sent into service or to work in the city by their families. Their work represented a continuation of practices customary in the family economy. When resources were scarce or mouths at home too numerous, children customarily sought work outside, generally with family approval.

Industrialization and urbanization created new problems for rural families but generated new opportunities as well. In most cases, families strategically adapted their established practices to the new context. Thus, daughters sent out to work went farther away from home than had been customary. Most still defined their work in the family interest. Sometimes arrangements for direct payment in money or foodstuffs were made between a girl's parents and her employer. In other cases, the girls themselves regularly sent money home. Commentators observed that the girls considered this a normal arrangement—part of their obligation to the family.

In some cases the conditions of migration for young working girls emphasized their ties to family in many ways limited their independence. In Italy and France, factory dormitories housed female workers, and nuns regulated their behavior and social lives. In the needle trades in British cities, enterprising women with a little capital turned their homes into lodging houses for pieceworkers in their employ. Of course, these institutions permitted employers to control their employees by limiting their mobility and regulating their behavior. The point is not that they were beneficial practices, but that young girls lived in households which permitted them limited autonomy. Domestic service, the largest single occupation for women, was also the most traditional and most protective of young girls. They would be sent from one household to another and thus be given security. Châtelain argues that domestic service was a safe form of migration in France for young girls from the country. They had places to live, families, food, and lodgings and had no need to fend for themselves in the unknown big city as soon as they arrived. It is true that servants often longed to leave their places, and that they resented the exploitation of their mistresses (and the advances of their masters). But that does not change the fact that, initially, their migration was sponsored by a set of traditional institutions which limited their individual freedom.

In fact, individual freedom did not seem to be at issue for the daughters of either the landed or the landless, although clearly their experiences differed. It seems likely that peasant families maintained closer ties with their daughters, even when the girls worked in distant cities. The family interest in the farm (the property that was the birthright of the lineage and not of any individual) was a powerful influence on individual behavior. Thus, farm girls working as domestics continued to send money home. Married daughters working as domestics in Norwegian cities sent their children home to be raised on the farm by grandparents. But even when ties of this sort were not maintained, it was seldom from rebellious motives. Braun describes the late eighteenth-century situation of peasants in the hinterland of Zurich. These peasants were willing to divide their holdings for their children because of new work opportunities in cottage industry. These young people married earlier than they would have if the farm had been held undivided, and they quickly established their own families. Braun suggests that the young workers soon lost touch with their parents. The process, as he describes it, however, was not rebellion; rather, the young people went into cottage industry to lessen the burden that they represented for the family. These motives were welcomed and encouraged by the parents. Family bonds were stretched and broken, but that was a consequence, not a cause, of the new opportunities for work.

Similarly, among urban artisans, older values informed the adaptation to a new organization of work and to technological change. Initially, artisans as well as their political spokesmen insisted that the old values of association and cooperation could continue to characterize their work relationships in the new industrial society. Artisan subculture in cities during the early stages of industrialization was not characterized by an individualistic, self-seeking ideology, as Thompson, Hufton, Forrest, Soboul, Gossez, and others have clearly shown. With no evidence that urban artisans adopted the values of the marketplace at work, Shorter's deduction about a "libertine proletarian subculture" has neither factual nor logical validity. It seems more likely that artisan families, like peasant families, sent their wives and daughters to work to help bolster their shaky economic situation. These women undoubtedly joined the ranks of the unskilled who had always constituted the urban female workforce. Wives and daughters of the unskilled and propertyless had worked for centuries at service and manufacturing jobs in cities. In the nineteenth century there were more of them because the proportions of unskilled propertyless workers increased.

Eighteenth- and early nineteenth-century cities grew primarily by migration. The urban working class was thus constantly renewed and enlarged by a stream of rural migrants. Agricultural change drove rural laborers and peasants cityward at the end of the eighteenth century, and technological change drove many artisans and their families into the ranks of the unskilled. Women worked outside the home because they had to. Changed attitudes did not propel them into the labor force. Family interest and not self-interest was the underlying motive for their work.

## Women's Work

What happened in the mid-eighteenth century with the spread of capitalism, the growth of markets, and industrialization? Did these economic changes bring new work experiences for women, with the consequences which Shorter describes? Did women, earning money in the capitalist marketplace, find a new sense of self that expressed itself in increased sexual activity? In examining the historical evidence for the effects on women's work of industrialization and urbanization, we find that the location of women's work did change—more young women worked outside the home and in large cities than ever before. But they were recruited from the same groups which had always sent women to work.

The female labor force of nineteenth-century Europe, like that of seventeenth- and eighteenth-century Europe, consisted primarily of the daughters of the popular classes and, secondarily of their wives. The present state of our knowledge makes it difficult to specify precisely the groups within the working classes from which nineteenth-century women wage earners came. It is clear, however, that changes in the organization of work must have driven the daughters and wives of craftsmen out of the family shop. Similarly, population growth (a result of declining mortality and younger age at marriage due to opportunities for work in cottage industry) created a surplus of hands within the urban household and on the family farm. Women in these families always had been expected to work. Increasingly, they were sent away from home to earn their portion of the family wage.

Shorter's notion that the development of modern capitalism brought new kinds of opportunities to working-class women as early as the middle of the eighteenth century is wrong. There was a very important change in the location of work from rural homes to cities, but this did not revolutionize the nature of the work that most women did. Throughout the nineteenth century, most women worked at traditional occupations. By the end of the century, factory employment was still minimal. . . .

Shorter is also incorrect in his assumption that the working woman was able to live independently of her family because she had the economic means to do so. Evidence for British working women indicates that this was not the case. Throughout the nineteenth century, British working women's wages were considered supplementary incomes—supplementary, that is, to the wages of other family members. It was assumed by employers that women, unlike men, were not responsible for earning their own living. Female wages were always far lower than male. In the Lancashire cotton mills in 1833, where female wages were the highest in the country, females aged 16–21 earned 7/3.5 weekly, while males earned 10/3. Even larger differentials obtained among older workers. In London in the 1880s, there was a similar differential between the average earnings of the sexes: 72 percent of the males in the bookbinding industry earned over 30/– weekly; 42.5 percent of women made less than 12/–. In precious metals, clocks, and watch manufacturing, 83.5 percent of the males earned 30/– or more weekly; females earned 9–12/–. Women in small clothing workshops earned 10–12/– weekly, while women engaged in outwork in the clothing trades made only 4/– a week. In Birmingham, in 1900, the average weekly wage for working women less than age 21 was 10/–, for men 18/–. Women's work throughout this period, as in the eighteenth century, was for the most part unskilled. Occupations were often seasonal and irregular, leaving women without work for many months during the year. Is it possible that there were many single women who could enjoy a life of independence when the majority could not even afford to live adequately on their personal wages? . . .

Women's work from 1750 to 1850 (and much later) did not provide an experience of emancipation. Work was hard and poorly paid and, for the most part, it did not represent a change from traditional female occupations. Those women who traveled to cities did find themselves free of some traditional village and family restraints. But, as we shall see, the absence of these restraints was more often burdensome than liberating. Young women with inadequate wages and unstable jobs found themselves caught in a cycle of poverty which increased their vulnerability. Having lost one family, many sought to create another.

## The Origins of Increased Illegitimacy

The compositional change which increased the numbers of unskilled, propertyless workers in both rural and urban areas and raised their proportion in urban populations also contributed to an increase in rates of illegitimacy. Women in this group of the population always had contributed the most illegitimate births. An increase in the number of women in this group, therefore, meant a greater incidence of illegitimacy.

A recent article by Laslett and Oosterveen speaks directly to Shorter's speculations: "The assumption that illegitimacy figures directly reflect the prevalence of sexual intercourse outside marriage, which seems to be made whenever such figures are used to show that beliefs, attitudes and interests have changed in some particular way, can be shown to be very shaky in its foundations." Using data from Colyton, collected and analyzed by E. A. Wrigley, they argue that one important component in the

incidence of illegitimacy is the existence of illegitimacy-prone families, which bring forth bastards generation after generation. Nevertheless, they warn, "this projected sub-society never produced all the bastards, all the bastard-bearers."

The women who bore illegitimate children were not pursuing sexual pleasure, as Shorter would have us believe. Most expected to get married, but the circumstances of their lives—propertylessness, poverty, large-scale geographic mobility, occupational instability, and the absence of traditional social protection—prevented the fulfillment of this expectation. A number of pressures impelled young working girls to find mates. One was the loneliness and isolation of work in the city. Another was economic need: Wages were low and employment for women, unstable. The logical move for a single girl far from her family would be to find a husband with whom she might re-establish a family economy. Yet another pressure was the desire to escape the confines of domestic service, an occupation which more and more young women were entering.

Could not this desire to establish a family be what the domestic servants, described by the Munich police chief in 1815, sought? No quest for pleasure is inherent in the fact that "so many young girls leave service. . . . But they do little real work and let themselves be supported by boyfriends; they become pregnant and then are abandoned." It seems a sad and distorted version of an older family form, but an attempt at it, nevertheless. Recent work has shown, in fact, that for many French servants in the nineteenth century, this kind of transfer to urban life and an urban husband was often successful.

Was it a search for sexual fulfillment that prompted young women to become "engaged" to young men and then sleep with them in the expectation that marriage would follow? Not at all. In rural and urban areas premarital sexual relationships were common. What Shorter interprets as sexual libertinism, as evidence of an individualistic desire for sexual pleasure, is more likely an expression of the traditional wish to marry. The attempt to reconstitute the family economy in the context of economic deprivation and geographic mobility produced unstable and stable "free unions."

. . . The central point here is that no major change in values or mentality was necessary to create these cases of illegitimacy. Rather, older expectations operating in a changed context yielded unanticipated (and often unhappy) results. . . . Women's work in the late eighteenth and early nineteenth centuries was not "liberating" in any sense. Most women stayed in established occupations. They were so poorly paid that economic independence was precluded. Furthermore, whether married or single, most women often entered the labor force in the service of the family interest. The evidence available points to several causes for illegitimacy, none related to the "emancipation" of women: economic need, causing women to seek work far from the protection of their families; occupational instability of men which led to *mariages manqués* (sexual intercourse following a promise of marriage which was never fulfilled). Finally, analysis of the effects of population growth on propertied peasants and artisans seems to show that the bifurcation of marriage and property arrangements began to change the nature of marriage arrangements for propertyless people.

---

**LOUISE A. TILLY** was professor of history and director of the women's studies program at the University of Michigan. She is the co-author of *Women, Work and Family* (Methuen, 1986) and the author of numerous articles on social history.

**JOAN W. SCOTT** was director of the Pembroke Center for Teaching and Research on Women at Brown University and was professor of social science at Princeton University's Institute for Advanced Study. She is the author of *Gender and the Politics of History* (Columbia University Press, 1988).

**MIRIAM COHEN,** Evalyn Clark Professor of History, has been at Vassar College since 1977. She received her BA at the University of Rochester in 1971 and PhD in history from the University of Michigan in 1978. Her specialities include the history of American women and the history of twentieth-century social reform.

# EXPLORING THE ISSUE

## Did the Industrial Revolution Lead to a Sexual Revolution?

### Critical Thinking and Reflection

1. Briefly describe the economic effects of industrialization and industrial capitalism in Europe.
2. Critically analyze the explanations provided by the YES and NO selections for the rise in illegitimacy rates between 1750 and 1850. Evaluate the arguments offered by each side.
3. How did the lives of the young women who entered the market economy change with industrialization? What did they gain and what did they lose? Critically discuss.
4. Based on the evidence provided in the selections, why did young women join the paid workforce? What types of work were they typically doing? Do the historians agree on the answers to these questions?
5. Critically analyze the evidence offered by each side. Which side seems more convincing? Critically discuss why you believe this to be the case.
6. On what basis does Professor Shorter believe the attitudes toward sexuality of these young women changed? Do you find his argument convincing? Critically discuss your evidence.
7. On what basis do Professors Tilly, Scott, and Cohen argue that the context, rather than attitudes, changed? Are their arguments convincing? Critically discuss your evidence.
8. Do all major economic changes lead to cultural and social changes? Critically discuss.

### Is There Common Ground?

The historians in this issue are all exploring history "from the bottom up." They have undertaken the challenges inherent in seeing the world from the point of view of the relatively powerless, often illiterate, people who constitute the majority in this time period and who did not leave written records. Although their conclusions differ substantially, all the historians who contributed to this issue also agree on a number of factors. All accept that there was a rise in illegitimacy rates in the 100 years between 1750 and 1850. All agree that significant numbers of young women entered the market economy, often leaving their homes and traditional villages to secure paid employment. The observable results provide the areas of common ground.

Where these historians differ is on what evidence is valid for making a reasonable set of assumptions that explain the behavior of these young women. They also disagree about what motivated the women to seek paid employment, and they make very different assumptions about what changed and what remained the same. While all agree that women often left places where family and village customs were in place, only the NO side finds the lack of these traditional supports to be significant.

*Question:* Would they agree that the young women who stepped into radically different lives than those lived by their mothers and grandmothers were demonstrating agency? *That is*: Were they acting as agents of their own lives, making decisions as active participants in an unfolding historical process?

### Create Central

www.mhhe.com/createcentral

### Additional Resources

To make your own decision consider the evidence offered in the following books and essays. Ivy Pinchbeck in *Women Workers and the Industrial Revolution, 1750–1850* (G. Routledge, 1930, 1969) argues that occupational changes played a significant role in women's legal and political emancipation. Rudolf Braun, in "The Impact of Cottage Industry on an Agricultural Population," in David Landes, ed. *The Rise of Capitalism* (Macmillan, 1966), describes an economic system in rural Switzerland in which the daughters in a family learned to spin and weave, contributing their earnings to the family economic unit as a matter of course. Olwen Hufton makes a similar point about the Parisian poor in the eighteenth century in "Women in Revolution, 1789–1796," *Past and Present*, LIII (1971) and about a broader segment of the population in "Women and the Family Economy in Eighteenth-Century France," *French Historical Studies* IX (1975). Lutz K. Berkner describes the pre-capitalist family lifecycle in "The Stem Family and the Developmental Cycle of the Peasant Household: An Eighteenth-Century Austrian Example," *American Historical Review* 77 (April 1972). Whether or not young, working women kept their own wages and had enough money to support an independent lifestyle is a key historiographical question. For more work by the authors, students may wish to read "Women's Work and the Family in Nineteenth Century Europe," *Comparative Studies in Society and History* XVII (1975) and *Women, Work, & Family* (Holt, Rinehart and Winston, 1978) by Joan W. Scott and Louise A. Tilly. Other essays by Edward Shorter include "Illegitimacy,

Sexual Revolution and Social Change in Modern Europe," *Journal of Interdisciplinary History* II (1971); and "Sexual Change and Illegitimacy: The European Experience," in Robert J. Bezucha, ed. *Modern European Social History* (Lexington, MA, 1972).

# *Internet References . . .*

### Industrial Revolution

Offers many primary documents on the Industrial Revolution. Some relate directly to women's experience during this time of dramatic change in Europe.

**www.historyteacher.net/APEuroCourse/WebLinks/
WebLinks-IndustrialRevolution.htm**

Selected, Edited, and with Issue Framing Material by:
Helen Buss Mitchell, *Howard Community College*
and
Joseph R. Mitchell, *Howard Community College*

# ISSUE

## Was the French Revolution Worth Its Human Costs?

**YES: Peter Kropotkin,** from *The Great French Revolution, 1789–1793* (Shocken Books, 1971)

**NO: Marisa Linton,** from "Robespierre and the Terror," *History Today* (vol. 56, no. 8, 2006)

---

### Learning Outcomes

**After reading this issue, you should be able to:**

- Describe and explain the political and social changes that resulted from the French Revolution, as well as its human costs.
- Understand the intellectual positions of English statesman, Edmund Burke, and English-born American citizen Thomas Paine, as well as those of the French revolutionary, Maximilien Robespierre.
- Describe how the values held in each historical period shape the interpretations given by historian writing from within that period and describing past events.

---

### ISSUE SUMMARY

**YES:** Peter Kropotkin (1842–1921), a Russian prince, revolutionary, and anarchist, argues that the French Revolution eradicated both serfdom and absolutism, and paved the way for France's future democratic development.

**NO:** Marisa Linton, a professor and writer, argues that Maximilien de Robespierre offers a lens through which to view the terror and the real human costs of the French Revolution.

Few historical events have created the volume of emotional responses and concomitant debates as has the French Revolution. Taking advantage of one of the largest bodies of historical data gathered, historians of the past two centuries have analyzed, synthesized, and evaluated every facet of this seminal event in the history of the Western world.

From this scholarship has come a myriad of important questions regarding the political, economic, social, religious, cultural, and intellectual aspects of the revolution—questions involving causation, behavior, outcomes, and assessments. Each generation of historians has taken the work of its predecessors, and used it to shape an understanding of the revolution that emanates from the uncovering of new sources of information, the creation of new tools to assist in the process, and the development of new schools of historical thought, which attempt to give a more contemporary, relevant slant to this important event. As a result of this historiographical process, many major questions regarding the French Revolution have been raised, and plausible answers given.

One of the most important questions that French Revolution scholarship has raised—a double-edged one that is both elemental and significant—is: What were its outcomes, and were they worth the human cost that was paid to achieve them?

The debate began before anyone knew what course the revolution would take. In a 1790 treatise entitled *Reflections on the Revolution in France*, English statesman Edmund Burke (1729–1797) uncannily predicted the future course of the revolution and its catastrophic consequences for both France and Europe. He also argued in favor of a slow, evolutionary style of political change, which was taking place in his own country, rather than the spasmodic one that was beginning to envelop France. Burke's message was clear: the revolution in France will be costly and counterproductive.

A year later, the French Revolution gained an articulate defender in the person of Thomas Paine (1737–1809), an English-born American citizen. In *Common Sense* (1776), a stirring call-to-arms to the American colonists to throw off the yoke of English oppression, Paine acquired a reputation as a foe of tyrannical government and a strong supporter of human freedom and equality. In Part I of his political pamphlet *The Rights of Man*, Paine argued that revolution was necessary to purge civilization of those elements that stood in the way of democratic reform. According to Paine, no price was too high to pay for the realization of those cherished goals.

As generations passed, the basic question debated by Burke and Paine faded into the background as historians began to explore other fertile areas of historical research. There was either a general acceptance of the French Revolution's importance in changing the course of history or a quiet acquiescence to its outcomes, regardless of their consequences.

Peter Alexeievich Kropotkin (1842–1921) was an early historical defender of the French Revolution. Obviously influenced by his radical, anarchistic background and his desire to see all people freed from the yoke of oppression, his view of the revolution was somewhat simplistic and uncritical. Coming from a nineteenth-century environment where revolutions were commonplace and were viewed by many as an inevitable part of political evolution, Kropotkin expressed opinions on the French Revolution that were representative of his time, and endured for generations to come.

The first few years of the French Revolution (1789–1792) have been referred to as the "The Moderate Phase." The storming of the Bastille, a political prison in Paris, by an angry mob on July, 14, 1789, marked the first organized defiance of authority and resulted in deaths from both authoritarian and revolutionary forces. But the country did not immediately break apart into a bloody civil war. Moderate political factions gained control of France's National Assembly. This body drew up and enacted radical changes in the structure and nature of the nation's political system. King Louis XVI was forced to acquiesce but was never totally supportive of any changes in France's political structure. However, despite some conflict and controversy over the next few years, France had weathered the storm caused by the revolution's first phrase.

But two events occurred, which would shatter whatever peace France had achieved. In June 1791, the French royal family, traveling in disguise, attempted to leave the country and join émigrés, French noblemen working in neighboring countries, to organize an overthrow of France's new government. They were recognized and stopped at the border and returned to Paris as political prisoners. The guillotine would be their ultimate fate.

There is a saying that "Whenever France sneezes, Europe catches cold." When France's neighboring nations feared that what was happening in France might spread to their lands, they declared war on France and immediately invaded its territory. The French responded with feelings of both ultra-patriotism and fear, and the ultimate result was the end of moderate rule and the beginning of the revolution's second or "Radical Phase." The ensuing "Reign of Terror" provided an irrationality seldom seen, as French citizens killed each other for little or no reason. The Terror was thankfully short-lived, and France eventually maintained peace with its neighbors and its own people.

The most controversial feature of the French Revolution was this infamous "Reign of Terror," and it is a subject that all toilers in the garden of the revolution have to confront. The horrors of the twentieth century (some committed in the name of revolution) demand that the Terror gets the fullest treatment possible. Only then can the question as to whether or not the revolution was worth its human cost be answered.

The bicentennial celebration of France's revolution in 1989 was somewhat muted in tone. While credit for it was duly given, in the background was a sense of caution and concern, perhaps brought on by reminders of the revolution's violent dark side, which had been noted by some historians and commentators. It certainly bore little resemblance to our own bicentennial celebration on July 4, 1976.

An analysis of Japan's nineteenth-century "Meiji Restoration," and whether it was a revolution in the classical sense can be found in an issue on McGraw-Hill Create™. To examine the French Revolution, we suggest a comparison of the Meiji movement with other revolutions (including the French), using the model established by Crane Brinton in *The Anatomy of Revolution* (Random House, 1966). A comparison of the Meiji Japanese and French revolutionary experiences would be a tool that could be used to analyze the nature of past and future revolutions.

# YES ↵

Peter Kropotkin

# The Great French Revolution, 1789–1793

When one sees that terrible and powerful Convention wrecking itself in 1794–1795, that proud and strong Republic disappearing, and France, after the demoralising *régime* of the Directory, falling under the military yoke of a Bonaparte, one is impelled to ask: "What was the good of the Revolution if the nation had to fall back again under despotism?" In the course of the nineteenth century, this question has been constantly put, and the timid and conservative have worn it threadbare as an argument against revolutions in general.

. . . Those who have seen in the Revolution only a change in the Government, those who are ignorant of its economic as well as its educational work, those alone could put such a question.

The France we see during the last days of the eighteenth century, at the moment of the *coup d'état* on the 18th Brumaire, is not the France that existed before 1789. Would it have been possible for the old France, wretchedly poor and with a third of her population suffering yearly from dearth, to have maintained the Napoleonic Wars, coming so soon after the terrible wars of the Republic between 1792 and 1799, when all Europe was attacking her?

The fact is, that a new France had been constituted since 1792–1793. Scarcity still prevailed in many of the departments, and its full horrors were felt especially after the *coup d'état* of Thermidor, when the maximum price for all foodstuffs was abolished. There were still some departments which did not produce enough wheat to feed themselves, and as the war went on, and all means of transport were requisitioned for its supplies, there was scarcity in those departments. But everything tends to prove that France was even then producing much more of the necessaries of life of every kind than in 1789.

Never was there in France such energetic ploughing, Michelet tells us, as in 1792, when the peasant was ploughing the lands he had taken back from the lords, the convents, the churches, and was goading his oxen to the cry of *"Allons Prusse! Allons Autriche!"* Never had there been so much clearing of lands—even royalist writers admit this—as during those years of revolution. The first good harvest, in 1794, brought relief to two-thirds of France—at least in the villages, for all this time the towns were threatened with scarcity of food. Not that it was scarce in France as a whole, or that the *sans-culotte* municipalities neglected to take measures to feed those who could not find employment, but from the fact that all beasts of burden not actually used in tillage were requisitioned to carry food and ammunition to the fourteen armies of the Republic. In those days there were no railways, and all but the main roads were in the state they are to this day in Russia—well-nigh impassable.

A new France was born during those four years of revolution. For the first time in centuries the peasant ate his fill, straightened his back and dared to speak out. Read the detailed reports concerning the return of Louis XVI to Paris, when he was brought back a prisoner from Varennes, in June 1791, by the peasants, and say: "Could such a thing, such an interest in the public welfare, such a devotion to it, and such an independence of judgment and action have been possible before 1789?" A new nation had been born in the meantime, just as we see today a new nation coming into life in Russia and in Turkey.

It was owing to this new birth that France was able to maintain her wars under the Republic and Napoleon, and to carry the principles of the Great Revolution into Switzerland, Italy, Spain, Belgium, Holland, Germany, and even to the borders of Russia. And when, after all those wars, after having mentally followed the French armies as far as Egypt and Moscow, we expect to find France in 1815 reduced to an appalling misery and her lands laid waste, we find, instead, that even in its eastern portions and in the Jura, the country is much more prosperous than it was at the time when Pétion, pointing out to Louis XVI, the luxuriant banks of the Marne, asked him if there was anywhere in the world a kingdom more beautiful than the one the King had not wished to keep.

The self-contained energy was such in villages regenerated by the Revolution, that in a few years France became a country of well-to-do peasants, and her enemies soon discovered that in spite of all the blood she had shed and the losses she had sustained, France, in respect of her *productivity,* was the richest country in Europe. Her wealth, indeed, is not drawn from the Indies or from her foreign commerce: it comes from her own soil, from her love of the soil, from her own skill and industry. She is the richest country, because of the subdivision of her wealth, and she is still richer because of the possibilities she offers for the future.

Such was the effect of the Revolution. And if the casual observer sees in Napoleonic France only a love of glory, the historian realises that even the wars France waged at that period were undertaken to secure the fruits of the

Kropotkin, Peter. From *The Great French Revolution, 1789–1793*, 1971, trans. N.F. Dryhurst (Schocken Books, 1971).

Revolution—to keep the lands that had been retaken from the lords, the priests and the rich, and the liberties that had been won from despotism and the Court. If France was willing in those years to bleed herself to death, merely to prevent the Germans, the English, and the Russians from forcing a Louis XVI, upon her, it was because she did not want the return of the emigrant nobles to mean that the *ci-devants* would take back the lands which had been watered already with the peasant's sweat, and the liberties which had been sanctified with the patriots' blood. And France fought so well for twenty-three years, that when she was compelled at last to admit the Bourbons, it was she who imposed conditions on them. The Bourbons might reign, but the lands were to be kept by those who had taken them from the feudal lords, so that even during the White Terror of the Bourbons they dared not touch those lands. The old régime could not be re-established.

This is what is gained by making a Revolution.

There are other things to be pointed out. In the history of all nations a time comes when fundamental changes are bound to take place in the whole of the national life. Royal despotism and feudalism were dying in 1789; it was impossible to keep them alive; they had to go.

But then, two ways were opened out before France: reform or revolution.

At such times there is always a moment when reform is still possible; but if advantage has not been taken of that moment, if an obstinate resistance has been opposed to the requirements of the new life, up to the point when blood has flowed in the streets, as it flowed on July 14, 1789, then there must be a Revolution. And once the Revolution has begun, it must necessarily develop to its conclusions—that is to say, to the highest point it is capable of attaining—were it only temporarily, being given a certain condition of the public mind at this particular moment.

If we represent the slow progress of a period of evolution by a line drawn on paper, we shall see this line gradually though slowly rising. Then there comes a Revolution, and the line makes a sudden leap upwards. In England the line would be represented as rising to the Puritan Republic of Cromwell; in France it rises to the *Sans-culotte* Republic of 1793. However, at this height progress cannot be maintained; all the hostile forces league together against it, and the Republic goes down. Our line, after having reached that height, drops. Reaction follows. For the political life of France the line drops very low indeed, but by degrees it rises again, and when peace is restored in 1815 in France, and in 1688 in England—both countries are found to have attained a level much higher than they were on prior to their Revolutions.

After that, evolution is resumed: our line again begins to rise slowly: but, besides taking place on a very much higher level, the rising of the line will in nearly every case be also much more rapid than before the period of disturbance.

This is a law of human progress, and also a law of individual progress. The more recent history of France confirms this very law by showing how it was necessary to pass through the Commune to arrive at the Third Republic.

The work of the French Revolution is not confined merely to what it obtained and what was retained of it in France. It is to be found also in the principles bequeathed by it to the succeeding century—in the line of direction it marked out for the future.

A reform is always a compromise with the past, but the progress accomplished by revolution is always a promise of future progress. If the Great French Revolution was the summing up of a century's evolution, it also marked out in its turn the programme of evolution to be accomplished in the course of the nineteenth century.

It is a law in the world's history that the period of a hundred or a hundred and thirty years, more or less, which passes between two great revolutions, receives its character from the revolution in which this period began. The nations endeavour to realise in their institutions the inheritance bequeathed to them by the last revolution. All that this last could not yet put into practice, all the great thoughts which were thrown into circulation during the turmoil, and which the revolution either could not or did not know how to apply, all the attempts at sociological reconstruction, which were born during the revolution, will go to make up the substance of evolution during the epoch that follows the revolution, with the addition of those new ideas to which this evolution will give birth, when trying to put into practice the programme marked out by the last upheaval. Then, a new revolution will be brought about in some other nation, and this nation in its turn will set the problems for the following century. Such has hitherto been the trend of history.

Two great conquests, in fact, characterise the century which has passed since 1789–1793. Both owe their origin to the French Revolution, which had carried on the work of the English Revolution while enlarging and invigorating it with all the progress that had been made since the English middle classes beheaded their King and transferred his power to the Parliament. These two great triumphs are: the abolition of serfdom and the abolition of absolutism, by which personal liberties have been conferred upon the individual, undreamt of by the serf of the lord and the subject of the absolute king, while at the same time they have brought about the development of the middle classes and the capitalist *régime*.

These two achievements represent the principal work of the nineteenth century, begun in France in 1789 and slowly spread over Europe in the course of that century.

The work of enfranchisement, begun by the French peasants in 1789, was continued in Spain, Italy, Switzerland, Germany, and Austria by the armies of the *sans-culottes*. Unfortunately, this work hardly penetrated into Poland and did not reach Russia at all.

The abolition of serfdom in Europe would have been already completed in the first half of the nineteenth century if the French *bourgeoisie,* coming into power in 1794 over the dead bodies of Anarchists, Cordeliers, and Jacobins, had not checked the revolutionary impulse, restored monarchy, and handed over France to the imperial juggler, the first Napoleon. This ex-*sans-culotte,* now a general of the *sans-culottes,* speedily began to prop up aristocracy; but the impulsion had been given, the institution of serfdom had already received a mortal blow. It was abolished in Spain and Italy in spite of the temporary triumph of reaction. It was closely pressed in Germany after 1811, and disappeared in that country definitively in 1848. In 1861, Russia was compelled to emancipate her serfs, and the war of 1878 put an end to serfdom in the Balkan peninsula.

The cycle is now complete. The right of the lord over the person of the peasant no longer exists in Europe, even in those countries where the feudal dues have still to be redeemed.

This fact is not sufficiently appreciated by historians. Absorbed as they are in political questions, they do not perceive the importance of the abolition of serfdom, which is, however, the essential feature of the nineteenth century. The rivalries between nations and the wars resulting from them, the policies of the Great Powers which occupy so much of the historian's attention, have all sprung from that one great fact—the abolition of serfdom and the development of the wage system which has taken its place.

The French peasant, in revolting a hundred and twenty years ago against the lord who made him beat the ponds lest croaking frogs should disturb his master's sleep, has thus freed the peasants of all Europe. In four years, by burning the documents which registered his subjection, by setting fire to the chateaux, and by executing the owners of them who refused to recognise his rights as a human being, the French peasant so stirred up all Europe that it is today altogether free from the degradation of serfdom.

On the other hand, the abolition of absolute power has also taken a little over a hundred years to make the tour of Europe. Attacked in England in 1648, and vanquished in France in 1789, royal authority based on divine right is no longer exercised save in Russia, but there, too, it is at its last gasp. Even the little Balkan States and Turkey have now their representative assemblies, and Russia is entering the same cycle.

In this respect the Revolution of 1789–1793 has also accomplished its work. Equality before the law and representative government have now their place in almost all the codes of Europe. In theory, at least, the law makes no distinctions between men, and everyone has the right to participate, more or less, in the government.

⸎

The absolute monarch—master of his subjects—and the lord—master of the soil and the peasants, by right of birth—have both disappeared. The middle classes now govern Europe.

But at the same time the Great Revolution has bequeathed to us some other principles of an infinitely higher import: the principles of communism. We have seen how all through the Great Revolution the communist idea kept coming to the front, and how after the fall of the Girondins numerous attempts and sometimes great attempts were made in this direction. Fourierism descends in a direct line from L'Ange on one side and from Chalier on the other. Babeuf is the direct descendant of ideas which stirred the masses to enthusiasm in 1793; he, Buonarotti, and Sylvain Maréchal have only systematised them a little or even merely put them into literary form. But the secret societies organized by Babeuf and Buonarotti were the origin of the *communistes matérialistes* secret societies through which Blanqui and Barb'es conspired under the *bourgeois* monarchy of Louis-Philippe. Later on, in 1866, the International Working Men's Association appeared in the direct line of descent from these societies. As to "socialism" we know now that this term came into vogue to avoid the term "communism," which at one time was dangerous because the secret communist societies became societies for action, and were rigorously suppressed by the *bourgeoisie* then in power.

There is, therefore, a direct filiation from the *Enragés* of 1793 and the Babeuf conspiracy of 1795 to the International Working Men's Association of 1866–1878.

There is also a direct descent of ideas. Up till now, modern socialism has added absolutely nothing to the ideas which were circulating among the French people between 1789 and 1794 and which it was tried to put into practice in the Year II of the Republic. Modern socialism has only systematised those ideas and found arguments in their favour, either by turning against the middle-class economists certain of their own definitions, or by generalising certain facts noticed in the development of industrial capitalism, in the course of the nineteenth century.

But I permit myself to maintain also that, however vague it may have been, however little support it endeavoured to draw from arguments dressed in a scientific garb, and however little use it made of the pseudo-scientific slang of the middle-class economists, the popular communism of the first two years of the Republic saw clearer, and went much deeper in its analyses, than modern socialism.

First of all, it was communism in the consumption of the necessaries of life—not in production only; it was the communalisation and the nationalisation of what economists know as consumption—to which the stern republicans of 1793 turned, above all, their attention, when they tried to establish their stores of grain and provisions in every commune, when they set on foot a gigantic inquiry to find and fix the true value of the objects of prime and secondary necessity, and when they inspired Robespierre to declare that *only the superfluity of food stuffs should become articles of commerce, and that what was necessary belonged to all.*

Born out of the pressing necessities of those troublous years, the communism of 1793, with its affirmation of the right of all to sustenance and to the land for its production, its denial of the right of anyone to hold more land than he and his family could cultivate—that is, more than a farm of 120 acres—and its attempt to communalise all trade and industry—this communism went straighter to the heart of things than all the minimum programmes of our own time, and even all the maximum preambles of such programmes.

In any case, what we learn today from the study of the Great Revolution is, that it was the source of origin of all the present communist, anarchist, and socialist conceptions. We have but badly understood our common mother, but now we have found her again in the midst of the *sansculottes,* and we see what we have to learn from her.

Humanity advances by stages and these stages have been marked for several hundred years by great revolutions. After the Netherlands came England with her revolution in 1648–1657, and then it was the turn of France. Each great revolution has in it, besides, something special and original. England and France both abolished royal absolutism. But in doing so England was chiefly interested in the personal rights of the individual, particularly in matters of religion, as well as the local rights of every parish and every community. As to France, she turned her chief attention to the land question, and in striking a mortal blow at the feudal system she struck also at the great fortunes, and sent forth into the world the idea of nationalising the soil, and of socialising commerce and the chief industries.

Which of the nations will take upon herself the terrible but glorious task of the next great revolution? One may have thought for a time that it would be Russia. But if she should push her revolution further than the mere limitation of the imperial power; if she touches the land question in a revolutionary spirit—how far will she go? Will she know how to avoid the mistake made by the French Assemblies, and will she socialise the land and give it only to those who want to cultivate it with their own hands? We know not: any answer to this question would belong to the domain of prophecy.

The one thing certain is, that whatsoever nation enters on the path of revolution in our own day, it will be heir to all our forefathers have done in France. The blood they shed was shed for humanity—the sufferings they endured were borne for the entire human race; their struggles, the ideas they gave to the world, the shock of those ideas, are all included in the heritage of mankind. All have borne fruit and will bear more, still finer, as we advance towards those wide horizons opening out before us, where, like some great beacon to point the way, flame the words— LIBERTY, EQUALITY, FRATERNITY.

---

PETER KROPOTKIN (1842–1921) was a Russian revolutionary who wrote his autobiography entitled *Memoirs of a Revolutionist* in 1899.

**Marisa Linton**

 **NO**

# Robespierre and the Terror

**M**aximilien Robespierre has always provoked strong feelings. For the English he is the 'sea-green incorruptible' portrayed by Carlyle, the repellent figure at the head of the Revolution, who sent thousands of people to their death under the guillotine. The French, for the most part, dislike his memory still more. There is no national monument to him, though many of the revolutionaries have had statues raised to them. Robespierre is still considered beyond the pale; only one rather shabby metro station in a poorer suburb of Paris bears his name.

Although Robespierre, like most of the revolutionaries, was a bourgeois, he identified with the cause of the urban workers, the *sans-culottes* as they came to be known, and became a spokesman for them. It is for this reason that he came to dominate the Revolution in its most radical phase. This was the period of the Jacobin government, which lasted from June 1793 to Robespierre's overthrow in July 1794; the months when the common people became briefly the masters of the first French republic, which had been proclaimed in September 1792. It is also known, more ominously, as the Terror.

The enigmatic figure of Robespierre takes us to the heart of the Revolution, and throws light both on its ideals, and on the violence that indelibly scarred it.

Born in Arras in 1758, Robespierre suffered loss early in his life. His mother died when he was six, and soon after, his father abandoned the family. The children were brought up by elderly relatives who continually reminded them of their dependent situation and their father's irresponsibility. Maximilien was the eldest, a conscientious, hardworking scholarship boy. As soon as he was able he shouldered the burden of caring for his younger siblings. He became a lawyer, leading a quiet and blameless life in his native town. He was best known for defending the poor, and for some rather lengthy and tedious speeches at the local academy.

In 1789, when he was in his early thirties, the Revolution transformed his destiny. He launched himself into the political maelstrom that would immerse him for the rest of his life. He was elected as a deputy for the Third Estate in the Estates General in May, and he witnessed the onset of the Revolution that broke the power of the absolute monarchy two months later. Painstakingly, he worked to forge a reputation for himself as a public speaker in the Assembly. He had his power base in the Jacobin Club, the most important of the revolutionary clubs where people debated events.

From the first, Robespierre was a radical and a democrat, defending the principle that the 'rights of man' should extend to all men—including the poor, and the slaves in the colonies. This stance won him a reputation among the *sans-culottes* and the radical left, but the earlier years of the Revolution were dominated by men who had no wish to see power in the hands of the propertyless. Robespierre was undaunted. As a spokesman for the opposition and critic of government, he was tireless and consistent. He was also for a long time a vehement opponent of the death penalty. Why did he later change his mind and become an advocate of Terror? Part of the answer to this question lies in the deterioration of the political situation between 1789 and 1792, and the failure of the attempt to set up a workable constitutional monarchy, under Louis XVI.

From the spring of 1792 onwards France was involved in a spiral of war, revolt and civil war. Counter-revolutionaries were plotting the restoration of the absolute monarchy with the support of the Holy Roman Emperor Leopold II (succeeded in March by Francis II). The Girondins, then the dominant revolutionary faction in the Legislative Assembly, spearheaded the drive for an aggressive war with the Empire, declaring war in April 1792. The avowed intention of their leader, Jacques-Pierre Brissot, was to polarize French politics, oblige the counter-revolutionaries to emerge into open opposition, and force the monarchy either to capitulate to the revolutionaries or to face its own destruction. In these circumstances, political views hardened, suspicion and fear increased, and the early optimism of the Revolution vanished.

Robespierre himself had long warned of the dangers of provoking counter-revolution. He had tried to oppose the war, because he thought it would divide France and rally support for the counter-revolutionaries. Nor did he believe, as Brissot did, that the ordinary people of Europe would welcome an invading French army, even one that claimed to deliver liberty and equality. 'No one,' said Robespierre, 'welcomes armed liberators.' He stuck doggedly to this position, though it was deeply unpopular and he became politically isolated.

By the summer of 1792, his worst fears were realized. The French army, far from being victorious, was on the verge of defeat and suffered from disorganization and raw and inexperienced troops. Many people thought (not without reason) that Louis was secretly on the side of the Austrian and Prussian armies, which were now threatening Paris itself. Many now felt that Robespierre spoke for them when he declared that the aristocrats were plotting a conspiracy to destroy the Revolution. In August the monarchy was overthrown in a pitched battle at the Tuileries palace. A new government, the National Convention, was formed in September 1792, which promptly declared France to be a republic. By now Robespierre's ascendancy in the Jacobin club was unrivalled. The Jacobins identified themselves with the popular movement and the *sans-culottes*, who in turn saw popular violence as a political right.

The most notorious instance of the crowd's rough justice was the prison massacres of September 1792, when around 2,000 people, including priests and nuns, were dragged from their prison cells, and subjected to summary 'justice'. The Convention was determined to avoid a repeat of these brutal scenes, but that meant taking violence into their own hands as an instrument of government.

When the Convention debated the fate of Louis XVI, now a prisoner of the revolutionaries, Robespierre and his youthful colleague, Saint-Just (1767–94)—also once an opponent of the death penalty—led the way in claiming that 'Louis must die in order for the Revolution to live'. Robespierre had not abandoned his libertarian convictions, but he was coming to the conclusion that the ends justified the means, and that in order to defend the Revolution against those who would destroy it, the shedding of blood was justified.

In June 1793, the *sans-culottes*, exasperated by the inadequacies of the government, invaded the Convention and overthrew the Girondins. In their place they endorsed the political ascendancy of the Jacobins. Thus Robespierre came to power on the back of popular street violence. Though the Girondins and the Jacobins were both on the extreme left, and shared many of the same radical republican convictions, the Jacobins were much more brutally efficient in setting up a war government. A Committee of Public Safety was established to act as a war cabinet. It became the chief executive power, with Robespierre—now moving from opposition to government for the first time—one of its twelve members. Like so many politicians making such a move, Robespierre's attitude to political power was to change dramatically from this moment. In June the Jacobins drafted a new constitution, the most libertarian and egalitarian the world had yet seen. Yet for some months they hesitated to implement it, as the pressures of war with Austria and Prussia, and of full-blown civil war in the Vendée in the west were compounded by revolts across the country by *départements* rejecting the authority of the radical government in Paris.

In September 1793, the impatient *sans-culottes* once again invaded the Convention to exert pressure on the deputies. They wanted economic measures to ensure their food supplies, and the government to deal with counter-revolutionaries. A delegation of the forty-eight sections of *sans-culottes* urged the Convention to 'make Terror the order of the day!' The Jacobins responded: the Law of Suspects was passed on September 17th, 1793, giving wide powers of arrest to the ruling Committees, and defining 'suspects' in broad terms. In October the Convention passed the Decree on Emergency Government. This authorized the revolutionary government to suspend peacetime rights and legal safeguards and to employ coercion and violence. Saint-Just decreed that the government 'would be revolutionary until the peace'. The constitution was shelved: the libertarian ideals of the Revolution were suspended, indefinitely. *Sans-culottes* formed armed militias to go out into the provinces to requisition supplies for the armies and the urban populace and to root out counter-revolutionaries. In October Brissot and other Girondin leaders, as well as Marie-Antoinette went to the guillotine.

For the first time in history terror became an official government policy, with the stated aim to use violence in order to achieve a higher political goal. Unlike the later meaning of 'terrorists' as people who use violence against a government, the terrorists of the French Revolution were the government. The Terror was legal, having been voted for by the Convention.

Robespierre, like a number of the Jacobin government, had been a lawyer. He clung to the form of law partly in order to prevent the *sans-culottes* taking the law into their own hands through mob violence. As fellow revolutionary Danton said, 'let us be terrible in order to stop the people from being so'. The resort to Terror also emerged out of relative weakness and fear. The Jacobins had only a shaky legitimacy and innumerable opponents throughout France, ranging from intransigent royalists to more moderate revolutionaries who had seen power centralized and their ideas superseded. Many people in France were already indifferent, if not openly hostile, to the Revolution. For many the Revolution now meant requisitioning of supplies, military conscription and the constant threat to their traditional ways of life, churches, even time—for the revolutionaries had even invented a new calendar. Throughout the year of Jacobin rule, it was the *sans-culottes* who kept them in power. But the price of that support was the blood-letting.

The number of death sentences in Paris was 2,639, while the total number during the Terror in the whole of France (including Paris) was 16,594. With the exception of Paris (where many of the more important prisoners were transferred to appear before the Revolutionary Tribunal) most of the executions were carried out in regions of revolt such as the Vendée, Lyon and Marseilles. There were wide regional variations. Because on the whole the Jacobins were meticulous in maintaining a legal structure for the Terror clear records exist for official death sentences. But many more people were murdered without formal sentences imposed in a court of law. Some died in overcrowded and unsanitary prisons awaiting trial, while others died in the civil wars and federalist revolts, their deaths unrecorded. The historian Jean-Clément Martin, suggests that up to 250,000 insurgents and 200,000 republicans met their deaths in the Vendée, a war which lasted from 1793–96 in which both sides suffered appalling atrocities.

Today the civil war in the Vendée is largely forgotten except by specialists. It is of the guillotine that most people think when they hear about the Terror. After so many bloodlettings of the twentieth century, why does that image still have the power to shock us? The historian Lord Acton once famously said that in terms of the time, the deaths under the Terror were relatively few in number (he was thinking of the official death sentences). As Acton pointed out, many millions were to die in Napoleon's wars for no better reason than his own glory. Yet the aura of the hero still clings to Napoleon, while Robespierre's name is synonymous with violence and horror.

Perhaps it is because of the stark contrast between Robespierre's ideals and what he became that the question of the Terror remains shocking. In the mind of Robespierre and many of his colleagues, the Terror had a deeper moral purpose beyond winning the civil war: to bring about a 'republic of virtue'. By this he meant a society in which people sought the happiness of their fellow humans rather than their own material benefit. France must be regenerated on moral lines. 'What is our aim?' he asked in a speech of February 1794:

> The peaceful enjoyment of liberty and equality; the reign of that eternal justice whose laws are written, not on marble or stone, but in the hearts of all men, even in that of the slave who forgets them and of the tyrant who denies them.

He came to the conclusion that in order to establish this ideal republic one had to be prepared to eliminate opponents of the Revolution. The irony of this idea rings through in the same speech, when he justified the Terror. He said:

> If the basis of popular government in peacetime is virtue, the basis of popular government during a revolution is both virtue and terror; virtue, without which terror is baneful; terror, without which virtue is powerless. Terror is nothing more than speedy, severe and inflexible justice; it is thus an emanation of virtue; it is less a principle in itself, than a consequence of the general principle of democracy, applied to the most pressing needs of the *patrie*.

Throughout his time in government Robespierre conducted his private life as a man of virtue. Far from living in palaces, amassing treasure, or allying himself with royalty, as Napoleon was to do, Robespierre lived a celibate life as a lodger, occupying simple rooms in the house of a master carpenter. He was known as 'the Incorruptible' for,

unlike many politicians, he refused to use a public position for private gain and self-advancement. He lived simply on his deputy's salary. He walked everywhere, never taking a carriage. He enjoyed walks in the country and musical *soirées* with his landlord's family.

Yet the other side of this benign, if dull, domestic life, was the public role he undertook as a spokesman for the Committee of Public Safety and the guiding hand on the policy of Terror. He had become an astute political tactician, and he used these means finally to achieve political power. He could be accused, justly, of political ambition, but he himself did not see this as inconsistent with his dedication to the Revolution. He had an unshakable belief that his own aims coincided with what was best for the Revolution. He was a man of painful sincerity. He was not a hypocrite. He really did believe that the Terror could sustain the republic of virtue. But he was naturally self-righteous, suspicious and unforgiving. All these qualities came to the fore as it became evident that while the Terror played a key part in winning the war and quelling the counter-revolution, it was having the reverse effect as far as installing the republic of virtue was concerned, undermining any genuine enthusiasm for the Revolution. Even Saint-Just, Robespierre's most loyal friend on the Committee of Public Safety, could not be blind to the way the Terror, with its neighbourhood surveillance committees and denunciations, encouraged an atmosphere of duplicity, cynicism and fear, even among the Revolution's most fervent supporters, the Jacobins. 'The Revolution is frozen', he wrote dispairingly in a private note in 1794.

Some of the victims of the last months of the Terror were Robespierre's former friends and colleagues, stalwarts of the Jacobin Club. They included Camille Desmoulins, Robespierre's comrade from his schooldays. Desmoulins had taken the fateful step of supporting Georges Danton, another former friend of Robespierre, in his call that the Terror be wound down, and the power of the Committee of Public Safety broken. In December 1793 he launched a journal, *Le Vieux Cordelier*, arguing that the Revolution should return to its original ideals. Up to a point Robespierre had supported Desmoulins and his campaign against the more violent extremism of the *sans-culottes*, led by the journalist, Hébert. Robespierre read, and approved, the first two issues of *Le Vieux Cordelier* in proof. But in the third issue of the journal, Desmoulins parodied the notorious Law of Suspects and its wide range of people who could be considered 'counter-revolutionary'. Under the Roman Empire, he said, paraphrasing Tacitus, people could be condemned as counter-revolutionary for being 'too rich . . . or too poor . . . too melancholy . . . or too self-indulgent'. Robespierre saw this satire—rightly—as a veiled attack on the Committee of Public Safety itself. Robespierre tried to persuade Desmoulins to burn the journal publicly in the Jacobin Club. Desmoulins refused, recklessly citing the words of Robespierre's hero, Jean-Jacques Rousseau, against him: 'burning is not an answer'. Robespierre was stung, and stopped trying to help his friend. When the

Committees decided to arrest Danton and Desmoulins in March 1794, Robespierre used his personal knowledge of the two men to supplement his notes for the official indictment against them. Desmoulins' wife, Lucille, tried to agitate for his release but she too was accused of conspiracy against the Revolution and followed her husband to the guillotine in April. The letter from her heart-broken mother to Robespierre, begging for his intervention to save her daughter, went unanswered. Robespierre had said that a man of virtue must put the good of la patrie before private loyalty, even to his friends. Never had his own virtue seemed so appalling and inhuman as at that moment.

Perhaps he thought so too, and the strain of what he had become was beginning to tell. In the last few weeks of his life he shut himself in his rooms, and did not attend the meetings of the Committee or the Convention. He was losing his grip, both on himself and on power. In his absence it is notable that it was 'business as usual' for the Terror: in Paris the executions intensified, based on the notorious Law of 22nd Prairial (June 10th, 1794) which, by depriving the accused of counsel and removing the need for witnesses to substantiate accusations, removed the vestige of justice from the Tribunal.

Robespierre was never the head of the government, nor the only terrorist: he was one man on the Committee—albeit its most high-profile member. Other members of the Committee, together with members of the Committee of General Security (responsible for the police, prisons and most of the arrests), were as much responsible for the running of the Terror as Robespierre. Some of his colleagues were hard, ambitious men, not averse to political corruption unlike Robespierre, and scornful of his dream of a virtuous republic. There were aspects of the Terror with which Robespierre disagreed. He was an opponent of dechristianization—a policy carried out by some militant sans-culottes of forcibly closing churches and preventing any kind of religious activity. In June 1794 he organized the festival of the Supreme Being, based on Enlightenment deist beliefs, intended to unify the people around broadly moral and vaguely religious principles. It made him a laughing stock with the atheists among the deputies and failed to conciliate devout Catholics, long since alienated from the Revolution by its anti-clericalism.

Robespierre also deplored the violent excesses of some of the Jacobin deputies sent out 'on mission' from the Convention to oversee the implementation of policy in the provinces and with the armies. While many of the deputies on mission were conscientious and restrained, others misused their powers to arrest, intimidate and execute local populations. Robespierre had some of these deputies, including Tallien, Fouché, Fréron, Barras and Collot d'Herbois, in his sights when he went to the Convention

for the first time in more than four weeks on the July 26th (8 Thermidor by the revolutionary calendar). It was the turning point. He had already quarrelled with men on both the ruling Committees, and, having rejected the reconciliation which Saint-Just tried to broker, he was left with little alternative but to try to destroy his enemies before they could do the same to him. He made a long speech in which he sought to justify the stand he had taken as a defender of virtue. But he also took the opportunity to demand another purge of suspect deputies. In a fatal miscalculation, he failed to name these men. Not unnaturally, many of the fearful deputies thought he might mean them. 'The names!' they shouted. But he refused. His enemies among the Jacobins spent that night in organizing their conspiracy. The next day Saint-Just was shouted down when he tried to speak in his friend's defence. Robespierre and his closest associates were arrested and, after a futile attempt to rally the sans-culottes to defend them at the town hall, they were executed the following day.

The men who overthrew Robespierre were more ruthless and cynical terrorists than he. They included Vadier, Elie Lacoste, Billaud-Varenne and Collot d'Herbois on the Committees, as well as the deputies who had carried out atrocities whilst 'on mission'. Initially they wanted the Terror to continue. But it rapidly became clear that the public had sickened of it. Since the overwhelming victory over the Austrians in the Low Countries at Fleurus on June 26th, the military justification for it had also diminished. In the reaction after Thermidor, as the coup is known, terrorist politicians rapidly restyled themselves. Members of the Committees now claimed that they had concerned themselves exclusively with the war: it was only the Robespierrists who had been terrorists. In the popular imagination Robespierre the enigma rapidly became the embodiment of the Terror. Yet he would never have been so influential had he not spoken for a wide swathe of society and government. When he spoke of conspiracies against the Revolution, of the threats to 'the patrie in danger', and the need for extreme measures, he voiced the fears of many at that time that France was about to be overwhelmed by foreign and internal enemies. The policies of the Jacobin Committees had, after all, been endorsed by the deputies of the Convention. Perhaps this is why he has been so vilified: in holding one individual culpable for the ills of the Terror, French society was able to avoid looking into its own dark heart at that traumatic moment. Robespierre, you might say, took the rap.

**Marisa Linton** is a senior lecturer in history at Kingston University and the author of *The Politics of Virtue in Enlightenment France* (Palgrave, 2001).

# EXPLORING THE ISSUE

## Was the French Revolution Worth Its Human Costs?

## Critical Thinking and Reflection

1. Briefly summarize the consequences of the French Revolution—both positive and negative. What would you include among its "human costs"?
2. Critically analyze the political differences between a monarchy and a republic. What freedoms and what challenges does a republic offer its citizens.
3. Were the people of France ready for the duties of citizenship? Critically discuss.
4. Analyze the points-of-view and perspectives of both Prince Kropotkin (1842–1921), born shortly after the revolution, and Marisa Linton, a professor writing in 2006, more than 200 years after the revolution. Critically discuss the political time period in which each wrote and the possible influences these two time periods might have had on the authors' assumptions.
5. In nineteenth-century Europe, revolutions were common and were often seen as the most effective way to change political systems. What are the advantages and disadvantages of a political or military coup?
6. Compare a coup with the process of electoral change currently used in most democracies. Is one or the other a superior way to change political systems? Critically discuss.
7. Investigate and evaluate the contributions of women (principally the wives of artisans) to the French Revolution. Some women joined in the storming of the Bastille. Does this information change your understanding of the revolution? Critically discuss.
8. Do you agree with Prince Kropotkin that "Liberty, Equality, Fraternity" are worth any cost? Critically discuss.
9. In the context of questions raised in this issue, critically analyze the films *La Nuit deVarennes* (for its study of the chaotic nature of French Revolutionary society before the Reign of Terror) and *Danton* (for the horror that the Terror would become).

## Is There Common Ground?

Both writers agree that serfdom and the monarchy were eliminated. France, today, is a republic that, like the United States, celebrates its revolutionary roots. An excerpt from Kropotkin's book and an article written by a contemporary historian, not long after the 200th anniversary of the French Revolution, provide not only opposing viewpoints on whether or not the French Revolution was worth its human costs, but also a clear example of how different eras can have different values, which can in turn affect how the past is interpreted. One element of the explanation for their differences lies in where each focuses his attention. Kropotkin celebrates the Moderate phase; whereas, Linton chiefly analyzes the Radical phase. Suppose France had not experienced the Terror and Louis XVI had provided some leadership during troubling times. If, in addition, European nations had not invaded France in 1792, might we be reading about a completely different, and less bloody, French Revolution?

Of all the books written about the French Revolution in recent years, none has been as popular as Simon Schama's *Citizens: A Chronicle of the French Revolution* (Alfred A. Knopf, 1989). Written in the year of the revolution's bicentennial celebration, the book aroused much controversy for many reasons; among them was his view that the French Revolution was not worth its human costs. Seeing violence as an endemic part of the revolutionary process, Schama also stated that the revolution produced few of the tangible results it had promised. This book encouraged others to question the nature and consequences of the French Revolution.

*Question:* If France had not undergone a revolution, with all its positive and negative consequences, could it have entered the modern world. How would France have overthrown the power of the clergy and the monarchy? How would serfdom have been abolished? Was there an alternative path or were both phases of the revolution necessary?

## Create Central

www.mhhe.com/createcentral

## Additional Resources

To list all of the major sources on the French Revolution is daunting, but two general accounts, readable and perfect, for the beginning student would be: William Doyle, *The Oxford History of the French Revolution* (Oxford University Press, 1989), and Donald M.G. Sutherland, *France, 1879–1815: Revolution and Counter-Revolution* (Oxford University Press, 1986).

As always, much can be learned from Alexis de Tocqueville, whose *The Old Regime* and the *French Revolution,* first published in the 1850s. These could be a useful starting point for a study of the causes and effects of the French Revolution from the point of one of that century's keenest observers.

Finally, two films whose visuals would provide an understanding of the French Revolution would be *La Nuit de Varennes,* for its study of the chaotic nature of French Revolutionary society before the Reign of Terror, and *"Danton,* for the horror that the Terror would become.

# Internet References . . .

### Internet Modern History Sourcebook: French Revolution

Looks at the French Revolution from those who experienced it; breaks the revolution into phases; and presents relevant primary source materials for each.

**www.fordham.edu/halsall/mod/modsbook13.html**

Selected, Edited, and with Issue Framing Material by:
Helen Buss Mitchell, *Howard Community College*
and
Joseph R. Mitchell, *Howard Community College*

# ISSUE

## Does Napoleon Bonaparte Deserve His Historical Reputation as a Great General?

YES: **Graham Goodlad**, from "Napoleon at War: Secrets of Success, Seeds of Failure? *History Review* (December 2009)

NO: **Jonathon Riley**, from "How Good Was Napoleon?" *History Today* (July 2007)

---

### Learning Outcomes

After reading this issue you should be able to:

- Understand how biography can support the "Great Man" theory of history, as well as the value of biography in helping us interpret historical events/eras.
- Evaluate Napoleon Bonaparte's role in France's attempt to establish an empire.
- Explain the criteria used to judge generalship and evaluate Napoleon, using those criteria.
- Understand how France rose and fell as an imperial power.

---

### ISSUE SUMMARY

YES: Professor Graham Goodlad argues that, because of his extraordinary military career, Napoleon Bonaparte deserves his reputation as a great general.

NO: Author and Military Commander Jonathon Riley argues that because Napoleon never succeeded in transforming a defeated enemy into a willing ally, his historical reputation as a general must be questioned.

---

In the nineteenth century, the English historian Thomas Carlyle wrote that "The history of the world is but the biography of great men." In doing so, he established a trend that would dominate historical writing for more than a century; it stated that history could best be understood by viewing it through the eyes of the great men who influenced the times in which they lived.

Carlyle was not the first to call attention to the contributions of "Great Men" to the world's story; in the first century C.E., the Greek writer Plutarch (46–120) became the world's first major biographer. In a book commonly referred to as *Plutarch's Lives,* he chronicled the exploits of the Greco-Roman era's most prominent men and how they influenced the times in which they lived. His work has influenced historians for centuries, including Thomas Carlyle.

It is not surprising that many of these "Great Men" have been military leaders. From the beginning of recorded history, men such as Alexander the Great, Julius Caesar, Charlemagne, and Genghis Khan (see CREATE Issue) have all had their exploits documented and evaluated.

Napoleon Bonaparte is certainly worthy of mention in the same context.

Napoleon Bonaparte (1769–1821) was born on the French island of Corsica. He attended a military school in France, which was followed by a stint at the Ecole Royale Militaire where he excelled, finishing his course of study in 1 year while others needed 3. He was commissioned a second lieutenant in 1785.

His rise in the French Army was meteoric. He distinguished himself at the Battle of Toulon and in 1795 he saved the French government from a counter-revolutionary mob by utilizing "a whiff of grapeshot." As a reward, he was given command of France's Army of Italy. There he excelled in defeating the Austrians, one of France's main continental enemies.

In 1798 he led a French army on a Middle Eastern campaign that was designed to threaten British control of India. This foray is considered by many to be a failure; Admiral Horatio Nelson destroyed the French fleet, limiting Napoleon's military options. When a change of government occurred in France in 1799, Napoleon left (some say deserted) his army and returned to France. Shortly afterward, he participated in a coup d'etat, which brought an end to the current French government, and was named one of the three Consuls who ruled France. He was 30 years old.

Napoleon was soon declared First Consul, making him the supreme ruler of France. He used the new century's first years to consolidate his political power and initiate a series of domestic reforms the likes of which France had ever seen. None of these bold moves endangered Napoleon's political power. In 1804 he had himself crowned Emperor. With domestic affairs in stern, powerful hands, he could now turn his attention to battle with France's continental allies.

Austria was the first to fall, when Vienna was occupied in 1805. In the same year, he defeated Russo-Austrian forces at the Battle of Austerlitz. In 1806, he warred against Prussia and Russia, beat both, and became the master of the European continent. A series of treaties certified that condition.

But Napoleon could never defeat Britain. Admiral Nelson, who destroyed the French fleet at the Battle of the Nile, also led a British–Spanish fleet to victory over the French at the Battle of Trafalgar in 1805. This a French invasion of the British Isles, formerly a mainstay in French military plans.

Later, Napoleon made several egregious military errors. From 1808 to 1813, he invaded the Iberian Peninsula to bring it under his control. The Spanish, aided by the British, fought a guerilla-style war, which sapped the strength of the French forces and robbed them of the big victory their superior forces were supposed to secure.

But Napoleon's greatest military error was the invasion of Russia in 1812. Extended supply lines, coupled with the freezing Russian winter, forced Napoleon to retreat. His army of 614,000 men had been reduced to 95,000. With France so weak, the nations Napoleon defeated ganged up on him and defeated the French army at the Battle of Leipzig. Napoleon was forced to abdicate and was exiled to Elba, a small island off the coast of central Italy in 1814. A subsequent escape, a return to power in France, and a defeat once again at the Battle of Waterloo proved to be Napoleon's last stand. Exiled to St. Helena, a remote South Atlantic island a thousand miles off the coast of Africa, he spent his last 6 years there, dying in 1821. Supposedly, he was poisoned by a Frenchman whose family Napoleon had ruined.

Napoleon Bonaparte was a remarkable historical figure. He was the first world leader to command both the military and political branches of a modern nation-state. For a while he was the dominant force on the European continent, and even placed relatives on the thrones of his conquered states. But eventually he spread himself (and France) too thin and suffered a final defeat in 1815. We may never see another like him.

In assessing Napoleon's career as a military leader, Graham Goodlad emphasizes the tactics he used and his ability to improvise in the heat of battle. Goodlad also gives credit to the generals who carried out his plans and were able to correct Napoleon's mistakes, turning what might have been a potential disaster into a glowing triumph. Jonathon Riley, himself a military commander, takes a broader view in his assessment of Napoleon's generalship. He won a lot, but he also lost. His tactics brought much blood-letting both to the French and to their enemies. And finally, despite defeating nations in war, he was never able to totally pacify them. "He won wars, but he never won the peace."

Recent times have created new interest in this debate regarding Napoleon's generalship. Two authors take different sides of the question. Graham Goodlad states that Napoleon's many victories are sufficient to support his reputation as a great general. Jonathon Riley argues that Napoleon's ultimate defeat by forces he had previously conquered lessens his reputation as a military commander

# YES

**Graham Goodlad**

## Napoleon at War: Secrets of Success, Seeds of Failure?

Even at a distance of two centuries, the extraordinary military career of Napoleon Bonaparte exerts a great fascination. His campaigns continue to be studied as exemplars in army staff colleges. The flood of academic and popular books and articles on his life and legacy shows no sign of abating. Yet there is considerable disagreement among historians over Napoleon's qualities as a commander. Some have accorded him the status of a military genius, pointing to his command of the battlefield, his skills as an organiser and his charismatic leadership. Others, however, have suggested that there were major blind spots in his strategic thinking, arguing that he depended heavily on the work of his predecessors and that he was an improviser who 'scrambled' to victory rather than an effective forward planner. A related line of argument is that his eventual downfall owed as much to his own weaknesses and mistakes as it did to the capacities of his opponents. Indeed it is possible to discern the roots of Napoleon's eventual failure in the very characteristics and qualities that originally helped him to dominate the continent of Europe.

### Command and Control

It is not hard to see why Napoleon has been numbered among the great commanders of history. A Napoleonic scholar, Gunther Rothenberg, has calculated that he personally commanded 34 battles between 1792 and 1815, of which he lost only six. For a period of ten years he dominated Europe, heading an empire that stretched from the Channel coast to the borders of Russia. The foremost military theorist of the age of Napoleon, Carl von Clausewitz, hailed him as 'the god of War' whilst in slightly more restrained fashion the modern historian Martin Van Creveld has described him as 'the most competent human being who ever lived' What were the distinctive qualities of leadership that brought such accolades?

Napoleon was essentially a practical individual, who did not commit his thoughts on strategy to paper in a systematic manner. His occasional observations on the subject simply underline his essential pragmatism: he declared that 'there are no precise or definite rules' and 'the art of war is simple, everything is a matter of execution'. Most historians would, however, agree that at the core of his philosophy was a belief in offensive action, aimed at a decisive clash with the enemy's forces. Napoleon's primary objective was the destruction of the opposing army rather than the seizure of territory or the capital city. This was demonstrated in the campaign of 1805, when he set out from France to crush the Austrian forces. In October, barely seven weeks after they left the camp at Boulogne, French forces surrounded General Mack's army at Ulm in southern Germany; forcing its surrender almost without bloodshed. Five weeks later, after marching a further 500 miles to the east, the French defeated a combined Austro-Russian army at Austerlitz. These victories effectively gave control of central Europe to France.

Rapid movement and the concentration of superior force were to a great extent dictated by practicalities. The French Revolution had seen a significant expansion in the size of armies—a trend which continued throughout the Napoleonic Wars. In 1805 Napoleon's Grande Armee numbered some 210,000 men: the French army that invaded Russia seven years later had practically trebled in size. Although the agricultural revolution of the eighteenth century created a food surplus, enabling armies to live off the land more easily than in previous generations, it was still necessary for them to continue moving to new areas in search of subsistence. It should be remembered that armies of this period depended heavily on horses for transport and that the daily food consumption of a horse was ten times that of a soldier. These considerations favoured a highly mobile, focused, and aggressive style of warfare. It is noteworthy that in the two theatres of war where Napoleon met with catastrophic defeat Spain and Russia—agricultural development was limited, forcing the French to rely on cumbersome supply trains. In the case of Russia in 1812, poor roads, combined with the enemy's willingness to deprive the French of resources through a deliberate 'scorched earth' policy, rendered the invasion unsustainable. Napoleon failed in Russia because he was unable to draw the enemy's principal force into the decisive battle that he always favoured.

### Master of the Battlefield

Napoleon's was an intensely personal and highly centralised style of waging war. Although his imperial headquarters evolved into a complex staff apparatus, its role was essentially the implementation of Napoleon's instructions.

Historians have frequently remarked on his impressive powers of work and his excellent memory, which enabled him to maintain a close oversight of numerous complex troop movements. His ability to direct and coordinate his forces was more impressive in an age when methods of communication remained rudimentary—a generation before the invention of the electric telegraph and two generations before the radio.

Napoleon's characteristic mode of operation was to have his army, divided into a number of self-contained corps consisting of infantry, cavalry and artillery, travel along separate but parallel routes. A cavalry screen ahead of the advancing army would gather intelligence whilst also confusing the enemy as to Napoleon's intentions. The formation would close up in a loose quadrilateral, the battalion carre, once the main enemy force had been located. The first corps to make contact would then seek to pin the enemy whilst the main French force would attack his rear, thereby threatening his line of communications—the so-called maneuvre sur les derrieres. The enemy would therefore face an unenviable choice between surrender and giving battle without a secure line of retreat. The Austrian capitulation at Ulm is a classic example of this technique in action. Another way in which Napoleon sought to isolate his opponents from their base camps was to use overwhelming force at one point in the enemy lines, punching a hole and then completing the encirclement from the rear.

An alternative method, used against an enemy who possessed superior numbers, was that of the 'central position'. The object was to divide the opposing forces into several parts and to win local superiority over each in turn. Whilst a portion of Napoleon's forces engaged one part of the enemy army, he would turn his main body against the other part and defeat it. The main force would then join the pinning force to finish off the second section of the opposing army. An early example of Napoleon's use of this method was his response to the Austrians' attempts to relieve the siege of Mantua, during his 1796 campaign in Italy. He dealt separately with the two Austrian columns that were converging on the city.

Mastery of grand tactics was not in itself sufficient to secure victory, it should be noted that the methods employed by Napoleon had been available to other generals of the French Revolutionary era. What distinguished Napoleon was his ability to grasp the essentials of a situation and to integrate all the elements of his response with speed and clarity. In this he was assisted by his effective intelligence gathering system, which informed him of enemy movements, and by his emphasis on the production of accurate and detailed maps. Added to these technical skills was a unique capacity to inspire and motivate his troops. This was achieved partly through staying close to them, as his nickname, le petit caporal ('the little corporal') testifies. The name derived from his performance at the Battle of Lodi in Italy in May 1796, when Napoleon drew on his own training as an artilleryman to site some of the French guns in person. Napoleon's personal charisma communicated itself in the addresses that he directed to his troops. Before the Battle of the Pyramids in July 1798, for example, he dramatised the event in memorable fashion: 'Soldiers, consider that from the summit of these pyramids, forty centuries look down upon you.' The issuing of individual rewards and recognitions of collective achievement consolidated his hold on his men's affections. It meant that he was able to make exceptional demands on them. The rapid reformation of Napoleon's 200,000 strong Grande Armee in the spring of 1815, after he returned to France from exile on tile island of Elba, is a tribute to his ability to project his personality.

## Planning and Improvising

In any analysis of Napoleon's skills as a commander we need to be aware of the extent to which he reacted intelligently to circumstances—sometimes with a certain amount of luck—rather than following through a predetermined plan of action. He himself stated, during his final period of exile, that the mark of a great general is the 'courage to improvise'. Prior to the encirclement at Ulm, for example, Napoleon first drove his army beyond the enemy's main position, across the River Danube to the south bank, before he discovered that the Austrians were actually behind him, on the north bank. He then ordered much of his army back across the Danube in order to trap the Austrians.

Nor should we imagine that Napoleon invariably secured military victory without the assistance of able subordinates. In the October 1806 Jena-Auerstadt campaign against Prussia, the emperor initially miscalculated but the day was saved by the skill of Marshal Davout. At the outset Napoleon characteristically took the offensive, seeking to cut the Prussian forces off from their capital, Berlin, and to crush them before their Russian allies could intervene. He mistakenly believed that the Prussians whom he encountered at Jena, and defeated with overwhelming numbers, constituted the main body of the enemy. The truth was that Davout, who had been dispatched to the north, had in fact met the bulk of the Prussian army, led by the Duke of Brunswick, at Auerstadt. It was a tribute to Davout that he managed to overcome the much larger Prussian force, bringing his three divisions into line to check the enemy advance. He then launched a ferocious counter-attack, causing the Prussian forces to break and flee towards Jena where the other wing of their army was disintegrating.

It is also important to be aware of the extent to which Napoleon owed his success to the mistakes and failings of his adversaries. At Austerlitz, for example, the Russian Tsar Alexander I accepted battle on terrain of Napoleon's choosing. He ill-advisedly took at face value a tactical withdrawal by the French forces, in the process overruling his more cautious but experienced general, Kutuzov. Similarly the outcome of the Jena-Auerstadt campaign can be attributed in part to weaknesses in the Prussian high command. The Duke of Brunswick was a poor choice as commander-in-chief and there was no unity among the senior figures in the recently created general staff. At Auerstadt the Prussians failed to bring their numerically significant reserve into play, which might have turned the tide if used appropriately. Napoleon's enemies certainly presented him with opportunities that he was able to exploit.

## The Author of His Own Downfall?

Some historians have detected a falling off in Napoleon's abilities as a general from about 1809. He himself privately reflected in 1805 that 'I will be good for six years more: after that even I must cry halt.' Before that time had elapsed, contemporaries noted that his reactions were deteriorating and his health was often poor. A corresponding decline in the quality of his army also began to have an effect. Yet the logic of conquest drove him to embark on more or less continuous warfare. A prayerful case can be made for the claim that Napoleon was ultimately responsible for his own downfall.

In the early years of the empire, Napoleon had profited from advances in tactics and organisation introduced before he attained high command. The ordre mixte, for example, which combined the advantages of shock and fire by linking formations in column with others in line, was established as French practice before his time. Napoleon also benefited from the experience gained by French troops in the fighting of the Revolutionary Wars. The men he led were far more professional and battle-hardened than those who had first been called upon to resist the enemies of the Revolution in 1792. The introduction of conscription moreover made available a much larger reservoir of troops. Warfare on a Napoleonic scale required a commitment of large numbers to the battlefield and a willingness to accept a high level of casualties. It has been estimated that by 1809 the number of dead, wounded and otherwise incapacitated French troops equalled the 210,000 who had made up the grande armee originally assembled four years earlier.

In order to fill the gaps the empire was obliged to recruit less skilled men, so that infantry tactics were at once less sophisticated and more wasteful in terms of lives. In battle troops were used increasingly to batter a way through the enemy lines, whilst artillery were used in greater quantities. The historian of battle tactics, Brent Nosworthy, dates this change from the Battle of Wagram (July 1809), where Napoleon gained success at the cost of heavy casualties. At the same time, growing demands for manpower in satellite states, such as the Kingdom of Italy, placed a strain on the acceptance of French rule by local populations. No more than half of the 600,000 troops gathered for the invasion of Russia in June 1812 were French. The inferior quality and motivation of these reluctant auxiliaries contributed to the weakening of Napoleon's power. In addition, the heavy losses sustained in the Russian campaign—fewer than one in ten returned to France—were extremely difficult to make good. The situation was exacerbated by the continuing loss of manpower as he strove unsuccessfully to reduce Spain and Portugal to obedience in the long-running Peninsular War of 1808–13. Once Austria, Prussia, and Russia had combined their forces in central Europe, Napoleon faced daunting odds. His defeat at the Battle of Leipzig in October 1813, in which 200,000 French faced 342,000 coalition troops an engagement which paved the way for the invasion of France the following year—was the unavoidable consequence.

Napoleon's fall was not, however, caused solely by purely military factors. At a deeper level, the nature of the empire and the personality of its leader were to blame. Napoleon's programme of conquest meant that he could never rest from conflict for long. His accommodations with other powers, such as the Treaty of Tilsit with Russia in July 1807, or his marriage alliance with the Austrian royal family three years later, were pragmatic arrangements, devised purely to serve French interests, rather than genuine harbingers of peace. His alliance partners never trusted him and the demands that he placed upon them bred a slow-burning desire for revenge. An additional complication was Napoleon's inability to defeat Britain, whose naval supremacy was demonstrated at the Battle of Trafalgar in October 1805. This led him to introduce the so-called 'Continental system', an attempt to cut mainland European states off from trade with Britain. The economic damage that was inflicted on Napoleon's unwilling satellites was a major source of grievance. Portugal's refusal to co-operate with the trade embargo drew Napoleon into the Peninsular War. Tsar Alexander I's decision to end his participation in it was an important cause of the rupture between France and Russia. Napoleon invaded Russia in an ill-fated attempt to compel its return to the Continental system and to reassert French dominance of Europe.

The reality of Napoleonic rule was that its extension generated increasingly powerful resistance, ultimately threatening its very survival. The emperor's refusal to acknowledge anything except French self-interest eventually drove the other powers to reorganise and to coalesce for long enough to ensure his defeat. His inability to compromise forced them to conclude that there was no prospect of a lasting settlement and that therefore renewed war was the only course of action.

## The Uniqueness of Napoleon

Later generals looked back on Napoleon with admiration, in spite of his eventual defeat, and sought to emulate his aggressive style of warfare. The Prussian commander Helmuth von Mohke, for example, who won three wars against Denmark, Austria and France in 1864–71, could certainly be described as 'Napoleonic' in his generalship. The wars of German unification were won through a combination of careful planning, rapid penetration of the enemy's defences, and concentration of force, suitably updated to take account of developments in firepower and railway communications. Moltke also shared Napoleon's flexibility, famously stating that 'no battle plan survives contact with the enemy'.

Never again, however, would a single individual combine, as Napoleon did, the political leadership of a major state with the professional command of armies in the field. The growing complexity of warfare in the nineteenth century—and still more in the twentieth—meant that the tasks he handled in person had increasingly to be delegated to trained military staffs. Even in the closing years of Napoleon's military career, it was not really feasible for one commander, however talented, to exercise direct personal control over battlefields on which hundreds of thousands of troops were now engaged. In a real sense his career and achievements were unrepeatable.

GRAHAM GOODLAD is head of politics at St. John's College, Southsea UK, and the author of several books, most recently an analysis of William Gladstone.

Jonathon Riley

 **NO**

# How Good Was Napoleon?

**B**y 1805, the year that Napoleon became sole head of state and supreme warlord of France, the notion of strategy was recognizably modern. Joly de Maizeroy had written in Theories de la Guerre (1777): 'Strategy . . . combines time, places, means, various interests and considers all . . . [Tactics] reduces easily to firm rules, because it is entirely geometrical like fortification.' Achieving strategic objectives through means as diverse as diplomacy, economic power, information warfare and military power is not too far from this line of thought. The sort of strategy practised by Napoleon, his allies and some of his opponents, should be distinguished from that of his implacable enemy, Britain. Its worldwide empire, economic base and naval reach, all meant that it was able to conduct strategy through other means than military power. Revolutionary and imperial France was not in this position—it had to use military force not in addition to the other instruments of national power, but in order to access them. Military power for Napoleon must be seen therefore as diplomacy, not merely, as in the Clausewitzian sense, an addition to it.

Napoleon's strategy aimed not just at establishing a stable limit to his empire in Europe through peace with Britain, but at global domination. The latent hostility of the European anciens regimes, Britain especially, forced him to keep expanding until no opponents were left. In 1811 he remarked that 'in five years, I shall be master of the world: there only remains Russia, but I shall crush her.' For Napoleon, greater and greater success was the means to achieving a favourable and lasting settlement; one that saw Napoleon and his empire in control of the international system. Here lay the seeds of his destruction, and three examples of such over-reach demonstrate the flaws in the system: the Continental System, the occupation of Spain, and the invasion of Russia.

This last was the biggest single factor in his downfall. Napoleon needed a speedy conclusion to force the Russians back into the Continental System before the odds began to tell against him in the field. The campaign had a massive impact on French military potential: the empire lost 570,000 men, 200,000 horses and 1,050 guns—while the guns could be replaced, the men and horses could not. More important, the defeat shattered the myth of Napoleonic invincibility and rekindled the coalition against him. In the final years of his reign, Napoleon won battlefield victories, but after Russia, he was irrevocably on the road to St Helena. There is no better example of the great truth that, if strategy is flawed then, no matter how brilliant the tactical manoeuvres, no matter how inspired the operational art, failure will be inevitable.

Napoleon would certainly have understood the modern notion of the operational level of command. Military theory at the time spoke only of strategy and tactics, but the campaign was a well-understood idea, as was the concept of operational manoeuvre, usually referred to as Grand Tactics. Modern notions of operational art focus on the idea of critical vulnerabilities within a centre of gravity, pitting strength against weakness. Napoleon understood this, although when he possessed overwhelming strength, as he often did, he chose attrition over manoeuvre.

For Napoleon, the centre of gravity at the operational level was almost invariably the enemy's army, and the decisive act in achieving his strategic objectives was its destruction in battle by the fastest means available. By this means he would break the enemy's will to resist so that all else—the conquest of territory in particular—would follow. 'I see only one thing,' Napoleon declared in 1797, 'namely the enemy's main body. I try to crush it, confident that secondary matters will then settle themselves.'

Much of the success of Napoleonic campaigning was founded on logistics. Although the emphasis in logistics has changed since Napoleon's day, as has the technology, the problem has not altered. Sustaining his army remains a key factor for any general in planning and executing a campaign and may, as with Napoleon in Russia, be decisive. It is a driving factor in the size of forces that can take and keep the field. Napoleon's armies were the largest that the Western world had yet seen, and his method of supplying it had to be innovative—hence his insistence on spreading out and foraging to supplement his depots.

It is ironic that, having succeeded in so many campaigns on the basis of just enough, just in time, he failed in Russia after the most extensive preparations undertaken in the history of warfare up to that point. He knew that living off the country would be impossible, and he knew the consequences of staying in one place for any length of time, but even his preparations were insufficient for the demand, distance and duration of the campaign. In modern campaigns, static operations in theatres like the Balkans,

Iraq and Afghanistan have brought their own problems in over-stretching military logistic units and military forces that rely on contractors to provide many functions. This situation is almost the reverse of Napoleonic times. Once the line of communication has been established, the use of contracts allied to food technology and other commodity storage have made it far simpler to maintain a static force than a mobile one. Given the conditions of his time, therefore, the fact that Napoleon overran most of Europe, and did not starve his armies in the process, is nothing short of a miracle.

For Napoleon, there was an inescapable connection between the campaign and the battle: the campaign was constructed to achieve his strategic objectives—that of bringing the enemy to a battle that would be the decisive act of any war. While distinctions may be drawn between strategy, operational art and tactics, strategy and operational art are by no means suspended when battle is joined. Manoeuvring throughout the theatre of operations, and in the realm of diplomacy, continues before, after, and during a battle. This is implicit in Karl von Clausewitz's celebrated but often misquoted (and still more often misunderstood) remark that 'war is simply a continuation of political intercourse, with the addition of other means.'

The close connection between strategic objectives, operational manoeuvre and battle was underlined by Napoleon's own position as head of state, head of government, and commander-in-chief: in such an unrivalled position, he could ensure the unbroken maintenance of the aim from the beginning to the end of a war. The same intelligence prepared the general strategic conditions and objectives, set the operational scenery, and joined the engagement. Today, the position of a commander at the strategic or operational levels is different. He may indeed assist in preparing the general conditions for engaging an enemy, he may exert influence on the course of battles by assigning resources, priorities, boundaries, rules of engagement and so on, but the execution of a battle will be entrusted to a subordinate combined arms commander.

Napoleon expected to be in a position to observe and control any battle personally from one or two key positions. Like a modern commander, he needed to separate himself and his tactical headquarters from the impedimenta of the much larger main headquarters. This gave him the flexibility to exercise command at wherever the decisive point of a battle might be—but for limited periods. Meanwhile the main headquarters kept control of the army. Napoleon could thus find out what was going on, communicate his intentions to his subordinates, and maintain contact with the staff so that problems could be solved.

Close co-operation on the battlefield was relatively simple at that period, not only between corps but between the various arms and services of the entire army. Napoleon, crucially, never allowed control of any battle to slip from his hand. On the few occasions he did so the outcome was a bad one for the French, as Marengo (1800)

almost proved, and Aspern-Essling (1809) and Waterloo (1815) certainly did. It is often said that Napoleon did not interest himself in tactics: this does not stand close examination. Whilst he only rarely issued detailed guidance on corps level tactical employment, Napoleon devised and issued the battle plans, and directed the combined attacks of infantry, cavalry reserves, and massed batteries of guns. What a modern corps or divisional commander carries out on the battlefield today within his own sphere of command, therefore, Napoleon himself performed on the entire field of battle.

If Napoleon was brilliant at the operational level, there was little glitter and less subtlety on the battlefield. True, he produced a run of successes in his early years, leading up to the triumph of Jena-Auerstadt (1806). Thereafter, for every victory, there was a disaster or near-disaster. He won at Friedland (1807), but only after the bitter winter battle of Eylau; Wagram recovered the near-disaster of Aspern-Essling at huge cost; and there was little to celebrate at Borodino (1812). His flash of genius was apparent at Lutzen (May 2nd, 1813), but Bautzen (May 20th–21st) was a draw, and the success of Dresden (August 26th–27th) was followed by the defeats of Kulm, the Katzbach and, finally and decisively, Leipzig (October 16th–19th). After the escape from Elba, Napoleon's success against the Prussians at Ligny (June 16th, 1815) was an illusion, shattered the same day by Quatre Bras and by Waterloo two days later.

One common aspect of Napoleonic battles was the blood-letting. Because of his insistence on rapid marching to gain time, the myth grew up that 'the Emperor uses our legs instead of our bayonets'. Nothing in the history of his campaigns shows this to be true. In battle after battle, the French conscripts would hold on in desperate combat, waiting for support from the rest of the army. Then, when the greatest possible mass had been assembled, the day would be settled—in victory or in a draw—by the crude application of force: massed artillery fire to blast holes in the enemy, and columns of infantry and cavalry pouring in. There is no subtlety here.

A key judgement for any general is to understand what his army is capable of doing, and what is beyond its abilities. In the early years, Napoleon's Grande Armee was the most capable battlefield force in the world; Napoleon could demand feats of endurance, sacrifice and complexity beyond those of his opponents. But the quality of its later performances declined as casualties took their toll on the troops and on his marshals. After the Russian campaign, Napoleon rarely tried to unite dispersed corps on the battlefield in the presence of the enemy during offensive operations because he could no longer rely on a high-quality holding action to buy time for the assembly of his main army. As performance declined, so the cost of fighting rose still higher. Bautzen cost Napoleon more than 20,000 casualties. Despite Dresden, the French army lost 150,000 men between June and September 1813. Leipzig cost him 70,000 men, including seventeen general officers. These figures equal the very worst days on the Western Front, yet the First World War generals are often vilified while Napoleon's reputation shines.

In the century after 1815 Napoleon's legend was dominant: every general wanted to be him, to crush his enemy's army, march into his capital, and attain the decisive victory. What did not dawn on his admirers, or on those responsible for teaching the military class of the future, was the simple fact that, in the end, Napoleon lost.

Of course, Napoleon himself, writing his memoir, on St Helena, did all he could to disguise this. It was the military theorist Basil Liddell Hart who reminded the world of the uncomfortable truth that 'it is as well to remember that St Helena became his destination'. To get Napoleon there took more than twenty years of ruinous war—against mixed opposition: Napoleon did not have to be faultless, he just had to be better than his opponents. Given this, and the edge that superior French organization and a unified command brought, it is not surprising that his legend grew as it did.

So large did it loom, in fact, the evolution of the nature of modern warfare over the next century became obscured. European armies after Napoleon were almost invariably large organizations raised through conscription, and the full impact of the industrial revolution—not felt until after 1815—equipped them with weapons closer to those of today's battlefield than to Leipzig or Waterloo. Of course, military technologies do not advance in complete capability leaps, and there is, in warfare, a relationship between the introduction of new technologies, and the employment and deployment of troops. This relationship is not constant, and without careful and frequent revision, trouble follows. By the American Civil War (1861–65), armies were equipped with powerful, rifled muskets and heavy artillery, and could be moved by rail, but the tactics were still those of Waterloo. The results, for generals seeking the Napoleonic decisive battle, were the casualty rates of battles like Antietam, Fredericksburg and Gettysburg, and the acceleration of trench warfare. The same process continued through the Franco-Prussian war, the opening stages of the South African War, and the early years of the First World War.

Today, armies still operate within what is described as a Napoleonic staff model and a corps structure when, once again, the employment–technology relationship is shifting. The IT revolution should mean that general staffs are organized in a way that cuts across traditional divisions in order to provide superior (not necessarily faster) information, and thus produce superior decisions. Generals in the West today are most likely to be opposed, not by states, but by non-state groupings whose command structures, as far as they can be said to have any, operate in the virtual realm. Bringing an army corps into action may succeed in the taking of ground, but as the Coalition has found in Iraq, the action is unlikely to be decisive. But the focus on destroying an enemy force remains.

This is, however, the wrong lesson to draw from Napoleon's legacy in the context of modern warfare. Napoleon was successful on many battlefields; and he may have been a master of campaigning. However, in strategic terms, he was a failure principally because he never succeeded in transforming a defeated enemy into a willing ally. He won wars, but he never won the peace.

---

**JONATHON RILEY** was the general officer commanding British forces in Bosnia and played a similar role in Iraq. He is the author of *Napoleon as a General* (Continuum Books, 2007).

# EXPLORING THE ISSUE

## Does Napoleon Bonaparte Deserve His Historical Reputation as a Great General?

### Critical Thinking and Reflection

1. Examine the "facts" of Napoleon's military career. Which author more accurately evaluates his accomplishments? Critically discuss.
2. How important are the criticisms that credit others with correcting Napoleon's errors and turning defeat into victory? Could this be said of every famous general? Critically discuss.
3. Professor Goodlad places more emphasis on personal qualities and style, whereas Military Commander Riley analyzes tactics and outcomes more thoroughly. Is one or the other of these sets of criteria more relevant than the other? Critically discuss.
4. A similar figure is Alexander the Great of Macedonia, subject of an issue in CREATE. How would you go about comparing these two men, each of whom dominated his respective era as leader and conqueror?
5. Since Napoleon aimed at global domination, how damaging is Military Commander Riley's criticism that Napoleon was never able to transform a defeated enemy into a willing ally? Must a successful general accomplish this? Critically discuss.
6. How would you evaluate Napoleon's role in France's imperial ambitions? Was he an effective champion? Critically discuss.
7. Despite numerous military victories, Napoleon was forced to abdicate and died in exile. Was he, as Professor Goodlad claims, the one responsible for his own downfall? Critically discuss.

## Is There Common Ground?

A careful reading of the YES and NO selections reveals that, although Goodlad focuses on Napoleon's personal qualities and style while Riley emphasizes tactics and outcomes, each writer deals with all these ingredients. Each praises some qualities from both sides of this equation. Perhaps we must consider a blend of military prowess and personal psychology if we are to do a fair evaluation of Napoleon. Both authors agree that later generals have emulated his aggressive military style and continue to operate within his staff model and corps structure in blending technology advances with troop deployment.

*Question:* What if Napoleon had died on the battlefield or in his bed as emperor? Would we be more likely to overlook his failings in the light of his dazzling victories?

## Create Central

www.mhhe.com/createcentral

## Additional Resources

The biographies written about Napoleon Bonaparte are too numerous to mention here. Some books that shed light on his generalship include: James Marshall-Cornwall, *Napoleon* *as a Military Commander* (Penguin Books, 2002); Owen Connelly, *Blundering to Glory: Napoleon's Military Campaigns* (Rowman & Littlefield, 2006); Jonathon Riley, *Napoleon as a General* (Hambleton & London, 2007).

Where you stand determines what you see. Looking only at tactics and daring, we might rate Napoleon highly as a battle commander. However, as Berthold Brecht pointedly asked: "Who built the Seven Gates of Thebes? Was it kings that hauled the craggy blocks of stone?" Many people paid a high price for Napoleon's victories.

Yehuda Bauer, who has spent a lifetime studying and writing about the Holocaust, put it this way in a speech before the German Bundestag: "In our schools we still teach about Napoleon, for example, and how he won the Battle of Austerlitz. Did he win it on his own? Maybe someone assisted him in this. A few thousand soldiers, perhaps? And what happened to the families of the fallen soldiers, to the wounded on all sides, to the villagers whose villages had been destroyed, to the women who had been raped, and to the goods and possessions that had been looted. We are still teaching about the generals, about the politicians, and about the philosophers. We are trying not to recognize the dark side of history—the mass murderers, the agony, the suffering that is screaming in our faces from all of history. We do not hear the wailing of Clio." (Yehuda Bauer, *Rethinking the Holocaust* [Yale University Press, 2001, p. 262]).

# *Internet References . . .*

### Napoleon at War

This PBS website examines the campaigns and battles led by Napoleon. Included are the following campaigns: first and second Italian, Egyptian, Ulm-Austerlitz, Prussian, Russian, and Waterloo. Also links to the Austrian War and From Lutzen to Elba.

**www.pbs.org/empires/napoleon/n_war/campaign/
page_1.html**

**Selected, Edited, and with Issue Framing Material by:**
Helen Buss Mitchell, *Howard Community College*
and
Joseph R. Mitchell, *Howard Community College*

# ISSUE

# Did British Policy Decisions Cause the Mass Emigration and Land Reforms That Followed the Irish Potato Famine of the 1840s and 1850s?

**YES: Christine Kinealy**, from *This Great Calamity: The Irish Famine 1845–52* (Roberts Rinehart Publishers, 1995)

**NO: Hasia R. Diner**, from "Where They Came From," *Erin's Daughters in America: Irish Immigrant Women in the Nineteenth Century* (The Johns Hopkins University Press, 1983)

---

## Learning Outcomes

**After reading this issue you should be able to:**

- Describe what happened agriculturally to cause the potato famine in Ireland.
- Understand the nature and scope of policy decisions made by the British government in response to the Irish potato famine.
- Describe the political and economic relationship between Ireland and the United Kingdom, including Britain's goal of long-term economic, social, and agrarian reforms, as well as effective long-term responses by the Irish people.
- Define and describe the distinctions made by the British between the "deserving" (English factory workers) and the "undeserving" (Irish farmers) poor.

---

### ISSUE SUMMARY

**YES:** Professor at Drew University Christine Kinealy argues that the British government's response to the Irish potato famine was deliberately inadequate because its "hidden agenda" was the long-term aim of economic, social, and agrarian reforms, which the famine accelerated; mass emigration was a consequence of these changes.

**NO:** Historian Hasia R. Diner argues that large-scale emigration occurred both before and after the famine and credits the Irish people with learning from their famine experiences that the near-total reliance of the poor on the potato and the excessive subdivision of land within families were no longer in their own best interests.

**B**eginning in 1845, a fungal disease repeatedly struck the potato crop of Ireland. Until the blight was finally eradicated in the early 1850s, the failure of the potato harvest, on which a majority of the rural population depended for sustenance, caused an estimated 1 million deaths, in a country with a population of 8 million, and the emigration of another million Irish people. On the eve of the famine, two-thirds of the population earned their living by working the land—for the most part land that they did not own. Still, Ireland fed its own people and exported food to feed 2 million Britons. During these years, Ireland was part of the United Kingdom, integrated within the British Empire by the Act of Union, which linked England, Scotland, and Ireland in 1801.

Initially, the British government responded to the failure of a third of the Irish potato crop in 1845 by purchasing and storing Indian corn from America, which it later sold to those who could afford to buy it. Unwilling to offer handouts, the British government provided subsidy only to those who entered the workhouses. As the crisis deepened, the government undertook public works projects, such as road and pier construction, offering the poor a means to earn money, and, ultimately it set up a network of soup kitchens.

By 1847, however, the British government had transferred responsibility to Ireland itself, insisting that outside aid (i.e., aid from Britain) would henceforth be available only after local resources were exhausted or if it could be demonstrated that without aid people would die. As the blight continued, British aid was provided to the manufacturing districts in the north of England, which were undergoing an economic slump, but not to the less "deserving" Irish.

More prosperous counties of Ireland, less dependent on the potato crop, resented being held exclusively responsible for the financial bailout of the poorest of their neighbors. If Ireland were truly part of the United Kingdom, they argued, all of the United Kingdom would be equally responsible for alleviating the suffering of any of its members. In fact, prevailing stereotypes frequently contrasted the "deserving" poor—industrious factory workers in England's manufacturing centers—with the "undeserving" poor—notably the Irish, believed to be lazy and without ambition. How much of a role did these prejudices, which appeared regularly in cartoons and print descriptions, play in the neglect that allowed a million people to die and forced another million to emigrate?

Another factor was the *laissez-faire* economic principles, pioneered by Adam Smith and others, which contended that government would be well advised to stay out of (literally to leave alone) the regulation of the economy. Without outside manipulation, this theory suggested, the "hidden hand" of economic forces, such as supply and demand, would regulate the economy efficiently. The prevalence of these well-respected theories gave the British government a solid justification for withholding economic aid to Ireland. The real question is why they selectively ignored this hands-off policy when an economic slump hit the north of England in 1847.

In 1849, Queen Victoria, the reigning monarch of the United Kingdom, paid a state visit to the cities of Cork, Dublin, and Belfast in Ireland. She attended receptions, balls, and fireworks displays, accepted a shamrock-topped salmon, and witnessed "a genuine Irish jig" danced by prettily attired "peasantry." Naturally, she did not witness the starvation and social breakdown in the hardest hit areas.

Stories from this time, which persist into the present, insist that the Irish starved because their home-grown food was all shipped to England. John Percival, in *The Great Famine: Ireland's Potato Famine 1845–51* (Viewer Books, 1995), calls this legend untrue. Six times as much grain was imported as exported, Percival claims. Still, in this balanced account, he concludes that even if exports (which were crucial to the Irish economy) had stayed in Ireland, those who needed it most could not have afforded to pay for them.

Ireland's leading economist, Cormac O'Grada, studies famine folklore, the limitations of medical science, the selection of who would emigrate (many through landlord-funded programs) and who would not, and even the role of the weather in intensifying the famine in *Black '47 and Beyond: The Great Irish Famine in History, Economy, and Memory* (Princeton University Press, 1999). This interdisciplinary work looks at stories and songs that suggest what it was like to live during famine times, explores the impact of famine-related diseases on the city of Dublin, and follows one group of emigrants to New York's Sixth Ward.

For a look at the experiences of Irish women who emigrated, see Hasia R. Diner's *Erin's Daughters in America* (Johns Hopkins University Press, 1983). The focus of the book from which our NO selection comes is the experiences of Irish women once they arrived in America as immigrants. Much more successful (in terms of marriage, work, educational achievement, and upward mobility) than other female immigrants, they benefitted, according to Diner, from a vibrant cultural tradition they brought with them from Ireland. *Emigrants and Exiles: Ireland and the Irish Exodus to North America* (Oxford University Press, 1985) by Kerby A. Miller documents both pre- and post-famine exoduses and explores the traditional Irish Catholic worldview that led the Irish to regard themselves as involuntary "exiles," forced to leave home by forces beyond their control.

Christine Kinealy faults British government policies for exploiting the chaos of the famine in order to implement what she calls a "hidden agenda." Seeing the failure of the potato crop as a golden opportunity to force conversion of the Irish economy to a more commercial system of agriculture, the British government, Kinealy explains, was able to rid itself of "nonproductive elements," including landless laborers and apathetic landlords. The million who emigrated, along with the million who died, improved the demographics and facilitated modernization of the Irish economy—but at a terrible cost.

Hasia R. Diner sees much more continuity than discontinuity in emigration patterns. While the famine may have accelerated this process, she writes, the Irish had been moving to other parts of the British Empire and the United States in large numbers at least since the late eighteenth century. Calling the famine the "great convincer," Diner attributes changes in agricultural diversity, land inheritance patterns, and marriage practices to the Irish people themselves, acting on their own behalf as agents of historical change.

Did British Policy Decisions Cause Emigration and Land Reforms Following the Irish Potato Famine? by Mitchell and Mitchell

49

# YES

**Christine Kinealy**

## This Great Calamity: The Irish Famine 1845–52

The Famine that affected Ireland from 1845 to 1852 has become an integral part of folk legend. In the popular imagination, the Famine is associated with nationwide suffering, initially triggered by the potato blight, compounded by years of misrule and consolidated by the inadequate response of the British government and Irish landlords alike. The resultant large-scale emigration took the tragedy of the Famine beyond the shores of Ireland to an international stage. Recent scholarly studies of the Famine have attempted to move away from this traditional view. In doing so, a sanitised alternative has emerged that has endeavoured to remove the patina of blame from the authorities involved in providing relief, while minimising the suffering of those who were most directly affected by the loss of the potato crop.

Several specific issues need to be addressed in order to evaluate the varying responses of those in power. At a broad level there are three questions. First, what relief measures were implemented? Second, what were the determinants of the measures that were introduced? Third, and most significantly, how effective were they?

These questions are fundamental to an understanding of the Famine. There is still a widespread view that the Famine relief measures were inadequate. Much of the blame is laid at the door of the British government, and to a lesser degree, Irish landlords. Is this an unfair assessment, especially when seen in the context of the perceived role of government in the middle of the nineteenth century?

Early in the nineteenth century, Ireland was widely regarded as a poor country, dominated by a stagnant subsistence agriculture based substantially upon the ubiquitous potato. On the eve of the Famine, the Irish economy supported a population in excess of eight million people which was large by European standards and represented a sizeable portion of the United Kingdom population as a whole—the population of England and Wales at the same period was approximately sixteen million, and of Scotland, under three million. On the eve of the Famine, the economy of Ireland supported its own population and supplied food for a further two million mouths in Britain. Ireland, therefore, should have been a significant consideration in any social or economic policies that affected the United Kingdom as a whole.

The onset of the Famine was unexpected although partial crop failures and food shortages were not unusual. In 1845, therefore, the potato blight, regardless of the lack of understanding of either its origins or an antidote, was not regarded with undue alarm. Although approximately 50 per cent of the main subsistence crop failed in 1845–6, the consequence of the resultant shortages was not famine, nor did emigration or mortality increase substantially. The role played by the government, local landlords, clerics, and various relief officials was significant in achieving this outcome. The second, more widespread, blight of 1846 marked the real beginning of the Famine. Ominously, the impact of the shortages was apparent in the period immediately following the harvest. Inevitably also, the people undergoing a second year of shortages were far less resilient than they had been twelve months earlier. The government responded to this potentially more serious situation by reducing its involvement in the import of food into the country and by making relief more difficult to obtain.

The distress that followed the 1847 harvest was caused by a small crop and economic dislocation rather than the widespread appearance of blight. The government again changed its relief policy in an attempt to force local resources to support the starving poor within their district. The government professed a belief that this policy was necessary to ensure that a burden which it chose to regard as essentially local should not be forced upon the national finances. This policy underpinned the actions of the government for the remainder of the Famine. The relief of famine was regarded essentially as a local responsibility rather than a national one, let alone an imperial obligation. The special relationship between the constituent parts of the United Kingdom forged by the Act of Union appeared not to extend to periods of shortage and famine.

To what extent was a famine or other disaster inevitable when viewed within the context of the general, and some would say increasing, poverty of Ireland? This assumption of Irish poverty, which underpinned political prescription during the Famine, perhaps owed more to distantly derived dogmas than to the reality. For example, a number of recent studies have suggested that height is a reliable indicator of 'nutritional status' (that is, 'the balance of nutritional intake with growth, work, and the defeat of disease'). Surveys of nineteenth-century British military records indicate that Irish recruits were taller than recruits from the rest of the United Kingdom. This implies a sustained nutritional advantage within Ireland. Also, it is now widely accepted that Ireland's pre-Famine economy was more diverse, vibrant, dynamic and responsive to change than has traditionally been depicted. In contrast to this situation, recent quantitative studies of the British economy have reassessed the impact of industrialisation in the first half of the nineteenth century and concluded that, throughout this period, Britain's economic growth remained 'painfully slow'. . . .

The slump of 1847 was a sharp reminder to the government of the problems on its own doorstep. During the autumn of 1847, news of Irish distress vied increasingly for column space in the English newspapers with stories of hardship, unemployment and bankruptcies in England, notably in Lancashire, the flagship of industrial Britain. Poverty and distress, therefore, were not confined to Ireland but were also evident in one of the wealthiest parts of the British Empire. The demands of the Irish poor were now in direct competition with the demands of the urban poor within Britain. An obvious comparison was drawn between the distress of the feckless Irish peasants and their irresponsible and greedy landlords, with the distress of the hard-working factory operatives and the enterprising entrepreneurs upon whom, it was believed, much of the success of the British Empire rested. Since the reign of Elizabeth I, Poor Law philosophy had drawn a distinction between the 'deserving' and the 'undeserving' poor. The English factory operatives, unemployed through no fault of their own, were regarded as deserving poor; it was apparent that the Irish peasants could be regarded with equal justification as falling into the latter category.

A hardening attitude to Irish distress was illustrated by the response to appeals for additional assistance as a third year of shortages became inevitable. An early indication of a resistant official response occurred in October 1847, when a group of Catholic bishops and archbishops appealed to the government for an increase in official aid. They were informed, in a widely published response, that such a request was unreasonable, particularly as it implied that:

> the means for this relief should be exacted by the government from classes all struggling with difficulties, and at a moment when in England trade and credit are disastrously low, with the immediate prospect of hundreds of thousands being thrown out of employment or being as destitute of the means of existence as the poorest peasant in Ireland.

An appeal for funds in the form of a second 'Queen's Letter' was also published in October 1847 and read out in all churches throughout England. It elicited more criticism than cash.

The government remained committed to the policy of forcing Ireland to depend on its own resources as far as possible, chiefly through the mechanism of the Poor Law. Within the domestic economy, however, the government did depart from its declared *laissez faire* policy and intervened to allow the terms of the 1844 Bank Charter Act to be relaxed in order to aid the industrial sector. By the end of 1847, the financial crisis in Britain was over and a period of prosperity was under way. The Great Exhibition of 1851 was a triumphant demonstration of Britain's international industrial and economic supremacy. In the same year, in a different part of the United Kingdom, the west of Ireland, a portion of the population was about to confront a seventh consecutive year of famine and shortages.

The contribution of outside charitable bodies was mostly confined to the early years of the Famine. By 1847, most of these sources had dried up or, as in the case of the Quakers, they had decided to use their remaining funds to concentrate on long-term improvements rather than immediate relief. Significantly, the Quakers' men on the ground who toured the west of Ireland in the winter of 1846–47 were critical both of absentee landlords and the policies pursued by the British government alike. The British Relief Association, which remained operative after 1847, allowed its funds to be allocated through the medium of the Treasury. This was not without problems. Count Strzelecki, the Association's local agent, fought a hard battle with the Treasury to ensure that a successful scheme to feed schoolchildren was continued, regardless of the disapproval of [Charles] Trevelyan.

A fundamental policy position of government, enforced rigorously throughout the Famine, as noted earlier, was the determination to make local resources support local distress. The Irish landlords were singled out continually as a group that needed to be reminded of, and occasionally coerced into, undertaking their duties to the poor. Following the 1845 blight, however, the money contributed voluntarily by the landlords and other subscribers was the highest amount ever raised. Regardless of this achievement, the Irish contribution was represented as derisory and the landlords increasingly targeted as the object of public opprobrium. Irish landlords undoubtedly provided an easy and obvious scapegoat both as a cause of, and as contributors to, the Famine. This was a view taken both by their contemporaries and by some later historians. . . .

To what extent, however, can any individual group, organisation or state body be blamed for the degree of suffering that resulted from successive years of potato blight? Would the outcome of the years of shortages and suffering have been different if the response of the authorities, various charitable organisations, and other key individuals to successive years of blight had been different?

There is no doubt that the part played by the government was pivotal within the whole relief endeavour. Was it, however, within the remit of the government—either ideologically or financially—to provide sufficient relief to keep suffering, emigration, and mortality to a minimum level? The policies of the government, and the way in which it perceived its role, are crucial to an understanding of the Famine years. The changing perceptions and strategies of the British government determined the type of relief provided and the methods and timing of its allocation. The role played by the Treasury, both in implementing the various relief policies and in advising the government, was critical. Charles Wood, the Chancellor of the Exchequer, together with his colleague, Charles Trevelyan, represented a school of economic orthodoxy which advocated both non-intervention and fiscal rectitude. A populist version of their views found a wider audience in the columns of *The Times* and the cartoons of *Punch*. It was also supported in the learned contributions to the *Edinburgh Review* and the fledgling *Economist*. In the wake of the financial and monetary crisis of 1847, the demand for retrenchment was also welcomed by a politically influential industrial middle class. The Treasury, in effect, became not only the guardian of the relief purse, but—mainly due to the energetic and prolonged involvement of Charles Trevelyan—was increasingly deferred to by members of the government as the oracle of all wisdom regarding Ireland. Although no one person can be blamed for the deficiencies of the relief policies, Trevelyan perhaps more than any other individual represented a system of response which increasingly was a mixture of minimal relief, punitive qualifying criteria, and social reform.

The Treasury's agenda for Irish relief went far beyond the mere allocation of government funds. Its imprint was evident throughout both the public and private sectors. Not only did it arbitrate on the crucial issue of who deserved to be given financial support and how much they should receive, but increasingly it attempted to control the day-to-day administration of relief. No other organisation played such a sustained role or showed such an obvious interest in the affairs of Ireland. The government, which was in the midst of a foreign crisis, an economic depression, and a year of revolutions and uprisings in Europe which extended both to Britain and Ireland, was no doubt glad to be able to allow the Treasury to shoulder such a large portion of the Irish relief burden. Also, despite evidence to the contrary, many officials, including even the well-informed Trevelyan, publicly declared the Famine to be over in 1848. The problems of Ireland, therefore, were necessarily a low priority to a government at the centre of a large and still expanding Empire. However, by allowing the Treasury to play such a pivotal role in the provision of relief, it was perhaps inevitable that the need to 'balance the books'— an excellent objective in Treasury terms—should at times overshadow the need to provide adequate relief. By using the Treasury in such a capacity, its role far exceeded that of guardian of the public purse and extended both to influencing public policy and, even more significantly, to final arbitrator in the provision of relief. . . .

The Famine was a disaster of major proportions, even allowing for an inevitable statistical uncertainty on its estimated effect on mortality. Yet the Famine occurred in a country which, despite concurrent economic problems, was at the centre of a still-growing empire and was an integral part of the acknowledged workshop of the world. There can be no doubt that despite a short-term cyclical depression, the combined resources of the United Kingdom could either completely or much more substantially have removed the consequences of consecutive years of potato blight in Ireland. This remains true even if one accepts Trevelyan's proud assertion that no government had done more to support its poor than Britain had done during the Famine years. The statement implies that not only was enough done to help the suffering people in Ireland, but that it was accompanied by a generosity that patently is not borne out by the evidence. To have fed in excess of three million people in the summer of 1847 was a worthy and notable achievement. It also dispels the frequent assertion that the British government did not possess the administrative capability to feed such a large number of starving people. But if the measure of success is judged by the crudest yet most telling of all measures—that of mortality—the British government failed a large portion of the population in terms of humanitarian criteria.

In this context, Trevelyan's comment reveals the separateness of Ireland from the rest of the United Kingdom. His perception mocked the precepts of the Act of Union. It should not, however, be forgotten that the government and the Treasury had to provide a system of relief that would satisfy both parliamentary and public opinion. If measured by this criterion alone—accepting, however, the individual criticisms of the opposition party—the relief measures were undoubtedly regarded as successful, and to some, even over-generous.

The policies of the government increasingly specified criteria that disallowed external assistance until distress was considerable and evident. The leit-motif of relief provided by the central government throughout the course of the Famine was that assistance would be provided only when it—or, in fact, its agent, the Treasury—was satisfied that local resources were exhausted, or that if aid was not provided, the distressed people would die. By implementing a policy which insisted that local resources must be exhausted before an external agency would intervene, and pursuing this policy vigorously despite local advice to the contrary, the government made suffering an unavoidable consequence of the various relief systems which it introduced. The suffering was exacerbated by the frequent delays in the provision of relief even after it had been granted and by the small quantity of relief provided, which was also of low nutritional value. By treating the Famine as, in essence, a local problem requiring a local response, the government was, in fact, penalising those areas which had the fewest resources to meet the distress.

The government response to the Famine was cautious, measured and frequently parsimonious, both with regard to immediate need and in relation to the long-term welfare of that portion of the population whose livelihood had been wiped out by successive years of potato blight. Nor could the government pretend ignorance of the nature and extent of human tragedy that unfolded in Ireland following the appearance of blight. The Irish Executive and the Poor Law Commissioners sent regular, detailed reports of conditions within the localities and increasingly requested that even more extensive relief be provided. In addition, Trevelyan employed his own independent sources of information on local conditions, bypassing the existing official sources of the Lord Lieutenant. This information revealed the extent of deprivation caused by the Famine. It also showed the regional variations arising from the loss of the potato crop; and it exposed the inability of some areas to compensate for such losses from their own internal resources. There was no shortage of detailed and up-to-date information. What was crucial was the way in which the government used this information.

While it was evident that the government had to do something to help alleviate the suffering, the particular nature of the actual response, especially following 1846, suggests a more covert agenda and motivation. As the Famine progressed, it became apparent that the government was using its information not merely to help it formulate its relief policies but also as an opportunity to facilitate various long-desired changes within Ireland. These included population control and the consolidation of property through a variety of means, including emigration, the elimination of small holdings, and the sale of large but bankrupt estates. This was a pervasive and powerful 'hidden agenda'. The government measured the success of its relief policies by the changes which were brought about in Ireland rather than by the quality of relief provided *per se*. The public declaration of the Census Commissioners in the Report of the 1851 Census, which stated that Ireland had benefited from the changes brought about by the Famine, is a clear example of this. . . .

The response of [Whig leader Lord John] Russell's government to the Famine combined opportunism, arrogance and cynicism, deployed in such a way as to facilitate the long-standing ambition to secure a reform of Ireland's economy. In the midst of dealing with a famine in Ireland, increasing reference was made to the need to restructure agriculture in Ireland from the top to the bottom. This had been the ambition of a succession of governments prior to 1845, but the Famine provided a real opportunity to bring about such a purpose both quickly and, most importantly, cheaply.

In the early decades of the nineteenth century, for example, state-sponsored emigration had been recommended by select committees, social theorists and government advisors alike, all of whom agreed that it would be beneficial to Ireland; but the government had refused to involve itself in the additional expenditure that an active pursuit of this policy would involve. The Famine, however, gave the impetus to emigration to flourish, without imposing an additional financial burden on the government. It, therefore, provided opportunities for change.

The Whig administration, through legislation such as the Quarter-Acre Clause and the Encumbered Estates Acts, ensured that such opportunities were not wasted.

If the potato blight had been confined to 1845, its impact would have been insignificant and it would have been remembered only as one of the many intermittent subsistence crises which affected Ireland and all agricultural societies. Even though over half of the crop was lost through blight in 1845, the increase in excess mortality and emigration was insignificant. In 1845–46, as had so clearly been demonstrated in the subsistence crisis of 1782–84, if the political and social will existed, a subsistence crisis did not necessarily have to become a famine.

In the 1840s, the policy of the British government was shaped by a prevailing economic dogma, inspired by a particular interpretation of free market economics. The champions of this philosophy were Adam Smith and his successors such as Nassau Senior and Harriet Martineau. In the context of providing poor relief in Ireland, this influential philosophy decreed that ultimately such relief was damaging and that genuine improvements could be achieved only through self-help. In its more extreme form, the principles embodied in this dogma denied any government responsibility for the alleviation of distress. Proponents of such theories even managed to suggest that during periods of extraordinary distress it could be better for those affected not to have access to extraneous relief lest the self-righting mechanisms of the economic system—the allegedly ubiquitous yet truly imperceptible 'invisible hand'—became ensnared by unwarranted interference. The outcome of a slavish adherence to these self-adjusting mechanisms would inevitably be human suffering. Yet this appeared to be of little consequence to those who worshipped at the altar of *laissez faire*. Short-term suffering appeared to be a small price to be paid for long-term improvement, especially if the theoreticians did not have to participate directly in the experiment.

Despite the fashionable adherence to these theories at the time of the Famine, they were only one of the many influences upon political decision-making. It is clear that such theoretical dogma could be dismissed when prevailing pressures demanded: the intervention by the government in the autumn of 1847 to alleviate the impact of a slump in the manufacturing districts of England providing a concurrent example. The philosophy of noninterference was in practice employed selectively and pragmatically. Its content and application changed as the government considered necessary. Within the Whig government itself, there existed differences of opinion regarding the level of financial intervention in Ireland. Significantly, those who favoured a minimalist approach, spearheaded by the men at the Treasury, were in the ascendant. Nevertheless, during the crucial period in the provision of Famine relief, that is, after the complete devastation of the potato crop in 1846, there is no doubt that this economic theory had powerful public support and, more significantly, enjoyed a popular appeal among many of the ruling elite,

Did British Policy Decisions Cause Emigration and Land Reforms Following the Irish Potato Famine? by Mitchell and Mitchell

**53**

particularly those most directly responsible for determining the extent and means of providing relief.

From the perspective of a political response to the Famine, the most substantial deviation from the purist theories of free market economics came about in Ireland itself. This deviation was motivated by the less than purist desire to seek a major reform of the Irish economy, especially in the 'potato economy' districts in the west. In these areas, the free market clearly had failed to deliver spontaneously the desired result, particularly in terms of larger, more efficient holdings, and the British government chose to use the Famine as a means of facilitating and imposing their own reforms. The Famine provided a unique opportunity to bring about long-term structural changes in Ireland's agrarian sector.

During the latter part of the Famine, notably following the transfer of relief to local responsibility through the mechanism of the Poor Law in the autumn of 1847, a 'hidden agenda' of reform is increasingly apparent. Much of this was covert. The government and its agents were not willing to admit openly that the suffering of many people in Ireland, and the consequent high levels of mortality and emigration, was being employed to achieve other purposes. The government was able to use the chaos caused by the Famine to facilitate a number of social and economic changes. In particular, it took the opportunity to bring about a more commercial system of farming within Ireland which no longer would offer refuge to a variety of non-productive elements—whether they were landless labourers or apathetic landlords. If, due to its ultimate aim, this policy could be judged as altruistic, its implementation, based on the prevailing view of the Irish, cannot be. Irish peasants, feckless and indolent as they were perceived to be, were judged less 'worthy' to receive relief than their counterparts in Britain. One consequence of this perception occurred in 1846 when Ireland was not allowed to receive imports of food until supplies had been delivered to Scotland first. . . .

In conclusion, therefore, the response of the British government to the Famine was inadequate in terms of humanitarian criteria and, increasingly after 1847, systematically and deliberately so. The localised shortages that followed the blight of 1845 were adequately dealt with but, as the shortages became more widespread, the government retrenched. With the short-lived exception of the soup kitchens, access to relief—or even more importantly, access to food—became more restricted. That the response illustrated a view of Ireland and its people as distant and marginal is hard to deny. What, perhaps, is more surprising is that a group of officials and their non-elected advisors were able to dominate government policy to such a great extent. This relatively small group of people, taking advantage of a passive establishment, and public opinion which was opposed to further financial aid for Ireland, were able to manipulate a theory of free enterprise, thus allowing a massive social injustice to be perpetrated within a part of the United Kingdom. There was no shortage of resources to avoid the tragedy of a Famine. Within Ireland itself, there were substantial resources of food which, had the political will existed, could have been diverted, even as a short-term measure, to supply a starving people. Instead, the government pursued the objective of economic, social and agrarian reform as a long-term aim, although the price paid for this ultimately elusive goal was privation, disease, emigration, mortality and an enduring legacy of disenchantment.

---

CHRISTINE KINEALY is a professor of Irish history at Drew University and the author of 14 books, including *A Death-Dealing Famine: The Great Hunger in Ireland* (Pluto Press, 1997).

Hasia R. Diner

 **NO**

# Where They Came From

If poverty, persecution, and violence seem to have been eternal elements of Irish life, changes in the economic and social structure nonetheless did occur. . . . Historians love watersheds: dramatic incidents that set off one epoch from another; major upheavals that loom as signposts along the historic path. The Great Famine of the late 1840s has generally been considered the event in Irish history which sent shock waves throughout Irish society, whose reverberations could be felt around the world, in Boston, London, Toronto, Sydney, and Melbourne, and whose intensity lasted over a century. Nothing remained the same after the devastation of the Famine. The harrowing memory of the starvation, disease, and destruction that engulfed Ireland after the potato blights of 1845–49 altered all relationships; the footing between landlord and tenant changed, as did that between priest and parishioner. The ruler and the ruled shifted ground as they faced each other. Entire classes of people disappeared. The Famine signaled the demise of the Irish cottier class, that landless mass on the lowest stratum of the social structure.

Sheer numbers also confirm the brutal impact of the Famine. After the four years of continuous blight on the potato crop, the Irish staff of life, at least one million people had vanished. Some were felled by starvation, typhus, and dysentery. In the same year three million were reduced to charity. Others fled the Emerald Isle. The Famine's shadow seems to have left no one untouched. The memory of the starvation and what was considered the inaction of the British (some saw it as pure malice) would, over the course of the next century, become a major weapon of nationalist propaganda. Irish journalists, poets, novelists, and playwrights would constantly cull the maudlin scenes of those years for pathetic and gripping material. Father Theobald Matthew, who led Ireland's highly popular temperance movement in the 1870s, invoked such wrenching scenes in sermon after sermon:

> There, admist the chilling damp of a dismal hovel see yon famine-stricken fellow-creature; see him extended on his scanty bed of rotten straw; see his once manly frame, that labour had strengthened with vigour, shrunk to a skeleton; see his once ruddy complexion, the gift of temperance, changed by hunger and concomitant disease to a shallow ghastly hue. See him extend his yellow withering arm for assistance; hear how he cries out in agony

> for food, for since yesterday he has not even moistened his lips!

> Who could forget the vision of a strange and fearful sight like what we read of in beleaguered cities; its streets crowded with gaunt wanderers, sauntering to and from with hopeless air and hunger-struck look—a mob of starved, almost naked women around the poor-house clamoring for soup tickets.

People around the world gasped at the horrors of the Famine. Relief poured in. Generous Americans collected money to send food to Ireland's starving millions. American magazine readers were fed a constant diet of grim details about "a widow with two children who for a week had eaten nothing but cabbage. . . . Another woman with two children, and not far from being confined again, stated that during the last week they had existed upon two quarts of meal and two heads of cabbage . . . famine was written in the faces of this woman and her children."

Intimate relationships between men and women, husbands and wives, parents and children, brothers and sisters, were not exempted from this massive restructuring of life. The qualities of personal ties and social bonds were swept away by the Famine's blast. The 1851 Census of Ireland surveyed the ruin of the countryside and lamented that

> the closest ties of kinship were dissolved; the most ancient and long cherished usages of the people were disregarded; the once proverbial gaiety and lightheartedness of the peasant people seemed to have vanished completely, and village merriment or marriage festival was no longer heard or seen throughout the regions desolated by the intensity and extent of the Famine. . . .

The watershed approach does have its pitfalls. Few of the changes that occurred after the cataclysm were totally unrelated to the nature of the earlier society. The great upheaval merely accentuated trends that had begun earlier and accelerated forces unleashed in more tranquil and stable times. For example, the great upsurge in religiosity that occurred in post-Famine Ireland, the devotional revolution with its tremendous growth in both the number and the power of the clergy, swept a society that was religiously oriented to begin with. Religion had been a powerful political identity for a long time, and the priest, the *soggarth aroon,* had long held a cherished place in the hearts of the masses.

So, too, the trends in Irish demography—constantly decreasing population with late and infrequent marriage and high rates of celibacy, a social environment of gender segregation and reluctant sexuality, the concomitant ethic of intense gender animosity—had roots that reached far back into Irish folk life and characterized some classes in the pre-Famine structure. Yet after the Famine these elements came to be synonymous with all of Irish culture and these trends became the norm of Irish behavior. Similarly, the Famine did not cause the massive emigrations. For one thing, the Famine of the late 1840s was not the first to ravage Ireland in modern times. In 1800, 1807, 1816, 1822, and 1839 massive crop failures and wide-ranging epidemics had shaken up the rural Irish. Immigration had in fact begun before the Famine and it continued well afterwards. At least seven hundred thousand people abandoned the thirty-two counties of Ireland between 1825 and 1844. As early as 1841 a half million Irish-born men and women had decided to settle permanently in England and Scotland, while in the same year over ten thousand new arrivals to the port of Boston listed Ireland as their birthplace. In the 1831–41 decade a half million Irish emigrated. Long after the Great Famine had become a memory and a closed chapter of Ireland's sorrowful history, twentieth-century Ireland continued to send its young men and women around the world, making people Ireland's chief export.

⟨⦿⟩

The legacy of the Famine as it shaped emigration to the United States, and particularly as it stimulated a massive female exodus, involved a demographic transition and an alteration in family relations much more subtle than millions of individuals merely fleeing their native land. Drawing upon older Irish traditions and social trends associated with the more stable classes in pre-Famine society, Ireland became a country that held out fewer and fewer attractions to women. By the last decades of the nineteenth century many young women had no reason to remain in the agricultural towns of Catholic Ireland. They had no realistic chances for marriage or employment. For Irish women to attain either, they had to turn their backs on the land of their birth.

Ireland became the Western world's most dramatic and stark example of a demographic pattern associated with the shift from traditional to modern societies. Ireland led the world by the 1870s as the nation with the latest age of marriage. Irish men and women decided more frequently than men and women elsewhere to eschew marriage and live out their lives in a single state. Ireland was, in fact, one of the only countries in Europe to enter the twentieth century unconcerned about overpopulation, because decades earlier it had achieved more than

"zero population growth." This, however, had not always been the case. Before the Great Famine, more likely than not an Irish peasant or laborer married young. Until the decade of the Famine Irish population figures had risen with alarming rapidity. Ireland's mushrooming—perhaps, more appropriately, exploding—population had, in fact, provided Thomas Malthus with his gloomiest example of the improvidence of the poor and the inexorable cycle whereby population grew far out of proportion to resources.

A large and controversial body of demographic literature has attempted to explain how this happened. The issues in the analysis of Irish population trends are clouded by the difficulty of obtaining accurate statistics on just how many births and deaths occurred in any given year before 1864, when compulsory registration of nationwide vital statistics was enacted. The first official head count of any kind was made in 1821, and that of 1841 is considered the first that approached reliability. Generally, it is accepted by demographers and historians that the 1821 Census counted fewer people than actually existed, whereas the 1831 count overstated the number. Despite the technical problems of portraying Irish demographic movement, scholars and commentators on the Irish scene have sought to come to terms with the ways in which the population changed and why The impact of the Great Famine is central to this endeavor, and from it we can begin to discern the nature of women's lives in Irish society.

On the eve of the Famine, over eight million people inhabited Ireland. Fifty years later the same island had been home to fewer than three million. This tremendous growth occurred without any industrialization or increase in economic opportunities and without any influx of foreigners. In fact, this staggering proliferation occurred while emigration had already become an established part of life. Over four hundred thousand Irish-born men and women lived in Great Britain in 1841, whereas between 1780 and 1845 more than one million Irish had made their way to the United States and Canada. Thus, despite a continuous stream of Irish leaving Ireland in this same half century, the rate of population increase constituted a major demographic revolution.

One strand of analysis which attempts to explain Irish population dynamics focuses on diet—on the impact of the lowly potato on mortality and fertility trends. The potato culture, which gradually came to characterize all Ireland, triggered a constant and seemingly unending process by which the land was broken into smaller and smaller holdings. Widespread was "the general practice with farmers to divide their land into portions, which were given to their children as they got married. The last married frequently got his father's cabin along with his portion of the ground, and there the parents liked to stop feeling attached to the place where they spent their lives." The fleshy tuber could be grown anywhere, even on the most miniscule of plots, and contained just enough nutrients to sustain the life of the poor.

As the Irish had become potato-eaters by the end of the eighteenth century, they also had become early marriers. The poor, in particular, saw no reason not to marry spontaneously, that is, without protracted negotiations between families, and certainly without the aid of a matchmaker. Young men and women married when they wanted, and since they could always grow potatoes, a family of hungry mouths was not a burden. A priest from Mayo generalized to the Commission of Inquiry on the Irish Poor in 1836 that "small holders are induced to marry by feeling that their condition cannot be made worse, or rather, they know they can lose nothing, and they promise themselves some pleasure in the society of a wife." This testimony typified the statements that were offered by the clerics and laymen alike to the commission, to the Devon Commission, which met in 1841, and to other, similar bodies. One man in County Galway confessed in 1835, "if I had been a blanket to cover her, I would marry the woman I liked; and if I should get potatoes enough to put into my children's mouths, I would be as happy and content as any man." Similarly, very few Irish men and women did not marry. The nature of the economy and the social structure left very little room for the unattached adult. Within marriage, fertility was high. There was no incentive for, or seeming interest in, contraception of any kind as there was in France at the same time. Some scholars even argue that, by providing a cheap and easily cultivated source of nutrition, the potato improved the health of women and gradually led to heightened fertility.

Even before the Famine this pattern of early and improvident marriage characterized the depressed peasants—the cottiers and the poor laborers—much more than any other class. Townspeople, tradesmen, and farmers with more than a potato plot demonstrated greater reticence about marriage. For those with hope of economic stability and with aspirations for a more "middle-class" kind of existence, improvident marriage could spell disaster. Marrying too young meant the expense of feeding and clothing a family too soon. Marrying too young was clearly associated with the reckless behavior of the poor, who inched closer and closer to doom as they subdivided and resubdivided their possessions.

A County Kilkenny observer noted that "those who are a grade above the cottier are more cautious as to marriage, and it is chiefly among small farmers that you will find bachelors." Similarly, in County Limerick one could have found "a greater proportionate number of unmarried men amongst the farmers and tradesmen than amongst the lowest classes of agricultural labourers." This same phenomenon could be plotted geographically. In the wealthier and more fertile East, which supported the cultivation of grains as well as potatoes, people generally married later than in the poverty-stricken West, which was home for the most destitute of laborers and cottiers. Thus, even in the early nineteenth-century, when Irish population grew rapidly, the growth was clustered in the bottom classes.

The late- and non-marriers of "higher" social status in Irish society provided the link between the pre- and post-Famine eras of Irish history. They undermine the more dramatic interpretation that sees the Famine as the central and defining event in Ireland's development. It is in part because of these more prosperous farmers that the rapid population growth had actually begun to slacken by 1821, and the 1831 Census registered a marked increase in the number of nonmarried adults. What the Famine did accomplish was to dramatically universalize trends that were already in operation. This happened in a number of ways. In the first place, the Famine could claim grim responsibility for the almost total elimination of the cottier class. Second, the memory of the Famine impressed the British lawmakers enough in the succeeding decades to enact legislation that outlawed subdivision and other practices associated with pre-Famine agriculture, thus transforming most Irish men into holders of small, although viable, farms.

The Famine might also be seen as the great convincer. It demonstrated to all the folly of agrarian practices that defined a postage-stamp-size piece of land as enough just because it brought forth potatoes. Irish agriculture was going to have to become much more diversified, and though potatoes could remain a central dish on the Irish family's table, that same farm family would also have to produce a cash crop as well as butter, eggs, and other dairy products for markets. The Famine also demonstrated to Irish parents that no one prospered if they cut up their holdings into equal portions for all their sons. An inheritance came to be the entire holding or nothing. Similarly, the Famine also convinced Irish men and women that early marriage was reckless marriage; that nonmarriage was an option, too. As the Irish changed their marriage patterns, they basically adapted the behavior of the more economically stable elements in the society, convinced that the devastation and destruction of the late 1840s had in part been caused by irrational, carefree marriage and family practices that failed to treat conjugal life as a fundamentally economic enterprise.

Whereas before the Famine commentators on Irish life—Catholic clergymen, economists, and British officials alike—lamented the reckless marriage patterns that seemed to accompany the Irish descent into poverty and destitution, after the Famine concern mounted that the Irish in Ireland were increasingly uninterested in remaining at home, marrying, and reproducing themselves. In 1902 one writer mourned, "In saying all this we are fully alive to the sadness of seeing a grand old race disappear as it were, off the face of the earth." Richard J. Kelly in 1904 shared this pessimism with readers of the *New Ireland Review* and chided the experts. "Economists, so-called, read lessons to us on our over-population and improvident early marriages and, as they said, consequent wretchedness. But they can no longer, with any regard for truth say so now, with a smaller population, lower marriage and a lower birth rate than most countries in Europe." Descriptions of Irish life in the last decades of the century all stressed the gloom of decay, the moribund quiet of a society in decline, although perhaps a decline accompanied by increasing prosperity. A magistrate of County Meath saw his home as

> one of the most melancholy counties I know. This grass grown road, over which seemingly little, if any, traffic passes, is a type of solitude everywhere found. Tillage there is none; but in its stead one vast expanse of pasture land extends. Human habitations are rarer than the bare walls of roofless cottages. Where once a population dwelt, and as consequence, see how lonely and untrodden are these roads.

Census figures painfully recorded the dwindling of Irish numbers. In the fifty years between 1841 and 1891, Ireland lost 3,470,374 residents, plummeting from the pre-Famine population of 8,175,124 in 1841 to 4,704,750 in 1891. Constant migration picked off many of these Irish men and women, but migration could not alone be blamed. The decline in Irish population stemmed most fundamentally from a change in family life and a major demographic shift. There were, to be sure, bad harvests in the last half of the nineteenth century which took their toll, somewhat reminiscent of the Famine, but they lacked the bite of the 1840s' devastation.

The bulk of the late-nineteenth-century population decline occurred in the rural areas, siphoning off the residents of farm regions much more rapidly than residents of towns. Ireland was becoming somewhat less overwhelmingly rural in the last half of the century. In 1841 only 17 percent of the population was urban; by 1891 over one-quarter of all the Irish could be found in cities like Dublin and Cork. Even the urban population of the country slumped, however, falling from over a million city dwellers in 1841 to eight hundred thousand in 1891. Only Dublin grew in that same time period, but that growth was hardly dramatic and clearly indicated the stagnation of Irish population and the absence of any industrial development or commercial rejuvenation to draw discontented farm people into the cities. Ireland had basically become a nogrowth nation. It had no urban-industrial attractions to stimulate a massive internal movement. It had in fact become a nation characterized by late and reluctant marriage as well as by a massive voluntary exodus.

In the early 1840s, before the Famine shocked and convinced the Irish out of impoverished, although perhaps comfortable, ways, the rate of marriage was 7.0–8.0 per thousand per year. It bore a close resemblance to the rate of marriage throughout Europe. From 1868, four years after compulsory registration of vital statistics, to 1870 the rate of marriage spiraled down to 5.1 per thousand and then fell to 4.0 in the years 1881–90. Clearly, in any given year or span of years during the second half of the century

fewer Irish men and women were setting up families than in years past. Many were merely deferring, that is, they were marrying later than they might have in earlier periods. In 1864, for example, 18.1 percent of all women who married were under twenty-one. In 1911 only 5.3 percent entered marriage by that age. Similarly, in 1864 71.1 percent of all wives in a first marriage were under twenty-five; in 1911 only 51.1 percent were similarly situated. But Ireland also came to be the home of large numbers of men and women who just chose not to marry or who were unable to. In 1861, 11 percent of all men in Ireland sixty-five or over were permanent bachelors; in 1926 that figure had risen to 26 percent. Again using 1841, or the last pre-Famine census, as the point of contrast, the percentage of women age twenty-five to thirty-four who were single in Ireland went from 28 percent to 39 percent in 1851. It did not change in 1891. Although fewer Irish women continued to be unmarried as they approached old age, among women forty-five to fifty-four the number of singles also increased from 12 percent in 1841 to 17 percent in 1891. Figures for men were significantly higher in both age categories, in all years. No longer did Irish society live under the specter of the impetuous young rushing off emotionally to marry and set up homes.

Not surprisingly, this matrimonial trend occurred in tandem with yet another development that characterized post-Famine Irish society. Parents increasingly became reluctant to subdivide their land among heirs, and Ireland as a whole came to have fewer and fewer holdings. In 1841, for example, there were 691,000 holdings in all of Ireland, the largest percentage being the smallest holdings, one to five acres. In 1861, 568,000 estates were primarily of the five- to fifteen-acre size, whereas in 1891 the number of holdings declined to 469,000, most of them over thirty acres. Evictions certainly help account for this trend toward land accretion. The poorest could no longer hold onto their tiny plots, and consolidation in Ireland became the basic trend. The cottiers were gone and increasingly the middling Irish farmer had control of a reasonably viable piece of land, which was to be used for pasture-farming, not for tillage.

These middling Irish farmers either had survived the Famine themselves or their parents had witnessed the harrowing devastation, commonly attributed to the wrath of God, or to the heartlessness of the Saxon ruler, or, importantly, to the impetuous romanticism of the poor. The middling Irish farmers were *not* going to err again. They were not going to find themselves in the same position as had the Irish in the 1840s. To ensure their continuous survival without want and destitution they finally sought to shake off the yoke of British rule. To ensure their continued survival with a degree of material comfort and security they sought to establish families that enhanced their economic needs. Land and the economic security it brought became obsessions with the Irish. A folk proverb suggested, "Let any man go down to hell and open an Irish man's heart . . . the first thing writ across it was land."

Whereas there is no agreement in sight for the lively and sparring scholarly debate over the cause of the pre-Famine population growth, there is unanimity as to the nature of post-Famine marriage: what it was and why it developed into a more discriminate and rationalized institution. Marriages were based now on economic calculation with parents figuring and weighing the financial benefits and liabilities of their children's marital futures. Land would not be divided. An estate would pass intact and undisturbed from one generation to another. Therefore, only one member of the family's younger generation could hope to inherit the land. No systematic or established pattern developed which designated that single heir. Primogeniture was not the rule, nor was the younger son the immediately designated heir. Who inherited the land became the decision of father and mother and they made that decision as late in their lives as possible. Parents held onto control of their fields until well into old age. (Interestingly, Ireland had among Europe's most impressive statistics on longevity.) At the same time they tenaciously held onto control of their children's futures.

---

Hasıa R. Dıner is a professor of history at New York University. Her research interests include American Jewish history, immigration-ethnic history, and women's history.

# EXPLORING THE ISSUE

## Did British Policy Decisions Cause the Mass Emigration and Land Reforms that Followed the Irish Potato Famine of the 1840s and 1850s?

## Critical Thinking and Reflection

1. What was the nature of the Irish potato famine that began in 1845, and why were its effects on Irish farmers so devastating? Were all parts of Ireland uniformly affected?
2. What role did Adam Smith's theory of *laissez-faire* economics play in Britain's withholding of economic aid to Ireland? Was this justified in your view? Critically discuss.
3. Which groups were included in what Professor Kinealy calls "nonproducing elements"? Either support or attack her claim that their loss facilitated the modernization of the Irish economy.
4. In either case, was this benefit worth the human cost? Critically discuss.
5. Historian Hasia Diner sees continuity in pre- and post-famine emigration patterns. Support or attack her claim that this offers proof of the Irish people's ability to act on their own behalf, as agents of historical change.
6. Which of the changing patterns, begun during the famine years, have continued? Why?
7. Why, in your view, did responses to Irish distress harden over time? Critically discuss.

## Is There Common Ground?

Both writers are in basic agreement about what happened in Ireland between 1845 and 1852. The question of this issue has more to do with attitudes of Britain and their effects on the people of Ireland. How would you go about evaluating these differing explanations of why events unfolded as they did? As in many issues, we find first that the YES and NO selections are focusing on different areas. Another consideration is whether we are looking at the issue from inside Ireland or from outside Ireland, in the relative prosperity of Britain. If one looks solely at economic systems and their long-term benefits, without "seeing" the effects of radical change on people, it might be possible to argue that the potato famine worked to Ireland's long-term benefit. However, it is difficult to ignore the people, a million of whom died and another million of whom emigrated. Revisionist historians, taking the long view of history, sometimes tend to minimize the suffering of those caught in the confusing middle of historical trends. How should historians fairly calculate degrees of suffering, and how might they fairly assign blame—both in Britain and within Ireland?

*Question:* Since many immigrants from Ireland contributed to the building of the United States, speculate about how the United States might be different if the potato famine had been handled differently by Britain.

## Create Central

www.mhhe.com/createcentral

## Additional Resources

*The Great Irish Famine*, edited by Cathal Poirteir and produced in association with Irish Television (Radio Telefis Eireann), has an especially interesting essay by Peter Gray on "Ideology and the Famine," which explores anti-Irish prejudice, the influence of economic theories on British policy, and the reality of political considerations. Two television series have explored this topic: "The Great Famine," produced by Arts & Entertainment (A&E) and "Ireland: A History," produced by British Broadcasting Company and Radio Telefis Eireann (BBC/RTE). Accompanying the latter is a well-illustrated book of the same title by Robert Kee (Abacus Edition, Sphere Books Ltd., 1982). Chapter 5, titled "Famine," is sprinkled with engravings and well documented with contemporary newspaper accounts of conditions in Ireland. A similar "you are there" feeling is available in *Famine Diary* (Irish Academic Press, 1999) by Brendan O'Cathaoir, author of *The Irish Times* column of the same name. It features longer, unabridged accounts from newspapers, official correspondence, and diaries that offer graphic descriptions of worsening conditions in the Irish countryside.

The 150th anniversary of the beginning of the potato famine has sparked a scholarly reassessment of the traditional interpretation that focused on nationwide suffering, years of misrule, and inadequate responses from both the British government and Irish landlords. Revisionist interpretations have tended to minimize the degree of suffering and are reluctant to blame the authorities for the crisis. Works such as the YES selection by Christine Kinealy are, in part, a response to what seems to be a "sanitized" version of the potato famine that trivializes the catastrophe and fails to acknowledge its causes.

# *Internet References . . .*

### The Great Irish Famine

A comprehensive guide to the Irish famine, covering all facets of the issue: Introduction, Before the Famine, The Blight Begins, The Great Hunger, Coffin Ships, Financial Ruin, Gone to America, After the Famine, Author/Bibliography.

**www.historyplace.com/worldhistory/famine/**

Selected, Edited, and with Issue Framing Material by:
Helen Buss Mitchell, *Howard Community College*
and
Joseph R. Mitchell, *Howard Community College*

# ISSUE

# Did the Meiji Restoration Constitute a Revolution in Nineteenth-Century Japan?

**YES: Thomas M. Huber,** from *The Revolutionary Origins of Modern Japan* (Stanford University Press, 1981)

**NO: W.G. Beasley,** from *The Meiji Restoration* (Stanford University Press, 1972)

---

## Learning Outcomes

**After reading this issue you should be able to:**

- Describe the nature and character of the Japanese Meiji Restoration.
- Understand the historical circumstances that led the Japanese to centralize political power and modernize on their own terms.
- Use the Japanese word *Ishin*, meaning "renovation," as a tool for understanding Japan's aims in this return to emperor rule, as well as an end to Japan's 250 years of self-imposed exile.

---

### ISSUE SUMMARY

**YES:** Historian Thomas M. Huber argues that the Meiji Restoration was revolutionary and should be recognized as "the most dramatic event of Japan's modern history."

**NO:** Historian W.G. Beasley argues that when compared with other revolutions like the French and Russian, the Meiji Restoration did not constitute a revolution in the classical sense.

In 1603, the Japanese closed themselves off from the rest of the world. Fearful of Western economic and religious influences, which could corrupt their traditions and mores, they banned foreign contacts and meted out severe punishments (including death) to any who violated the ban. Part of this process was the outlawing of Christianity as a recognized religion in Japan. This self-imposed exile was to last for more than 250 years.

The decision to isolate was made by the Tokugawa Shogunate (1603–1868), Japan's ruling power during that period. Since the feudal period of Japanese history, the country had been ruled by *shoguns*, who were hereditary leaders. Like dynastic rulers anywhere, their right to rule lasted as long as their ability to maintain control, and they could always be replaced by another leader who could then establish his family's rule over the country. Thus, for most of the second millennium, Japan was ruled by successive shogunates: Kamakura (1192–1333), Ashikaga (1335–1673), and Tokugawa (1603–1868). During this time civil wars became prevalent, as there was no shortage of ambitious men eager to test the waters of political supremacy.

The shoguns were assisted in their rule by *daimyo*, feudal lords who sometimes posed threats to their masters.

The *samurai*, Japan's legendary warrior class, provided the power base for any shogun. Under this system, the Japanese emperor, whose office dated back to the fifth century C.E., had been reduced to that of an isolated figurehead. With the modern world casting covetous eyes around the globe, many wondered how long Japan's self-imposed exile would last, and whether it would end by outside force or national choice.

The warrior class that had developed in Japan between the ninth and twelfth centuries and that had supported the shogunates that ruled Japan prior to the nineteenth-century Meiji Restoration was also called bushi, and the code by which they lived and died became known as *Bushido*—the way of the warrior. As skilled fighting men, the *samurai* were, above all, loyal to the emperor, to an overlord or daimyo, and to other *samurai* of higher rank. Skilled in swordsmanship, horsemanship, and hand-to-hand combat, many were often also adept at painting, calligraphy, and poetry. They lived spartan lives marked by honor, pride, patriotism, and honesty. Prepared at any moment to lay down their lives for their lord, the *samurai* preferred ritual suicide (known as seppuku or hara-kiri, meaning disembowelment) to capture in battle or to dishonor. Later scholars have also found elements of Confucianism, and Shinto in the Bushido Code.

From Shinto comes reverence for the emperor as a God-like father of the nation. Out of this loyalty to the imperial family flows an intense patriotism as well as the promise that to die for one's country in a battle is to become like a God. This absolute fidelity of the *samurai* may be seen continuing into the modern era. Kamikaze pilots and suicide torpedoists who willingly sacrificed their lives for the success of the nation and to honor the emperor during World War II were following their own version of the Bushido Code.

Confucianism draws attention to the five constant relationships—between parent and child, husband and wife, older and younger sibling, older and younger friend, and ruler and subject—as models for achieving harmony with the Way of Heaven. To know one's place, to do one's duty, to honor those above and act kindly toward those below, this was the way to live a life of balance, to serve the common good, and to please the ancestors. Samurai loyalty to emperor and overlord may be understood within this context of properly lived human relationships. All of these elements of the traditional Japanese worldview were severely challenged by Japan's encounter with the modern West.

In 1853, U.S. Commodore Matthew Perry arrived in Tokyo, seeking and receiving a treaty from the Japanese government. Although its terms were not seriously detrimental to Japanese hegemony, it did start a trend that resulted in similar treaties with other foreign nations. In Japan, these actions had the dual effect of forcing the Japanese to consider what they could do to limit further Western intervention and causing the rise of nationalist sentiment against these foreign elements. This resulted in an overthrow of the Tokugawa shogunate by an alliance of feudal lords and samurai in 1866, which returned the emperor to a position of authority in the new Japanese government. The new emperor took the name Meiji (enlightened government) and since that time, the period in Japanese history from 1868 to 1912 has been known in the West as the Meiji Restoration. Thus began Japan's modern history.

The transformation of Japan seemed to be profound; no part of Japanese life escaped the winds of change. Although those who overthrew the Tokugawa government had no set plan—and many of them had diametrically opposed goals and objectives—change was the order of the day. Some of the most important results of Meiji rule were the growth of Japan's industrial and military power, presumably accomplished to counter balance Western power in Asia. This was done under the aegis of a highly centralized government that featured a "top down" power structure. Under such a system, a premium was placed on nationalism as a unifying force. Some of the Meiji-made decisions were to have a positive impact on Japan's modernization; others, such as imperialism, were to have drastic consequences for the nation and its people.

One basic historical question about the Meiji Restoration concerns the nature of the movement. How much and what type of change did it have? Was it revolutionary in nature? How does it compare with its French and Russian counterparts? A problem facing one who attempts to answer those questions lies in definition, and in this case, an accurate translation of words. The Japanese word to describe the Meiji movement is *Ishin*, which may be closer in meaning to renovation than the Western-translated restoration.

Keep this in mind as we assess the revolutionary nature of the Meiji restoration through the work of Thomas M. Huber and W.G. Beasley who present complementary, yet differing, opinions on the subject. The former refers to the Meiji Restoration and its reforms as a revolution that rescued Japan "from the bondage of colonialism, and from the feudal encumbrances of her own past." The latter agrees that the Meiji Restoration was revolutionary, but argues that it "lacked the avowed social purpose that gives the 'great' revolutions of history a certain common character." Instead Beasley finds that Japanese nationalism was the force that made the Meiji movement possible.

# YES

**Thomas M. Huber**

# The Revolutionary Origins
# of Modern Japan

## Introduction

The creation of the Meiji Restoration government in 1868, and the sweeping reforms that followed, constitute the most dramatic event in Japan's modern history. Within a decade Japanese leaders established a system of universal education, formed a modern army and navy, and recruited an efficient administrative bureaucracy, both nationally and locally. They developed a network of telegraph and rail communications, and laid the broad fiscal and financial foundations that were needed for rapid industrialization. The Restoration transformed Japan into a modern society by the standards of the day, and rescued her alone among her Asian neighbors from the bondage of colonialism, and from the feudal encumbrances of her own past.

Western scholarship on Japan has been at pains to explain why this amazing transformation happened to take place, and in recent decades a scholarly consensus on the question has emerged. Since it is my purpose to reopen this issue by offering a differing analysis of the Restoration experience, let us begin by examining the basic assumptions of what is now the most commonly accepted view. First, it is argued by scholars that the leading restorationists, those who seized power in 1868 and set about constructing the new regime, were enlightened statesmen motivated by a shared concern over the growing threat of Western power. Since most of them came from the samurai hierarchy's middle and upper portions, and were therefore already privileged under the old order, social and class grievances played little part in bringing them to act. Rather, it was their traditional loyalty to domain and nation, daimyo and emperor, that spurred the Meiji leaders to action after Perry's fleet arrived in 1853.

Second, the political turbulence of the 1850s and 1860s is seen by historians as unrelated to the institutional reforms worked out by statesmen after 1868. The strife-ridden decade of the 1860s represented little more than two false starts: xenophobic terrorism (1860–63) and militant loyalty to domain (1863–68). According to the established view, these exhausted impulses gave way after 1868 to a more sophisticated, pragmatic nationalism.

Third, the Meiji reforms after 1868 are seen as being primarily imitative. Having no clear program other than the desire not to be overborne by the West, Meiji leaders understandably turned to the West to discover how Japan might best be strengthened against the Western challenge.

Being rational bureaucrats as well as nationalists, when they found economic and social institutions in the West that served their purposes, they simply imported them.

The now widely accepted explanation represented by these three assumptions is ptolemaic in the sense that each set of occurrences in the crucial Restoration years has to be accounted for by a different principle of historical motion. Is it really likely that the fanaticism of the early 1860s simply vanished, or that the leaders who fought so hard from 1864 to 1868 to establish the hegemony of their own domains would work just as hard in 1869 to disestablish those same domains? (There is a paradox in this view that parallels that of the Japanese Marxist thesis, advanced in the 1920s, that "lower-class samurai" abolished the samurai class and the Tokugawa Bakufu in order to preserve as much of the feudal order as possible!) Something seems to be missing from this approach. Either the substance of public life in this period was disjointed to a very unusual degree, or else there was some underlying historical principle giving unity to the events of this era that has somehow escaped scholarly analysis.

I shall argue in these pages that the three propositions stated above are fundamentally mistaken. They are mistaken because they do not adequately explain either the extraordinary events that led up to the Restoration or the massive changes that followed it. I will try to offer fresh concepts that may more satisfactorily explain Japan's great transformation, and will present a new hypothesis with respect to the central cause and mechanism of that transformation.

The premises of this study are as follows. First, the Restoration leadership acted on behalf of a distinctive social category or class, namely Japan's early modern service intelligentsia. Second, the leading members of this class in late Bakuhan society were both materially deprived and spiritually tormented by the workings of an antiquated system of aristocratic privilege and lavish ceremonial waste. Third, these leaders refashioned elements of their own intellectual tradition to construct iconoclastic and compelling ideological support for their social complaints. Fourth, on the basis of empirical principles derived from these traditional sources, the reformist leaders developed notions of social change similar to those implemented in Meiji, and evolved a coherent social program some years before they had meaningful access to Western models. Fifth, the seemingly disjointed violence of the Bakumatsu period reflected what was in reality a continuous escalation of political hostilities, during which reformers were driven to rely in succession on polemic, terror, and civil warfare in their relentless struggle against conservative power. Sixth, the Meiji transformation represented the actual implementation of reforms and reformist principles that had been advocated for decades by Japan's indigenous service intelligentsia.

In sum, I shall argue that the Meiji Restoration was in essence a blow struck at pervasive patterns of social injustice by a frustrated and ultimately embattled service intelligentsia. It was a domestic affair, in which the Western challenge figured only as a convenient instrumentality, used by the reformers to win broader approval for the basic structural changes they had long favored.

Twenty-five years ago, when Tokugawa Japan was typically seen as a "feudal" and relatively backward society, this kind of explanation could not have been easily sustained. In recent years, however, scholars such as Ronald Dore, John Hall, Conrad Totman, Tetsuo Najita, and Thomas C. Smith have shown that late Tokugawa institutions and thought were more highly developed in every sphere than had previously been believed. This book, which pursues some of the implications of their revealing studies in the context of the Meiji Restoration, is greatly indebted to their work.

Intelligentsia-oriented analysis has long been familiar in European historiography, where a political intelligentsia commonly figures as the leading element or "vanguard" of a bourgeois or proletarian movement. Japan's insurgent intelligentsia did not conform to this pattern; although motivated in part by idealistic perceptions, it was the vanguard primarily of itself. Whatever benefits its triumph may have gained for other groups, its own interests and perceptions were the main dynamic force behind Japan's modern transformation. (One of the intelligentsia's perceived interests was, however, the welfare of the whole national community, for reasons that will be discussed below.) The case of the Restoration is thus an interesting one in theoretical terms, suggesting as it does that the bureaucratization processes emphasized by Weber may tell us more about some revolutionary upheavals than is revealed by the proletarianization processes described by Marx. This study will allow us ultimately to explore some of the complex issues raised by this suggestion.

In the pages that follow I will make the above arguments by examining the political careers of a prominent group of Restoration leaders known as the Chōshū activists. Chōshū was one of the larger "outer" domains of the Tokugawa system, and in the decades after the Restoration several of her sons came to dominate the highest levels of the new government. Men like Kido Kōin, Itō Hirobumi, Yamagata Aritomo, and Inoue Kaoru wrote the new constitution, founded the new military, created a modern diplomatic corps, and in general supervised the building of the new society.

Earlier, these men had been members of a larger group of militant restorationist sympathizers in Chōshū. This larger group had been continuously active in the movement for reform from the 1850s on. They figured prominently in the terrorism of 1860–63, and it was their mobilization of the Chōshū army in 1866 that brought the Bakufu to its knees. The Chōshū reformers were perhaps the most vigorous and effective opponents of the Tokugawa regime, and it was their actions that ultimately proved decisive in bringing it down.

My main concern is with relating the Chōshū activists' social origins to their values, goals, motives, and strategies in the 1850s and 1860s. I will concentrate in particular on the Sonjuku group, a political association of several dozen persons within the Chōshū movement that produced Itō and the Meiji statesmen. During the 1850s, the famous teacher Yoshida Shōin ran a school called the Shōka Sonjuku in the Chōshū capital of Hagi. Itō and the others were at one time students of this school.

The Sonjuku group was characterized by a high degree of political engagement throughout, and the casualty rate among its members was high. Three men in succession served as its leaders between 1853 and 1868, and each man perished doing so. The martyrdom of these leaders was for their companions part of a larger pattern of political endeavor, however, and it is the purpose of this study to grasp the essential "cause" of the Restoration by revealing what that endeavor was.

My findings take the form of a sequence of political biographies, one for each of these three remarkable leaders. Chapters 2 through 4 deal with the early life, thought, and leadership of Yoshida Shōin, prior to his execution by the Bakufu in 1859. Chapters 5 and 6 explore the promising early career of the young physician Kusaka Genzui, and the years of his political leadership from Yoshida's death in 1859 until his own in a hail of rifle fire at the Forbidden Gate in 1864. Chapters 7 and 8 set forth the early life and political career of Takasugi Shinsaku, who finally led the reorganized Chōshū military to victory against vastly superior conservative forces in the years between 1864 and 1867. The implications of these events are discussed in Chapter 9.

This treatment will show that the Meiji transformation was accomplished only after a long and daring political insurgency, by men dedicated to reformist principles that were articulated in the 1850s and even earlier. It was over these principles, representing as they did the vision of a new society and the aspirations of a new social class, that the bitter struggles of the 1860s were waged, and for the sake of these principles that the Chōshū men and others put their lives at risk. The Chōshū leaders probably did not see themselves at first as being the foremost champions of these new values, but when fortune so decreed, they proved worthy of the task. In this book the origins of the Meiji state are characterized as revolutionary. If the explanation offered here is correct, they were nothing less.

---

**THOMAS M. HUBER** is an international historian and Japan specialist on the history faculty of the U.S. Army Command and General Staff College in Fort Leavenworth, Kansas.

W.G. Beasley  **NO**

# The Meiji Restoration

## Introduction

During the middle decades of the nineteenth century China and Japan both faced pressure from an intrusive, expanding West. This entailed, first, a political and military danger, manifested in two Anglo-Chinese wars and in the use of force on many other occasions, threatening their independence; and second, a challenge to their traditional culture from one that was alien in many of its fundamental concepts, as well as superior in technology and science. Emotionally and intellectually, Chinese and Japanese reacted to the threat in similar ways: with simple hostility, with manifestations of cultural chauvinism, with a grudging recognition of their own inferiority in "wealth and power." Yet they differed greatly in the kind of actions that this response induced. In China, the Confucian order proved strong enough to inhibit change, whether in polity or ideas, thereby bringing about a union of conservatism at home with concession abroad that led eventually to dynastic decline and an age of revolutions. In Japan, men succeeded in "using the barbarian to control the barbarian" so as to initiate policies that produced a "modern" state, powerful enough in the end to meet the West on equal terms. Hence Japan, unlike China, moved to empire and industry, not poverty and civil war.

The Meiji Restoration is at the heart of this contrast, since it was the process by which Japan acquired a leadership committed to reform and able to enforce it. For Japan, therefore, the Restoration has something of the significance that the English Revolution has for England or the French Revolution for France; it is the point from which modern history can be said to begin. For this reason it has been much studied. Equally, it has been the subject of enduring controversy, for its significance—and thus the way in which it is to be explained—has changed with every change of attitude toward the society that it brought into being. . . .

## Conclusions

The history of the Meiji Restoration . . . is relevant to a number of themes that are important not only for Japan. In part it was a response to the nineteenth-century expansion of the West in Asia. Hence studying it raises questions about the nature of imperialism and nationalism and of their relationship to change in the modern world. Equally, the Restoration was at least in some respects a revolution. One must therefore ask, what kind of revolution was it?

How does it compare with other great political upheavals in other parts of the world at other times? And are the features that mark it off from them idiosyncratically Japanese, or do they arise from the fact and nature of the West's involvement? Finally, since the Restoration is the historical starting point for the modernization of Japan, a process that is highly significant for theories of economic growth, it poses yet another question, to wit: How far is a radical restructuring of society a necessary condition—and not merely a consequence—of the transformation of a premodern into a modern economy.

Clearly, though the example of Japan is an element in the discussion of all these matters, it is not necessarily a decisive one. Therefore a [selection] like this, which approaches the Restoration from inside, as it were, that is, as a part of Japanese history, ought not to offer itself as providing answers that are universally valid. What it *can* do, what these closing remarks are intended to do, is to present its conclusions in such a way that others might be able to use them to these ends. As a preliminary to this, it might be helpful to recapitulate the story in a rather more generalized form than was possible when setting out the detailed narrative.

Under the Tokugawa, Japanese society was gradually modified by economic change in such a way as to bring about by the nineteenth century a disjunction between contemporary reality and the inherited ideal. This was manifested in a number of phenomena for which the traditional order had no place: samurai whose debts turned them into ambitious office-holders or impoverished umbrella-makers; farmers abandoning subsistence agriculture to become commercial producers and rural entrepreneurs or laborers and quasi-tenants; and city merchants enjoying feudal patronage in a kind of symbiosis with authority or escaping into an urban subculture of their own.

Because these things happened at different speeds in different areas, they disturbed the balance of power between the Bakufu [or "tent government" because soldiers lived in tents] and the domains, which had depended originally on a carefully calculated distribution of land. Because they happened at all, they produced social upheaval: a blurring of status distinctions, stimulating samurai unrest; and economic disruption, provoking peasant revolt. These were reflected in turn in a "what-is-wrong-with-the-world" literature and attempts at "reform," the latter seeking either to reconstitute an ideal past (a restoration of feudal authority and its agrarian base) or to exploit commercial growth for the benefit of the ruling class (if at some cost to its ethos). One result was to give more samurai a degree of participation in active politics than hitherto. Another was to make the concept of "reform" familiar and to prompt a feeling that society was in danger of destruction from within.

Yet the country's social and political institutions proved to be remarkably durable: eroded but far from demolished, they did not seem in 1850 to be on the point of being swept away. Not least, this was because the system of institutional checks and balances coupled with deliberate regional fragmentation that had been devised to restrain the anticipated disaffection of samurai and feudal lords proved capable also of imposing controls on the new "men of substance" who might have challenged the established order from outside the samurai class. Accordingly, most of these men sought their opportunities of advancement through conformity, not revolution, acquiring status by purchase or marriage, but remaining politically passive.

It was into this situation that there were injected the West's demand for trade relations in the years 1853–58, leading to "unequal" treaties. The manner in which the treaties were obtained, that is, by gunboat diplomacy, was as important as their content, for it helped to produce in Japan an upsurge of emotion greater than any that had been aroused by domestic issues. Its importance was not merely that the blow to Japanese pride led to a call for "action" (not necessarily of any specific kind); it was also that this was a "national" dishonor in the sense that it could be felt in all areas and at all levels in Japanese society. It thereby helped to break down the regional and social fragmentation that had been one of the foundations of Tokugawa power.

Moreover, the humiliation at the hands of the West precipitated struggle and controversy. The struggle arose when men questioned the efficiency of the country's leaders, especially their ability to defend Japan; and it brought to the surface many of the latent divisions in the national polity by asking, if only implicitly, who their replacements should be in case they failed. The controversy concerned both short-term diplomatic issues and long-term cultural ones, but it had a single, central thread: the extent to which Japan must abandon custom in order to save herself, first in the context of technology, or particular institutional devices to serve particular ends, and then, more generally, in the context of radical changes in society, such as industrialization had induced in the countries of the West. . . .

History offers many different examples of the kind of motivating force that is capable of overcoming inertia and the bonds of tradition: imperial ambition, religious faith, the pursuit of social justice, the aspirations of a newly emergent class. For Japan in the nineteenth century, nationalism had this function. Again and again in the documents of the years we have been considering there are phrases that put policy of every kind—economic and political, as well as diplomatic—into the context of the "national" interest, justifying proposals on the grounds that they would "restore our national strength" or "make the imperial dignity resound beyond the seas." What is more, most of the major political crises centered on the question of Japan's relations with the outside world: that of 1858, when the signing of the treaties became linked with the question of the Tokugawa succession; that of 1863–64, when the fate of the "men of spirit" was decided against a background of foreign bombardment; that of 1873, when the debate about Korea brought into the open a struggle about priorities at home. Throughout, Japanese opinion was moving from a consciousness of foreign threat to an awareness of national identity, expressed in demands for unity and independence.

The contrast with China underlines the extraordinary speed and thoroughness of Japan's response. Despite widespread anti-foreign feeling among gentry and officials, Chinese continued to behave, at least until the end of the nineteenth century, as a people defending a civilization that was threatened, not a nation defending a country that was under attack. Long before then, the Japanese, subscribing to a more articulate and sophisticated version of the Restoration's search for "wealth and strength," had found in nationalism a means of reconciling the conflict between cultural tradition and imperative circumstance.

The "liberal" constitutional movement was heavily influenced by that new-found nationalism. "The one object of my life is to extend Japan's national power," Fukuzawa Yukichi wrote in 1882. "Compared with considerations of the country's strength, the matter of internal government and into whose hands it falls is of no importance at all. Even if the government be autocratic in name and form, I shall be satisfied with it if it is strong enough to strengthen the country." This is Fukuzawa the nationalist overcoming Fukuzawa the liberal, if only temporarily.

Taking a wider framework, the newspaper *Nihon* celebrated the announcement of the Meiji Constitution in 1889 by urging that a limit be set to the adoption of foreign ways. It had no desire "to revive a narrow xenophobia," *Nihon* declared, for "we recognize the excellence of Western civilization. We value the Western theories of rights, liberty and equality. . . . Above all, we esteem Western science, economics and industry." Nevertheless, it continued, these things "ought not to be adopted simply because they are Western; they ought to be adopted only if they can contribute to Japan's welfare." In Tokyo in 1889 this was a conservative warning not to go too fast or too far. In contemporary Peking it would have been reformist.

One is bound to ask, why did Japan evolve in a generation a nationalism that in China came much more slowly and with much less effect, given that both countries had long traditions of political and cultural unity? Difference of size was a factor, of course. In Japan, which was smaller and had a very long coastline, the presence of the foreigners and their ships was evident to a higher percentage of the population, making the danger from them easier to believe and act on. China was not only larger, but more varied—in spoken language, social patterns, types of crop—so that there were great practical obstacles to imposing administrative and economic unity in the nationalist sense, just as there were in India and the Ottoman Empire, for example. China did not lend herself very readily to being made into a "country," Japan did.

In addition to all this, however, there are historical differences between the two that have a particular relevance to the study of the Meiji Restoration. One is Japan's relative freedom of cultural choice: she was less bound than China to a single view of her society and her place in the world. Japan had already imported elements of Chinese civilization, which coexisted with others that were her own; thus to adopt a part of Europe's civilization was not to damage an entity that was whole and unique, but to add a third possibility to an existing two, one of which was in any case "foreign." For instance, medicine was a Chinese science in pre-modern Japan, using many Chinese drugs, hence accepting a Western alternative was not so very shocking. Warfare, the samurai's trade, was studied in a Chinese classic text (albeit embodied in a thoroughly Japanese mystique) and was conducted with the help of a seventeenth-century "Dutch" technology. There was nothing in this to inhibit following alien models. As Rutherford Alcock noted of the Japanese when he first became acquainted with them, "they have little of the stupid conceit of the Chinese, which leads them to ignore or deny the superiority of foreign things."

It was the same with political institutions. No educated Japanese of the Tokugawa period could fail to be aware that the political structure of his country differed from that of China, which the philosophers he read upheld as an ideal. His country had a Shogun as well as an Emperor; it was administered through a feudal system, not a bureaucratic one. This helped to heighten his sense of Japaneseness, which was an element in nationalism, but it also made him aware that substantial variations could exist within the limits of what was known and acceptable.

In other words, in abolishing the Bakufu, reasserting the Emperor's authority, and instituting a centralized bureaucratic state, the Japanese could see themselves as making a fresh set of choices among the variables that their history already contained, however much they reinterpreted them. Hence renovation (ishin) could be coupled with restoration (fukko) in a manner that causes the least offense. This was especially so because of the nature and ethos of the ruling class. In China, civil officials held office by virtue of being Confucian, that is, as exemplars of a structure of belief on which their whole society was founded. To tamper with part of that structure was to undermine the whole, weakening their power. This was not so in Japan. The samurai, it is true, had accepted the Confucian ethic and some of the bureaucratic habits that went with it. He did not depend on these, however, to validate his rule. As a feudal lord or retainer, his position rested on birth, on inheritable status received as a reward for past military prowess. His code, Bushidō, though it coexisted with Confucianism, emphasized different virtues, the specifically military ones. Accordingly, he did not feel a need to accept or reject Confucianism as a whole. He could employ it—as Meiji society did—in the context of personal and family behavior while turning to other concepts for his political and economic life: nationalist ones, which could be given a Shintō coloring; or Western ones, explaining the new phenomena of industry and commerce. And the fact that the new amalgam was not a conspicuously logical one worried him less because of the equal irrationality of the old.

Finally, one must note the significance of Japan's having entered this phase of her history, unlike China, under a *military* ruling class. This relates to nationalism to the extent that soldiers were more inclined to think of defending a territory than defending a system of ideas, more of defending country than culture. It also relates to modernization, since it contributed to the identification of agreed priorities, where individuals had a multiplicity of views. Indeed, it may well be that a military habit of mind, variously applied, was the samurai's most important contribution to Meiji society—and hence, to the making of the modern Japanese state.

What has been said [earlier] amounts to an assertion that nationalism had a double function in Japan in the twenty years after 1853: first, that it provided a motive compelling men to act; second, that it shaped their aims and priorities. Unhappily, this pleasingly simple explanation of what took place is incomplete. Side by side with the story of nationalism and the foreign threat, there is another, that of social change; and in turning to it, we move from a discussion of men's purposes to a discussion of the circumstance in which they found themselves. It was from the interaction of the two that history was made.

. . . [H]ow, then, are we to set political struggle and social change in relation to each other? I would suggest, as follows:

1. The class composition of the politically active minority in late-Tokugawa Japan already reflected the results of economic change in that it did not accord with the *formal* allocation of authority in society: a few daimyo, a few upper samurai, a good many middle samurai, a much larger number of lower samurai and "men of substance" from outside the samurai class. Proportionately, this corresponds fairly well with the number of men within each of these groups. Yet no Japanese of the time would have been prepared to argue that participation in decision-making should be

proportional to numbers in this way; traditionally, it should have been almost entirely the prerogative of lords and senior retainers. Departure from traditional norms in this respect therefore suggests that at the *beginning* of the period with which we have dealt, the outlines of a new ruling class were emerging from within the old. It was *within* this class that most of the crucial debates took place.

2. In the various proposals for curing the country's ills after the conclusion of the treaties, there was usually an element of class or group interest, though not necessarily a dominant one. Bakufu and feudal lords, despite their rivalries, both sought to defend Japan without much disturbing its society; by promoting "men of talent," the middle samurai meant principally themselves; and the "men of spirit," despite an inability for the most part to get away from feudal terminology, clearly envisaged that the success of their plans would bring them a status they did not already have. Thus the defeat of kōbu-gattai, "unity of Court and Bakufu," and of kinnō, "serving the Emperor," were defeats for socially conservative and politically radical formulations of reform, respectively, as well as for particular ideas about how Japan could best be defended from the foreigner.

3. The men who emerged as leaders in succession to the reforming lords and dissident samurai, mostly after 1864, were realists, pragmatists, bureaucrat-politicians whose social origins matched their role: that is, they were nearly all middle or lower samurai, not high enough in the feudal hierarchy to be bent on preserving it, nor excluded from it to the point of wanting above all to break it down. Moreover, they were convinced that national defense required national unity. Accordingly, they believed as much in conciliation as reform, and so began to bring together the components of what was a social, as well as a political, alliance. Edo intransigents and rebellious peasants they would not tolerate, because both were obstacles to order and unity in their different ways. But the rest could all find a place: Court nobles, feudal lords, samurai, landlords, influential merchants, even servants of the Shogun in the end. To belong, one needed only to subscribe to the national objectives, as the inner group defined them.

4. Victory over the Tokugawa made these men responsible for government, that is, for implementing on a national scale the policies that would bring Japan "wealth and strength." In much of what they then did they acted still as samurai-bureaucrats trained in Confucian ideas: manipulating the Emperor as they had their lords; caring for the people's welfare, subject to the tax

needs of the state; framing an education system that contributed to good order and to the citizen's skills. Concepts of government and its functions did not change as much from Tokugawa to Meiji as the emphasis on modernization sometimes makes us think. Yet some of the differences were vital. Since feudalism contributed nothing to efficiency and was an obstacle to military strength, it had to go. Equally, since land tax was an essential resource and defining it involved the recognition of what had happened in the village, landlords got confirmation of their landed rights. Indirectly, they also obtained an extension of their economic opportunities. In fact, though the purpose of it all was not to change society, but rather to identify the least degree of social adjustment that would make possible fukō kukyohei—a militarily strong Japan rich enough to sustain a position of independence in the world—the application of these policies produced something very different from the Japan of twenty years before. For the minimal change, once identified, proved to be substantial. Consciously, there was an attack on samurai privilege; but consequentially this made possible the emergence into a position of influence of a new class, the well-to-do commoners whose power had until then been only latent.

5. Several factors came together to ensure that the society which emerged at the end of these years would be a capitalist one. Some of the long-term trends in the Tokugawa period were already moving in that direction, providing a basis on which to build. They were given a stimulus by contact with the capitalist West, initially through the effects of foreign trade, then because of the nature of the advice Japan received and the models she studied; the Western solutions that were applied to Japanese problems were inevitably those of the contemporary industrial state. Development was also given a particular direction by the nature of the policies that were devised for the promotion of national strength—the encouragement of industrial and commercial growth, coupled with an unusual degree of government intervention in the country's economy—so that Japan's transition from the "centralized feudalism" of Tokugawa days was to a similarly centralized form of capitalism. This resolved one Tokugawa anomaly, that of merchant wealth, by bringing the entrepreneur, like the landlord, into the dominant class and giving him a means to fulfill his aspirations legally. It left another, that of peasant unrest, aside. In the short term the second issue was settled by force; but as the pressures on the cultivator increased with the growth of industry it re-emerged to become a problem of the twentieth century in a different form.

Does all this amount to a revolution? Perhaps to ask the question is to invite an argument about the meaning of words, since the reader is likely to have and to apply criteria of his own in finding an answer. Nevertheless, there are a number of points that can be made by way of a final gloss on what has been said [earlier]. For example, the Bakufu had some of the classic characteristics of an ancien régime; it had grave financial problems; it tried unsuccessfully to effect reform; it was indecisive and ineffective at the end in suppressing opposition; and for a variety of reasons it lost the confidence of a considerable segment of the ruling class. Also, those who overthrew it included men of many social origins (but not the lowest); they were generally of some respectability and experience; and they produced what might well be called "a dictatorship in commission." One could even argue that Restoration politics moved through appropriate stages of moderation and extremism before eventually bringing about, not "a brand-new ruling class," but "a kind of amalgamation, in which the enterprising, adaptable or lucky individuals of the old privileged classes [were] for most practical purposes tied up with those individuals of the old submerged classes, who, probably through the same gifts, were able to rise."

There are other tests, too. There was a considerable shift in the locus of political power, which was downwards by pre-Restoration standards. Broadly speaking, there was—if one takes a long enough time base—a change from feudalism to capitalism as the organizing principle of Japanese society. There was even an application of force to politics to bring about these things, or at least to bring about some of the specific decisions that went to make them up.

Yet, despite it all, I am reluctant to call the Restoration a revolution in the full meaning of the term. In part, this is because what happened in Japan lacked the avowed social purpose that gives the "great" revolutions of history a certain common character. But it is also because of the nature of the society to which the Restoration gave rise, in which "feudal" and "capitalist" elements worked together in a symbiosis dedicated to acquiring national strength. The political movement that brought this society into being cannot properly be called "bourgeois" in view of the dominant role samurai played in it and the power they retained when it was done. It was certainly not "peasant," given the fate of peasant revolt. Nor was it "absolutist" or "rightist," if that is to imply that the primary stimulus was a fear of popular unrest. What then is left, when none of these standard categories satisfactorily apply? Only to call it a nationalist revolution, perhaps, thereby giving recognition to the nature of the emotions that above all brought it about.

---

**W.G. Beasley** is an emeritus professor of the history of the far East at the University of London. He is the author of many works on Japan, including *The Rise of Modern Japan* (St. Martin's Press, 1995).

# EXPLORING THE ISSUE

## Did the Meiji Restoration Constitute a Revolution in Nineteenth-Century Japan?

## Critical Thinking and Reflection

1. Having studied the French Revolution, how would you comparatively evaluate the changes made during the Meiji Restoration?
2. Which areas of Japanese life were most dramatically changed? Critically discuss.
3. How sweeping, in your view, were the political, military, cultural, and economic changes undertaken during this era. How much does modern Japan owe to these reforms and renovations?
4 To what extent do you agree with historian W.G. Beasley's suggestion that expansion by the West may have played a precipitating role? Critically discuss.
5. To what extent do you agree with historian Thomas M. Huber's assertion that the Meiji changes were articulated in the 1850s and even earlier? Critically discuss.
6. It has been widely argued that the Meiji Restoration permitted Japan to modernize on its own terms. Critically discuss the extent to which this is so.
7. Consider this counterfactual scenario: What might have happened had Japan permitted change to unfold evolutionarily rather than revolutionarily? Critically discuss.

## Is There Common Ground?

An interesting question raised by this issue is the nature and scope of the term "revolution." The criteria used in defining this term would likely have an impact on the debate. In the search for possible common ground, a good starting point might be a brief exploration of the term "revolution," using references to and comparisons with other noted world revolutions. Crane Brinton (1898–1966), in *The Anatomy of Revolution*, rev. ed. (Random House, 1966) presents an interesting model for studying the nature of revolutions, using the English, American, French, and Russian revolutions as case studies.

Consider what you have learned from reading the YES and NO selections. Then, consider this: From his data, Brinton drew the following conclusions regarding the revolutionary process:

1. The countries were generally prosperous prior to the revolution; however, government machinery was clearly inefficient. Discontent was strongly felt by those wealthy citizens who felt restrained by the titled aristocracy who contributed little to the country's well-being. The intellectuals eventually transferred their loyalty from the ruling monarchy to the discontents.
2. The revolutions generally passed through three phases: (a) the moderate stage where reformers who overthrew the monarchy and now controlled the government, worked to gradually solve the country's problems in a moderate, nonviolent way; they are opposed by the extremists who argue for immediate change, if necessary,

through violent means; (b) the radical phase in which the extremists take control of the government, get rid of the moderates, and begin a radical restructuring of society; they are assisted by the people who demand a strong central government to bring stability at home and provide the military forces to deal with foreign countries who oppose their revolution; (c) the counter-revolutionary phase in which the tyranny of the extremists is overthrown by a coalition of forces who desire an end to the violence and a return to a peaceful, secure society.
3. *Results*: while the revolution brings many changes to the country, it ends with a government that is similar to the one in place before the revolution. Using the material provided in both selections, consider the following:

*Question:* How does Japan's Meiji Restoration match or not match Brinton's model? Do Brinton's criteria still seem valuable in assessing potential "revolutions" of the present day?

## Create Central

www.mhhe.com/createcentral

## Additional Resources

Sources of modern Japanese history abound. A general reference work would be: *The Cambridge History of Japan*, vol. 5: *The Nineteenth Century*, Marius B. Jansen, editor (Cambridge University Press, 1989). W.G. Beasley's *The*

*Rise of Modern Japan* (St. Martin's Press, 1995) is a readable volume, written by one who has contributed much to an enlightened understanding of Japan and its history. Some specific sources on the Meiji era would be: Carol Gluck, *Japan's Modern Myths: Ideology in the Late Meiji Period* (Princeton University Press, 1985); Kenneth B. Pyle, *The New Generation in Meiji Japan, 1885–1895* (Stanford University Press, 1969); and two works by W.G. Beasley, *The Meiji Restoration* (Stanford University Press, 1972) and

*Japanese Imperialism, 1894–1945* (Oxford University Press, 1987), which concentrate on late Meiji diplomacy and its influence on Japan's future twentieth-century course. A specialized study is: *Japan in Transition: From Tokugawa to Meiji*, Marius Jansen and Gilbert Rozman, editors (Princeton University Press, 1986), which contains scholarly essays on related aspects of Japanese history during this important time period.

# *Internet References . . .*

### The Meiji Restoration and Modernization

This website covers all aspects of the Meiji Restoration. This site also includes documents and discussion questions.

http://afe.easia.columbia.edu/special/japan_1750_
meiji.htm

Selected, Edited, and with Issue Framing Material by:
**Helen Buss Mitchell,** *Howard Community College*
and
**Joseph R. Mitchell,** *Howard Community College*

# ISSUE

# Was Popular Opinion a Significant Ingredient in Nineteenth-Century British Imperialism?

**YES: John MacKenzie,** from "Another Little Patch of Red," *History Today* (August 2005)

**NO: Bernard Porter,** from "What Did They Know of Empire?" *History Today* (October 2004)

| Learning Outcomes |
| --- |
| **After reading this issue you should be able to:** <br> • Define "imperialism" and trace its roots from ancient times to the late nineteenth century. <br> • Identify those factors in the nineteenth century that allowed Britain to become the world's major imperial power. <br> • Evaluate the effects that British imperialism had on England, its colonies, and the rest of the known world. <br> • Evaluate the effects that British public opinion had on the development of that nation's imperialism. |

## ISSUE SUMMARY

**YES:** Professor Emeritus, John MacKenzie, argues that both imperial rule and the possession of an empire were essential components of British identity, life, and culture during this period.

**NO:** Professor of modern history, Bernard Porter, argues that, through most of the nineteenth century, most Britons knew little and cared less about the spread of the Empire.

From the earliest stages of recorded history, civilizations have extended beyond their boundaries to conquer neighboring peoples. The term "empire" has been used by historians to describe this process of domination and the political and economic systems that it produced. In fact, it is easy to chronicle human history as a series of eras in which one or more civilizations display dominance and maintain it until they, themselves, are conquered by a more powerful force. With the development of nation-states in the early modern period, the nation replaced the civilization. But the process of conquest and dominance continued; perhaps there were more players in the game, but larger realities remained largely unchanged.

In the English language the term "imperial" was created to characterize empire building. Derived from the Latin word *imperium* (command), it came to denote the process by which a group of people extended their control over a larger area than they had originally controlled. For example, when the Romans expanded from a small republic and extended their control over vast territories, they assumed the title of Imperium Romanum. In modern times, the term "imperialism" has been used to describe the process of empire building.

The later half of the nineteenth century is considered to be imperialism's apex. During that era European nations (and ultimately the United States) began to extend their influence over the non-Western world. The results were swift and decisive; within a generation there were few areas in Asia and Africa that remained free from European intrusion. The mad scramble for colonies had begun.

For what reasons did these Western nations begin this process of domination? Historians have offered many explanations, among them: the development of global capitalism; nationalistic imperialism; strategic protection for national interests; religious missionary zeal; and the capacities of new technology that made it all possible. Despite the fact that modern imperialism is little more than a century old, it has received a lot of attention from historians due to its far-reaching national and global consequences.

Since nineteenth-century imperialism accompanied the rapid rise and development of capitalism, the first historians wrote of the two as being symbiotic in nature. The

West expanded in order to procure raw materials, establish foreign markets for their domestically produced goods, and provide additional venues for investment capital. The English economic historian, John A. Hobson, was the first to state this viewpoint in 1902, citing as additional factors the restless energies of entrepreneurs and an excess of competition and production from neighboring countries that spurred the need for ever greater expansion into new markets. The Russian theoretician, Vladimir I. Lenin, took the argument one step further; borrowing an idea from Marx that capitalism by its nature must expand in order to survive, Lenin, however, saw imperialism as capitalism's last spasm, before the communist revolution would bring it to an end.

This economic interpretation of imperialism held sway within the scholarly community for many years until fresh examinations began to uncover other possible reasons for imperialism's rise. National rivalries, for instance, which ultimately led to World War I, caused some historians to look at imperialism as an example of nationalism gone mad; Western nations used the acquisition of colonies as manifestations of their national pride. Other historians offered the need for strategic outposts as an excuse for the acquisition of overseas territories. Once some were acquired, others were ultimately needed to protect and defend them. It became unthinkable that a rival nation could be in a position to endanger any nation's colonial possessions!

No historian who has researched nineteenth-century imperialism will discount any of the factors—economic, political, social, strategic, religious, and cultural—that were influential in its development and perseverance. Rather each historian's work concentrates on discovering which ingredients were either more or less important than others. History seldom provides monocausal explanations for events and movements.

In recent years, historians have developed several new theses for the development of nineteenth-century imperialism. Some have pointed to the power of national identity and the effects of popular culture on the citizenry as generators of support for imperialism and empire. The creation of a fervent patriotism, rooted in part in fear of the "other," produced a passionate defense of national ambition and national destiny, according to this viewpoint. And, missionary societies promoted imperialism at home and abroad, as part of their effort to end what they termed "barbarism" and "savagery" in far-flung outposts of the empire. Cultural images of non-Western peoples in Western literature and music (which are usually untrue and condescending) have created a "white man's burden" mentality that has been used both to promote and justify imperialism. Finally, there are those who have stressed the role of the military and diplomatic corps in producing heroes that captured the popular imagination and that ultimately led businessmen, missionaries, and others down the primrose path of imperial conquest.

The question in this issue centers on the extent to which the attitudes and images outlined in the last paragraph permeated British society. Although examples may be found, how pervasive were they? And, were they absorbed equally by all classes in society or primarily (even exclusively) by the upper class—those who expected to rule? Were school children and members of the middling and working classes offered alternative visions of their identity as British citizens and their expected roles as members of society? And, in the case of the adults, were they too absorbed in survival issues, such as earning a living and caring for their families to have the leisure time to read literature or popular novels or even to visit the popular music halls and theatres?

In the YES selection, John MacKenzie refers to maps of the British Empire in which imperial "possessions" were colored red. For a long time it could be said that "the sun never sets on the Union Jack," referring to the British flag that flew in many outposts around the world. Professor MacKenzie cites numerous examples of the embeddedness of both imperialism and empire in the British psyche. In the NO selection, Professor Porter chronicles the perhaps surprising absence of these themes from literature, opera, and school textbooks and classrooms, arguing that Britain was "an imperial nation, but never a truly imperial society." He does, however, acknowledge the efforts of imperialist propagandists and the pageantry of the "Empire Day Movement."

# YES ↵

John MacKenzie

## Another Little Patch of Red

A remarkable portrait from the late eighteenth century depicts a wealthy Glasgow merchant, John Glassford, surrounded by his family and with a black servant standing behind. Or it should show the servant behind. In fact, at some point in the nineteenth century, the servant was painted out. We only know about this because modern X-ray techniques have rediscovered the image of the black attendant. No one is quite sure why: was it because of sensitivities during the anti-slavery campaign or did it arise from a desire to render the portrait 'racially pure'?

This example reflects the wider debate about the role of the British Empire in British culture and society. Just as the servant was literally brushed out, there have been many attempts to divest domestic British society of its imperial connections. Many committed imperialists in the late nineteenth and early twentieth centuries were convinced that the British were not really interested in their empire. But the fully committed always worry about the commitment of others. Those who espouse a cause with quasi-religious fervour—as imperialists in the high noon of empire did—are always on the lookout for tangible evidence of such commitment, in membership of associations, adherence to specific causes, or voting patterns at elections. But the influence of empire upon British culture and society did not always take such obvious forms.

In the early twentieth century, J.A. Hobson, the economic theoretician of empire, wrote passionately about the extent of contemporary jingoism in British society during the Anglo-Boer War of 1899–1902. But by the middle years of the twentieth century a new breed of historian was emerging that actively wished to distance imperialism from British society. Radical scholars sought to study empire in fresh ways, yet they often remained more interested in the 'official mind' of imperialism rather than its 'popular psychology'. To a certain extent, all of them reacted against Hobson; some later conceded that there might have been an outburst of imperial fervour at the turn of the century, but insisted that this was an aberration, a deviation from the norm of indifference.

Historians of Britain were keen to suggest that the working class, much more concerned with such hard-headed concerns as workers' rights and the amelioration of depressed labour and social conditions, had been untainted by imperial ideologies. Marxist and quasi-Marxist interpretations suggested that imperialism had seduced the 'aristocracy of labour' into compliance with elite objectives or had served to blunt any revolutionary urges of the British, but these views were discounted by historians on what we would now call the 'soft left'.

In the last few decades of the twentieth century, there was a further diversification of historical interests. Older concerns with political, administrative, constitutional and economic pasts were supplemented by new specialisms in social, gender, and cultural history. Cultural history was the new kid on the historical block and its practitioners became fascinated, among other things, with questions of identity, connecting such key areas as race, class, gender and nation.

The notion that British society could be described as an essentially imperial culture developed from this, and was partly influenced by the fact that the former colonial territories had produced sophisticated schools of historians. They were aware of the manner in which British culture had been everywhere projected into colonial life. A 'British world' had emerged from the myriad cultural forms dispersed around the colonies. Surely the British themselves could not have been immune to this cultural assault, so characteristic of imperial rule?

It is of course a matter of definition. The British Empire is difficult to define, precisely because of its complex history, the variety of its territories, and the diversity of their function. Some might see empire as reflected essentially in the colonies of white settlement, which seemed to offer so much opportunity to British migrants. Others might view it as resting principally on the 'jewel in the Crown', India, often described as a separate empire in itself. Some might see the colonies of the later nineteenth century, representative of the so-called 'new imperialism', as being characteristic. Or again, some might consider the fortresses, garrisons, and naval bases, dotted around the world as the bastions of an imperial seaborne system, as reflecting the true essence of imperial power.

Certainly, the latter seemed to fit with the ideas that emerged from the sixteenth and seventeenth centuries, that empire was about dominion over the oceans. The acquisition and retention of territories in North America, the Caribbean, and Asia were based upon that essential belief. The absence of such maritime power rendered colonial enterprises difficult, as the Scots discovered with their ill-fated Darien scheme of the 1690s. The failure of that colony helped to propel them into the Union of 1707 and from then the term 'British' became more common. Moreover, the interests of large numbers of cities and towns

MacKenzie, John. From *History Today*, vol. 55, no. 8, 2005, pp. 20. Copyright © 2005 by History Today, Ltd. Reprinted by permission. References omitted in Scotland, England and Wales became bound up with the business of seaborne trade and commerce, much of it imperial. These conditions affected the ports and many towns which were soon connected to the coast by the new canal network.

By the second half of the eighteenth century, particularly after the Jacobite revolts, Scots became major 'entryists' into the whole imperial enterprise, through the 'm' professions: medical, military, maritime, mercantile, and later missionary. Many of the celebrated Scottish regiments—which governments have recently been laying down and amalgamating—were founded at this time. Ideas emanating from Scottish Enlightemnent figures like William Robertson or Adam Smith became highly influential in North America and in India. Scots established potent patronage networks that gave them an extraordinary access to governorships and other forms of officialdom. They also soon established notable rates of migration. Indeed, so obvious were the Scots in all imperial ventures of the day that they became extremely unpopular among the English.

The Scottish historian Tom Devine has written that by the early nineteenth century:

> So intense was the Scottish
> engagement with empire that it
> affected almost every nook and
> cranny of Scottish life:
> industrialization, intellectual activity,
> politics, identity, education, popular
> culture, consumerism labour
> markets, demographic trends,
> Highland social development and
> much else.

But if this was the case in Scotland, can it really be suggested, as some have done, that the English somehow remained 'uncontaminated'? Can such a powerful ideological infection have flourished in one part of the island and not in another? The evidence suggests that English identities and cultures were indeed not immune.

Seaborne power, and the victories in the wars of the eighteenth century, came to occupy a highly significant place in British (including English) culture in the period. Progressive acquisition of colonies, including Quebec in 1759, as well as their loss in the American crisis of the 1770s and early 80s, was well known among the British public. Throughout the period, European wars had distant actions and global consequences. The voyages of James Cook (1768–79), with their intimation of the extension of power into the Pacific, were also a familiar triumph of the age. Cook brought back the Tahitian Omai who became the central figure of a celebrated theatrical presentation on the London stage. Developments in the progressive extension of East India Company power in India were also familiar.

The Napoleonic Wars confirmed the relationship between European war and imperial power. Actions took place in North America, the Caribbean, the Indian Ocean, on the coasts of India, as well as in Europe and the Mediterranean. Nelson was unquestionably an imperial figure. In the West Indies, he wrote to island governors proclaiming his anxiety to protect British colonies from the French. He also served during his career in India, Canada, and visited South Africa. His victory at Aboukir Bay (the Battle of the Nile) catapulted him to truly heroic status and few would have been ignorant of the full meaning of that victory: Napoleon was trying to use Egypt as a stepping stone to India. Although further military campaigns were to ensue in the region, the serious damage inflicted on his fleet removed the French threat to the East.

The outburst of Nelson hero-worship after Trafalgar was extraordinary. In Glasgow, a monument was organized with extraordinary speed and the town came to a halt for the laying of the foundation stone and its eventual unveiling. The subscribers were almost all merchants and ship-owners. Glasgow's principal trade was trans-Atlantic: few could have been ignorant of the significance of Nelson's victories in keeping open the seas for trade and therefore maintaining the flow of wealth to the rich and employment to the poor.

The penetration of imperial and colonial questions was apparent throughout British life. The new disciplines of geography, ethnography, philology and what would later come to be called 'comparative religions' were closely implicated with the development of imperial rule. This was also true of botany, forestry and geology. The major institutions of the day, botanic gardens like Kew, the Royal Society, the Linnaean Society, and the Royal Geographical Society (founded in 1830), together with the journals associated with them, were full of studies and theoretical discussion made possible by the exotic laboratories that were the colonies.

Moreover, as military historian Hew Strachan has pointed out, it is impossible to understand the development of the British army without comprehending its role within imperialism. Indeed in London and the major provincial centres, the army, the missionary lobby, scientists, mapmakers, and statisticians, among others, conducted their activities in such a way that the colonial dimension was a vital conditioner and energizer of intellectual and practical developments. Colonial and domestic affairs were closely intertwined.

These were of course the concerns of political and intellectual elites, the equivalents of today's 'chattering classes'. But they were also the means by which the upper classes and the bourgeoisie found common cause and interacted, in ways that were not entirely divorced from the working class. It is true that the latter would have had more immediate concerns. Yet the lid was kept on the social turmoil between 1815 and the 1840s as well as upon the trade union activities and the major strikes later in the century. In many respects, the possession of empire and its inhabitants led politicians and social reformers to see the working class as internal 'others' and directed colonial-style policies at them, for example in Christian missions and university extension in slum areas.

Unsurprisingly, many among the elite saw the colonies as a convenient dumping ground for the problems of labour. Such schemes were not always successful, but between 1789 and 1914 around ten million people left Britain for the Empire (over half a million had gone to the colonies in the eighteenth century). A larger figure went to the United States before 1914, but in the twentieth century immigrant quotas in the US again ensured that a higher proportion went to the colonies, encouraged by the subsidies of the 1922 Empire Settlement Act.

In any case, an extraordinary cultural continuity can be identified in the nineteenth century. In the theatre the two principal forms of the century were melodrama and spectacle, both of which lent themselves to colonial subject matter (and many productions went on national tours). Spectacle's fascination with realism, with mechanical contrivance, and with grand and exotic display ensured that it was perfectly adapted to the display of imperial events, naval victories and colonial campaigns. India featured on the stage in 1818; the Burma war in 1826; and the South African frontier wars in 1853. But this was but the tip of a vast agglomeration of colonial plays that were generally successes. Melodrama had some class-conscious comment earlier in the century, but soon featured differences in race as more significant than those of class.

The young Henry Irving, soon to be the Victorian era's most celebrated actor, appeared in a country-wide tour of The Indian Revolt or, the Relief of Lucknow in 1860. There were many other plays with imperial content, examples include The Great Mogul, the Nabob's Fortune, The Begum's Diamonds, the Saucy Nabob, The Zulu Chief or Cetewayo at Last, The Cousin from Australia, The Cape Mail, The Diamond Rush, The Raid on the Transvaal, which date from the 1880s and 1890s. All of these constituted 'faction', a popular blend of fiction and topical events. But in many cases titles are a inadequate guide. Youth in 1881 featured Rorke's Drift in the Zulu War. Human Nature dealt with the Sudan campaign of 1884–85, and several other plays featured this climactic event. Pluck and Cheer Boys Cheer are entirely imperial in content. Even traditional pantomimes could develop imperial content. Sinbad the Sailor in the Christmas season of 1882 featured the British bombardment of Alexandria earlier in the year with the Khedive of Egypt as the villain. Many other pantomimes injected their performances with colonial episodes, to the apparent delight of the audiences.

Moreover, the illustrated press, like the Illustrated London News (ILN) or The Graphic, contained almost 'wall-to-wall' imperial comment and illustrations at climactic points, like the 'Mutiny' of 1857, the death of Livingstone in Central Africa (which was to stimulate a wave of missionary activity as well as aspects of the scramble for Africa), the events in Zululand and Afghanistan in 1879, the death of Gordon at Khartoum in early 1885, the later re-conquest of the Sudan and much else. The ILN also issued supplements at key moments. Even when it was disaster that was being chronicled, this constituted a rallying cry to a more successful and sometimes more honourable imperialism. Such pricey journals had a middle-class readership, but they must have percolated down to other classes, whether 'below stairs' or in libraries, mechanics' institutes and other reading rooms.

National and local papers (all of which carried international news) increasingly offered 'colonial intelligence', featuring the major imperial events of the later years of the century (including the royal visits, of Victoria to Ireland and her sons to Canada, India and South Africa). Queen Victoria, trained by Prince Albert, turned the monarchy not only into a bourgeois institution in tastes and morals, but also eagerly transformed it into an imperial symbol. Disraeli flattered the Queen with the Royal Style and Titles Bill in 1875 by creating her Empress of India (when her son, the future Edward VII, was embarking on a grand tour of the Indian subcontinent, exciting much press interest).

Many in Parliament were uneasy about these developments, fearing that the title of Empress might be extended to Victoria's other functions and that the autocratic tendencies of imperial monarchies, like those of Russia or Austria-Hungary, might emerge in Britain. This might seem to offer evidence of anti-imperial sentiment. But all the ceremonies connected with Victoria, the jubilees, the grand openings of exhibitions, the Imperial Institute in South Kensington and the like, were imperial in their trappings, in the colourfully uniformed soldiers of colonial regiments escorting her, the Indian princes who were often present, the music performed, the national and local spectacles organized like grand Indian durbars. She repeatedly received rulers from the colonial empire who came to offer their allegiance. She took this role very seriously, commissioned paintings of Indians and India, commissioned an Indian durbar hall to be built as her Osborne dining room, and employed Indian servants. The monarch was central to the depiction of an essentially imperial polity well into the twentieth century. Victoria as imperial monarch was repeatedly illustrated in paintings, statuary and memorials. Most members of the British public would have had little difficulty in visualizing her in this way.

Literature unquestionably responded to imperial opportunity. The writings of Anthony Trollope are full of empire. In Phineas Finn (1869), the colonies are the central interest of the leading character. Later Victorian writers like Wilkie Collins, Rider Haggard and Arthur Conan Doyle projected images of colonial places and peoples. Juvenile literature adopted imperial themes to wean children away from the 'sensational' material which caused alarm to the middle classes. Charlotte M. Yonge, a prolific author whose career spanned over half the nineteenth century, wrote interlocking family sagas. Her Mays, Mohuns, Merrifields and Underwoods always have family members serving in the colonies: farmers, administrators, army officers, clergy and missionaries.

W.H.G. Kingston, G.A. Henty, and Gordon Stables, writing between the 1870s and the First World War, focused almost entirely on contemporary and historic empire, selling vast numbers of books. Henty, an imperial war correspondent, and Stables, formerly a medical officer on the East African anti-slavery squadron, knew what they were writing about. Henry wrote that he abandoned classical subjects because his readership wanted imperial wars. Readers cannot have been immune to the central ideology of imperialism, particularly as they increasingly saw black and brown people around them in port cities, fairs, seaside shows and working as peddlers. As far back as the 1830s, boys in Bristol were said to have followed the Hindu reformer Rammohan Roy calling out 'Tippoo', a reference to the South Indian wars of the 1790s and the defeat of the King of Mysore.

The later nineteenth century also saw the flowering of the mass market. The images of the Queen and members of her family were frequently used in advertising, and so were those of the army and of imperial events. Advertisers were looking for signs and symbols that would ingratiate their products with a buying public. In journals, newspapers, posters and public places products were associated with imperial territories or with qualities that were said to make the empire great. Such advertising images and marketing techniques like cigarette cards, offer a set of vital clues to the penetration of an imperial culture.

There were other key ways in which colonial activities were transmitted to a wider public. The effect of the relatively small number of missionaries overseas was greatly amplified by activities in churches, sermons, lectures by those on furlough, articles in religious magazines, and exhibitions. Pressure groups such as the British and Foreign Anti-Slavery Society (founded in 1839) were capable of whipping up extraordinarily lively popular agitations, often involving working-class men and women. When in 1889 it was proposed that a Scottish missionary area south of Lake Nyasa (Malawi) should be handed over to the Portuguese, a petition was signed by 11,000 ministers and elders of the Church of Scotland, publicized in every pulpit, and Salisbury's government duly declined to ratify the treaty.

Music halls, the most popular medium of entertainment throughout the country, took on imperial and patriotic song scenes as a universal feature. These were certainly much satirized, as 'the Great' MacDermott's famous jingo song was after 1878. But the point of satire is that the original is well known, and satirical pastiche is often as much affectionate as undermining. There is substantial evidence that workingmen's clubs adopted such imperial material, often to the disgust of those who thought that it militated against more ideological behaviour. Regiments, associated with specific towns and counties, were visibly connected to their imperial campaigns.

During the Boer War, there were dramatic explosions of popular fervour. Press accounts make it clear that these were not confined to the upper and middle classes. The working class took part in almost every town, causing widespread disruption as they did so. After the Relief of Mafeking, the Glasgow Herald surveyed such activities throughout Scotland and England, commenting that the war had given workers additional income to celebrate and to buy flags and bunting.

This may have been a high point of such activity, but it was not an aberration. The sense of an imperial identity had been with the British since the eighteenth century. As it permeated almost all forms of popular culture in the nineteenth, it came to a climax, but it continued to have a considerable profile—as advertising, films, broadcasting, posters, and other material demonstrate—until beyond the end of the Second World War. For many decades, all three political parties, Conservative, Liberal, and Labour, were essentially imperial in policy. The British may not have known a great deal about their empire, but most knew relatives or friends who had migrated to or served in it. British culture was essentially imperial, and this was projected to, and imbibed by, a cross-section of all the social classes. Some might say that the effects are still with us today.

JOHN MACKENZIE is a professor of imperial history at Lancaster University in England. He is the editor of *Imperialism and Popular Culture* (Manchester University Press, 1986).

**Bernard Porter**

# What Did They Know of Empire?

The idea that British society was thoroughly infused with 'imperialism' in the nineteenth and early twentieth centuries has gained broad currency in recent years. Influential here have been John MacKenzie's works on the wide spread of imperial propaganda in the later part of this period, at least; and the late Edward Said's exposure of the hidden imperial content of much of the 'high' culture of the earlier nineteenth century. Some have taken these findings much further to justify imperialist readings of just about every feature of modern British society before the 1960s. Travel, science, exhibitions, zoos, boys' adventure stories, even nude paintings (Empire as rape), were all essentially imperialist activities. Modern film and TV adaptations of Victorian novels and documentaries about nineteenth and early twentieth-century subjects regularly interpolate imperial references, even when they do not appear in the original texts, on the ground, presumably, that the Victorians must have been thinking about their Empire even when they did not talk or write about it, rather like sex, and that this needs to be brought out for a modern audience. (An example is Sarah Curtis's 1999 film version of Jane Austen's *Mansfield Park* of 1814.) The impression given is that almost everyone was an imperialist of one kind or another. They must have been, seems to be the assumption behind this; the Empire was so vast and great and vital to them. It also must have needed their commitment; otherwise how could it have survived?

Of course the Empire left its marks on British society. This is especially so materially. It provided work for Britons, for example, manufacturing things for colonial markets; or—another way of looking at it—helped keep their wages low. It may also have contributed to Britain's long-term industrial decline, by masking it for so long. It furnished an escape route for the poor and disaffected, through emigration, thus possibly defusing civil unrest. It kept the British supplied with much of their ubiquitous tea and sugar (and so helped rot their teeth). It had an input into domestic social reform, the 'woman question', the public schools, and the development of policing in the UK. It puffed up the monarchy. It was responsible for the violent early deaths of many Britons, mostly men, especially if we believe that its existence was partly to blame for the outbreak of the First World War. Latterly, it made a terrific show: celebrations, processions, lots of dressing up in silly clothes. This is quite apart from its repercussions on the wider world it served or tyrannised

(according to one's point of view), which is not under discussion here. The Empire's huge impact on Britain is undeniable. So is the fact that it left its footprints in many areas of British culture, including even *Mansfield Park*, though far more lightly in the novel than Sarah Curtis implies on screen. Influence, however, is something else. The Empire could have impacted on Britons without their really noticing it, let alone enthusing over it. Surprisingly, to a great extent this seems to have been the case.

There are several reasons for thinking this. One is empirical. There are vast areas of British society and culture, especially during the first three-quarters of the nineteenth century, where the most remarkable fact is how relatively bereft of obvious imperial references or allusions they are. This is especially true of 'high' culture; which is why our postcolonial cultural theorists—followers of Said—have to tease them out. Not a single 'canonical' novel of the nineteenth century features the Empire significantly. The same applies to all the other arts. One would have thought that opera composers, at least, would have relished Indian or African settings; but not in Britain's case. There is no empirical evidence to suggest that nudes were meant as metaphors for colonial conquest; that is simply a modern construction placed upon them. If painters yearned for the exotic, they usually found it in the English Middle Ages, not the colonised East. The taste for 'oriental' architecture hardly survived the death of George IV, and very few of London's public buildings were as 'imperial' in other ways—grandiose and Roman, for example—as in many other capital cities of the world, including republican Washington. Imperialists used to complain of this. London was just not worthy of the Empire. In 1904 a couple of patriotic architects mooted a new project to remedy this: an 'Imperial Monumental Halls and Tower', dwarfing the adjacent Houses of Parliament and Westminster Abbey—state and church—symbolically. It was never built, of course. London did not even have many statues of imperialists, and none who were not soldiers as well. More popular forms of culture were equally bereft of imperial content. The people's favourite novels, plays and songs were on other themes entirely; shows of the Empire's 'savage' subjects, though they did exist, were few and far between. Why was this great, apparently overwhelming Empire not celebrated more openly in the literary and artistic culture of the time? France, after all, had no qualms about celebrating hers.

There are special explanations in the case of the 'higher' forms of art. Serious artists and the *literati* were atypical of British society as a whole. They regarded themselves as 'above' it, and were likely to avoid topics regarded as 'popular' for that reason alone. Colonies were a particular anathema because they represented rude action rather than refined feeling and thought. Imperialists returned the compliment, being generally unsympathetic to 'art'. Men of action regarded art as 'effeminate'. Britain did not need to paint or sculpt or carol her Empire, wrote Thomas Carlyle:

> . . . thy Epic, unsung in words, is written in huge characters on the face of this Planet—sea-moles, cotton-trades, railways, fleets and cities, Indian Empires, Americas, New Hollands: legible throughout the Solar System.

That was more than sufficient. The British were a strong, silent, undemonstrative and practical people. Obviously this did not make them non-imperialists; rather the reverse.

This may help explain the imperial deficit in the 'higher' and more refined forms of culture; but hardly in the cruder, more popular kinds. Why do nineteenth-century boys' adventure stories before G.A. Henty, for example, also avoid the British Empire so deliberately? (A noncolonised 'Coral Island'—as in R.M. Ballantyne's novel of 1858—was not the same.) Could it be because the lower classes were not particularly interested in it, either?

More evidence for this lack of interest comes from what we know of the education system of the time. The Empire was hardly ever a subject for study in schools. Some scholars have been misled about this by a number of contemporary history (and to a lesser extent geography) school textbooks that did touch on it; but most of those are highly unrepresentative. Fletcher and (Rudyard) Kipling's oft-cited and notoriously imperialistic *A School History of England* (1911), for example, was widely derided in its own time ('almost too bad to be true' is one of the milder criticisms), and in any case was far too expensive for most schools to buy.

Public schools rarely taught any modern history at all. This was because of their emphasis on the Classics. The only way the upper classes formally learned about the British Empire was indirectly, through the Roman. Elementary schoolchildren did not even get that. History and Geography had no place at all in most state school curricula for most of the nineteenth century, and only a small niche for several years after that. The history that was taught in the 'middling' schools—the ones the textbooks were written for—usually had a different agenda from the 'imperialist' one; its main theme was the growth of individual 'liberty' in Britain, with the Empire—which fitted uneasily with this, of course—pushed to the margins. The idea that Victorian schoolrooms all sported red-bespattered world maps on their walls is also a myth; colour-coding the British Empire in this way only caught on in the 1880s, and the maps did not start appearing widely until the 1900s, when they were donated to the schools by imperial propagandists.

As a result, the vast majority of nineteenth century English children could have received no serious education in imperialism at all. In 1902 an MP recounted how, when he asked a class of school leavers who among them had heard of the Indian Mutiny, only one boy raised his hand. This was at a school where history was taught, but stopped at the Tudors (just before the Empire proper, therefore). That was apparently common. It is this kind of thing that the historian J.R. Seeley was referring to when he wrote in 1883, famously, that the empire seemed to have been acquired 'in a fit of absence of mind'. What he meant was that this was the impression one got from reading the accounts of it in the history books then available; not that it *had* been acquired absentmindedly. Seeley felt this was all wrong. He argued that the issue of a Briton's 'freedom' had been settled in the seventeenth century, since when the history of Britain had been essentially an imperial one, centred 'not in England but in America and Asia'. But that is emphatically not what British schoolchildren before the 1900s were taught.

This may seem strange. If the Empire was a matter of national pride, you would have expected it to have been rammed down the throats of children at school. Patriotism, after all, is generally one of the things schooling is about. In many countries this is quite open, as in the flag-raising ceremonies that start the day in many American schools. This is one of the ways society is held together. In nineteenth century Britain, however, it was not. 'Patriotism' was considered dangerous. Early on it was mainly associated with radical ideas like 'citizenship'—'*aux armes, citoyens*'. Britons were never 'citizens', of course, but 'subjects' of the Crown—something that only changed officially in 1983. They also belonged to *classes*. It was the mutual obligations between those classes that bound society together. The working classes needed to respect and obey their betters; the upper classes to serve and protect those beneath them; the middle classes to create the wealth that trickled down and up to both. This, therefore, was what was drummed into children in their schools: their class roles, rather than their 'Britishness'. The upper classes were taught how to rule—at home as well as abroad. This is why they did not need to be taught about their Empire; ruling was the same everywhere—they could learn about the people they had to rule on the job. In their schools the workers were mainly taught their social role too: hard work, obedience, frugality, the errors of socialism. The middle classes were taught individual 'freedom'. (Hence the bias of their history books.) There was no possible use for imperialism, or indeed any kind of patriotism, in any of this. Even imperialists did not see any point in it. In 1893 a former Colonial Secretary, Lord Kimberley, speaking on the question of whether schoolchildren ought not to be given some education in imperial patriotism, opined that they would be better off 'given practical lessons in the geography of their own localities', rather than 'being shown maps [of the empire] they are not well versed in, and which do not convey much to their minds'.

Behind all this was a deeper upper-class fear of any kind of broader education for the 'masses', expressed in this quotation from *The Times* in 1880: 'is it going to turn the heads of ploughboys, and make them look down on their destined walk in life?' That says it all, and largely explains why imperial education was not officially promoted among—indeed, was actually kept from—at least 80 per cent of the English population in the nineteenth century.

If a national imperial commitment was not necessary to keep the people on-side politically, it was no more necessary from the point of view of Empire. Those red-painted world maps are misleading in another way. They give an entirely false impression of British imperial power. Most of the Empire was ruled through accommodations with local people: settlers in places like Canada and Australia, traditional rulers elsewhere. This does not make it any less 'imperial'; but it does mean that Britain's imperialism could be managed in a way that had a minimal impact upon the British people, in terms of cost and personnel. It took only a handful of men to rule the Empire, and even—relatively speaking—to police it, when the accommodations broke down, as in India in 1857–58. It did not need a national effort to sustain it. The imperialists themselves did not want this. This was another reason why there were so few calls for a more widespread imperial education before the end of the century. On the whole, the small class that was directly involved with it preferred to keep it to themselves. It was their empire, not the 'people's'.

This may have been just as well, for the 'people' clearly had other priorities. The working classes had to struggle to keep alive for most of the century; nearly all their time was taken up with that. This was also where they channelled their political energies: into improving their condition collectively. The empire had no relevance to this, except as a place of exile in the last economic resort, or worse if they were reduced to serving (and dying) as soldiers there, which was not likely to warm them to it as an idea. The middle classes had more time for the empire; but it was marginal to most of their basic concerns too. We have seen where their dominant values lay, from the sort of history they were taught in their schools. Those values might support an entrepreneurial, hard-working, settler type of colonialism at a pinch, but not the 'ruling', Indian sort.

Indeed, a careful study of middling-class attitudes to the colonies during the bulk of the nineteenth century shows that they distinguished strictly between what Peter Marshall calls the 'libertarian' and 'authoritarian' kinds of colonial rule. Nearly all their enthusiasm, such as it was, went to the former—and also, incidentally, to the United States of America, as representing its culmination. So it was not British *rule*—the imperialism, strictly speaking—that interested them about these lands. The only class that really went for the 'ruling' sort of empire in this period was the one whose function was to rule. They were the genuinely imperialist section of British society.

This suited the Empire for most of the nineteenth century, as we have seen. Towards the end of that century, however, this changed. The Empire started coming under threat from other European powers, as well as from nationalists in the colonies themselves. Quite suddenly it looked as though the imperialist classes might need some broader popular support after all. This was when the big imperial propaganda movement started, particularly after the scare of the Anglo-Boer War in 1899–1902. In itself, of course, this suggests that popular commitment to the Empire was weak at that time. This is certainly what zealous imperialists felt. From them one gets a very different picture of the state of popular imperialism in the late nineteenth and early twentieth centuries than from certain modern scholars. The workers, especially, were entirely unreliable. You wait, warns one of Galsworthy's upper-middle-class characters caught up in the 'Mafeking' mob in London in May 1900 in *In Chancery* (1920); they might seem encouragingly imperialist now:

> . . . but some day they would come in different mood! . . . One of these days we shall have to fight these chaps, they're getting so damned cheeky—all radicals and socialists. They want our goods.

Scarcely any contemporary imperialist regarded 'jingoism' as any indication of a reliable popular imperialism. As late as 1931 the chairman of the Empire Day movement, founded at the turn of the century to encourage imperial patriotism, was still grumbling that there were:

> . . . still many dark comers in Great Britain, especially in the industrial areas, where the rays of our Empire sun have not yet been able to penetrate.

Hence the propaganda.

It is difficult to be certain about its impact. Of course one should not take the imperialists' word for it; right-wingers tend to be pessimistic, and most of these ones hardly knew the bulk of their compatriots well. (Some of them weren't even compatriots. A surprising number of the leading imperialists of the early twentieth century were either foreigners, brought up in India, or educated in Germany.) Much of the propaganda certainly met with a cool response:

> Audience gave the impression of suspicion, of hostility to the subject and of considerable indifference to the conditions prevailing in the colonies,

was the Victoria League executive committee's note on one awkward attempt to reach a 'lower-class' audience, through the Workers' Educational Association, in 1911.

Imperial propaganda was at its most successful when there was plenty of sugar to cover the pill; as with Empire Day (a half-holiday), all those imperial stories for boys by Henty and co. (the derring-do), Scouting (the games and the camping out), Empire exhibitions (the fun-fairs), and so-called music-hall imperialism (the tunes). (In fact only a very tiny number of music hall songs even during the Boer war years were unambiguously imperialist. Most longed for sweethearts left at home, worried about fathers at the front, or bemoaned the ordinary squaddie's lot.) How much of the pill went down with the sugar is hard to say. Jeffrey Richards thinks the workers were too 'unintellectual' to resist it. Many working-class autobiographers claim to have resisted it nonetheless; but they were certainly unrepresentative—'intellectual' almost by definition. There are no objective measures of public opinion from this time. (The first systematic government survey, in 1948, revealed an amazing ignorance of and lack of commitment to the colonies *then*.) In any case people could have imbibed Empire-related attitudes unconsciously, without realising their implications. Racism is an obvious example, although the connection between this and imperialism is not at all straightforward. So we cannot know for certain.

What seems likely, however, is that imperialism in a strict, or narrow, sense of the term did not permeate British society very much more in the early twentieth century than it had in the nineteenth. This was for some of the same reasons, though not all. Society was still divided by class. This still determined people's main interests and priorities, as we can see from the major domestic events of the time: the General Strike, the depression, the rise of Labour and so on. So were the schools. Great efforts were made to bolster imperial education after the 1880s—free distribution of the maps was one—but there continued to be obstacles here. A Salford schoolboy called Robert Roberts recalled in his memoir being indoctrinated with imperialism at school in the 1900s, and is often quoted as evidence of this; but he is almost the only such example. A problem with elementary schools at the time was supposed to be their teachers, who generally came from the pupils' own class and had the reputation of being dangerously left-wing. There is little solid evidence that any substantial degree of 'imperialism' got through to girls and boys in these schools before the First World War. Working- and middle-class autobiographies (apart from Roberts') suggest the same with respect to people's adult lives.

Certainly the dominant values of British society, apart from its highest reaches, were not particularly Empire-related. Some of those values seemed to fly in the face of imperialism: British 'freedom', for example, which was still the main message of the history books even after 1900. It is noticeable that this did not give rise to any very widespread anti-imperial feeling (though there was some); but it cannot be inferred from this that people necessarily supported the Empire. Most appear to have been apathetic to it, or too busy with their lives to care much about it.

The way in which it was presented was also important. Here the propaganda may have had an effect. After the First World War, in particular, both school textbooks and imperial propaganda in general radically shifted their ground. The Empire was pictured differently from before: no longer as a matter of conquest and glory, but as a 'family', peacefully acquired and lovingly nurtured in liberalism; an example, if you like, of 'internationalism', the new buzzword of these League of Nations years. The new term 'Commonwealth' expressed this. It was mainly a travesty, but it was a significant one. It suggests that imperialism *pur*—in the usual meaning of the word, implying subjection and control—was still not widely acceptable in Britain. The thing had to be disguised to make it so. Even most Britons who were imperialists, therefore, may not have been so for strictly imperialistic reasons. Other 'discourses' were far more powerful.

It is a mistake, therefore, in studying the social history of Britain in this period, to focus on imperialism too much. It existed, but was thinly spread, patchily distributed, and never dominant. Britain was an imperial nation, but never a truly imperial society. It is important to bear this in mind, and not be too misled by the footprints. The relative lack of imperial commitment could, after all, have been a factor behind the Empire's eventual fall.

**BERNARD PORTER** is a professor of modern history at the University of Newcastle. He is the author of several books on British imperialism.

# EXPLORING THE ISSUE

## Was Popular Opinion a Significant Ingredient in Nineteenth-Century British Imperialism?

### Critical Thinking and Reflection

1. Examine both authors' descriptions of British society and culture during the age of imperialism. Critically discuss both the similarities and the differences that exist in their works.
2. Both authors list existing class distinctions as a factor in British society's interest/disinterest in imperialism. Critically examine which author makes the better case and provide evidence to support your judgment.
3. Although both authors offer examples of what elementary and middle school children might have been learning during this period, they differ in evaluating the influence of schools and textbooks. Critically examine and discuss their differing conclusions.
4. Identify cultural examples—artistic, literary, musical—that are used by both authors. Critically examine whether such examples should be used as reliable historical evidence.
5. Bernard Porter states that nineteenth-century British imperialism "existed, but was thinly spread, patchily distributed, and never dominant." Critically examine the ways in which Professor Porter substantiates/does not substantiate this claim.
6. John MacKenzie states that, during this time, "British culture was essentially imperial, and this was projected to and imbibed by a cross-section of all the social classes." Critically examine the ways in which Professor MacKenzie substantiates/does not substantiate this claim.
7. Think about the wars in Iraq and Afghanistan that have been labeled "American imperialism" by some observers. Critically evaluate them in the context of this issue, focusing specifically on the role of popular culture in either influencing or not influencing U.S. national aims abroad.

### Is There Common Ground?

There are many instances in which these two historians cite similar examples, yet reach differing conclusions. These areas of common citation might constitute the common ground for this issue. Perhaps we are seeing a disagreement over relative emphasis, rather than a stark conflict in thesis. One way to begin assessing the question posed by this issue might be to list the areas of common citation and do further research into them.

If we look at our own present-day culture, for instance, how would we assess the impact of films on popular opinion? Could the same film generate both pro- and anti-war views? If this is possible or even likely, how can a historian evaluate what influenced British school children a century ago? We are unlikely to find the ideas of school children expressed in their own words.

*Question:* What other factors must be considered in evaluating the relative influence of music, textbooks, images, and literature on the ways in which people no longer alive to speak saw themselves and their culture? How does the work of historians—even when, or maybe especially when, they disagree—offer us a deeper and more multifaceted understanding of cultures from the past?

### Create Central

www.mhhe.com/createcentral

### Additional Resources

Two older works that should be consulted for economic factors and imperialism are: John A. Hobson, *Imperialism: A Study* (1902) and V.I. Lenin (Ulyanov), *Imperialism: The Highest Stage of Capitalism* (1916). Recent economic analyses include: Lance E. Davis and Robert A. Huttenback, *Mammon and the Pursuit of Empire* (Cambridge University Press, 1987) and Patrick K. O'Brien, "The Costs and Benefits of British Imperialism, 1846–1914," *Past and Present* (August 1988, pp. 163–200), both of which find imperialism less than profitable, but still consider economic factors crucial to its development.

A seminal book in the study of nineteenth-century imperialism has been Ronald Robinson, John Gallagher, and Alice Denny, *Africa and the Victorians: The Climax of Imperialism* (Doubleday, 1968), which argues that British imperialism's main impetus came from national security and diplomatic rivalry sources. A work of ancillary value would be Daniel R. Headrick's *Tools of Empire: Technology and European Imperialism* (Oxford University

Press, 1981), which relates technology to the entire process of imperialism.

Exploring the relationship between culture and imperialism has been a hot topic recently, and the work in the field has been dominated by the presence of Edward Said. His *Culture and Imperialism* (Alfred A. Knopf, 1993) shows how nineteenth-century Western misperceptions of non-Westerners in cultural venues such as literature and grand opera played a role in imperialism's development. On a lighter side (culturally speaking), John M. MacKenzie's edited volume *Imperialism and Popular Culture* (St. Martin's Press, 1989) relates the fascination of the masses with exotic people and places, and sees it as a motivating factor in imperialism's maturation.

Since many of the world's contemporary problems can be traced to the effects of imperialism on indigenous peoples, we would be remiss not to include some sources which deal with that subject. Eric Wolf *Europe and the People Without History* (1982) explores the subject, as does the more recent *The Wealth and Poverty of Nations: Why Some are so Rich and Some so Poor,* by David S. Landes (W.W. Norton, 1998), which has provoked interesting responses from its reviewers.

## Internet References . . .

### The British Empire: Where the Sun Never Sets

Created by a British teacher (who has also taught in France, the Middle East, and Japan) in 1996, this site includes many sections and sub-sections, arranged in easy-to-navigate arrays. Particularly relevant to this issue are the sections on "Art and Culture," "Armed Forces," and "Articles." This web resource has grown to more than 11,000 pages.

**http://britishempire.co.uk/**

# Unit 2

# UNIT

# The Early Twentieth Century

*In this unit, we explore the first half of the creative, chaotic twentieth century, which was marked by great technological improvements and two disastrous world wars. The events of the twentieth century prove that societies in every century face the same problems. However, as the world becomes more technologically sophisticated, the stakes seem to become ever higher.*

*We have seen how the West exploded technologically in the last unit. Ironically, Chinese scientists had developed the concepts of mechanization and mass production as early as the eleventh century. Unlike the British, however, the Chinese chose not to pursue their initial advantage. For reasons that remain unclear, the implications of this technology were never explored. Within a relatively short time, China fell behind in the race toward technological mastery. Today, of course, China is again an economic tiger. Heavily influenced by Confucianism, China has had centuries of a hierarchical, communal worldview. Are these values compatible with Western capitalism? Or, must one give way to the other?*

*In areas of British influence, such as China, resistance to distant control and to aggressive Christian missionary activity led to rebellion. The so-called Boxer Rebellion offers insight into the pushback against imperialism in Britain's far flung empire. Britain was also a major player in the Treaty of Versailles that punished Germany for its role in starting World War I. Did this punitive treaty help precipitate World War II? Or, should the primary responsibility be assigned to Prussian militarism?*

*In the period between the world wars, Russia erupted into a revolution that overthrew czar and church and instituted a communist economic and political system. Though radical changes occurred, the entrenched gender system remained unchallenged. Women were granted legal rights and encouraged to define themselves as "workers." However, their traditional roles as housewife and mother were not shared by husbands or lovers. In the aftermath of World War II, the world was shocked to learn about "death camps" and the willingness of seemingly ordinary citizens to participate (or at least acquiesce) in the killing of millions of people. Labeling some people in society as "the other" has always made killing easier and perhaps made it seem justifiable in war. Genocide, based on ethnic hatred run wild, has become a pattern that we will examine in the next unit. Sigmund Freud's contention that we are prisoners to our subconscious urges has caused us to examine the roots of our darkest impulses. Despite our technological progress, have our social systems kept pace? Are we more enlightened than our counterparts of hundreds of years ago?*

Selected, Edited, and with Issue Framing Material by:
**Helen Buss Mitchell,** *Howard Community College*
**and**
**Joseph R. Mitchell,** *Howard Community College*

# ISSUE

# Was China's Boxer Rebellion Caused by Environmental Factors?

**YES: Paul A. Cohen,** from "Drought and the Foreign Presence," *History in Three Keys: The Boxers in Event, Experience, and Myth* (Columbia University Press, 1997)

**NO: Henrietta Harrison,** from "Justice on Behalf of Heaven," *History Today* (September 2000)

---

### Learning Outcomes

**After reading this issue, you should be able to:**

- Name and describe the multiple factors that historians believe precipitated China's Boxer Rebellion of 1898–1900.
- Understand and explain the role of Western commercial and missionary expansion in Asia during this period.
- Trace the roots of "The Fists of Righteous Harmony" and explain why its members were incorrectly named "Boxers."
- Explain the key features of the Chinese worldview and the role weather conditions might have played in creating conditions of unrest.

---

### ISSUE SUMMARY

**YES:** Professor Paul A. Cohen argues that while antiforeign and anti-Christian attitudes played a role in the start of the Boxer Rebellion, a more immediate cause was a severe drought and its impact on Chinese society.

**NO:** Historian Henrietta Harrison argues that, while the Boxers were motivated by more than a single factor, opposition to Christian missionary activity was at the core of their rebellion.

CREATE contains an issue on British imperialism, by which the West attempted to extend its influence over the peoples of the non-Western world. This issue provides a case study of the opposition that resulted from it: the Chinese Boxer Rebellion (1898–1900).

Western domination of Asia and Africa took different forms, the establishment of colonialism, which brought direct Western rule to much of Asia and Africa being the most prevalent. In China, however, geographic size and a large population made this impossible. There European nations established "spheres of influence" and recognized zones of China controlled and exploited by various Western nations. In these areas, China's rule was in name only.

Accompanying those coming to Asia for economic gains were missionaries who came to gain converts for evangelical Christianity. In China, with so many souls to save, this missionary zeal was a powerful force, and to many Chinese, a particularly odious one.

What made this domination of China possible was the weakened nature of the Chinese government. The Manchu dynasty and its Empress Dowager Tsu Hsi appeared to be powerless to stop this Western tidal wave sweeping over its country. When the Chinese did fight back, they were soundly defeated.

During the late 1830s, the Chinese government made an attempt control the Western commerce within its borders, especially the opium traded there by the British. The latter went to war to guarantee their right to sell the drug in China and won. As a result, the Chinese were forced to grant trade concessions, and a pattern of subservience was established. Any Western nation interested in trade with China would now demand the same deal the British received. In 1857, Britain and France went to war to force China to grant further diplomatic and commercial concessions, and once again the Chinese government was forced to accede to their demands.

By the turn of the century, a seemingly intolerable situation became worse, made so by more Western nations becoming involved in Chinese affairs, their increasing demands for further concessions from the Chinese, and the large number of Christian missionaries who entered China since 1860. These conditions were exacerbated by the Sino-Japanese War of 1895, which China lost and which resulted in the signing of another humiliating treaty. The Chinese government not only seemed powerless to stop Western encroachment; it couldn't stop the encroachments of one of its Asian neighbors. If China's government was powerless, perhaps some of China's citizens would have to fight to win back control of their country and bring an end to Western imperialism within its borders. The Boxers were a product of such conditions and concerns.

The Boxer Rebellion had its roots in the economically depressed Shandong province, made so by a devastating drought that not only caused massive starvation, but also brought its people to a psychological breaking point. Many young people turned to secret societies to vent their anger and disillusionment. Eventually they coalesced into a group known as the "Fists of Righteous Harmony." Because its members practiced martial arts, the term "Boxer" was applied to the movement by Westerners. It is a misnomer, which has endured to this day.

The movement began with sporadic attacks in the countryside, aimed primarily at Western missionaries and Chinese converts to Christianity. As the movement grew and its influence spread to some of China's urban centers, many wondered what the Empress Dowager Tsu Hsi would do. She was under intense pressure from Western officials to suppress the insurrection. But she also recognized in the Boxers a useful tool in fighting against Western influences and restoring Manchu hegemony in China. After a period of fence-straddling, she decided to openly support the Boxer cause. Thus, when the rebellion was suppressed by Western forces, she had to bear responsibility for their actions.

Another humiliating treaty was forced on China's dynastic government by outsiders. It would be the last. In 1912, the Manchu dynasty was removed from power by Chinese nationalists who had grown weary of governmental incompetence and Western domination.

Many problems arise when current interpretations of the Boxer uprising as a historical movement are attempted. One is motivation, the subject covered in this issue. Another concerns how the Boxers themselves should be viewed. Were they, as Henrietta Harrison states in the NO selection, "loyal and patriotic enforcers of the moral order or superstitious and xenophobic peasants"? Finally, as Paul A. Cohen points out in his book, how do we separate Boxer myth from Boxer reality? All of these questions form the basis of current historical inquiry, and answers to them must be sought if we are to accurately understand what occurred during this period.

Complicating matters is China's status today as a communist nation, adhering to a strict Marxist interpretation of history. There is strong pressure in such a society to fit historical events into this predetermined historical theory, and sometimes the truth can be lost within that process. But even as China's needs change, so does its history. According to Henrietta Harrison, during the Cultural Revolution of the 1960s, "The story of the Boxers was rewritten as one of peasant rebellion against foreign imperialism," a departure from previous Chinese interpretations of the movement. See Hu Sheng, *From the Opium War to the May Fourth Movement*, 2 vols. (Foreign Language Press, 1991) for an analysis of the major events in Chinese history from 1840 to 1920 from a Marxist perspective.

Joseph W. Eshrick, *The Origins of the Boxer Uprising* (University of California Press, 1987) was an important modern work, which encouraged others to pursue the Boxers-as-history movement. Paul A. Cohen's *History in Three Keys: The Boxers as Event, Experience, and Myth* (Columbia University Press, 1997) provides an interesting companion, and when combined with Hu Sheng's work mentioned above, provides the reader with three different points of view on the Boxer uprising.

What motivated the Boxers United in Righteousness to act as they did seems a simple enough question to answer—they were fighting to rid their country of the "foreign devils" who were causing it irreparable damage. However, some recent scholarship on the subject points to the severe drought and its psychological impact on Chinese society as an overriding factor. In the YES and NO selections, Paul A. Cohen stresses the latter, while Henrietta Harrison emphasizes the former.

# YES

**Paul A. Cohen**

## Drought and the Foreign Presence

### Drought, Anxiety, and the Spread of the Boxer Movement

Prayer, . . . even when offered up by the most powerful people in the realm, does not always work. And, as a drought continues and people become more and more desperate, restlessness, anxiety, and ultimately panic easily set in. To imagine how profound the panic can be among impoverished farmers and poor city folk living in a society with little in the way of a "safety net," it is illuminating to look at the reactions of the newly unemployed in California in the early stages of the recession that began in the latter half of 1990. "The hardest thing," observed the part owner of a small marketing company in Huntington Beach that had recently gone out of business, "is to see how panicked people are. . . . Right now, I don't have a dime. I'm worried about buying things like sugar. I'm that close to losing my home. Now is when the nerve systems are really going." A young film editor from Hollywood, noting the "prevailing air of uncertainty," expressed a lack of confidence "about the future."

Uncertainty about the future governs virtually all phases of human experience. But it does not always produce anxiety. For anxiety to result, the uncertainty must bear on an aspect of life that is of vital importance: a child's safety, one's performance in a play or a sporting event, the fate of a loved one engaged in combat, the time frame of one's own mortality, the security and dependability of one's livelihood. It was the last-named area of uncertainty that was shared by Californians in 1990 and Chinese farmers in North China almost a century earlier. Different societies, however, are differentially susceptible to the effects of natural or social disasters, and in the case of the drought of 1899–1900 in China (or that of 1899 in western India), because of the absence of a well-functioning crisis support system, it was much more a matter of life and death.

A wide range of sources, including gazetteers, diaries, official memorials, oral history accounts, and the reports of foreigners, indicate a direct link between the spread and intensification of the Boxer movement, beginning in late 1899, and growing popular nervousness, anxiety, unemployment, and hunger occasioned by drought. As early as October 1899, Luella Miner [American Board of Commissioners for Foreign Missions] (ABCFM) identified drought as one cause of growing Boxer-related unrest in northwestern

Shandong. In the Beijing area, where for many months very little rain had fallen and the wheat seedlings had completely withered, popular feeling was described as unsettled and volatile, owing to drought-induced hunger, and from late April 1900 contagious diseases began to break out with increasing frequency and seriousness. In other parts of Zhili it was much the same. American legation secretary W. E. Bainbridge, noting that during the preceding year "there had been insufficient rain" and that "the entire province was on the verge of famine," concluded that conditions were "peculiarly favorable to its [the Boxer uprising's] friendly reception. . . . As Spring advanced and early Summer approached with no rains to aid the crops, the excitement . . . reached a fever heat." From Zhuozhou, just southwest of Beijing, apprehensions were expressed in early June that, if it did not rain soon, it would become increasingly difficult to control the thousands of Boxers who had gathered in the area. A gentry manager of a *baojia* [local level mutual security system] bureau just west of Tianjin reported that in the spring of 1900 young farmers idled by the drought often took up boxing because they had nothing else to do with their time. The relationship among drought, idleness, and augmented Boxer activity found blunt corroboration in the testimony of a former Boxer from the Tianjin area: "*Gengzi* [1900] was a drought year and there was nothing to do, so we began to practice Yihe Boxing." . . .

Drought conditions in large areas of Shanxi had by summer 1900 become, if anything, even worse than in Zhili. In many places there had been no rain at all since winter. Farmers were without work. The prices of wheat and rice had shot up. Hunger was widespread and popular anxiety at a high pitch. A missionary report stated that the "organization of the Boxer societies spread rapidly throughout the province when so many were idle because of the drouth." The gazetteers of Qinyuan, Quwo, Lin, Jie, Linjin, Xiangning, and Yuci counties all connected the first emergence of the Boxers in mid- or late June to the protracted drought in their areas. Moreover, it was alleged that famine victims regularly joined in when the Boxers stirred up trouble.

I do not at all want to suggest that the expansion of the Boxer movement in the spring and summer of 1900 was due to drought alone. Within a given area, the official stance toward the Boxers, pro (as in Shanxi) or con (as in Shandong), played a role of perhaps equivalent weight. Nevertheless, drought—and the range of emotions associated with it—was a factor of crucial importance. It is significant, in this connection, that in a number of instances when rain fell to interrupt the drought and possibly bring it to an end, Boxers (as well as Big Sword Society members) dropped everything and returned to their fields. Esherick observes that when "a substantial penetrating rain" fell in early April along the Zhili-Shandong border, peasants went home to plant their spring crops, "quieting things down considerably." After being defeated by the foreign forces in Tianjin during a torrential downpour on July 4, fleeing Boxers are reported to have said to one another: "It's raining. We can return home and till the soil. What use is it for us to suffer like this?" The following day, accordingly, most of them dispersed.

Oral history accounts from Shandong tell a similar story. In late June 1900, during the drought in the western part of the province, a Big Sword Society leader from Zhili named Han Guniang (Miss Han) was invited to a Big Sword gathering at the hemp market at Longgu, just west of the Juye county seat. Rumored to be a Red Lantern with extraordinary magical powers—it was said that, in addition to being able to withstand swords and spears, "when she mounted a bench it turned into a horse, when she straddled a piece of rope it turned into a dragon, and when she sat on a mat it turned into a cloud on which she could fly"—Han Guniang took charge of food distribution. Within a short time, upwards of a thousand people joined her Big Swords. The grain she handed out had been seized from the supplies of rich families. "After two or three days," one account continues, "there was a big downpour. The next day there were no Big Swords anywhere in sight. They were all gone. The reason these people had come in the first place was to get something to eat. As soon as it rained, they all went back to tend their crops."

Lin Dunkui, who has made a special study of the role of natural disasters in the history of the Boxers, concludes that "from the time of the first outbreak of the Big Sword Society right up to the high tide of the Boxer movement, a sizable number of peasants were prompted to take part in these movements mainly by the weather.". . .

## The Boxer Construction of the Drought

What is fascinating is the degree to which contemporary Chinese—non-Boxers as well as Boxers—also viewed everything that happened in the world, including whether it rained or not, as being in the control of Heaven or "the gods." Indeed, although the Chinese construction of reality differed greatly in specifics from that of the missionaries, in a number of broad respects it formed almost a mirror image of the missionaries' construction. Where the missionaries saw themselves as representatives of the Lord, sometimes describing themselves as "God's soldiers" and often believing quite literally that they had been called by

Jesus Christ to go to China to labor for that country's salvation, in jingles repeated and notices circulated throughout North China in 1900 the Boxers were often portrayed, in comparably salvific (as well as martial) terms, as "spirit soldiers"(*shenbing*) sent down from Heaven to carry out a divine mission or, which amounted to the same thing, as mortals whose bodies had been possessed by spirits (thereby rendering them divine) for the identical purpose.

Again, where the missionaries constructed the Boxer movement as a satanic force, whose capacity for evil knew no bounds, the Boxers (and, one presumes, millions of Chinese who were not active participants in the movement) saw the missionaries, and by extension all other foreigners (as well, of course, as Chinese Christians and other Chinese who in one way or another had been tainted by foreign contact), as the root source of evil in their world, the immediate reason for the anger of the gods. The explanation of the drought found in Boxer notices was embedded in a full-blown religious structuring of reality; the notices also provided participants in the movement with a clear program of action designed to mollify the gods and restore the cosmic balance. Such notices began to be widely circulated at least as early as the beginning of 1900. (It is doubtful that one would encounter drought-related notices much before this date, as it was probably not until the late months of 1899 that people in North China began to experience the protracted dry weather as a "drought.") In February of this year the Tianjin agent of the American Bible Society reported the following text to have been "posted everywhere" in North China: "On account of the Protestant and Catholic religions the Buddhist gods are oppressed, and our sages thrust into the background. The Law of Buddha is no longer respected, and the Five Relationships are disregarded. The anger of Heaven and Earth has been aroused and the timely rain has consequently been withheld from us. But Heaven is now sending down eight millions of spiritual soldiers to extirpate these foreign religions, and when this has been done there will be a timely rain.". . .

## Boxer Motives: Anti-Imperialism, Antiforeignism, or Anxiety Over Drought?

The crisis remedy proposed by the Boxers in 1900 reveals a close kinship to that described by [Norman] Cohn for the millenarian movement of 1420. In one placard after another, the Chinese people are enjoined to kill off all foreigners and native Chinese contaminated by foreigners or foreign influence. Only after this process of physical elimination of every trace of the foreign from China has been completed will the gods be appeased and permit the rains once again to fall.

What is peculiar here and needs somehow to be accounted for is why at this particular moment in Chinese history there was such an extreme response to the foreign presence. Chinese had often shown a tendency, during times of military or cultural threat, to lapse into a form of racial thinking that categorized outsiders as fundamentally different and called for their expulsion, and this tendency had been greatly magnified in the nineteenth century with the appearance of "physically discontinuous" Westerners, who also happened to be carriers of a symbolic universe that diverged radically from the Chinese and, directly and indirectly, challenged the validity of the Chinese cultural world. From the early 1800s, people who had had contacts of any sort with Westerners were regularly referred to as "Chinese traitors" (*Hanjian*). More specifically, there had been efforts prior to the Boxer era to link natural disasters (as well as the failure of Chinese prayers to relieve them) with the presence of Christians. And of course there had been no end of anti-Christian and antiforeign incidents in China in the decades leading up to 1900. Never before, however, had there been a movement like the Boxers, uncompromisingly dedicated to the stamping out of foreign influence and backed, all the evidence indicates, by the broadest popular support. How do we explain this?

The reasons are without doubt very complex. Chinese historians, insisting upon the "anti-imperialist and patriotic" (*fandi aiguo*) character of the Boxer movement, tend to assign primary responsibility to the intensification of foreign imperialism in the last years of the nineteenth century. My own view is that the vocabulary of anti-imperialism is so deeply colored by twentieth-century Chinese political concerns and agendas that it gets in the way of the search for a more accurate, credible reading of the Boxer experience. This is not to deny that imperialism was a fact of life in China at the turn of the century or that it formed an important part of the setting within which the Boxer movement unfolded. It was only one causal agency among several, however, and its gravity relative to other causal forces varied considerably from place to place and over time. Furthermore, action taken against the more tangible reflections of imperialism—missionaries and Chinese Christians, railways, telegraphs, foreign armies, and the rest—could, when it occurred, derive from a range of possible motives; it need not have been inspired by either "patriotism" or "anti-imperialism." To superimpose this vocabulary on the Boxer movement, therefore, is to risk radical oversimplification of the complicated and diverse motives impelling the Boxers to behave as they did.

. . . We have hundreds of samples of Boxer writing—handbills, wall notices, charms, slogans, jingles, and the like. And even though most if not all of these may be assumed to have been composed by Boxer leaders or elite Chinese sympathetic to the Boxer cause rather than by rank-and-file participants in the movement, there is, as argued earlier, little doubt that they incorporate values and beliefs widely shared among the Boxers in general, not to mention millions of Chinese who witnessed and often supported, but were not directly engaged in, the activities of the Boxer movement. Still, as crucially important as these materials are in establishing the mindset of the Boxers, they fall well short of supplying the kind of intimate tracking of experience that we get, say, from the memoir literature of participants in the Cultural Revolution or the heresy trial testimony of the sixteenth-century Italian miller Menocchio or the letters, journals, and even poems composed by British soldiers in the trenches in World War I. In fact, it was not until after 1949 that elderly survivors of the Boxer uprising, mainly in western Shandong and Tianjin and other parts of Hebei (Zhili) province, were finally given a chance to describe more or less in their own words their experiences at the turn of the century. As useful as these oral history materials can sometimes be, however, their value is circumscribed by the advanced age of the respondents, the remoteness in time of the events under discussion, the political and ideological constraints built into the environment within which the interviewing was conducted, the specific questions the interviewers posed, and the editorial process by which the resulting responses were structured.

Consequently, in attempting to get at the range of motives that impelled the Boxers to attack foreigners, foreign-made objects, and foreign-influenced Chinese, we are regularly faced with the necessity of inferring these motives from Boxer actions, of reading back, as it were, from behavior to intent. This is one of the more dangerous kinds of business in which historians must unfortunately all too often engage, as it presents us with an open invitation to discern in the experience of the past the values, thought patterns, and psychological orientations that make the greatest sense to us in our own day.

Although on a macrohistorical level we hear much of the intensification of foreign imperialism that took place in China in the years following the Sino-Japanese War of 1894, it is arguable that, unlike drought, a conspicuously growing foreign presence was not, in 1899–1900, the common experience of the vast majority of Chinese inhabiting the North China plain. Whether we train our sights on expanded communities of native Christians or the growth in strength of the Catholic and Protestant missionary bodies or the construction of railways and telegraphs or the intrusion of foreign armies, the experience of direct confrontation with the foreign or foreign-influenced remained, for those living away from large urban centers, a sporadic and highly localized one in these years. Despite a substantial increase in the numbers of Protestant and Catholic converts in China as a whole in the 1890s—from approximately 37,000 Protestants in 1889 to 85,000 in 1900, and from about 500,000 to over 700,000 Catholics between 1890 and 1900—there were still, in 1899–1900, large stretches of North China that had Christian communities of negligible size or none at all. Similarly, in the case of both the Catholic and Protestant missionary efforts in the empire, although impressive growth occurred in the last decade of the century, this growth was far more in evidence in certain areas—the greatly expanded Catholic presence in southern Shandong, for example—than in others. Again, as of 1899–1900, the only railway lines that had been completed in North China were the Beijing-Baoding line, the Beijing-Tianjin line, and the line extending northeastward from Tianjin, through Tangshan, into Manchuria. And, leaving out the military activities of the Russians in Manchuria, foreign troop movements in the Boxer summer were largely confined to Tianjin and Beijing, their immediately surrounding areas, and the corridor connecting these two cities (although in the months following the lifting of the siege of the legations, . . . punitive expeditions were carried out in other parts of Zhili and in eastern Shanxi).

In other words, despite an overall expansion in the opportunities for direct contact with foreigners, foreign-influenced Chinese, and foreign technology in the last years of the century, these opportunities were not evenly distributed throughout North China. Furthermore, there is the curious circumstance—curious, at least, if one interprets the behavior of the Boxers as having been guided in significant measure by anti-imperialist impulses—that the areas where the impact of imperialism was greatest often did not coincide with those areas in which the Boxers were most active. This was especially true in Shandong, where the arenas of greatest foreign economic activity—the eastern and southern coasts—were conspicuously free of Boxer involvement and where approximately half of the missionized areas also were left untouched by the Boxers. Mark Elvin, who includes southern Zhili as well as Shandong within his purview, is so struck by the weakness of the link between "Boxerism and the religious and foreign irritant usually supposed to have caused it" that he questions whether it can serve as "a convincing sufficient explanation" of the movement's origins.

I am not particularly concerned here with the origins of the Boxer movement. I do, however, believe that there is room for a fresh understanding of the range of motives that lay behind what was perhaps the Boxers' most distinctive and defining characteristic: their antiforeignism. The reality of Boxer antiforeignism—and the antiforeignism of many millions of Boxer supporters and sympathizers—is not at issue. What is at issue is the underlying meaning of this antiforeignism. Was it a reflection of simple hatred of foreigners owing to their foreignness? Or did it result from anger over specific foreign actions? Or did it spring from fear and anxiety and the need for a credible explanation for the problems—above all, drought—occasioning this fear and anxiety?

My own view is that antiforeignism, in the sense of fear and hatred of outsiders, was there all along in China in latent form, but that it needed some disturbance in the external environment, a rearrangement of the overall balance of forces within a community or a geographical area, to become activated. Chinese antiforeignism thus functioned in much the same way as fear of witchcraft in late seventeenth-century Salem or anti-Semitism in 1930s Germany. In each of these instances outsiders—Westerners in China, people accused of being witches in Salem, Jews in Germany—lived more or less uneventfully within their respective communities when times were "normal." But when something happened to create an "abnormal"

situation—economic insecurity in Germany, apprehension concerning the enormous economic and social forces transforming New England in the late 1600s, anxiety over drought in turn-of-the-century North China—and people sought in desperation to address their grievances and allay their insecurities, outsiders became especially vulnerable.

The specific circumstances favoring outbreaks of antiforeignism in North China in 1899–1900 varied from place to place. In Shandong, escalating Boxer anti-Christian activity in late 1899 resulted (under foreign pressure) in the replacement as governor of Yuxian, who had followed a policy of leniency toward the Boxers, with Yuan Shikai, who, after the killing of the British missionary S. M. Brooks on December 31, pursued an increasingly strong policy of suppression. In Zhili province, especially in the Beijing and Tianjin areas and the corridor connecting the two, there was a relatively high level of exposure to the full range of foreign influences and, from the winter of 1899–1900, to rapidly growing numbers of Boxers. In Shanxi, where there were no significant manifestations of foreign influence apart from the missionaries and native Christians, there was a governor (Yuxian having been transferred there in March) who was deeply antiforeign and pro-Boxer.

Although the precise mix of factors was thus variable, the drought was shared in common throughout the North China plain. It was this factor, more than any other, in my judgment, that accounted for the explosive growth both of the Boxer movement and of popular support for it in the spring and summer months of 1900. Missionary reports and oral history accounts occasionally used the term "famine" to describe conditions in North China at the time. This was, for the most part, a loose usage; severe famine did not appear until the early months of 1901, mainly in Shanxi and Shaanxi. The evidence is overwhelming, on the other hand, that *fear* of famine, with all its attendant bewilderment and terror, was extremely widespread. As has often been the case in other agricultural societies, moreover, the uncertainty, anxiety, and increasingly serious food deprivation accompanying the Chinese drought—the *delírio de fome* or "madness of hunger," in the arresting formulation of Nancy Scheper-Hughes—seem to have inclined people to be receptive to extreme explanations and to act in extreme ways. The year 1900 was not a normal one in China. The menace of inopportune death was everywhere. And, as can be seen in the periodic eruptions of mass hysteria and the apparent readiness of many members of society to give credence to the most spectacular religious and magical claims of the Boxers, there was a strong disposition on the part of the population to depart from normal patterns of behavior.

**PAUL A. COHEN** is professor of Asian studies and history at Wellesley College, Massachusetts. He is the author of *Discovering History in China: American Historical Writing on the Recent Chinese Past* (Columbia University Press, 1984).

Henrietta Harrison

# Justice on Behalf of Heaven

On the fifth day of the seventh month of the twenty-sixth year of the Guangxu Emperor, Liu Dapeng, a tutor and diarist, stood at the door of his family home in the village of Chiqiao in Shanxi province and watched an army of a thousand Boxers pass through. Liu was a brave man; some forty years later during the Second World War he was to stand on the roof of that same house watching the bombs falling from Japanese planes on his neighbours' houses. When the Boxers passed through, most of the other villagers had fled to the hills or were hiding behind the locked doors of their houses in fear that the Boxer forces would loot and extort money and goods. Liu himself had taken leave from his job as a private tutor in a grand house some twenty or thirty miles away and come home to look after his mother, wife and children because of the crisis. At the head of the Boxers came a young man known as Third Prince, who Liu guessed was less than twenty years old. Two banners before him proclaimed 'Bring justice on behalf of Heaven!' and 'Support the Qing! Destroy the foreign!' Then came rank after rank of men marching down the narrow street that ran through the centre of the village. There were men of all ages, but Liu reckoned that at least two-thirds were not yet adults. All of them wore red belts and red cloths tied around their heads. They marched in an orderly fashion, divided into companies and brigades, and did not, after all, do any damage in the village.

Liu's attitude to the Boxers was divided. On the one hand he approved of their loyalty to the Qing dynasty and their opposition to the expansion of foreign power in China. He was particularly supportive of their campaign against the local Catholics, whom he perceived as having sold out to the foreigners. On the other hand, he was dubious about the movement's religious elements and particularly concerned about the threat they posed to law and order. While he approved of the provincial governor's efforts to force Catholics to renounce their religion, he found it hard to condone the murder of travellers suspected of poisoning wells, let alone pitched battles between Catholic villages and Boxer forces. Liu's feelings, in this respect, were typical of the time and were shared across a wide social spectrum. Indeed, it was just such conflicting attitudes at court that allowed the Boxer movement to spread on such a wide scale. Although events in the northern coastal province of Shandong where the Boxer movement originated are better known, some of the worst violence in the uprising took place in the adjoining Shanxi province, witnessed by Liu.

The Boxers' opposition in the foreign powers and especially to Christianity struck a chord with many Chinese and drew widespread support. China's defeat by Japan in the war over Korea in 1894 was a turning point in perceptions of the foreign threat. The country's perception of itself as the Middle Kingdom, a central realm of civilisation surrounded by tributary states, and by savages and barbarians beyond that, had been affirmed by Korea, which had conducted an elaborate tributary relationship with China. The loss of Korea, moreover, brought with it humiliating defeat by the Japanese, hitherto often dismissively referred to as 'dwarf pirates'. In the Treaty of Shimonoseki, which concluded the war, China not only agreed to Korean independence, but ceded Taiwan to Japan and gave the Japanese the same treaty rights as those of Westerners. These were the events that roused Sun Yat-sen, later China's first President, to plan his first revolutionary uprising. But it was not only members of China's tiny reformist elite who were concerned at this outcome. The news was carried across the country and was talked about by the farmers in Chiqiao village, all of whom, Liu reported, opposed the terms of the treaty. Li Hongzhang, who had been the chief negotiator on the Chinese side, became extremely unpopular, with rumours circulating in the countryside that he had married his son to the daughter of the Japanese emperor, and satirical rhymes attacking him for selling his country. It is important to remember that, though often condemned as ignorant, superstitious and xenophobic, the Boxers were acting in an environment where China's changing international situation was widely known and resented.

Popular opposition to foreign power was confirmed in Shanxi when news came through in the summer of 1900 that the government had declared war on the foreign powers. Liu heard that governors had been ordered to kill collaborators, that is to say Christians, and to arrest any foreigners and execute them if they planned to make trouble or plotted with the Christians. Shanxi's governor, Yu Xian, was said to be delighted at the news and immediately sent soldiers to round up those foreigners residing in the province and bring them to the provincial capital. Less than a month later some forty unfortunate foreigners were formally executed outside the provincial government building. The Chinese leaders of the Catholic community were ordered to renounce their faith and one who refused was executed. It was thus clear that the government declaration of war on the foreign powers included not only foreign civilians but also Catholic villagers. When the Boxers marched through the countryside carrying banners that said 'Restore the Qing! Destroy the foreign!' their claims that they were loyal forces obeying the orders of the dynasty were hard to deny.

Catholics were seen as potential collaborators in a war with the foreign powers because Christianity had been introduced into China by foreign missionaries. Indeed the right for Christian missionaries to reside in the interior had repeatedly been the object of treaty negotiations between the Qing dynasty and the foreign powers. In Shanxi, the Protestant missionaries had only a handful of converts, but Catholicism was firmly rooted in many rural areas and had been widespread since the eighteenth century. The heart of the problem lay in the contradictions between Christianity and the belief system that underlay the structures of the state. In the villages—where the Boxers operated—the problems of integrating Christianity in the imperial state were focused around the issue of temple festivals and opera performances. Temple festivals were funded by contributions from all members of the local community. In addition to a market they included sacrifices to the deity in whose honour the festival was held and often theatrical performances on a stage facing the temple. Wealthy villages would hire a travelling opera company who would perform for three to five days. Poorer villages might only have a puppet theatre for a single day. The festival performances were intended for the deity but were also a source of entertainment. Friends and relations came from miles around to see the operas, meet and chat, while the market drew large crowds. The funds raised to pay for the opera, meanwhile, also provided a working budget for such village level local government as existed. They might, for example, be used to pay for the dredging of dikes for a communal irrigation system or a law suit against a neighbouring village. Christians, however, refused to pay the levies on the grounds that they would be used to support idolatrous practices.

By refusing to contribute to the festivals, Shanxi Catholics were excluding themselves from the local community. At the same time locals were aware that allowing Christians to opt out of paying taxes made Christianity, which was generally seen as a heterodox religion, a financially advantageous option for the poor, who often turned out to enjoy the festivities even if they had not helped to pay for them. As a result, the 1890s saw an increasing number of legal cases being brought by village leaders against recalcitrant Catholics. The Catholics were able to fight these suits because the foreign consuls, backed by the threat of arms, negotiated with the central government for the right of Christians not to pay for religious practices in which they did not believe. Both the village leaders and the magistrates, however, saw the cases as resting on matters of loyalty and obedience to the state rather than on religious toleration. An extract (translated by

Roger Thompson) from one magistrate's interrogation of a Catholic named Yang accused of refusing to pay village levies gives a sense of the way in which Christians were seen as alienating themselves from the state:

*Magistrate:* You are a person of what country?

*Yang:* I am a person of the Qing.

*Magistrate:* If you are a person of the Qing dynasty then why are you following the foreign devils and their seditious religion? You didn't pay your opera money when requested by the village and you were beaten. But how can you dare to bring a suit? Don't you know why Zuo Zongtang went to Beijing? In order to kill—to exterminate—the foreign devils. You certainly ought to pay the opera subscription. If you don't you won't be allowed to live in the land of the Qing. You'll have to leave for a foreign country.

Liu Dapeng, watching the Boxers pass his front door on their way to join an attack on Catholic villages, shared this view. In his opinion:

> When the foreign barbarians preach their religion, they say they are urging men to do good, but in fact they are disrupting our government, creating turmoil in our system, destroying our customs, and deceiving our people; that is to say that they want to turn the people of China into barbarians.

The issue of Catholic refusal to participate in the religious practices of the local community became particularly powerful and problematic in the summer of 1900 because of the fear of drought. Drought was a constant threat to the North China Plain, where farmers rely on rain falling at precisely the right times of year. In Shanxi many remembered with fear the great famine of the 1870s when in Chiqiao one in ten of the population died, and in parts of the south of the province the death toll was worse still. Drought like this was widely seen as divine punishment for immorality and people reacted with ritual and prayer. In Chiqiao men went with bare heads and bare feet to a spring high up in the mountains to pray for rain. The villages through which they passed set up altars in front of their homes laid out with candles, cakes, branches of willow and dragons' heads carved from gourds. As the procession passed through the village the men would repeat the words 'Amitabha Buddha' and the onlookers knelt and used the willow branches to scatter water on them. For three days the men stayed at the temple beside the spring, eating only thin gruel and praying constantly for rain. Such rituals were commonplace throughout northern China in times of drought and were believed to require the sincere participation of the whole community in order to be effective. Catholic refusal to participate in the rituals needed to save the local community from famine accentuated an already problematic relationship.

The conflict between Catholics and villagers meant that the Boxers could be seen as representing and embodying the community even as they attacked and burned their neighbours' homes. With their banners 'Bring justice on behalf of Heaven!' and 'Support the Qing! Destroy the foreign!', they claimed to uphold the moral and social order where the dynasty, because of foreign pressure, was unable to do so. As Liu Dapeng put it, 'the court could not kill the Christians and the officials dared not kill them, so the Boxers killed them.'

However, the people of Chiqiao village, which had no Catholic families at all, nevertheless fled in panic when they heard the Boxers were approaching the village. Doubts lingered about the beliefs and rituals of the Boxers, and about their violence. People expected that boxing, or martial arts, techniques would be learned from a teacher over many years, but these were mostly young boys with hardly any training. Liu Dapeng went to see them practising at a large temple near Chiqiao. They set up sticks of incense and kowtowed to them. Then they stood facing southeast, put their hands in a certain position and recited an invocation to several deities. Immediately they fell on the floor, as if asleep. Then, as the crowds of spectators gathered, their hands and feet began to move and slowly they stood up and began a kind of dance sometimes with weapons, all the time keeping their eyes closed. Although their expressions were terrifying, they somehow looked as if they were drunk. After keeping up these strange movements for a while they fell to the ground again, and eventually awoke. Later they said that they did not remember what they had done while they were in the trance. When one of the onlookers asked what would happen if they had to face guns, they replied that Heaven was angry and had sent them as soldiers to warn the people. This was the 'spirit possession' that was central to the Boxer movement. Spirit possession by semi-professional mediums is a feature of Chinese folk-religious practice, but mass spirit possession of this sort was, as Liu commented, very strange indeed.

But the strangeness of Boxer claims was not limited to spirit possession. As at other times when drought threatened, bizarre rumours were rife. In Shanxi it was said that the wives of the foreign missionaries stood naked on the roofs of their houses fanning back the winds that would have brought rain. Other rumours concerned the Catholics, who were said to be poisoning village water supplies. Western power, and particularly science, was considered to border on black magic in the eyes of much of the population. The same black magic was also attributed to the Chinese Catholics. Rumours spread through Shanxi that Catholics had painted blood on doorways, and where they had done this the entire family would go mad within seven days. The Boxers claimed to have the power to oppose this Catholic magic and Liu saw people washing the blood off their doors with urine as the Boxers instructed. Strange stories told of full-scale battles between the Catholic and the Boxer magic. In a large town near Chiqiao there was a panic one night that

the Catholics had come and many of the townspeople went to guard the city walls. When they were there they heard a huge noise like tens of thousands of people attacking and then suddenly a green hand as big as a cartwheel appeared in the air. The local Boxer leader pointed at it and there was a crash of thunder and rain began to fall. He explained that the green hand had been a form of Catholic magic and he had destroyed it. Outside the city wall the villagers saw the lights, heard strange noises and fled from their homes in panic to hide in the fields. It is clear that such stories were widely believed at the time, and yet there was always an underlying distrust. The next morning, when the villagers cautiously emerged from their hiding places, they realised that there had been no Catholic army and no battle. The fear of drought inevitably gave rise to rumours, but many, including Liu, were not wholly convinced by the magical claims of the Boxers.

Distrust of the Boxers' spiritual powers was increased by a growing realisation of the threat they posed to law and order. This began with the murder of people accused of poisoning wells. Most of these were not even Catholics, but were accused of being in their pay. Magistrates, unsure of how to respond to the movement, failed to investigate the crimes and Boxer confidence grew. Large groups of men assembled and began to fight their Catholic neighbours. The army of men that Liu saw marching through his village had gone out to a nearby village which had a sizable Catholic population. The Catholics had hired men from another province to protect them and had withdrawn to their solidly-built stone church. The Boxers besieged the church and the battle lasted for six days. More than thirty of the mercenaries were killed before the church fell. A few of the Catholics survived the seige and escaped, but the rest were massacred and the church burned.

Magistrates' failure to act in the face of such disorder was due to the weakness and indecision of the central government, which vacillated between support for the Boxers and fear of the foreign powers. For more than fifty years the foreign threat had been at the centre of factional divisions within the court. At the heart of this debate was the question of whether a modern, well-equipped army or popular feeling should be more important in withstanding the foreign powers. The leaders of the bureaucracy were examined and trained in Confucian thought and for many of them it was an article of faith that victory in battle would be the result of the people's support. On the other side stood a faction, many of whom were drawn from the Manchu ruling ethnic group, who had accepted the strength of the European powers and believed that it was necessary to approach them cautiously until such time as China had built up the technical expertise to face them. The radical Confucians saw the growth of the Boxer movement as a sign that the people were at last aroused to fight the foreigners. Putting their trust in this, they were prepared to overlook the folk-religious aspects of the movement, which were clearly at odds with Confucian rationalism, and also the inevitable threat to law and order that would arise if the people were allowed to bear arms outside state control. With the support of the ruling Empress Dowager the court declared war on the foreign powers. However, the more cautious modernisers, many of whom had power bases in the southern provinces, believed that China was still unable to defeat the foreign powers; the governors general of the southern provinces refused to enter the war. Instead they drew up private agreements with the foreign powers, giving protection to foreigners and Christians in return for a promise that the foreigners would not invade. Although the Confucian radicals had won at court the central government was not strong enough to control the regions. The result was indecision and a series of conflicting orders. The Qing army never really engaged with the foreign troops, but country magistrates dared not arrest the Boxers, and thus appeared to be encouraging the movement to spread.

The debate over whether the Boxers should be seen as loyal and patriotic enforcers of the moral order or superstitious and xenophobic peasants has remained at the heart of Chinese perceptions of the uprising. In the early years of the twentieth century the modernisers, who had added a desire for the adoption of Western culture to their Qing predecessors' perception of the need for Western technology, continued to criticise the movement. Indeed, for this group in the 1910s and 20s, the failure of the uprising to solve China's problems by driving out the foreigners was symbolic of the failure of China's encounters with the West. The Boxers embodied what the modernisers saw as the very national characteristics that had led to China's international weakness. They were depicted as ignorant and conservative, a group whose folly and credulous belief that they could be saved from bullets by reciting magic rhymes had ultimately led to the imposition of the huge Boxer Indemnity that sunk the nation in the burden of debt.

However, from the 1920s onwards, a new generation of historians and politicians began to rewrite history in terms of China's resistance to Western imperialism, rather than of its development towards modernity. The events of 1900 came to be known, as they are in China today, not as the Boxer Uprising but as the invasion of the Eight Allied Armies, thus shifting the focus from the Boxers themselves to the foreign response. In addition, the Communists took over the mantle of the radical Confucians in their belief in the centrality of mass popular movements as the foundation of resistance to foreign powers. During the Cultural Revolution in the 1960s the Boxers were depicted as heroic, anti-imperialist fighters while the threat they posed to law and order was reconstructed as rebellious opposition to the forces of feudalism. The mass spirit possession and other elements of folk religion at the centre of the movement were completely ignored. The story of the Boxers was rewritten as one of peasant rebellion against foreign imperialism.

Since the 1980s there has been renewed interest in the Boxers. Chinese social historians are beginning to integrate popular folk religion and mass spirit possession into their interpretations of the movement. However, the ambivalence between interpretations of the Boxers as patriots or a superstitious and disorderly rabble has continued to form the framework of the argument. The ambivalence of contemporaries who observed the Boxers and which in many ways created the movement as a national phenomenon has continued to inform Chinese interpretations of the uprising.

---

**HENRIETTA HARRISON** is a lecturer in Chinese at the University of Leeds, England. She is the author of *The Making of Republican China: Political Ceremonies and Symbols in China, 1861–1911* (Oxford University Press, 2000).

# EXPLORING THE ISSUE

## Was China's Boxer Rebellion Caused by Environmental Factors?

### Critical Thinking and Reflection

1. According to Professor Paul A. Cohen, how did the Chinese worldview contribute to the way Boxers understood the drought?
2. What are the effects of drought today? Find examples of drought conditions, in the United States or around the world, and research the economic and psychological effects these droughts produce in populations.
3. Research the term "Mandate of Heaven" to understand why Chinese rulers find natural disasters anxiety-producing. To what extent might this worldview persist even today, especially in rural China? Critically discuss.
4. What role did Western commercial and missionary expansion play in precipitating the Boxer Rebellion? Critically discuss.
5. According to historian Henrietta Harrison, in what way were the actions of Christian missionaries most disruptive? Critically discuss why this was the case.
6. Research the role of martial arts in China. In what ways might the acquisition of "spiritual powers" seem threatening? Critically discuss.
7. Today, in China, a martial arts practice, Falun Gong, has been prohibited; many of its members have been jailed. It was said that Falun Gong had more active members than the Communist Party. Might this help us understand the Boxer Rebellion? Critically discuss.

### Is There Common Ground?

This issue offers the possibility of exploring a multiple-factor model of causation. Though each of the authors in this issue places more emphasis on one factor, multiple factors are acknowledged as possible causes of the Boxer Rebellion of 1898–1900. Carefully examine the evidence provided by each of these scholars in support of various potential causes. Separate groups of students might research and explain each of the proposed causes. If all these factors were, indeed, present, how might a historian decide on a chief or predominant factor?

*Question:* One test that might be useful asks: Is this cause both necessary and sufficient? Dry wood is necessary for a wood fire. However, by itself, it is not sufficient. Flame is also necessary, and also not sufficient. Is it possible that all these factors might have been necessary to spark the rebellion and yet no one of them was sufficient to ignite the rebellion by itself?

### Create Central

www.mhhe.com/createcentral

### Additional Resources

The centenary anniversary of the Boxer uprising has produced a number of interesting articles on the subject. R.G. Tiedemann, "Baptism of Fire: China's Christians and the Boxer Uprising of 1900," *International Bulletin of Missionary Research* (January 2000), views the Rebellion as a "tragic anomaly" in China's relationship to Christian missionaries. Robert Bickers, "Chinese Burns Britain in China, 1842–1900," *History Today* (August 2000), places the blame for the Boxer Rebellion squarely on the shoulders of British and European imperialism.

Finally, for a more popularly written account of the Boxer uprising, see Diane Preston, *The Boxer Rebellion: The Dramatic Story of China's War on Foreigners that Shook the World in the Summer of 1900* (Walker & Company, 2000).

## Internet References . . .

**The Boxer Rebellion**

A short essay is followed by links to the Qing Dynasty, several maps of China, and general information on China during this time period.

**www.smplanet.com/imperialism/fists.html**

Selected, Edited, and with Issue Framing Material by:
Helen Buss Mitchell, *Howard Community College*
and
Joseph R. Mitchell, *Howard Community College*

# ISSUE

# Did Prussian Militarism Provoke World War I?

**YES: Peter H. Wilson**, from "The Origins of Prussian Militarism," *History Today* (May 2001)

**NO: Christopher Ray**, from "Britain and the Origins of World War I," *History Review* (March 1998)

## Learning Outcomes

After reading this issue you should be able to:

- Identify and describe the four major long-range causes of World War I.
- Describe the division of Europe into allied and central powers, following the assassination of Archduke Franz Ferdinand of Austria-Hungary by a Serbian nationalist.
- Trace the aims and policies of the major powers on behalf of national states, during the decades leading up to World War I.
- Define militarism and trace its rise in Prussia and later pathway into a unified German national state.

### ISSUE SUMMARY

**YES:** History Professor Peter H. Wilson argues that Prussian militarism, though not a direct cause of later horrors in the two world wars, posed a threat to Europe in the prewar period.

**NO:** History Professor Christopher Ray argues that threatened German actions represented a challenge to English interests and honor, mobilizing public opinion in favor of Britain's declaration of war in 1914.

**I**t could be argued that World War I was the twentieth century's most cataclysmic event. It was responsible for the destruction of four major empires—Turkish, Russian, Austrian, and German—tied inexorably to the rise of fascism and communism—and caused more death and carnage than any event prior to that time. It also created an age of anxiety and alienation that shook the foundations of the Western artistic, musical, philosophical, and literary worlds. No wonder World War I has attracted the attention of countless historians who have scrutinized every aspect in search of lessons that can be derived from it.

As with all wars, the major historical questions are: Why did it occur? Who was responsible for it? Answering these questions can be a daunting task, yet an important one, if we are to learn any lessons from the mistakes of the past. Historians have identified four major long-range causes of the war: nationalism; militarism; imperialism; and the alliance system. But these represent only a partial answer to the question of why in August 1914, after the assassination of Archduke Franz Ferdinand of Austria-Hungary by a Serbian nationalist, Europe divided into two armed camps—the allied governments: Britain, France, and Russia (and later Italy)—and the central powers: Germany,

Austria-Hungary, and the Ottoman Empire—and engaged in a conflict that would involve most European countries and spread to the rest of the world.

Important as these factors are, they fail to include the human factor in the equation. To what extent were the aims and policies of the major powers, formulated by individuals acting on behalf of national states, responsible for the war? Is there enough culpability to distribute among many nations? Or was one nation and its policymakers overwhelmingly responsible for the onset of the Great War? Of course, the Treaty of Versailles, which brought an end to the war, officially answered the question of responsibility. In the now-famous Article 231, Germany and her allies were held accountable for the war and all concomitant damages, since the war was imposed on the Allied and Associated Governments ". . . by the aggression of Germany and her Allies." Little or no historical investigation went into the making of this decision; it was simply a case of winners dictating terms to losers.

The first to write of the war were the diplomats, politicians, and military leaders who tried to distance themselves from responsibility for what they had allowed to happen, and offered explanations for their actions suited to their country's needs and interests. Historian Sidney

Bradshaw Fay was the first to offer an unbiased interpretation of the war's onset. In a monumental two-volume work, *Before Sarajevo: The Origins of the World War*, and *After Sarajevo: The Origins of the World War* (The Macmillan Company, 1928), he stated that the liability for the war had to be shared by all involved parties, and that to find Germany and her allies solely responsible for it, ". . . in view of the evidence now available, is historically unsound" (vol. II, p. 558).

Unfortunately, the influence of Fay's work was minimized by the effects of the world-wide economic depression and the fast-approaching second world war of the century. The historiography of the World War I was temporarily put on hold. It would be reopened in the post-1945 era—and with some surprising results.

In 1961 German historian Fritz Fischer's *Germany's Aims in the First World War* (W.W. Norton & Company, translated 1967) reopened the debate in a startling fashion. While holding that no nation involved in the war was blameless, he found primary culpability for the war in the expansionist, militarist policies of the German government. The book first sparked a national controversy, which later moved into the international historical arena. Thus two works published more than 30 years apart established the framework of the debate.

Recent historical scholarship seems to balance both sides of the World War I historical pendulum. University of Sunderland History Professor Peter H. Wilson traces the rise of militarism in Prussia, including the maintenance of a large standing army, the glorification of military ideals, and the creation of a kind of military patriotism that shaped the German nation and created loyalty to the "fatherland." Writer and lecturer Christopher Ray argues that Germany's actions in the late nineteenth century and especially its threat to invade Belgium in early August 1914 were perceived as a threat to British interests and mobilized public opinion behind England's declaration of war against Germany and its allies in 1914.

It's possible that more current events in the former Yugoslavia have spurred renewed interest in World War I since that conflict represented the first time that the Balkan "powder keg" had exploded on the world's consciousness and provided the immediate cause for Great War. Yugoslavia was a creation of that war's aftermath, and some see its recent problems as a failure of the Versailles settlement.

Regardless of the veracity of this assumption, it is certainly true that the last few decades have seen the publication (and republication) of a number of important works on the Great War. Volker Berghahn's *Germany and the Approach of War in 1914* (London, 1993), and Samuel R. Williamson's *Austria-Hungary and the Origins of the First World War* (London, 1991) both have had second printings. David G. Hermann's *The Arming of Europe and the Making of World War I* (Princeton University Press, 1996) concentrates on the size and strength of land armies and their role in the genesis of the war, a subject that has been neglected in the past as historians tended to concentrate on the build-up of naval armaments as examples of militarism's role in the origins of the war.

Many of the recently published books on World War I either have been written by English historians or have England's role in the war as their primary concentration. One of the latter is Edward E. McCullough's *How the First World War Began: The Triple Entente and the Coming of the Great War of 1914–1918* (Black Rose Books, 1999), a revisionist work that holds the creation of the Triple Entente as a prime force among the causes of the World War I. Comparing the condition of Germany today to England, France, and Russia, McCullough questions not only the folly of the war, but how its results seem to have been counterproductive.

# YES ⤶

**Peter H. Wilson**

## The Origins of Prussian Militarism

The story of Prussia's transformation from potential victim of hostile international forces into a dominant and aggressive state often seems miraculous. To those who viewed it in the eighteenth century, it inspired a mixture of admiration and apprehension. These feelings gave way in the nineteenth century to a rather less critical glorification fostered by the authorities and German nationalist historians like Heinrich von Treitschke (1834–96), who saw Prussia's rise as the foundation of a united and dynamic imperial Germany. This vision disintegrated in the horrors of the first half of the twentieth century, after which Prussia's earlier rise appeared a historical 'wrong turn' (Sonderweg) on the path to modernity. It remains nonetheless a compelling tale tha[t] requires explanation.

Known as the 'sandbox of the Holy Roman Empire' on account of its poor soil and limited natural resources, the lands of the Prussian Hohenzollern dynasty were scattered across northern Europe from what is now modern Poland along the southern Baltic shore through to isolated enclaves on the Dutch border. When Frederick William (1620–88) became Elector or ruler of Brandenburg in 1640, he inherited a collection of different provinces lacking in common bonds or a uniform administration. Even the army, numbering a few thousand unreliable mercenaries, was split into regiments funded separately by the different provincial administrations. By his death in 1688, Frederick William had faced off his Polish and Swedish enemies, ruthlessly suppressed domestic opposition, imposed new taxes, forged common institutions and established a permanent army of no fewer than 29,154 men. He would go down in history as the 'Great Elector'. His son and successor, Frederick I (1657–1713), would receive a less prominent place in Prussian history, but nonetheless acquired a royal title for Prussia itself in 1701 and added another 10,000 men to the army. This force was effectively doubled during the reign of King Frederick William I (r. 1713–40), known to posterity as the 'soldier king' for his obsession with all things military and his passion for his 'giant grenadiers', a special regiment of exceptionally tall men stationed at his palace in Potsdam who, when the King was feeling unwell, would march through his bedroom to cheer him up. However, it was only under his son, Frederick II 'the Great' (r. 1740–86), that this well-drilled army was really tested in battle. Whereas only 15,000 sq km of new territory had been added to the Hohenzollern domains between 1648 and Frederick's accession in 1740, over 75,000 sq km

were acquired by the time of his death in 1786 through the conquest of new lands, particularly at the expense of Poland and the Austrian Habsburg monarchy. A further 113,500 sq km were seized in 1793–95 during the final carve-up that removed Poland from Europe's map until 1918. These gains increased the overall size of the Hohenzollern monarchy from around 1.6 million inhabitants in 1713 to at least 8.5 million by 1795. Impressive as these figures were, they failed to explain the phenomenal growth of the Prussian army, which already ranked fourth in size in Europe by 1740, while the country was only in thirteenth place in terms of population.

Contemporaries felt that this transformation was due to something more than the gritty determination and tactical skill of the Prussian monarchs and pointed to a deeper, underlying militarisation of Prussian state and society as the reason for the country's emergence as a great power. Among the most perceptive was the Austrian chief minister, Wenzel Anton von Kaunitz (1711–94), who identified the 'canton system' introduced between 1713 and 1733 by Frederick William I as the cause of a new militarism. This system was a form of conscription which divided the entire Prussian monarchy into cantons, or recruiting districts assigned to each regiment. In a practice known as enrolling, lists were kept of all males from the age of religious confirmation. The regiment drew men from the list as required to keep it up to strength, training them for about a year before giving them furlough; in other words discharging them on unpaid leave. Industrial zones and those individuals who were wealthy or deemed of value to the state were exempt from service. The regiments remained in being thanks to a cadre of paid professionals serving throughout the year, many of whom were recruited from outside the Prussian monarchy, while the conscripts were recalled annually for a period of intensive training. This system enabled Prussia to maximise its military potential without destabilising its labour-intensive agrarian economy since the discharged conscripts were free to work their landlords' fields for most of the year, thus sustaining productivity and with it state taxes, while also mollifying the Junkers, the feudal aristocracy on whom the crown depended for its officers and administrators.

While recognising that it had certain technical military advantages, Kaunitz felt the canton system was 'repulsive' as it led to the total subordination of all civil life to military requirements, creating 'unending oppression and extortion', a slavish mentality on the part of the population and suffocating the freedom and patriotism he believed flourished in more progressive countries like Britain and the Dutch Republic. Moreover, the 'Prussian military state' was inherently unstable with an in-built propensity to war as it could only sustain itself through external aggression to acquire ever more territory and resources. This had led to a new kind of total war in 'that the king does not just exploit his own population, money and military potential, but also all the inhabitants, money, food and other materials of innocent and neutral neighbours as far as force enables him'.

Emperor Joseph II (r. 1765–90) rejected Kaunitz's advice and introduced Prussian-style conscription into the Habsburg lands after 1771 in an effort to match the threat posed by Frederick the Great. However, subsequent historians have tended to agree with the minister's assessment of the fateful consequences of the canton system. In an influential thesis, the German post-war historian Otto Busch argued that it consolidated the compromise between the Hohenzollern dynasty and the feudal Junker aristocracy that underpinned Prussian absolutism since the reign of the Great Elector in the later seventeenth century. In return for voting taxes for the army and surrendering their say in determining foreign policy in the 1650s, the Junkers received confirmation and extension of their powers over their peasant tenants, tying them to perpetual servitude and forced labour. The subsequent expansion of the army under Frederick William after 1713 consolidated this by offering the Junkers socially prestigious and financially rewarding positions in the officer corps. The canton system completed the process by tightening the Junkers' grip on their serfs, especially since their monopoly of officer posts ensured that many aristocrats were simultaneously both captain and landlord over the same group of serf-conscripts. Since the army now regarded every man as a potential recruit, attempts to leave the country were equated with desertion so that military discipline reinforced feudal jurisdiction, creating what some have called a 'military-agrarian complex' or community of interest between monarchy, army and feudal aristocracy.

Though this system enabled Prussia to wage war successfully in the mid-eighteenth century, it became increasingly inflexible—as change to any part of this structure threatened the web of vested interests. This appears to account for the rigidity that contemporaries noted in the Prussian army after the Seven Years' War (1756–63) as it became a force drilled to perfection but unable to cope with any serious reverse. These weaknesses were exposed by the crushing defeat at the twin battles of Jena-Auerstadt in 1806 at the hands of the forces of dynamic Napoleonic France. The catastrophe led to a brief period of liberal reforms which partially modernised the army without seriously disturbing the social order. The canton system was replaced by what was heralded as patriotic universal military service in 1814, but the aristocracy reasserted its hold on the officer corps and the militarisation of society continued unabated once Napoleon had been defeated.

Busch's views proved highly controversial and were rejected by the still largely conservative German historical establishment in the 1950s, delaying the publication of his thesis by a decade. However, when it first appeared in 1962 it coincided with a wider trend in historical revisionism which sought not to explain the Nazi era as an aberration in an otherwise blameless German past, but as the direct culmination of earlier militarism. Rather than only briefly departing from the European norm in 1933–45, Germany now seemed to have been heading in the wrong direction since the early eighteenth century.

Busch's explanation of what he termed 'the origins of German social militarisation' fitted so well with the wider assumptions of the 'wrong turn' theory that no one has seriously questioned it until comparatively recently. Improved access to the archives of the former GDR after German reunification in 1991 has been instrumental in this reappraisal since these contain material relating to the feudal heartlands of Brandenburg and Pomerania. New research has incorporated different methodologies, including historical anthropology and detailed 'microhistorical studies' of individual Junker estates. A greater readiness to compare Prussia to other German territories has also been important. Even by 1800 the Hohenzollern monarchy still only contained a fifth of the inhabitants of the Holy Roman Empire: clearly German history cannot be written simply by generalising from the Prussian experience.

Taken together, these findings reveal a very different picture of the relationship of army and society in old regime Prussia than presented by Busch. In purely technical military terms, Prussia now appears less innovative than once thought. Key elements of the canton system like the practice of enrolling, furlough and assigning recruitment districts to individual regiments were all in use in other German territories, in some cases decades before their introduction in Prussia. Moreover, Prussia was not uniquely militarised as many smaller territories including Hessen-Kassel, Munster and even tiny Schaumburg-Lippe maintained more troops in proportion to their populations. Perhaps more significantly, the core assumptions behind the social militarisation thesis have been undermined and there is little evidence that serfdom and canton recruitment were necessarily mutually-reinforcing systems. Conscription was implemented throughout the Prussian monarchy, including in towns and areas like the Westphalian enclaves where serfdom and Junker manorial agriculture were not practised. More crucially, Junkers were rarely captains of their own serfs. Even in East Prussia, bastion of feudal Junkerdom, locally-born noblemen made up only half of the captains of regiments stationed in that province, while elsewhere the proportion could be as low as ten per cent. Being a native of that province did not mean one necessarily held land there. Many aristocratic officers were landless while those who still had estates generally had them outside the canton of their own regiment. Indeed, this was a necessity since tying officer appointments to only particular groups of estate owners would have rendered any kind of promotions and personnel policy impossible.

Far from militarising society, the practice of discharging conscripts for most of each year partly civilianised the army which assumed many of the characteristics of a militia, despite the fact that Frederick William abolished the Prussian militia structure and even banned the use of the word Milk in 1713. By regulating conscription, the canton system also made recruitment more predictable and easier to bear by the population. The internal administration of the canton was largely determined by the civilian settlement pattern of individual 'hearths' and communities which were permitted some role in the selection of recruits. Though obliged to serve for life if drafted, many conscripts were discharged early if others of a more suitable stature became available. All were permitted to return home for most of the year, enabling something approaching a 'normal' life despite military service. Soldiers retained their own homes and a relatively large proportion were allowed to marry, factors which gave the system considerable stability and discouraged desertion. The rules for surveillance and supervision by the military and civil authorities, though strict on paper, were not completely enforceable in practice and were open to manipulation from below as well as abuse from above. Some Junkers even connived at draft dodging to prevent the loss of valuable workers while the army's interest in preserving a pool of healthy recruits acted as a break on the excesses of tyrannical landlords. It is also telling that a significant minority of cantonists actually volunteered for service, joining the army as full-time paid professionals where they received a guaranteed minimum wage and were free to earn more money as hawkers, servants and building workers in their long off-duty hours. Those who were successful in finding such work could quadruple their basic pay, while those who were not could still supplement their wage by standing extra watch duty while their more entrepreneurial comrades engaged in more profitable civil employment.

These findings should not be taken as an attempt to return to the Hohenzollern legend propagated by nineteenth-century historians like Treitschke. The Prussian monarchy was far from being an impartial, strict yet benevolent guardian of common German interests. Canton conscription represented a heavy burden with at least five per cent of potential recruits serving in peacetime and double that number in war. Though service could be accommodated by those it took, it hardly offered a comfortable life: neither conscripts nor professional Prussian soldiers received a pay raise between 1713 and 1799! Frederick the Great's brilliant strategy may have ensured his country's survival during the Seven Years' War against impossible odds, but his battle tactics demanded a heavy price. Over 180,000 Prussian servicemen died in the conflict in addition to perhaps as much as ten per cent of the civil population. The army served the crown whose policies the bulk of the population had no say in determining and with which many, particularly the new Polish subjects acquired after 1772, could not identify.

Nevertheless, the recent research does raise questions about the degree of continuity between eighteenth-century conditions and subsequent German militarism. The aggressive militarism after 1871 has been regarded as a product of the marriage brokered by Bismarck of the old Prussian tradition represented by the Hohenzollern dynasty and Junker aristocracy with liberal capitalists and the big industrialists like the arms manufacturer Friedrich Alfred Krupp (1854–1902). Continuity with the eighteenth century was sustained by the resilience of the old regime which rode out the storms of Napoleonic defeat in 1806 and the Reform Era of 1807–14 and survived the violent socio-economic change unleashed by rapid industrialisation by introducing sham democracy after 1871 and pursuing increasingly reckless diversionary strategies such as Kaiser Wilhelm's Weltpolitik bid for colonial empire and, ultimately, launching world war in 1914.

Like all teleological arguments, this is seductively persuasive but flawed in the light of the recent research into eighteenth-century Prussia. The lines of continuity, though surely still present, now seem less clear or straightforward and Frederick the Great no longer appears the direct antecedent of Kaiser Wilhelm, let alone Hitler. The eighteenth century nonetheless left a fateful legacy, but it was not the fabled canton system. The army did enjoy unusually high social prestige in Prussia—something that was deliberately fostered by the crown as part of its efforts to reconcile the Junkers to service in the officer corps. Prussia also witnessed a new kind of militarised patriotism which first flowered in the Seven Years' War and intensified with the experience of the 'War of Liberation against Napoleonic France 1813–14. This re-evaluated the soldier's tragic death on the field of slaughter as the hero's glorious sacrifice for the fatherland. Significantly, this fatherland was no longer defined in terms of the decentralised, pacific, non-aligned and cosmopolitan Holy Roman Empire, but increasingly by reference to blood, soil, language and Protestantism.

However, this was not yet the exclusively reactionary, xenophobic nationalism associated with the Wilhelmine and Nazi eras which, in retrospect now appears more the product of the mid-nineteenth century experience. It was only the experience of revolution, especially that of 1848 when Prussian troops fired on crowds in Berlin and other cities, that heightened consciousness of the army as pillar of an increasingly obsolete social and political order. Additionally, the short and spectacularly successful wars of German unification in 1866 and 1871 left a very different memory of martial conflict than the prolonged bloodletting and near disaster of the Seven Years' War or Frederick the Great's last military engagement, the inglorious 'Potato War' of 1778–79 against Austria when deserters exceeded battle casualties by a factor of ten to one. It was these factors, rather than the experience of the eighteenth century, that conditioned the militarism that was to have 'such fateful consequences for Europe after 1914.

# For Further Reading

Otto Busch, *Military System and Social life in Old Regime Prussia 1713–1807: The Beginnings of the Social Militarisation of Prusso-German Society* (Humanities Press, 1997); Christopher Duffy, *The Army of Frederick the Great* (2nd ed., The Emperor's Press, 1996); Dennis Showalter, *The Wars of Frederick the Great* (Longman, 1996); Peter H. Wilson, *German Armies: War and German Politics 1648–1806* (UCL Press, 1998); Peter H. Wilson, 'Social militarisation in eighteenth-century Germany'. *German History,* 18 (2000), pp.1–39.

**PETER H. WILSON** GF grant professor of history at the University of Hull and the author of many books, including *From Reich to Revolution: German History 1558–1806* (Palgrave, 2004).

Christopher Ray

 **NO**

# Britain and the Origins of World War I

Accounts of the outbreak of World War One often communicate a sense that Britain was propelled into the conflict by force of circumstance, that it was, in some way, an accidental belligerent or a bystander 'dragged' into war by forces beyond its control. Certainly, the events in the Balkans that led to hostilities were far removed from Britain's normal concerns and had little direct bearing on its relations with other powers in Europe. And, if the mood of detachment in Britain, which prevailed throughout July 1914, had continued unchanged, then there might he grounds for viewing its eventual participation in the war as 'accidental'.

This, however, is not the case for, on Monday 3 August 1914, London witnessed an uncharacteristic public clamour for intervention that decisively pushed Britain into war. Until that day the majority of Britons seemed resolved that their country had no business becoming involved in a Continental war and, as the European Powers began to mobilize against each other, that it was yet another case of 'six of one and a half dozen of the other'. There can be little doubt that it was news that Germany intended the invasion of neutral Belgium, guaranteed by Britain under the treaty of 1839, that tilted the balance in favour of a British intervention, changed the public mood from indifference to war fever and propelled the nation towards action.

Yet, if this appears to provide an overall explanation for British intervention, it actually explains very little. While the British people seemed content to see their Continental friends, if not actual allies, march to Armageddon with few qualms, why did the fate of Belgium weigh so heavily with them? And, was it conceivable that, if the French had marched into Belgium in order to forestall an expected German attack aimed, primarily at them, then Britain would have joined with Germany and declared war on France? This proposition seems highly unlikely and to discover Britain's real motivation for entering the war it is necessary to explain why British public opinion reacted so strongly to German actions and, in so doing, to discover what Britain's true role had been in the generation of the conflict.

## Britain Turns Against the Germans

For most of the nineteenth century British defence planning was aimed primarily at France and Russia. Both posed threats to British colonial possessions overseas, France in Africa and Russia in the Far East. And, during the course of the century Britain had gone to war with both, with

France from the end of the eighteenth century until 1815 and with Russia in the period 1854–5. British interests were also best served by the maintenance of a balance of power in Europe and in the prevention of the Continent being dominated by any one state. The large ground forces at the disposal of France and Russia were, consequently, a further factor in Britain's animosity towards these two countries. However, from the middle of the century, the rise of Germany into the ranks of the first-class powers helped to counterbalance this threat and allowed Britain to keep its distance from events on the Continent while remaining in 'splendid isolation'.

It was not until the late 1890s that this began to change as tensions grew between Britain and Germany. To a certain extent this was based on the time-honoured principle in Britain of maintaining the balance of power in Europe and the consequent fear that Germany, after its defeat of France and its subsequent unification under the leadership of Prussia in 1871, might rise to dominate the Continent. It was, however, also based on the disappointment in Germany that Britain did not seek closer relations and remained somewhat condescending in its dealings with it. This was further compounded by Britain's preference for friendly relations with the United States, often at the expense of Germany, which became apparent after 1898. During the Spanish–American War of that year, Germany had sought to limit the extent of the American victory by raising a united European front against the United States in support of Spain. This failed largely because Great Britain refused to take part in any such diplomatic initiative and chose, instead, to give what support it could, within the confines of official neutrality, to the Americans. A further effort by Germany to flex its naval muscles at Manila Bay, and intimidate the American squadron which had arrived there to do battle with the Spanish fleet, was again thwarted by the British.

The resentment this caused in Germany was only compounded by the events surrounding the Venezuelan crisis four years later in 1902. In an attempt by Britain, Germany and Italy to force the Venezuelan government to honour its European debts which they had refused to meet, these three countries sent a combined naval squadron to enforce a blockade of the South American republic. This in itself caused little diplomatic friction with the United States, which recognised the principle that nations should honour their debts. However, when German naval forces actually opened fire on Venezuelan ships, President Roosevelt vigorously condemned what he saw as a violation of the Monroe Doctrine which claimed an American Veto over European interference in the Western Hemisphere. Germany, which had never recognised the legitimacy of the Monroe Doctrine, was ready to fight over this principle, but the British reaction was to promptly recall its naval forces leaving Germany to face the wrath of the United States alone. Germany, too, was eventually forced to retire and, as a consequence of the humiliation it felt, all attempts to forge a closer relationship with Britain were abandoned in favour of concentrating on a naval building programme designed to give it more diplomatic room for manoeuvre.

However, this programme also represented a challenge to the Royal Navy's claim to mastery of the seas and, in mounting such a challenge, Germany touched a raw nerve in Britain. Maintaining communications by sea was the key element in the defence of the British Empire which took precedence even over maintaining the balance of power in Europe. Germany, just beginning at this time to expand abroad and establish colonies in Africa, the Far East and the Pacific, could defend an expansion of its fighting navy on the same basis, but its naval expansion programme was based on a premise that was all too obviously aimed directly at Britain. Unable to challenge the Royal Navy directly in terms of size, the expansion of the German High Seas Fleet was based on what Grand Admiral von Tirpitz described as the 'risk-fleet' theory. The aim of this was to build a fleet based in the North Sea of sufficient size to pose a serious threat to Britain if it found itself at war with a third party. When the Royal Navy left home waters to do battle with such an enemy in defence of the Empire, it risked not only exposing the British Isles to invasion from the Continent but also, the theory suggested, loss of its overall naval superiority. If the British were to suffer grave losses in such a war, then the German navy might snatch a lead over its rival which Britain might find difficult to claw back. In order to facilitate this 'risk-fleet' strategy, Germany began building a formidable new naval base on Heligoland and embarked on an ambitious, though not extravagant, naval building programme. At the same time the Kiel Canal, through which the German fleet could be transferred from the Baltic to the North Sea, was widened to take the new, bigger, German battleships.

The implications of this were quickly recognised in Britain where, under the energetic leadership of Admiral Sir John Fisher, measures were taken to counter these German moves. A new naval base at Rosyth, facing the German base across the North Sea in Heligoland, was begun and Fisher was able to push through the building of a new class of super-dreadnought armed with twelve-inch guns that would make all of Germany's warships, which were armed with ten-inch guns, obsolete.

## Britain's Diplomatic Revolution

At the same time diplomatic moves were made to augment Britain's defensive posture. The Anglo-Japanese alliance of 1902 allowed the return of British warships from the Far East to home waters, while the growing entente with France allowed a parallel movement from the Mediterranean. The entente with Russia after 1907, which settled their differences over Persia, Afghanistan and Tibet, had the two-fold effect of relieving defence concerns over India and the Middle East. And the support given to the United States during the Spanish–American War also paid dividends by building a new relationship with that country which allowed for the withdrawal of warships from the Caribbean. By 1910 it was clear, therefore, that Tirpitz's 'risk-fleet' strategy had failed and had merely forced Britain into closer relationships with Japan, France, Russia and the United States. While this added to German feelings of insecurity, the British Isles themselves were actually more secure than they had ever been before.

## Anti-German Hysteria

Apart from forcing Britain into a diplomatic revolution that dismantled the false and rather dangerous policy of 'splendid isolation', German naval expansion had also caused a complete change of mood within the British population itself. Throughout the nineteenth century those in Britain who wished to see the maintenance of a strong Royal Navy had used the fear of possible invasion by a continental enemy as their chief instrument of propaganda. Much of this propaganda was carried in the right-wing press which continually ran news reports and editorial comment on the implications of various imperial and diplomatic moves by the French and Russians. However, such newspapers also hit on the novel idea of carrying works of fiction in serialised form, designed to act as parables, in order to get their message across. This gave birth to a whole genre of literature that may be termed 'invasion stories'.

Throughout the 1880s and '90s these stories naturally tended to concentrate on the threat posed by Britain's nearest continental rival, France, although some also envisaged a combination of French and Russian forces pouring across the Channel. The amount of suspicion that such stories aroused may be gauged by the public demand for the abandonment of a cross-Channel tunnel which was being planned in Britain during the 1880s. While H.G. Wells' *The War of the Worlds* (1899), was the most outlandish of these invasion stories, envisaging a Martian rather than a French invasion, it was, nevertheless, only a single example of a very popular genre. It also introduced a new 'scientific' element that would find echoes in later invasion stories and which took them to new levels of absurdity. While one of the common elements in the stories of French and Russian invasions was the use of treachery to affect an invasion of Britain, this new element introduced the concept of a 'secret weapon' which could nullify Britain's naval predominance.

These elements were still very much in evidence when, in 1903, the stories took on a new dimension. In that year Erskine Childer's book, *The Riddle of the Sands*, was published which introduced a new enemy—Germany. As with previous invasion stories, the enemy was portrayed as devious and without any real sense of honour; the exact opposite of the traits supposed to characterise the Anglo-Saxon, with his sportsman's sense of fair play. However, great emphasis was also laid on the importance of sea power and in keeping a developmental edge against future enemies. From 1903 onwards invasion stories, which continued to he highly popular in Britain, were almost exclusively concerned with the danger represented by Germany.

Works with titles like *The Invasion of 1910, The Enemy in Our Midst, When England Slept, An Englishman's Home,* and *When William Came,* told of secret armies of German reservists living undetected in Britain, clandestine concrete gun emplacements in London suburbs and blockades by fleets of German submarines. The extent to which these stories gripped the imagination of even sensible people may be gauged by the reaction of Frederick Harrison, the positivist philosopher, who wrote a letter outlining his concerns to *The Times* during this period. There was in existence, he warned, a German army 'trained for sudden transmarine descent on a coast', while Britain's only defence lay in keeping its navy at a high level of readiness at all times. 'What the Spanish danger was to the Elizabethans', explained the *Quarterly Review,* with obvious reference to England's heroic stand against the Armada, 'that is the German danger to this generation'. And, if this were not enough, then the recognised master of the 'future romance', H.G. Wells, was happy to underline the message in a letter of his own to the *Daily Mail* in 1908. 'I can imagine the day of reckoning coming', he darkly predicted, from 'all the millions just over there, who seem to get busier and keener every hour.'

## British Self-Interest

The effects of all this were not just apparent in Britain, however. While, during the Algeciras crisis of 1905–6, the French had cause to be grateful to the new entente with Britain arranged in 1904, by 1911, when the Agadir crisis erupted, they were beginning to have second thoughts. Although the crisis was originally one between Germany and France, the British reaction to it was both surprising and alarming. In his speech at the London Mansion House on 1 July 1911, the Chancellor of the Exchequer, Lloyd George, made it clear that Britain regarded the crisis as one between Britain and Germany and he warned that if 'peace could only be preserved by the surrender of the great and beneficent position Britain has won by centuries of heroism and achievement', then such a peace 'would be a humiliation intolerable for a great country like ours to endure'. And, as it became clear that Britain had made little provision for an intervention on land in Europe, French officials began to wonder if it might not be their country that would be 'dragged' into a war they did not want and for purposes not their own.

There were grounds for such reservations. It is clear that the British did not regard the ententes with France and Russia as implying a clear obligation to intervene on behalf of either if attacked by the Central Powers. Rather, they were regarded as a means of minimalizing the threat to the Empire if an Anglo-German war became inevitable. As such, while Britain had not been harnessed to the Franco-Russian alliance, France and Russia had been harnessed to the defence of British interests abroad. And, as Anglo-German tensions rose and their naval competition intensified, it was this, as much as anything, that fuelled the division of Europe into two armed and opposed camps with fatal consequences for the maintenance of peace.

On the morning of 2 August 1914 thousands of ordinary British citizens flocked into London to attend an anti-war demonstration being held that morning in Trafalgar Square. They were there to make plain their belief that Britain should not go to war for the sake of either Russia or France. They need not have worried for, in prolonged cabinet meetings the previous day, the Asquith government had shown itself to be extremely reluctant to come to the aid of France even if invaded by the Germans. The idea of intervening on behalf of Russia was not even discussed. That same day the Governor of the Bank of England let it be known to Lloyd George that the financial institutions were totally opposed to war under any circumstances. The public mood changed later on 2 August, however, when it became widely known that Germany was threatening the invasion of Belgium as the opening phase of its campaign against France. British opinion was outraged, although it was widely hoped that the Belgian government would simply allow the passage of German troops through its territory and any cause for British intervention would consequently be removed. The British, it seems, were quite content for the letter of its treaty with Belgium to be observed while its spirit was openly violated. Only when Belgium refused to yield and German troops prepared to cross into its territory during the night of August 2–3, were Britain's armed forces mobilized and, even then, no decision was taken to send the Expeditionary Force to France.

On the afternoon of 3 August Sir Edward Grey, the British Foreign Minister, addressed parliament. There was no question, he told the packed House of Commons, of Britain being dragged into war by its entente with the Franco-Russian alliance since there was no obligation to do so under any agreements with either of these powers. However, he went on, the crisis in Europe should be regarded from the point of view of 'British interests, British honour and British obligations'. British interests were in peril because of the threat that Germany might seize control of the entire continental side of the Channel thus jeopardising its imperial lines of communication. Honour was at stake because Germany was ready to disregard the treaty obligations that Britain had undertaken in guaranteeing Belgian neutrality. And, he suggested, Britain could not idly stand by while Germany sailed down the

English Channel to bombard the 'unprotected coasts of France', since such an action would constitute an affront to British naval power and a challenge that could not he ignored.

While Grey felt strongly that Britain should come to the aid of France, indeed he had threatened resignation if the British government refused to do so, he had, nevertheless, couched his speech in terms calculated to appeal to his audience. Britain, he had implied, must go to war against Germany to protect its own interests and to uphold its honour against a country determined to trample this in the dust. He had judged that audience well. At the end of his speech he was wildly cheered and, by the time the Prime Minister, Herbert Asquith, walked from Downing Street to the House of Commons the next day to issue Britain's ultimatum to Germany, he, too, was loudly cheered by the waiting crowds who stood waving miniature Union Jacks. The hysteria that had been directed against Germany for over ten years had finally borne fruit. It was the assembled multitude of ordinary men and women, convinced that they were being called on to defend British honour and prestige against a treacherous and barbaric foe and not to defend France or Russia, who would drink its bitter brew.

---

CHRISTOPHER RAY is a writer and lecturer who has contributed to English historical journals.

# EXPLORING THE ISSUE

## Did Prussian Militarism Provoke World War I?

## Critical Thinking and Reflection

1. Briefly describe the sequence of events that ultimately led to World War I. At what point, in your view, did World War become truly inevitable? Critically discuss a possible "tipping point."
2. Critically examine the role this first explosion of the Balkan "powder keg" and the subsequent Versailles Peace Treaty that created Yugoslavia might have played in creating modern conflicts in this part of the world. Be specific in your evidence and explanation.
3. The war in Bosnia-Herzegovina could offer a rich area of research. Make a case for and against its roots in the events of World War I. Critically discuss.
4. Research and analyze the role that large land armies can play in the genesis of war. A debate on the potential risks versus benefits of having a large standing army could be an effective introduction to this part of the issue. Are there other, modern examples of large standing armies being drawn into conflicts?
5. Critically analyze the role of a militarist ideology in predisposing a nation to war. How powerful are ideologies in shaping the ways in which we see events? Give examples and counter examples.
6. Critically examine the role of public opinion in Britain in early August 1914. Why was it so strongly condemning Germany's plans to invade neutral Belgium? Can public opinion play a key role? Critically discuss.
7. Can you think of more recent examples of the role of public opinion in the United States either pushing the nation into war or demanding that the nation pull out of a war? Critically discuss.

## Is There Common Ground?

Analyzing and evaluating the responsibility for a war that involved so many nations and spread to all parts of the world, caused so much death and carnage, and led to results that may have led to another war more heinous than the first, is a daunting and complicated task. Each nation made its own decision and must share in the responsibility question. Germany may have been the prime mover, but others must share culpability. France sought revenge against Germany for the loss of the Franco-Prussian War of the 1870s. England felt her interests were threatened by a rising German superpower. Austria's aggressive policies against Serbia for the assassinations at Sarajevo could have played a role, as could Russia's military mobilization on Germany borders.

The most recent scholarship on the subject centers on England. In past analyses, she escaped culpability for the war. But as Christopher Ray points out in this issue, British public opinion could have forced Lord Gray's hand and led to a declaration of war. Two books—Christopher Clark's *The Sleepwalkers: How Europe Went to War in 1914* and Sean McMeekin's *July 1914: Countdown to War*, each published in 2013, suggest that World War I may have been a decade or more in the making and remind us that hereditary monarchs in Britain, Russia, and Germany were related by blood.

*Question:* Would you agree that a case might be made for many precipitating causes of World War I?

## Create Central

www.mhhe.com/createcentral

## Additional Resources

In *The Pity of War* (Basic Books, 1999), Scottish historian Niall Ferguson takes the revisionist viewpoint to a higher level. Arguing that the World War I was hardly inevitable, he claims that it was the British declaration of war that turned a continental conflict into a world war. He further argues that not only was Britain's participation in the war a colossal error, it was also counterproductive to the interests of the British nation and its people. He sees proof of this in the causes and results of World War II and the present condition of Great Britain.

Eminent British military historian John Keegan's *The First World War* (Alfred A. Knopf, 1999) may well prove to be the most widely read and influential volume on the Great War published in recent times. As a general work written with the utmost of skill, scholarship, and readability, it is a strongly recommended first choice selection. *World War I: A History* (Oxford University Press, 1998), edited by Hew Strachan, contains 23 chapters (each written by a different historian) that cover many aspects of the war from origins to memory and everything in between. William Jannen's *The Lions of July: Prelude to War, 1914* (Presidio Press, 1997) is an extremely readable account of Europe's last month of peace as its statesmen and military men blundered the continent into war.

Also, one should not forget the pioneering works of Fay and Fischer which have already been cited in the Issue Introduction. Both still ring with relevance today.

# Internet References . . .

### German Responsibility for the Outbreak of the War

Despite its title, the author of this lengthy essay-based website finds plenty of blame to go around. Its scope extends beyond the war itself to include its effect on the postwar decades. Also includes a World War I Document Archive.

**www.colby.edu/personal/r/rmscheck/ GermanyC1.html**

Selected, Edited, and with Issue Framing Material by:
Helen Buss Mitchell, *Howard Community College*
and
Joseph R. Mitchell, *Howard Community College*

# ISSUE

# Was the Treaty of Versailles Responsible for World War II?

**YES: Derek Aldcroft**, from "The Versailles Legacy," *History Today* (December 1997)

**NO: Mark Mazower**, from "Two Cheers for Versailles," *History Today* (July 1997)

---

## Learning Outcomes

**After reading this issue you should be able to:**

- Outline the key provisions of the Treaty of Versailles, dictated by the victorious allied powers—England, France, and Italy.
- Describe the alternative peace plan, offered by President Woodrow Wilson and the United States, a late entry (1917) in to the War on the allied side.
- Understand the roles played by English Prime Minister, David Lloyd George; French Premier, Georges Clemenceau; Italian Prime Minister, Vittorio Orlando; and U.S. President, Woodrow Wilson.
- Describe the League of Nations and its failure to ensure a lasting peace.

---

### ISSUE SUMMARY

**YES:** Historian Derek Aldcroft argues that a combination of the flaws present in the postwar Versailles Treaty and the resultant actions and inactions of European statesmen created a climate that paved the way for World War II.

**NO:** Historian Mark Mazower argues that, while the Treaty of Versailles contained weaknesses, it failed due to a lack of enforcement of its principles by a generation of European leaders.

---

The previous issue covered the causes of World War I and who was responsible for it. The war lasted 4 years and the loss of lives, property, and psychological well-being was staggering. Even before the war's end, statesmen were already making plans for the peace, which would follow. Not surprisingly, there were differences of opinion as to what shape that peace should take.

For the European allied powers—mainly England, France, and Italy—the answer was simple; Germany and its allies must be held accountable for their belligerence. In their minds this would include: accepting responsibility for the war, enduring a severe reduction in military forces to prevent future conflicts, making substantial reparation payments to its victims, and suffering substantial losses in territory and resources. All of these punitive measures would eventually result in the end of old empires and the subsequent creation of many new nations. Having suffered so much during the war, getting even and preventing future wars was all the allied powers could imagine coming out of the peace process.

The United States, also an allied power, had a different peace plan to offer. Entering the war in 1917, its sacrifices in life and property were minimal compared with those of its European allies. This allowed President Woodrow Wilson to propose a different type of peace. Describing it as "a peace without victory," Wilson urged his fellow allies to pursue a peace plan that would anger no nation, thus preventing future wars through its just settlement of the present one.

The cornerstone of Wilson's plan was the creation of an international congress of nations, which would meet regularly in order to ensure the absence of war and the continuance of peace. This was a radical proposal, the likes of which the world had never seen. However, when the war ended in 1918 and the allied nations convened in Paris to draw up the new peace plan, the defeated central powers were not invited. The Paris Peace Conference would be dominated by four men: English Prime Minister David Lloyd George, French Premier Georges Clemenceau, Italian Prime Minister Vittorio Orlando, and U.S. President Woodrow Wilson. The world's future was in their hands.

When the Paris Peace Conference began in 1919, it soon became clear that three of these men would be making the major decisions and each had specific provisions in mind. For France's Clemenceau the treaty had to ensure France's security; this would mean Germany's power had to be severely limited. Britain's Lloyd George's agenda contained reparations for war losses and the safety and maintenance of his nation's sprawling empire. U.S. President Woodrow Wilson's goals were more idealistic: the creation of an international organization whose purpose was to ensure world peace through diplomacy, not war. His most fervent hope—that the Treaty of Versailles not produce resentful nations that bore grudges against other nations—was frustrated. The defeated nations—Germany, Austria-Hungary, and Turkey—received what amounted to little more than a dictated document that they, as losers, were required to sign. So much for Wilson's dream of a peace without victory.

When the terms of the treaty were made public, the losers, especially Germany, were shocked at their vindictiveness. Germany was forced to pay reparations for war damages; the amount was eventually settled at $33 billion. Territorially, Germany lost all of its overseas colonies. On the European continent, Germany was forced to return the provinces of Alsace-Lorraine (taken during the Franco-Prussian War in 1871) to France. To protect France from future German aggression, the territory between them, referred to as the Rhineland, was to be demilitarized (free of military personnel and fortifications). To further limit Germany's ability to wage war, its army was reduced to 100,000 men; it was to be a volunteer army; no draft was allowed. Its navy was reduced to a small fleet and the building of submarines was forbidden.

Germany was also forced to cede other European lands to its neighbors. The newly created Poland received German territory that would allow that nation access to the Baltic Sea. When the new country of Czechoslovakia was created, German was also forced to cede some of its territory to the Czechs. All in all, Germany lost approximately 10 percent of its population and resources. In addition to all these losses, there was one final blow: Article 231 of the Treaty of Versailles forced Germany to accept full responsibility for the World War I.

Traditionally, it has been easy to speak ill of the Treaty of Versailles. Making Germany eager for revenge, paving the way for Adolf Hitler's rise to power, and creating inconsistent boundary lines drawn up by uninformed statesmen—all these provisions have been cited as evidence of the peace conference's weaknesses. And we now know what resulted from them. But, did the fault lie with a flawed treaty or with the actions and inactions of a generation of Europeans who were not up to the task of enforcing the treaty's provisions? Although the treaty created the League of Nations, that body proved incapable of using its power to enforce the treaty's provisions or to create a lasting peace. Sometimes institutions fail; sometimes individuals fail; oftentimes both share responsibility for the failures that occur.

The peace process had been marked by disagreements, debates, and eventual compromises. In the end, the Treaty of Versailles was a compromised document that satisfied no one. And within a generation of its passage, the world's nations were at war again, repeating the mistakes made by their elders a generation before.

Was the Treaty of Versailles responsible for World War II? Two historians offer differing opinions on this question. Derek Aldcroft contends that the treaty left major issues unresolved and left Germany bitter and resentful. The failure of the postwar leaders to deal with these issues exacerbated an already volatile situation. Mark Mazower offers a qualified endorsement of the Versailles Treaty, stating that it did a credible job and created a model world order under which Europe still lives today.

# YES ⤶

**Derek Aldcroft**

# The Versailles Legacy

**B**oth Sir Edward Grey and Maynard Keynes were remarkably perceptive about Europe's future in the aftermath of war. On the eve of hostilities the former commented: 'The lamps are going out all over Europe; we shall not see them lit again in our lifetime'. Keynes, in his vitriolic denunciation of the peace settlement with Germany, wrote as follows: 'The Treaty includes no provisions for the economic rehabilitation of Europe—nothing to make the defeated Central Empires into good neighbours, nothing to stabilise the new States of Europe, nothing to reclaim Russia; nor does it promote in any way a compact of economic solidarity amongst the Allies themselves; no arrangement was reached at Paris for restoring the disordered finances of France and Italy, or to adjust the systems of the Old World and the New'.

The war itself seriously weakened Europe both economically and politically and she never fully recaptured her former glory before a second conflagration occurred. However, while hostilities undoubtedly caused serious damage to the economic landscape, we shall argue here that it was what came afterwards that ultimately determined the fate of the Continent. It was primarily the actions of statesmen and policy-makers in the 1920s which were to blame for Europe's weakened state and which left her vulnerable to external shocks and exposed to internal collapse. The manner in which this happened can be illustrated by reference to the response to a number of key issues thrown up by the war and which failed to be resolved satisfactorily. These include (1) the reshaping of Europe; (2) the treatment of Germany; (3) relief and reconstruction; (4) international monetary stabilisation; and (5) the leadership issue.

## New States for Old Empires

Old Empires collapsed and fledgling states took their place in one of the biggest exercises in the reshaping of the boundaries of Europe ever undertaken. Even without a war there would no doubt have been some important changes in the map of Europe, since the Austro-Hungarian, Romanov and Turkish Empires were near the point of extinction. Hostilities speeded up the process and allowed nationalist groups to lay claim to territories out of which emerged several new or reconstituted states, many of which were confirmed by the Allied powers in the postwar settlement. The main problem was that in giving free reign to ethnic claims the European map came to resemble a patchwork mosaic which had no real coherence and which shattered the balance of power that had prevailed in the nineteenth century. The collapse of the Austro-Hungarian Empire, which had once been the bulwark between East and West, played into German hands since it left the way open for Germany, once she had recovered from the war, to further her aims of finding living space in the East. A serious vacuum emerged in Central/East Europe which the new states could never fill. With the partial exception of Czechoslovakia, which had done well out of the peace settlement, the new states were weak in every sense of the word. They were very backward economically, they lacked experience in parliamentary institutions, their administrations were poor and open to corruption, and despite the good intentions of the peacemakers they contained an assortment of different nationalities and religions, which inevitably gave rise to political and social tensions, while nationalist sentiments were rife. Even more significant was that most of them contained pockets of Germans anxious to unite with the mother country.

Thus by the early 1920s the European political and economic landscape had become decidedly fragmented and this effectively provided the breeding ground for the Second World War. Newman has no doubts about the crucial role of the region in determining the future distribution of power within Europe and ultimately the fate of the Continent. The new and reconstituted states, he says, were 'extremely weak reeds to place in the path of Germany, and they possessed few features that could lead to any hope of their being anything else but satellites . . . of Germany, Hitler or no Hitler'. The question is why Germany became the predator nation.

## The Path to German Hegemony in Europe

In theory any one of a number of European powers could conceivably have filled the vacuum in East/Central Europe: the possible contenders were Britain, France, Russia (Soviet Union), Italy and Germany. Britain ruled herself out since she regarded Europe with somewhat benign indifference and in any case her imperial interests took precedence.

France was too weak to play an effective role despite her machinations in the region. Russia had her own internal problems after the Bolshevik revolution in 1917, while Italy, much as Mussolini would have loved to pose as a world leader, was a non-starter. This left Germany and Germany had the resources, the motives and the ambition to lay claim to the East.

Though Germany lost the war and had to pay the price of a transgressor, she could by no means be written off as a great power. The country still had enormous potential and in fact emerged from the war as the strongest power on the continent. The collapse of the Austro-Hungarian Empire and the nationality principle in peacemaking served to strengthen her hand in Europe. For the first time the way was clear to gain space in the East.

The terms of the Versailles peace settlement provided the resolve to further her ambitions since it saddled Germany with what seemed to be iniquitous penalties. She lost significant amounts of territory and resources in Europe (including West Prussia which especially rankled) and overseas, she was saddled with a huge bill for reparations and a war guilt clause, while security provisions entailed demilitarisation and allied occupation of key zones in Germany.

This harsh treatment was no doubt understandable from the Allied point of view, especially by the French who had every reason to fear the worst if Germany was not successfully contained. Whether a more moderate settlement would have ensured a more compliant loser is a moot point. However, the fact is that the damage had been done and Germany harboured a burning resentment against the victors and was determined to secure revenge for such ignominious treatment by whittling down the original demands made upon her.

The crucial issue proved to be the reparations burden. Not only did it have important long-term political implications, but it provided the test case for demonstrating that Germany was not prepared to accept the treaty provisions without protest. Once she had achieved some measure of relaxation on this issue, it was only a matter of time before she gained other concessions.

The final reparations bill was presented in May 1921 in the famous London Schedule. It was a heavy but not an impossible burden, though there is still much debate on this issue. Prior to the final tally Germany had been making interim payments equivalent to some 10 per cent of her national income. However, the precise figures are less important than the fact that Germany perceived the burden to be unreal. Failing to secure any relief by verbal argument, the German government resorted to the printing press to prove their incapacity to pay, the results of which were one of the most spectacular inflations in history.

From the longer-term point of view it is the political consequences of the debacle that are the most significant, rather than the fact that Germany gained some concessions in the revised payment schedules under the Dawes Plan of 1924. The inflationary experience probably contributed more to the disintegration of democracy in Germany than any other factor. By destroying the savings of many middle-class citizens, it effectively undermined the bourgeois political consensus of Weimar Germany. In particular, the subsequent failure to implement a fair and equitable system of compensation for creditors who had borne the burden of inflation left many people extremely embittered and disenchanted with the Weimar regime, thereby resulting in 'a fundamental breakdown of voter identification with the traditional parties of bourgeois centre and right'. This led to the emergence of splinter parties composed of interest groups, shifting voter preferences and political instability. Ultimately it was the extreme right which became the major beneficiary of the alienated middle groups who were the chief losers from inflation. Estimates suggest that members of the Mittelstand (which included the bulk of the former creditors) accounted for a very substantial part of the Nazi Party's electoral support.

## The Reconstruction Fiasco

Curiously, the Allied powers, having carved up Europe to almost no one's satisfaction, did little to ensure the viability of the new configuration. It was recognised that German recovery was important for the future prosperity of Europe, though initially the Allies did their best to suppress it. It was also recognised, especially by the French, that security was equally important but again little was done to secure it. However, arguably the most urgent task initially was that of ensuring the viability of the smaller and weaker states.

Apart from famine and relief deliveries in the immediate post-war period, which proved totally inadequate, there was never any serious attempt to plan the reconstruction of Europe. The United States had no desire to get embroiled in European affairs on a permanent basis, while Allied cooperation disintegrated soon after the ending of hostilities, partly because of Anglo-American rivalry. Hence relief aid, most of which came from the United States, was sharply curtailed after the summer of 1919. To make matters worse, the sharp boom in commodity prices of 1919–20, followed by deflationary policies in the Anglo-Saxon countries, added to the difficulties of war-torn Europe.

Thus the new states of Europe were left to fend for themselves and desperate conditions called forth desperate remedies, including trade control, inflation and currency depreciation. Inflationary financing of budgetary deficits became a convenient way of easing the task of reconstruction in the short-term, since it gave a boost to economic activity and employment which was paid for by a tax on people's cash balances. Whether the benefits outweighed the costs is a debatable point given the fact that when stabilisation finally occurred employment and output were checked, while many creditors lost their savings. It is significant that by the mid-1920s industrial output in many countries was still well below the 1913 level, while the one country that showed solid advance was Czechoslovakia, which had stabilised her currency and eliminated inflation at an early date.

Moreover, the drastic measures did little to solve the fundamental economic problems of the successor states and in fact they may well have weakened their political viability. The League of Nations in one of its later reports explained how the economic and social fabric of many countries was allowed to rot away and when it was finally faced, it had ceased to be a general problem of transition and reconstruction and had become a problem of cutting the gangrene out of the most affected areas. Reconstruction in fact had to start afresh once stabilisation was achieved and this time it was dependent on private foreign lending. This in turn added to the instability of the region: growing debt burdens at a time of weakening commodity prices eventually spelled disaster in the early 1930s.

## The International Monetary System

International currency matters exercised the minds of statesmen continually during the 1920s and beyond. The pre-war gold standard, on which so much faith had been placed, disintegrated during the war and there was no plan to devise a new system as occurred in the closing stages of the Second World War. Once wartime control was removed most currencies depreciated sharply against the dollar, now the strongest currency unit, and for the next few years the exchanges in Europe 'danced and jumped with tireless and spasmodic energy'.

On one point there was fairly universal agreement: that stabilisation of exchanges and a return to the gold standard were essential for trade revival and world prosperity. Yet despite several resolutions to this effect at international conferences in the early 1920s, no plan for coordinated action ever materialised. The result was that countries stabilised their currencies and returned to gold as and when it best suited them and largely without reference to the relative changes in costs and prices that had occurred since the war began. Inevitably therefore, restoration was a piecemeal affair with countries stabilising their exchanges throughout the decade at different dates and at different parities relative to pre-war rates. Britain, the Netherlands, Switzerland and the Scandinavian countries regained their pre-war parities, Austria, Germany, Hungary, Poland and Russia introduced new currency units after the old ones had become worthless through hyper-inflation, France, Belgium and Italy stabilised at one quarter to one fifth of their pre-war values, while other countries adopted even more devalued rates.

What materialised was a largely unworkable system of exchange rates, since so few were in equilibrium from the start. As the League of Nations commented:

'The piecemeal and haphazard manner of international monetary reconstruction sowed the seeds of subsequent disintegration. It was partly because of the lack of proper co-ordination during the stabilization period of the Twenties that the system broke down in the Thirties'. The pre-war parity countries had overvalued currencies, as did Italy, while France and Belgium had undervalued rates. No fixed exchange rate system can work satisfactorily when currencies are seriously misaligned; the essential feature of the pre-war system was that rates of exchange, among the major countries at least, were for the most part in equilibrium. Moreover, under the pre-war system there was a fair degree of harmony in rates of development and costs and price structures between countries, so that few really serious pressures emerged. This balance no longer prevailed post-war, due to the differential impact of war on European economies and the distortions caused by inflation and inter-country debts, among other things.

There were other factors making for a less effective international monetary system. The dispersion of leadership among three main financial centres (London, New York and Paris, whereas before 1914 Britain's hegemonic role had been important in orchestrating the system) was one important factor. In addition, failure to abide by the rules of the game, the increasing reluctance of countries to sacrifice domestic stability on the altar of the exchanges, and the greater volume and volatility of short-term capital movements between financial centres, all added to the problem.

The resurrected gold standard was not of course the prime cause of the Great Depression of the early 1930s. But, once begun, the links forged by the fixed exchange rate mechanism helped to transmit recessionary forces from one country to another. Some countries removed the constraint by going off gold and devaluing at an early date, but this only made things worse for the countries remaining on gold. Initially many countries were reluctant to abandon it for fear of the inflationary consequences, with recollections of the first half of the 1920s close to hand, and this in turn conditioned their policy reaction to the depression. In fact it was those countries which avoided inflation and returned to gold at the pre-war parity that were less averse to breaking the links with this system. Britain's departure in September 1931 effectively spelled the beginning of the end of the gold standard since many other countries followed suit, culminating in America's departure in 1933. By then only a few diehard countries such as France, Belgium, the Netherlands and Switzerland clung to gold, but they were forced to relinquish it by the middle of the decade.

## The Leadership Issue and the Role of the United States

The European settlement as it emerged in the course of the 1920s had two main defects: it did not satisfy anyone, and it lacked firm leadership. France, Germany and Italy, for different reasons, were extremely disgruntled—France over compensation and the security issue, Germany because of the harsh treatment inflicted on her by the victors, and Italy as a result of unfulfilled promises of territory for joining the war. None of these countries was willing to promote the European cause. The remnants of the Austro-Hungarian Empire and the new and reconstituted states each in their turn had their grievances, all of which led to fragmentation rather than unity. This left Russia and Britain. The former, not having been invited to the Paris Peace Conference, was not particularly happy with the territorial arrangements arising from the peace settlement; but in any case her exclusion policy and domestic problems precluded her from playing a European role of any significance. And even when she did at a later date it took the form of clandestine communist infiltration into East European countries. Britain, the one country which might have been in a position to take an active role, was more concerned with her imperial connections, which meant that she preferred to view the affairs of Europe with benign indifference when it suited her to do so. The independence of the new states was welcomed so long as it did not involve active intervention. The attitude was summed up by the British Foreign Secretary (Simon) in a communication to the Prime Minister (MacDonald) in July 1934 over the question of Austria: 'Our policy is quite clear. We must keep out of trouble in Central Europe at all costs. . . . There are circumstances in which Italy might move troops into Austria. There are no circumstances in which we would ever dream of doing so'. In fact a year later Simon was of the view that the ramshackle regime was only worth tolerating 'for fear of meeting something worse'.

The result of this fissiparous tendency, in contrast to the situation after 1945, was that competitive national sovereignties dominated the scene in the 1920s to such an extent that there was little prospect of achieving unity and stability in Europe.

The question is why did America not take over the European mantle and reshape the destiny of Europe as she was to do after the Second World War? America's entry into the war and Woodrow Wilson's grandiose designs for Europe initially augured well for the future. Yet the United States was subsequently to play a very equivocal role in the affairs of Europe. She refused to ratify the Versailles Treaty, failed to endorse the League of Nations, abandoned the relief of Europe with almost indecent haste, and rejected proposals to link reparations and interallied war debts. Moreover, though America professed a belief in the importance of European recovery, her own economic policy often ran counter to the interests of European countries, for example on matters of tariffs, immigration, overseas lending and monetary policy. It is true that her attitude towards Germany was more lenient than that of either Britain or France, but this only served to antagonise the French since it offered little in the way of security against a recalcitrant Germany.

America's isolationist approach towards Europe has to be seen within the context of her domestic politics. The United States had entered the war reluctantly in April 1917. After the conclusion of hostilities there was a wave of revulsion against war and military activity, together with an unwillingness to get involved in the affairs of other countries which might lead to further conflict. This largely explains why the United States found herself in such a low state of military preparedness at the outbreak of the Second World War. The United States also felt remote from the European scene, both geographically and politically, and her own domestic interests were affected only marginally by what happened in Europe. Unlike the situation after the Second World War, America did not perceive any immediate power threat from Europe, and though European recovery was regarded as intrinsically important it was never seen as crucial to her own well-being. Thus, when it suited her own needs, the United States could afford to turn a blind eye to the problems of Europe, especially as these seemed likely to entail direct involvement in the affairs of that continent. America's refusal to assume a hegemonic role had several unfortunate consequences. It meant first of all, that certain aspects of the post-war settlement, such as reparations and territorial rights, emerged as international issues. Secondly, it left Europe stranded in the early and later 1920s when American credits ceased to flow. For a time private benefaction in the form of international lending emerged to fill the gap, but over which there was little control. As Hogan comments: 'The toothless loan control programme left the American government with no way to ensure that capital exports really contributed to recovery'. Thirdly, it robbed Europe of the leadership it so badly needed in the 1920s, especially with regard to currency stabilisation. Finally, the absence of US backing meant that the League of Nations played a diminutive role in the affairs of Europe. Apart from its work in rescuing several countries on the point of disintegration, perhaps its most lasting contribution was the large number of papers and documents it produced for the benefit of later historians.

## Conclusion

Cleaning up after a major war is always a messy business. Unfortunately the Allied statesmen did not do a very good job in the aftermath of the First World War. Had the Allied powers made a more concerted effort to provide for the reconstruction and stability of Europe, things might have turned out differently. As it was Europe remained in a fragile state both politically and economically and hence was unable to withstand later shocks. The Allies themselves were divided on many issues and it was all too easy therefore for nations to plough their own furrow with little regard for the greater good of Europe as a whole. Sovereignty rights and national issues counted for more than the sum of the parts. As Ross noted, 'There were few good Europeans'.

**DEREK ALDCROFT** is a research professor in economic history at Manchester Metropolitan University, London, and the author of *Europe in the International Economy, 1500–2000* (Edward Elgar Publishers, 2003).

Mark Mazower  **NO**

# Two Cheers for Versailles

Some suggest that Versailles was based on principles inconsistently applied. The charge is obviously true. The right of national self-determination was granted at Germany's expense, and the Anschluss with Austria, which Social Democrats in Vienna wanted in 1918, was prevented by the Great Powers and only achieved after the Nazis broke the League of Nations system and marched in twenty years later. But international affairs are not a matter of logic alone, and the principle of consistency must be matched against considerations of power politics or geography. National self-determination could never have been applied across the board; the basic issue is whether a better principle existed for the re-ordering of Europe.

More serious an accusation is that the peace settlement was not so much inconsistent as ineffective: it was based upon an inaccurate appraisal of the European balance of power and deprived of the means of its own defence by American withdrawal and British indifference. At Paris the Great Powers ignored the fact that the almost simultaneous collapse of Germany and Russia had produced an anomalous situation in Eastern Europe. The French, who of all the Great Powers felt most immediately threatened, thought the only safeguard of their own security—if the League was not to be equipped with an army of its own—was alliance with grateful clients like the Baltic states, Poland, Czechoslovakia, Romania and Yugoslavia. But it should have been obvious that the newly independent states formed there would be unable alone to ensure stability in the region once these two Great Powers reasserted themselves. The Treaty of Brest Litovsk of early 1918 had shown what intentions the Germans of the Kaiserreich harboured in that area; after 1939, Hitler's New Order pushed the principle of German (and Russian) hegemony one brutal stage further. But this is less an argument against the Versailles settlement itself than against the refusal of the Great Powers who sponsored it to back it up with armed force before 1939.

It is often felt that the whole approach to Germany after the Treaty was flawed. The enemy was humiliated but not crushed, burdened by reparations yet unopposed when it rearmed and marched into the Rhineland. It is true that the contrast is striking with the policies pursued towards Germany after the Second World War when long-term economic assistance was provided and by governments not the

markets, and when the Bundeswehr was quickly incorporated within West European defence arrangements. But the economic problem after 1919 was not so much reparations as the shaky structure of international lending and, in particular, the shock of the world depression. The Allies were helped to learn from the mistakes of the inter-war era by the Cold War, which divided Germany, and made Europe's German problem a question of reunification rather than of territorial expansion and revanche in the East.

Finally, there is the accusation common to conservatives and Communists alike that the Versailles peace settlement was overly ideological. For some, it was an extension of nineteenth-century liberal moralising, a combination of British utilitarianism and American idealism—a basically philosophical approach to the world which lacked realism or understanding of the political passions which animated people in Europe.

Alternatively, it was—behind the veil of noble sentiments—an anti-Communist crusade whose liberalism masked a fundamentally reactionary and deeply conservative goal: the containment, if not the crushing, of Bolshevism. Outflanked gradually by other more determined and forceful anti-Communist movements of the right, European liberals lost their enthusiasm for defending the Versailles order and sat back to watch fascism take over the task of saving Europe from red revolution.

One question, however, confronts the critics of Versailles: what were the alternatives? It was not, after all, as if the Powers had willed this new liberal order of independent, democratic nation-states into existence. They had certainly not been fighting the Great War to this end. On the contrary, as late as 1918 most Entente diplomats still favoured the preservation of the old empires in Central Europe in the interests of continental stability. Of course, after 1919 the conflicts and tensions produced by the new states of the region made many people nostalgic for what the Austrian writer Stefan Zweig, looking back to the Habsburg era, called 'the world of yesterday'. Fragmentation since the war seemed to have harmed the region both politically and economically, especially once the world depression forced countries into an impoverished self-sufficiency.

Yet it was a rare blend of nostalgia and realpolitik which lay behind much of the antipathy to Versailles. The makers of America's new role in Europe after 1945, for example,

Mazower, Mark. From *History Today*, vol. 49, issue 7, July 1999, pp. 8–14. Copyright © 1999 by History Today, Ltd. Reprinted by permission. References omitted.

who had grown up looking closely at these problems, held Versailles responsible for the instability of inter-war Europe. Adolf Berle, Roosevelt's assistant secretary of state between 1938 and 1944, believed that French generals had been responsible for breaking up the Austro-Hungarian Empire and wanted some kind of reconstitution of that entity to ward off the Russians. Hitler, he advised the president on the eve of Munich, was perhaps 'the only instrument capable of re-establishing a race and economic unit which can survive and leave Europe in balance'.

George Kennan, a younger man but more influential than Berle in defining the Cold War policy of containment, took a very similar view in the late 1930s. In his despatches from Prague he wrote:

> It is generally agreed that the breakup of the limited degree of unity which the Habsburg Empire represented was unfortunate for all concerned. Other forces are now at work which are struggling to create a new form of unity. . . . To these forces Czechoslovakia has been tragically slow in adjusting herself. . . . The adjustment—and this is the main thing—has now come.

It did not take long for someone as astute as Kennan to realise that the Nazi New Order was not going to stabilise Central Europe in the way the Habsburgs had done. But the reason for this, in his mind, was not the apparently obvious one that Hitler's whole upbringing had turned him into a German nationalist critic of the Austro-Hungarian monarchy. It was, rather, what Kennan conceived as the excessively democratic character of Hitler's Germany and the limited involvement of Germany's aristocracy in the Third Reich. More aristocratic government was Kennan's answer to Europe's problems. It is hard to imagine a more far-fetched or unrealistic approach—the Habsburgs were marginalised between the wars even by Hungary's reactionary regent Admiral Horthy, and the most successful Habsburg aristocrat of that era was the bizarre and premature proponent of European union, Count Coudenhove-Kalergi. Perhaps only an American conservative intellectual like Kennan could have taken the prospect of a Habsburg restoration seriously. European conservatives, closer to the ground, had fewer illusions. 'The Vienna to Versailles period has run its course', wrote the historian Lewis Namier in February 1940.

Whatever the weaknesses of the system created in 1919, a return to previous forms is impossible. They have been broken, and broken for good.

It was not aristocrats that had kept the old empires together but dynastic loyalty, and this had vanished. If dynasticism no longer offered an alternative principle to the Versailles order, then what of the rival ideologies of right and left? This was where root-and-branch critics of Versailles had to bite the bullet. Most anti-Communists between the wars had no difficulty in swallowing the idea of an authoritarian revision of the Versailles settlement. What made them hesitate was a quite different proposition;

the reality of life under the Nazi New Order. The difference between a right tolerable to most conservatives and an extreme and ideological fascism was that, for instance, between King Alexander's royal dictatorship in Yugoslavia, and Ante Pavelic's genocidal Ustase state in Croatia, or between King Carol's Romania and that of the Iron Guard, with its bloody pogroms, in the winter of 1940–41. Above all, the New Order was based on the idea of German racial superiority, and few anti-Communists could stomach this once they saw what it meant in terms of practical politics.

If one agreed with Namier that 'no system can possibly be maintained on the European Continent east of the Rhine which has not the support either of Germany or of Russia', then the only ideological alternative to Nazism was Communism, or more precisely the extension of Russian rule westwards into Europe. Just as Versailles's critics on the right had seen Germany's move east after 1933 as confirmation of their own prejudices, so critics on the left similarly interpreted the course of events after 1943 as a happy necessity. Historians like E.H. Carr saw this as realism replacing the idealism of Versailles. It was apparently not felt to be realistic to point out that all the historical evidence pointed to the unpopularity of Communism among the majority of the populations who now had to endure it. In only one country in Central Europe, Hungary, had a Bolshevik regime held power for any length of time before 1945, and that still brief experience—the Bela Kun regime of 1919—had only confirmed how unpropitious the soil was for such experiments. Today we are unlikely to see Communism as an attractive alternative to the principles embodied in the Versailles order: yesterday's 'realism' looks riddled with its own form of wishful thinking.

One of the reasons Bela Kun fell from power in 1919 was that he had not understood the strength of Hungarian nationalist feeling. So long as it had appeared to Hungarians that Bolshevik Russia might help them get back their traditional lands, they were prepared to tolerate Kun. But once it appeared that the Allies would not let this happen, Kun lost any popularity he had once enjoyed and he was easily defeated. The power of nationalism was the chief force to emerge from the First World War in Europe, and was the main political factor facing the architects of a new post-war settlement. From our perspective at the century's end, it hardly looks as though fascism and Communism were able to handle European nationalism better than the peacemakers at Versailles. Hitler's New Order proceeded by ignoring all nationalisms except the German, and lost Europe in consequence. Communism believed that eventually nationalist antipathies would vanish, subsumed within an internationalist struggle: but time ran out for the Communists before this happened. If we want to find guidance in the past for how to tackle the problems of nationalism that remain in Europe, we cannot do better than return to the diplomats who gathered in Paris eighty years ago.

In the Bukovina (a former province of the Habsburg Empire), Paris seemed very far away in the spring of 1919.

But events were occurring there which help us chart the trajectory of antisemitic violence from the unorganised pogroms of the nineteenth century to the more systematic population engineering of the twentieth. A manifesto was posted up in the village of Kamenestie, written in Romanian:

> Order to all the Jews in the village.
> Those Jews who are still in the village are asked to go to the city or somewhere else. You can leave in good condition [sic] and without fear in ten days. It will be made unbearable for those who stay beyond the limit.

Throughout the little villages of the Bukovina, pogroms were taking place in late 1918. 'Following the example of the neighbouring villages', runs an account from Petroutz,

> The peasants decided to drive the Jews out of this place. On the night of November 17th, they attacked the Jewish families Hermann, Feller and Schubert, broke doors and windows and took away everything they found. A scroll of the Law was torn to pieces by the marauders. After the robbery they burned everything that remained. All three families fled to Suczawa.

The Jews were the chief targets of ethnic violence in the Bukovina, as they were elsewhere in Eastern Europe, in Galicia for instance, or in Lithuania. But the war of nationalities could not be reduced to antisemitism: Poles were fighting with Ukrainians, Germans and Lithuanians. Across much of Europe there fell, a double shadow: ethnic as well as class war. Bolshevism was contained by a combination of land reform, reformist social democracy and the military defeat of the Red Army in the Russo-Polish war. But the nationalist enmities and suspicions which exploded into violence as the First World War ended, and which generated casualties on such a scale that some historians have compared them with the violence which erupted under Nazi rule after 1941, these proved harder to tackle.

Ethnic civil war emphasised in the most unmistakable way that the peacemakers in Paris were not sketching their maps on a tabula rasa. On the contrary, they were as much responding to circumstances as shaping them. East European critics of Great Power arrogance often forget today how far the Versailles settlement was brought into being, not by the Powers, but by local nationalist elites and their supporters. New nations were pressing their claims on paper, in the streets and by force of arms, as the war approached an end. Serb, Croat and Slovene delegates issued the Corfu Declaration in July 1917 and declared the new tripartite Yugoslav nation 'a worthy member of the new Community of Nations'.

The Provisional People's Government of the Polish Republic proclaimed 'the authority of Polish democracy' in its November 1918 manifesto. The Czech National Committee seized power in Prague as early as October 28th of the same year in the name of the infant Czechoslovak state. Much of the subsequent fighting from the Baltic to the Balkans was designed to conquer as much territory as possible for the new states, to see off rival claimants and to settle scores with Jews, Germans, Muslims and other hated, despised or feared peoples. Between 1920 and 1923, the Treaty of Sèvres was signed, scrapped and replaced by the Treaty of Lausanne as the struggle between Greece and Turkey shifted first one way then the other, culminating eventually in the forced population exchange of some two million people.

It is to the credit of the Versailles peacemakers that they confronted the problem of ethnic violence head on. They were aware of the chief defect of the Wilsonian principle of national self-determination—namely that if it was interpreted territorially and not merely as a grant of cultural autonomy, then on its own it ruled out either an equitable or a geographically coherent settlement of the problems of Central and Eastern Europe. No one, after all, was proposing to give the Kashubians, the Polesians, the Pomaks, or any of the other small ethnic groups of the region a state of their own. They, and several other larger peoples like the Jews, the Ukrainians and the Macedonians, would remain under the rule of others. In other words, the creation—or better, the recognition—of nation-states at Versailles was accompanied by its inescapable shadow, the problem of minorities.

Fearful in particular that Poland's appetite for territory might destabilise the whole area, the Powers obliged the reluctant Poles to sign a treaty granting the country's very sizeable minority population certain rights. The Polish treaty formed the basis for a series of similar treaties imposed in 1919 and 1920 upon most of the states of Central and Eastern Europe. The result was that for the first time an international organisation—the League of Nations—assumed the right to intervene in a member state's internal affairs on behalf of minority populations.

This right, however, was very limited and scarcely used at all by the League. Most countries feared doing away with the idea that a state was sovereign within its own borders, and even the Great Powers who had sponsored the Minority Rights Treaties trod warily. They had resisted calls to universalise the regime of minority rights on the grounds that 'the League cannot assume to guarantee good government in this matter throughout the world'. By 1929 they were very reluctant to act at all against member states accused of rights violations. British foreign secretary Austen Chamberlain warned that,

> We have not reached such a degree of solidarity in international affairs that any of us welcome even the most friendly intervention in what we consider to be our domestic affairs.

This attitude discouraged the most dynamic lobbyists for Europe's minorities, the Germans and the Jews. Until

1933, they worked together in the European Congress of Nationalities to try to give the Minorities' Treaties teeth. Thereafter their paths diverged. But Hitler's rise to power can be seen in the context of the failure of the League to protect Europe's minorities. Where the League's rather timid use of international law had failed, the Nazis used force; their 'solution' involved forced population transfer, resettlement and ultimately genocide. And after 1944 many of these instruments were turned on the Germans themselves as they were driven out of Poland and the former Habsburg lands.

Yet we should not write off the peacemakers of Versailles too quickly. Despite the horrors of the 1940s, which virtually eliminated both the Jews and the Germans from much of Eastern Europe, many minorities remained across the region. However, instead of building on the League's tentative efforts to construct an international regime of minority rights, the architects of the post-war order enshrined in the United Nations deliberately retreated from the problem and tried to dress up its reluctance to deal with it with meaningless persiflage about 'human rights'. As a result, when issues of minority rights came to the fore after the collapse of Communism in Eastern Europe in the decade after 1989, most obviously in the context of the disintegration of Yugoslavia, the international community possessed no coherent strategy for tackling the problem.

The consequences have been all too visible in Bosnia and Kosovo. The United Nations was less equipped to tackle the fundamental problem of minority rights than its predecessor, the League, had been. It delivered food and tried to keep the peace without a clear doctrine of what kind of peace it should keep. The contrast between the self-confident and articulate liberal universalism of the 1920s and the post-modern evasions of the 1990s was all too conspicuous. In Kosovo, too, the contrast with the Versailles generation does not flatter our own times. NATO intervention in Kosovo could, as articulated somewhat optimistically by Tony Blair, be interpreted as marking a new doctrine of foreign affairs, according to which state sovereignty may be overridden to prevent massive violations of minority rights. Yet, NATO's attacks on the Serbs, in the absence of any UN mandate, do not indicate any great confidence in international law and institutions. The United States, which has been leading the charge, is, after all, opposed to the creation of an International Criminal Court. If inter-war Europe suffered because international guarantees were never acted upon, we may suffer in the 1990s through military action taken without any reference to international law at all, the late twentieth-century equivalent of gunboat diplomacy handled by a post-Holocaust generation of politicians.

The very least, then, that we can say for Versailles is that it recognised and articulated the major problems for European stability at that time. What was more, there was no palatable alternative to the nation-state then, or since. Where the peace was found wanting between the wars was in the will to uphold it. Today NATO is turning itself into the kind of force which the peacemakers of 1919 lacked. But do its political masters have a clear grasp of what kind of Europe they wish to defend? They could do worse than cast their eyes back to the work of their predecessors eighty years ago. . . .

---

**MARK MAZOWER,** a professor of history at Birbeck College, University of London, and Columbia University, is the author of *Dark Continent: Europe's Twentieth Century* (Vintage, 1998).

# EXPLORING THE ISSUE

## Was the Treaty of Versailles Responsible for World War II?

## Critical Thinking and Reflection

1. Do you believe that the International Congress of Nations, proposed at Versailles by President Wilson, laid the foundation for the United Nations? Critically discuss.
2. Examine historian Derek Aldcroft's assertion that, having left major issues unresolved and Germany bitter and resentful, Versailles paved the way for World War II. Critically discuss.
3. Examine historian Mark Mazower's claim that Versailles, despite its flaws, created a model world order under which Europe lives today. Critically discuss this claim.
4. What evidence does each of these historians use to support his thesis? Is the evidence based on fact, deduction, anecdotal example, statistical data, or other data? Which of these types of evidence do you find more persuasive? Critically discuss.
5. Many historians fault Versailles for creating conditions that made possible Hitler's rise to power. What evidence for this charge do you find in the YES and NO selections? Critically discuss.
6. Research the League of Nations, established by Europeans after World War I. Did it have the potential to prevent the World War II? Why did it fail? Critically discuss.
7. If the United States had joined the League of Nations, would this have made a difference? Why did the Senate fail to ratify this treaty? Research and critically discuss.

## Is There Common Ground?

Europe's history has been marked by postwar treaties that have placed their stamp upon the generations that followed: the Peace of Augsburg (1555), which temporarily ended the continent's religious wars; the Peace of Utrecht in 1713, which stopped French King Louis XIV's domination of Europe; the 1815 Congress of Vienna, which brought an end to Napoleon's domination of Europe and established a new continental governing order; and the Treaty of Versailles in 1919, which marked the end of the World War I. One thing all these treaties had in common was that the peace they brought was only temporary. Some comparative research into these attempts at peace might produce an interesting discussion or debate.

Research the League of Nations, established by Europeans after World War I. Did it have the potential to prevent a second world war? Why did it fail? If the United States had joined (the U.S. Senate refused to ratify the treaty), would this have made a difference?

*Question:* What hints do you find in both the YES and NO selections that point the way by showing agreement

on errors that could have been avoided? Statesmen, both historians agree, would have overseen the reconstruction and stabilization of Europe.

## Create Central

www.mhhe.com/createcentral

## Additional Resources

For sources on the Treaty of Versailles, see John Maynard Keynes, *The Economic Consequences of the Peace* (Vintage Classics, 1995), written by a man who was a member of the British delegation to the Paris Peace Conference, but eventually resigned to show his disgust and disapproval for its process and results. His book is a classic in the field. More recently, Manfred F. Boemeke, Gerald D. Feldman, and Elizabeth Glaser, eds., *The Treaty of Versailles: A Reassessment after 75 Years* (Cambridge University Press, 1998) provide a more balanced account of the Treaty of Versailles' strengths and weaknesses.

## Internet References . . .

### The Treaty of Versailles

This site contains extensive background on the Treaty of Versailles, beginning with the attitude toward Germany of the "Big Three," the actual terms of the treaty, Germany's reaction to the treaty, the consequences of

Versailles, and other peace settlements with Austria, Hungary, Bulgaria, and Turkey. Exam questions on the peace settlement are included.

**www.historylearningsite.co.uk/treaty_of_versailles.htm**

Selected, Edited, and with Issue Framing Material by:
**Helen Buss Mitchell**, *Howard Community College*
**and**
**Joseph R. Mitchell**, *Howard Community College*

# ISSUE

# Did the Bolshevik Revolution Improve the Lives of Soviet Women?

**YES: Richard Stites**, from "The Russian Revolution and Women," in Marilyn J. Boxer and Jean H. Quartaert, eds., *Connecting Spheres: Women in the Western World, 1500 to the Present* (Oxford University Press, 1987)

**NO: Lesley A. Rimmel**, from "The Baba and the Comrade: Gender and Politics in Revolutionary Russia," *The Women's Review of Books* (September 1998)

---

## Learning Outcomes

**After reading this issue you should be able to:**

- Explain the changes to agrarian Russia brought about by the Bolshevik Revolution of 1917—the shift from 300 years of domination by the Romanov dynasty and the Orthodox Church.
- Enumerate the legal rights granted to Russian women, when they became "workers" first, as participants in a socialist revolution.
- Describe the theory and reality of the Zhenotdel or Women's Department of the Communist Party and the role it played, especially in the early years of the revolution.
- Describe the effects of the Stalinist takeover in the 1930s.

---

### ISSUE SUMMARY

**YES:** Former history professor Richard Stites argues that in the early years of the Bolshevik Revolution the Zhenotdel or Women's Department helped many working women take the first steps toward emancipation.

**NO:** Russian scholar Lesley A. Rimmel argues that the Russian Revolution remains unfinished for women, who were mobilized as producers and reproducers for a male political agenda.

Compared with life under the czars, life for women after the Bolshevik Revolution was certainly characterized by greater variety and freedom. The Romanov dynasty had ruled Russia for 300 years and the Orthodox Church for a much longer period. Both had reinforced a world of patriarchal authority, class structure, and patterns of deference. While the revolution overthrew the power of both church and monarch, the new communist state had a power and authority of its own. Between 1917 and 1920 Soviet women received equal rights in education and marriage, including the choice to change or keep their own names and the opportunity to own property, the rights to vote and hold public office, access to no-fault divorce, common law marriage, maternity benefits, workplace protection, and access to unrestricted abortion. They were the first to gain these rights, ahead of women in France, England, and the United States, but the question is whether these legal rights translated into improvement in their day-to-day lives.

A feminist movement had developed in urban areas as early as the 1905 workers' revolution and women joined men in leading strikes and protest demonstrations. By the time of the Bolshevik Revolution in 1917, however, the goals of the leadership were primarily economic, and feminism was dismissed as bourgeois or middle class. In a workers' revolution, women and men were to be equal. Housework and child care were to be provided collectively, and the family, like the monarchy, was to be replaced with something new. Giving women access to economic independence, by making them workers, was supposed to provide them the basis for equality within marriage.

Karl Marx had argued that the family reflects the economic system in society. Under capitalism, the bourgeois family exists to reproduce workers and consumers; it exploits women by unfairly burdening them with full responsibility for housework and child care. If similarly exploited workers, what Marx called the proletariat, overthrew the capitalist system that allowed factory owners to grow rich from their workers' labor, Marx believed the family would undergo an equally dramatic transformation. No one would be "owned" by anyone else. Prostitution would disappear and, as the state took responsibility for childrearing and education, women would be free to work and become economically self-sufficient. People would then be free to marry for love or sexual attraction rather than economic considerations.

The man who emerged as leader and architect of the new order, V.I. Lenin, was committed to women's rights. First and foremost, however, he was committed to a socialist revolution. When the struggle to make legal changes in women's lives came into conflict with the goals of the revolution, there was no question about which would have to be sacrificed. In this early period, a fascinating group of women briefly held highly visible leadership positions and had the chance to put their ideas into practice, at least during the first decade. Alexandra Kollontai was one of the most articulate and effective leaders of the Zhenotdel, or Women's Department of the Communist Party, whose purpose between 1919 and 1930 was to educate and mobilize the women of the Soviet state to participate fully in the revolution.

Former Georgetown University historian Richard Stites focuses on what he calls the "idealistic foreground" of the revolution—the part this is so often overlooked. Although poverty, cynicism, bureaucratic resistance, rural superstition, and urban blight ultimately thwarted many early dreams of reformers such as Alexandra Kollontai, bold efforts undertaken by the Zhenotdel and experiments in sexual equality raised the consciousness of women and men. A brief glimpse of what might be possible in a stable society kept the dreams and experiments alive—at least for a time, Stites concludes. The work of Zhenotdel as an official arm of the Party during its brief 11-year existence was able to improve significantly the lives of Soviet women especially in the cities. However, as Stites points out, its abolition in 1930 reveals that political equality for women had not yet been achieved.

Russian scholar Lesley Rimmel uses the contrasting images of the *baba*—an ignorant peasant woman—and the comrade—a full-fledged human and citizen, to describe how Russian women were targeted as workers in a class revolution while gender roles remained firmly in place. Rimmel sees the long-delayed gender goals, articulated during the Russian Revolution, including the right of women to define comradeship on their own terms, as finally being addressed in contemporary Russia. Although Soviet women were granted unprecedented legal rights, almost without a struggle, the real task was to translate these rights into a new way of life.

It is one of history's ironies that Soviet women were granted, with the stroke of a pen, all the legal and political rights that women in Britain and the United States were struggling to achieve. First to win the rights to vote and hold public office, Soviet women struggled to translate those paper rights into improved lives for themselves and their children. It has been a conviction of Western feminism that legal and political equality pave the way for full emancipation of women. The Soviet case raises interesting questions about the confusion that arises when there are conflicting revolutions. Real political power belongs to those who can assure the goals of their revolution receive first priority. It was the socialist revolution, not women's emancipation, that the party leadership worked to achieve.

Popular accounts of the Russian Revolution may be found in John Reed's *Ten Days That Shook the World* (Penguin, 1977) and *Louise Bryant's Mirrors of Moscow* (Hyperion Press, 1973). The story of Reed and Bryant, two Americans who find themselves eyewitnesses to the Bolshevik Revolution, is captured in the film *Reds*. Another film covering the same period is *Doctor Zhivago*, which is based on the book of the same title by Boris Pasternak (1958). For Lenin's views on women, one of the best sources is his book *The Emancipation of Women* (International Publishers, 1972). *The Unknown Lenin: From the Secret Archives*, edited by the eminent Russian historian Richard Pipes (Yale University Press, 1996), dips into the secret archives and brands Lenin a ruthless and manipulative leader. Robert McNeal's *Bride of the Revolution* (University of Michigan Press, 1972) focuses on the fascinating marriage and revolutionary relationship between Lenin and Bolshevik propagandist Nadezhda Krupskaya. And Sheila Fitzpatrick, in *The Russian Revolution* (Oxford University Press, 1982), surveys the critical 1917–1932 period with special emphasis on the work of Zhenotdel.

# YES

**Richard Stites**

## The Russian Revolution and Women

Based on his wide experience researching and writing Russian history. Richard Stites offers a broad synthesis of women's place in the Russian revolutionary tradition and post-revolutionary society. His story begins with the reforming sentiments of the 1850s and 1860s, at a time of debate over the nature and course of the emancipation of serfs. He identifies mid-century as the first phase of women's participation in the reforming movements and identifies three influential, if distinct, approaches: the feminist, which was essentially a movement by women for women; the nihilist, which was a countercultural current stressing the personal values of equality; and the radical, which sought total emancipation of all through socialism. The second phase was inaugurated by the tsarist government's commitment to industrialization and shift to parliamentary politics. It saw the growth of political parties, and many on the left, including the Marxists, feared the feminist revival as diversionary. In 1917, however, the significance of the half-century debate over the woman question became clear. Women's equality was among the many promises made by the new Bolshevik leadership, as were workers' control over factory production, educational advances, and ethnic self-determination. Despite the regime's public commitment to women's rights, however, the persistence of older notions of women's subordinate role hampered greater strides toward gender equality, as did continuous priority dilemmas that placed women's issues secondary to other societal and developmental goals. Besides, the regime was poor and could not afford extensive social support. It was only in work—as wage earners in social production—that the possibility of individual independence was extended to Russian women. There was less success in transforming family relationships and role divisions within the family.

The participation of women in the Russian Revolution of 1917 was conditioned—both in its successes and in its failures—by a long and interesting prehistory. The explosive events of 1917 can be explained only partially by the physical, military, and social environment of the moment; to this picture must be added a legacy of images, beliefs, feelings, and attitudes shaped in the two generations preceding the Revolution: the Populist Revolt (1860–1881), an almost purely upper-class affair; and the Revolution of 1905 (1890–1914), a nationwide, all-class uprising. Recent scholarship on peasants, workers, nationalities, soldiers, sailors, and other groups has demonstrated clearly that long-standing attitudes and circumstances of life are as important as any other factor in the molding of revolutionary (and counterrevolutionary) behavior. The same applies to the history of women: although deep study of the social structure of women's lives among the working class has just begun, research on the development of women's consciousness and women's movements in the major revolutionary episodes of the nineteenth and early twentieth centuries indicates the main peculiarities of women's political activity in the great Russian Revolution of 1917.

Though there is evidence of the growth of various forms of "women's consciousness"—that is, a refusal to accept traditional social roles—in early nineteenth-century Russia, it is generally accepted by Western and Soviet scholars that the woman question as a social issue burst onto the public scene in the late 1850s and early 1860s. There is no consensus as to why this happened. Some have stressed the general atmosphere of a political "thaw" under a new, reforming tsar, Alexander II (r. 1855–1881), the deep shame over the Russian defeat in the Crimean War (1854–1856), and a sense of euphoria connected with the imminent emancipation of the serfs (1861). Some have also suggested that social and economic factors were at work: the specter of serf emancipation and the prospect that dependent females might now be thrown onto the economy might have awakened an impulse to prepare for economic and personal independence. But no less important than these was the emergence of a new generation of intelligentsia males whose social outlook—often described as "nihilism" or a sweeping negation of accepted values—included egalitarianism, an attack upon elitist manners and conventions, and a determination to practice their beliefs in everyday life. From such males, many of whom became radicals of the 1860s, came the first important writings on women's equality. The Russian radical scene was almost unique in its inclusion of a demand for equal opportunity for women among its earliest political and social programs. This appeal by nihilist and radical males coincided with a new stage of women's perception and self-perception and set the stage for a movement for the emancipation of women.

But just as the motivations and impulses were complex and diverse; so were the responses of the women themselves. Almost simultaneously, there arose three distinct approaches to the woman question: feminism, nihilism, and radicalism. Though there was much overlapping, shifting, and interlocking of these three currents at first, they eventually sorted themselves into separate ways. The feminists of Russia were in many ways similar to Western feminists. They sought not revolution or even personal sexual emancipation but rather a legal and moderate movement led by women on behalf of women. By social origin, the leaders and founders were upper-class—mostly of the nobility. One should not be tempted to construct a deterministic sociology of their mentality because of this: the early nihilists and radical women came essentially from the same background. If the feminist leader Anna Filosofova was the wife of a tsarist general, Sofya Perovskaya, assassin of the Tsar in 1881, and Alexandra Kollontai, a Bolshevik Commissar in 1917, were daughters of generals—all of affluent and successful families. But the feminists chose very consciously to define the needs of women as something separate from general social struggle and the liberation of all the people. Their aims were modest and their achievements impressive: charity for poor girls, mutual assistance to themselves, experience in self-directed activity in a land where this was in short supply, and educational and professional opportunities for those women possessing the talent and the energy for careers. Largely through their efforts, universities and medical courses became available to Russian women in the 1870s, a notable feat for any European country at that time.

Nihilism was not a political or a formal intellectual movement in the 1860s—it was rather an ethos and a style of personal liberation. Like their male colleagues, nihilist women stressed their independence, their modernity, and their contempt for the established order by means of physical appearance and symbolic gestures: short hair, plain (sometimes dirty) clothes, a defeminized manner, cigarette smoking, and brusqueness in speech. This was part of a countercultural revolt like those of nineteenth-century European bohemians, *fin-de-siècle* decadents, or American hippies of the 1960s. Their values were equality, science worship, a general belief in progress, and a moralistic disdain for old Russian ways and customs—including religion, the family, and the highly stratified and visible class system. Wives and daughters broke with their families, migrated to the big capital cities—St. Petersburg and Moscow—enrolled in courses, joined circles and communes, and in general scandalized polite society. Many women who went through this counterculture moved on to political radicalism and even terrorism. But many of them did not. Nihilism was not coterminous with revolution for people of either sex. Even among women who admired Nicholas Chernyshevsky's *What Is to Be Done?* (1862)—a political novel and a utopia about women's emancipation—were those that remained deaf to its radical message and contented themselves with borrowing its devices (fictitious marriages, women's cooperatives, communes) for personal, social, and sexual emancipation.

Nihilist and radical women are often linked in the study of the revolutionary movement of the 1860s. But as far as women are concerned, radicals had more in common with active feminists than with those nihilists (often accused of egoism) who defined emancipation as a personal affair. Both the feminists and the radical women had larger goals; for the former, emancipation of women of their own class and assistance to many women of the urban lower orders (prostitutes, orphans, shopgirls); for the latter—emancipation of all the people, especially the toiling peasants, through socialism. They also seemed to share an almost religious sense of service and self-sacrifice. In a brilliant book on the subject, Barbara Engel has analyzed the sense of religious devotion and service among radical women of this generation and shown how their strategy of sacrifice and martyrdom—while extremely valuable in giving the revolution a symbolic halo—diminished their feminist sensibilities and led them to downplay or ignore special problems of the female population. This does not mean, however, that the feminist impulse was absent among radical women. Engel has shown in detail how many of the most active women in the populist movement of the 1870s went through an important phase of consciousness-raising and womanly self-definition before turning the "personal" into the "political." Female revolutionaries also maintained what we now call networks of moral and psychological sustenance, a phenomenon that has survived strongly into the present.

But who were the radical women and what did they do? Most of the several thousand females who participated in the revolutionary movement between the 1860s and 1880s were from privileged Russian families—gentry, professionals, government officials, and military officers—with an increasing admixture of merhants' and priests' daughters, women of the lower classes, and Jews, Poles, and other nationalities. In the minuscule circles of the 1860s, women acted as adjuncts, recruiters, messengers, and were sometimes treated by radical men—such as Sergei Nechaev—in a rather manipulative way. In the 1870s, with the "Movement to the People," women came into their own, migrating into factories and into villages in search of the "socialist" peasant, propagandizing, and falling into police dragnets. Hundreds were arrested and incarcerated or sent into Siberian exile. An era of assassination was inaugurated when Vera Zasulich fired a shot at a high police official in the capital in 1877. When disillusionment with peasant revolutionary potential and fear of open exposure led a branch of the movement—the People's Will—to a campaign of terror in the years 1879–1881, women were even more prominent numerically, constituting about one-third of that body's all-powerful Executive Committee. It was Sofya Perovskaya, after the arrest of her comrades, who led the final assault on the Tsar that took his life in March 1881, after which she and her co-conspirators were hanged. But failure attended the symbolic victory: no revolution occurred, peasant socialism did not emerge, and the People's Will gradually disintegrated.

The Populist episode left a dual legacy for radical women: it encircled them with the aureole of martyrdom and revolutionary honor and it endowed them with a myth of moral courage and indomitable power. But it often led their followers to continue the "pure radical" notion of the Great Cause, to the detriment of feminist concerns; and it also failed to win women a place of equal power and creativity in the revolutionary movements.

The second phase of the revolutionary movement in Russia occurred in an altered social context. Russia's rapid industrialization added dramatically to the number of urban factory women, prostitutes, and domestic servants. Peasant women followed their menfolk—and sometimes went independently—into the work force in the cities, the slums, and the proletarian working-class quarters. Female domestics were the most ignored by social critics (and the least studied to this day), though they were very prominent in the urban housing revolution that erupted in Russia after the Bolshevik Revolution. The prostitutes became a veritable symbol—in the eyes of cultural observers—of the moral decadence that was overcoming Russian society. Factory women, as Rose Glickman's superb new study has shown, had to face hostility and abuse on two fronts: in the exploitativeness of the factory system itself; and in the home where male "proletarian virtue" did not always include decent treatment of wives and daughters.

The partially successful Revolution of 1905, which produced civil rights, a free press, a parliament, and dozens of new public institutions, also thickened the social and political texture of Russia. Into the maelstrom of revolutionary politics rushed peasants, workers, the middle classes, and national minorities of many levels of cultural development. To represent their interests and those of the forces of order and stability, a whole spectrum of political parties appeared, most of which deliberated openly in the Duma, or parliament, created in 1906. As might be expected, the parties that inscribed fatherland, faith, and tsar on their banners were wholly opposed to feminism and woman suffrage. Conservatives sometimes fudged the issue but were generally hostile. The Liberal Party (Kadets) divided at first—thinking other matters more important than votes for women—but grudgingly came round to support them. The parties of the left—the Marxist Social Democrats (both Bolsheviks and Mensheviks), the Socialist Revolutionaries, and the anarchist groups supported equal rights for women in principle, though only the Marxists proclaimed it publicly and unambiguously. But in practice many leftists often ignored the woman question or were simply hostile to it, seeing it (as did the Liberals) as a luxury, a special cause that should be subsumed under a grander perspective of all-Russian liberation and the destruction of the tsarist system. The radical generation of 1905 was distinctly less interested in living sexual equality in part because its cohort rested comfortably on the radical myth that these things had already been decided in the 1860s.

While women were accepted as equals in the parties of the left, as individuals they were much less prominent in the leadership than they had been a generation earlier. The steady influx into the socialist parties of workers whose attitude toward women was not as advanced as those of the intelligentsia may also have been responsible for a certain downgrading of the role of women. It must be kept in mind, however, that for many women who sought a role in political life, the socialist parties seemed the only genuinely hospitable home.

One development—but not the only one—that made some Marxists suspicious of what they called "feminist" concerns was the emergence of the Russian women's suffrage movement around 1905 outside the context of socialism and large-scale revolution. The feminist movement of 1905 was very complex. In one sense it was a continuation of "classical" feminism of the 1860s—a movement of women for women and emphatically not simply the female component of one of the opposition movements, and consequently, not ready to bury its separate cause under some larger cause as defined by men. This focus on *women* as a constituency that cut across class lines and the willingness of some feminist groups to accept a limited (property) suffrage was quite enough to besmirch it in the eyes of most Marxists as bourgeois. The charge was not wholly accurate (quite aside from the utter meaninglessness of the word "bourgeois" in any Russian context).

In the first place, almost all feminists—conservative, liberal, or "social"—saw women's emancipation as part of a larger cause also: the liberation of all oppressed peoples, but not via a simple formula of "proletarian" revolution or neopopulism. They upheld the revolution and supported a whole range of reforms that benefited everyone. Secondly, an important component of the feminist movement was specifically interested in the labor movement, working-class women, factory conditions, the right to strike, and so on. Some of these feminists were even socialist party members. But they usually found themselves rebuffed by party leaders who frowned upon "separatist" tendencies. By 1906, the feminists—rearranged and reshuffled several times—had parted company with the revolutionary movement and continued their fight for the vote. They did not get it until 1917, but in the course of their campaigning they continued what their mothers had started—building self-confidence, gaining organizational experience, and winning valuable reform for women in matters of education, law, and social protection.

The Populist tradition of "pure radicalism" and devoid of organized feminism continued into this era. It was very strong among those women who shared with radical men the belief that everything about the emancipation of women had already been said and that there was, therefore, no need for a special movement for women. For Maria Spiridonova, a fiery schoolteacher from Tambov province, the hallmark of a political woman was personal valor and action: during the 1905 Revolution she avenged the scourged peasants of her province by shooting dead the General who had led the punitive expedition against them. After ten years in exile she returned to European Russia in 1917 and became a leader of the ultra-radical left Socialist Revolutionaries. Through it all, she evinced no interest whatsoever in organized feminism, seeing herself as already the equal of men and seeing the Revolution as the focal point of her life. Vera Zasulich, ex-terrorist and now a Menshevik Marxist, shared this opinion: special meetings and organizations for women within Social Democracy were unnecessary. In many ways these women (and there were many more) harbored some of the short-sightedness of successful women of the past (monarchs and writers, for example) who viewed their own record as "proof" of women's ability and who thought that there was nothing more to be done about the matter. The multitude of professional revolutionary women of all parties in the revolutions of 1905 and 1917 who shied away from the suffrage movement distinguished the Russian experience from that of England where violence found a place inside the feminist movement itself. It also reinforced male notions that attention to women's problems was provincial and harmful.

The "proletarian women's movement" in contrast was an attempt to synthesize one brand of radicalism—Marxism—with feminism. Formulated by the German Marxist, Clara Zetkin, and adapted to Russian conditions by Kollontai and Nadezhda Krupskaya (Lenin's wife), this synthesis rejected "bourgeois" feminist movements of women for women, reaffirmed the alliance of men and women in the class struggle for a proletarian revolution, but insisted on the special needs and concerns of women within the proletarian movement. Working-class women in particular were beset by problems of illiteracy, low political consciousness, unequal pay, absence of maternity benefits, sexual harassment on the job, and even abuse from their proletarian husbands. The Marxist feminists believed that these concerns were real, that organized feminism—with its suspected class bias—could not alleviate them, and that male socialist leaders poorly understood them and gave them insufficient attention. In 1905, Kollontai, still a Menshevik, helped to launch a special campaign to enlist women workers in the Social Democratic labor movement and to fight the feminist organizations in Russia. This struggle culminated at the first Women's Conference in 1908 when the two currents confronted each other in a mood of hostility. Thereafter, feminism in all its parts declined rapidly. The Marxist women's movement revived on a very modest scale, in 1912–1914, when the Bolsheviks launched a newspaper called *The Woman Worker* and began celebrating the European Marxist holiday, International Women's Day.

Three years of bloody European war (1914–1917) threw many of these controversies into the shadows, reduced old organizations to shambles, and kept many revolutionary leaders out of touch with Russian reality. Thus, on the eve of the 1917 Revolution, the woman question, having won important successes in the last years of the monarchy, was practically dormant.

The revolutionary year 1917 was actually only eight months long. It began with the overthrow of the monarchy, was followed by an uneasy and undefined alliance of the "bourgeois" parties in the Provisional Government and the moderate socialist leaders in the Soviets (workers' councils), and ended in October with the Bolshevik seizure of power and the creation of a new revolutionary regime under Lenin. At no time did the women's struggle dominate the proceedings, but a struggle there was nonetheless. All the old factions went to war again. The urban uprising in the capital that caused the collapse of the monarchy was begun by a demonstration in support of International Women's Day; and both Mensheviks and Bolsheviks attempted to organize and recruit women workers throughout the year. The feminist organizations came out of the doldrums, united, and petitioned the Provisional Government for the vote—which they received along with sharpened barbs from the Bolshevik women's organizers for presuming to speak for lower-class women. All the rhetoric and the insults of 1905 were trumpeted again by both sides.

But the feminists found a fresh cause with an ironic twist: the Women's Batallions of Death. If women of the revolutionary tradition could shunt feminism aside in favor of the Great Cause of social revolution, other women could do the same for another Great Cause: defending the fatherland. In the summer of 1917, while regular troops were melting away during the Provisional Government's last and ill-fated offensive against the Central Powers, Russian women volunteers, organized into batallions, were trying to stiffen the lines against the invaders. In the last act of 1917, the dramatic but anticlimactic storming of the Winter Palace, headquarters of the Provisional Government, a unit from the Women's Batallions defended while Bolshevik Red Guards, some women among them, assaulted and took the palace.

For the Bolsheviks the moment had at last come when, after generations of postponement of "smaller" questions for the sake of the larger, these questions had to be faced and solved: "the day after the Revolution." But the day after the Revolution never came. As there had been in the past, there were always good reasons why certain things had to wait—equality, harmony, cooperation, abundance, social justice, all the furnishings of the utopian dream. The first inkling that the "revolution" was not over but only beginning was the Civil War (1918–1921), where perhaps as many as 80,000 women served in combat, medical, support, espionage, partisan, and administrative roles. For these women the Great Cause arose once again as the all-embracing mission in life, and not the rights of women. They fought, they suffered, and they died—sometimes horribly—as they had done in the struggle against autocracy, once again projecting an unparalleled image of nobility and sacrifice, an image reflected in the posters and stories of the Civil War. It was in fact one of the greatest sagas of women at war in modern times—a saga to be repeated in excruciating and terrible detail when Nazi Germany invaded Russia in 1941. But as in all the previous episodes of the revolutionary tradition, the women were more often deputies, auxiliaries, assistants, nurturers, and teachers, than the possessors of raw power and monumental stature.

This is not to say that the Marxist-feminist synthesis of the prerevolutionary years was forgotten or abandoned. Lenin proclaimed again and again the complete equality of the sexes in all realms of life—and was the first political leader in power ever to do so. His regime, with the assistance of women advisors, promulgated a series of measures that legalized equal pay for equal work; proclaimed full political, juridical, and educational equality; legalized abortion; and liberalized the divorce system, making woman a full partner in the family. More important than this, recognizing that laws do not make a social revolution and that the best arbiters of women's affairs were women themselves, Lenin blessed the launching of a new experiment in women's self-activity—the Zhenotdel, or women's section, of the Communist Party (1919–1930). Under the general leadership of Inessa Armand and Kollontai, the Zhenotdel attempted through a national network of women organizers to spread the news of the Revolution, to enforce its laws (especially against errant and brutal husbands), to give political education and apprenticeships to working-class and peasant women, to launch literacy classes, to campaign against prostitution (which was now outlawed), and to lift the veil physically and metaphorically from the faces of Muslim women of the eastern regions of the Soviet republic—groups that had been all but untouched by the currents of women's liberation thought before 1917. The energy of Zhenotdel leaders was prodigious and their social ambitions vaulting; but their organization always remained weak, their efforts underfinanced, and their aims held in dubious repute by many male Bolshevik leaders, especially after death of Lenin. Why?

All Bolshevik leaders proclaimed in principle the equality of the sexes, but most of them had no interest in the rapid emancipation of women. Those who did often thought in terms of what one scholar has called "mobilization for modernization"—the deployment of women's energies in modern productive labor for the sake of the regime or of society (the Great Cause once again). It would be easy and natural to attribute this to the "treachery" or "hypocrisy" of the Bolsheviks, but name-calling does not add much to historical understanding. All revolutions, in a sense, cheat their supporters and mass participants, just as almost all societies exploit their poorest and weakest members. The communist revolutions of our time in Yugoslavia, China, Cuba, Vietnam, and other places that have gone back on their promises to women are hardly different in this than previous revolutions, except that perhaps they promised more and thus found it more difficult to keep their word. Like many revolutionaries in Russia before them, the Bolsheviks interpreted "equality" as complementarity, specialization, or division of labor. Since there were no titles or rules of entry that mentioned

gender, Bolsheviks came to assume that theirs was a community of equals even though some had more power, did more writing, or, after coming to power, had bigger rations. Bolshevism could not break—and to this day has not broken—with the deep conviction that women, though "equal" in valor and revolutionary consciousness, were by nature better at support, sustenance, nurturing.

In their public statements and symbols, Bolsheviks neither demeaned women nor put them on a pedestal (there is no equivalent to the French Marianne, symbol of the Republic, in Soviet heraldry). The posters, medallions, and symbols of the Revolution show man and woman, side by side, apparent equals in struggle and in labor. But a closer look at those symbols of the earliest months and years often shows women (sickle in hand) depicted as representing rural life, agriculture, the peasantry, fertility, while men (hammer in hand) represent the city, industry, workers, production. In a subliminal way, early Bolshevik symbolism reflected a view of women as passive, pliant, and reproductive. Although the Bolsheviks proclaimed from the very outset a moral and social alliance between peasants and proletarians, between town and country, the alliance was always an unequal one in favor of the urban over the rural.

From 1917 to the end of the 1920s Bolshevik men and women tried through public statements and institutions to reduce this dichotomy. But with the emergence of Stalinism in the 1930s, all but the thinnest of ideological pretenses were laid aside. Conservative divorce and abortion laws were issued, the Zhenotdel was abolished with the explanation that women were now actually equal to men and that its work was no longer needed—a palpable misstatement; wives of engineers and managers were publicly exalted for their work in beautifying the home and adorning their husbands' offices. The old ideal of the ascetic, thin-lipped, and determined women revolutionaries gave way to gushing images of supermothers and heroines of domesticity. If the early Bolshevik male leaders were conditioned by a cultural block to renege on the promises of women's equality, some of them at least had made an effort to recall these promises. With Stalin, an unabashed repudiation of old intelligentsia norms of political respect for women took place, and Soviet Russia reverted to many of the patriarchal attitudes and life patterns of the old regime. The heavily authoritarian style of politics under Stalin, the brutal warlike atmosphere of strife, and the economic imperatives set during the five-year plans were partly responsible for this; but so also was the industrial revolution of the early 1930s that pushed peasants into the cities and workers and lower-class urban elements up into positions of power and responsibility. With them came still unreconstructed attitudes toward women, the family, and sexuality. The result can only be called a counterrevolution in women's emancipation.

Post-Stalinist reform in the status of women was, like much else after 1953, partial and selective. On the one hand, the divorce and abortion laws were altered and certain legal and educational disabilities and inequities of women were removed. But attitudes and structures remained as in Stalin's time: women were to work in the economy and were expected to work a second shift as well in the home; they were segregated into lower-paying professions and into lower-paying ranks in all professions. Nothing except pallid and formulaic statements about male responsibilities and the ritual claims of equality was done to remove or diminish the strong Russian patriarchal attitudes toward women on the part of males. In recent years patriarchalism has even been expressed in official and semi-official journals.

In retrospect, the Revolution—and the revolutionary movement that preceded it—seems a failure in respect to women's position in Russian society. This is not wholly true. Until a few years ago, Soviet women enjoyed certain rights and wide opportunities in science, technology, medicine, and other professions that were rarely found in the West. That gap has almost closed and women's activism in Europe and the United States has—to use a favorite Soviet expression—"caught up and overtaken" that of Soviet women. Yet there is ferment. Some of it is quiet and indirect—newspaper campaigns and lobbying for an upgrading of facilities that are central to women's lives. More recently, there are signs that a genuine independent feminist movement has arisen among dissident women, one group of whom has published an almanac of grievances and aspirations that is truly moving and reminiscent of bygone feminist currents in Russian history. For any new feminist movement that may emerge from this ferment, the lessons of the Russian Revolution are quite clear: "larger" issues and causes—however noble—cannot be permitted to swallow the women's issue per se or to dismiss the purely feminist emphasis; males will have to look hard at the reality of women's lives, a reality that is clearly visible behind the tatter of overused slogans and symbols. Ultimately everyone will have to recognize—as painful as that may be—the fact that revolution and revolutionary movements and regimes, however lofty and libertarian their ideals, often generate their own kind of authoritarianism in their solution to the ills of social history.

---

**Richard Stites (1931–2010)** was a professor of history at Georgetown University. He is the author of *Revolutionary Dreams* (Oxford University Press, 1989), and *Russian Popular Culture* (Cambridge University Press, 1992).

**Lesley A. Rimmel**

# The Baba and the Comrade: Gender and Politics in Revolutionary Russia

**D**uring the nearly two years that I lived in Palo Alto, California, I translated several grant proposals from Russian into English for the Global Fund for Women, based nearby. As a longtime student of the USSR and Russia, I was fascinated to see how even in the farthest reaches of the former Soviet Union, women had organized on their own behalf and were writing to this explicitly feminist foundation for support. While all of the groups understandably focused on the need to counter the detrimental effects of recent economic changes on women, how they understood "feminism," and women's "nature" and role in society, varied considerably. This is not surprising, as the idea of gender is contentious in most societies. But what is most encouraging is that in Russia and the Newly Independent States, the issue of gender itself is being seriously grappled with for the first time. As these . . . books . . . indicate, women in Soviet times were defined as "the same as" or "different from" men according to the current needs of the regime, with gender-specific or gender-neutral policies then applied as the particular situation (war, peace, labor shortages) warranted. Only recently have post-Soviet women begun the difficult but necessary work of claiming agency and making themselves their own first priority.

These . . . books— . . . written or edited by scholars of distinction—diverge in their approaches and intended audiences. The one that addresses the earliest period of Communist Russia, Elizabeth A. Wood's long-awaited and richly documented *The Baba and the Comrade*, is also the most explicitly scholarly. Nonscholars should not be put off, however, for the book is clearly written and organized, and mostly free of jargon.

*The Baba and the Comrade* takes as its central theme the question that confronted Bolshevik (after 1918, Communist) activists: were women and men the same or different? Could a baba, generally defined as an ignorant peasant woman, become a comrade, a full-fledged human and citizen? Wood notes how reluctant the Bolsheviks were to target women separately in their propaganda and organizing efforts; only the competition with feminist groups and other socialist parties forced them to do so in the last years before the February and October 1917 revolutions and for several years thereafter.

The dilemma for the Communists was that their revolution was to be class-based, and "any special efforts on behalf of women threatened [the revolution's] class nature." Nadezhda Krupskaia, partner and wife of Bolshevik leader Lenin and usually a stalwart defender of women's interests, illustrated this reluctance (and some typical Communist condescension) in a draft editorial for the party paper Rabotnitsa ("Woman Worker") in 1913:

> The "woman question" for male and female workers is a question [of] how to draw the backward masses of women workers into organization, how best to explain to them their interests, how best to make them into comrades in the general struggle. Solidarity among the male and female workers, a general cause, general goals, a general path to that goal—that is the solution to the "woman" question in the working class environment. . . . The journal Rabotnitsa will strive to explain to unconscious women workers their interests, to show them the commonality of their interests with the interests of the whole working class.

Yet, for practical and historical reasons, women, who were less literate than men and who were charged with all household and childcare duties, in addition to whatever work they might have outside the home, could not be reached by Communist activists as easily as men. Many women could not or would not attend meetings with men, nor would they speak out with men present. But the Communists needed to appeal to women in order to mobilize their support (especially during the crucial years of the civil war, from 1918 to 1920). And if the backward baba was not made to support the new regime, then she might hinder the revolution and even become a source of counterrevolution (defined in practice as any opposition to Bolshevik policy). And as women would be raising the next generation, it was critical that they understand and support the new order. The spectre of the baba who would harm the revolution if not won over became the justification for focusing activism on women separately.

Wood concentrates on the period from 1918 to 1923, when woman-centered activism was most pronounced, but she begins by placing Communist ideas and stereotypes about women and reform in their Russian historical perspective. Beginning in the late [seventeenth] century under Tsar Peter I, who attempted to orient Russia to the West, women were viewed as surrogates for the backwardness of Russia; integrating them into male society would be a step toward "civilizing" Russia and turning women into human beings. The Bolsheviks basically continued in this vein, giving the tsarist interpretation a Marxist gloss. On the one hand, the Communist regime enacted legislation mandating sexual equality, with the only "special treatment" being pregnancy and maternity leaves for women in the workplace. On the other hand, the culture's traditional gender essentialism remained, to be resurrected when needed.

This dialectic of gender became evident during the civil war, when the Communists appealed to women's supposedly inherent traits as caregivers and homemakers to take on work as nurses and inspectors, to use their "sharp eyes and tender hearts" to care for wounded soldiers and root out any corruption or misdeeds. At the same time, local women's sections of the Communist Party were established, as well as a national organization, the Women's Department of the Party, the Zhenotdel.

Theoretically, the women's sections were to be "transmission belts" (a favorite Bolshevik metaphor) for bringing party policy to ordinary women. They did indeed function this way. However, as the civil war gave way to the era of the New Economic Policy, a time of some economic privatization with greater political centralization (somewhat like the situation of China today, and economically similar to present-day Russia), many women lost their jobs and their health benefits, and the women's sections began lobbying the government on women's behalf. Labor and enterprise leaders, seeing women more as mothers than as workers, were unsympathetic, and the state continued to curtail its "social programs." Zhenotdel activists countered by bringing out the threat of the baba: the NEP was forcing women into "domestic slavery" or prostitution in order to survive (a not untrue contention), and in their regression from comrade to baba, they would take men down with them.

If there was any regression, however, it was on the part of the government in general and men in particular, who by 1923–24 feared not that women would be a drag on the revolution, but that the housework would not get done. Women's section activists, whose political and material support from authorities was being cut, strove to assure men of the party that female comrades would not desert their posts—at the stove. Thus Bolshevik backlash against gender transformation began long before Stalinist family values became institutionalized in the 1930 and 1940s—a time often referred to as the "Great Retreat."

Wood's convincing work is a welcome addition to the growing literature on the gender-role traditionalism the Communists reinstitutionalized with their revolution. Women's opportunities—and workload—may have increased after 1917, but the culture's scepticism about women's "essential nature" did not. For those of us who for years have attempted to point this out (and were vilified, by some on both the Right and the Left, for doing so), Wood's readable narrative and copious examples bring further validation.

How did women in the Soviet Union negotiate their country's contradictory gender expectations? Mostly, it seems, they ignored them and concentrated on survival. Historian Barbara Alpern Engel and demographer and feminist activist Anastasia Posadskaya-Vanderbeck have collected eight interviews with women whose only commonality was (with one exception) that they were born before the Bolshevik Revolution, and survived to see the USSR's demise. The title of their book, *A Revolution of Their Own,* is [somewhat misleading], since it seems to imply that women actually got "their" revolution. In fact, as their stories indicate, most of these women did not benefit from the revolution, and for many the Soviet experience was a largely negative one.

Most interesting, however, is that neither the women's experiences nor their attitudes can be predicted from their backgrounds—a clear retort to the Communists' near obsession with people's "social origins." The interviews took place not just in Moscow but in Siberia and in Ekaterinburg in the Urals; the women themselves were born in a variety of places. While the eight are not a representative sample demographically, their experiences are varied enough to make for a rich and provocative portrait of a generation that lived through one of history's greatest dramas.

Each chapter consists of a thorough introduction to the woman being interviewed, complete with a description of the physical setting, followed by a portion of the interview (edited for length and variety), including abbreviated versions of Posadskaya's questions. The latter reveal Posadskaya's ability to prod the woman being interviewed—for example, on their views on abortion, which was not a topic these women normally discussed. (One area where Posadskaya did not prod was that of lesbian rights, which may have been an issue for one of the women.) Sometimes the questions illuminate more about Posadskaya and her generation's concerns than about her interviewees': when she asks Anna Dubova about who decided how the family income would be spent in the 1930s, Dubova responds, almost with surprise, "we had so little money, there was nothing to decide."

Neither family background nor individual efforts can totally explain each woman's fate or her orientation toward the Communist regime. Among those interviewed, the women with peasant backgrounds shared little except unpromising beginnings. Elena Ponomarenko was the youngest of seventeen siblings (from the same mother), and could rarely attend school because she did not have shoes and had to work. But joining the party gave her life structure and helped her to get a start in journalism, for which she repaid the regime with her consistent loyalty, even to the point of defending the Terror and leaving her dying mother to go on an assignment. Irina Kniazeva, on the other hand, knew nothing but hardship in her peasant life, from the father and husbands who mistreated her, the constant hard labor that was never rewarded, and even the burden of "sin" she carried for years for having stolen a handful of grain to feed her children during the famine of the early 1930s. Reading this woman's words, and seeing her careworn face (each interview includes pictures of the women, usually at various stages of their lives), I was moved to tears.

All the stories are dramatic and even novelistic—Communist activist Sofia Pavlova's nighttime escapes on horseback during the civil war, Ponomarenko fighting off wolves in her travels, Vera Malakhova's experience as a frontline doctor during World War Two—and it's no wonder that they can be disdainful of today's younger generation and its seeming worship of luxury. Nearly all the women had difficult family lives—drunken and abusive husbands, wonderful but brief relationships with lovers or second husbands who suddenly disappeared in one of the convulsions of the Stalin era, and long periods of single motherhood in conditions of extreme poverty.

In fact, as Engel and Posadskaya observe, "the 'new Soviet family' essentially consisted of a mother who 'saved the children,' [. . .] raising one or two by herself, often with the help of her own mother or a nurse but with no evident support, financial or otherwise, from the government." (At the end of World War Two there were 26 million more women than men in the Soviet Union.) Some of these women had to renounce their families of origin in order merely to survive, while others found it necessary to marry men of "correct" backgrounds so as to "lose" their pasts—or even just to gain a place to live. But no amount of "family values" legislation, which the Stalin regime provided in abundance during the 1930s and 1940s, could overcome the problems of hunger, crowded housing, fatigue, and policies that separated people from their loved ones and mined "family" happiness for so many.

What did give meaning to most of these women's lives was a love of work. Only a few of them, when prodded, complained about limited opportunities for women; but even party loyalist Pavlova had to admit that women could not get any farther than she had, as head of a department of the Communist Party's Central Committee (its second-highest decision-making body): "There was a ceiling. It's the tenacity of tradition, and unfortunately, to this day, we haven't broken its hold. I don't know how long it will take to overcome it." Under the personal, economic, and political conditions that these women lived through, however, their survival and the survival of (most of) their children seems nothing short of miraculous—they were truly "heroes of their own lives," to use Linda Gordon's phrase.

That these women tend to downplay any long-suppressed resentment at limitations they experienced because of their sex—the overt discrimination and the practical obstacles engendered by single motherhood and poverty—is probably because class-based discrimination affected them more deeply, for better or for worse. . . .

Russian history is full of ironies, and nothing is more ironic than the fact that women's freedom to discuss and protest their situation arrived in the late 1980s and early 1990s, just as most women's lives really began to worsen. The contradictions of gender essentialism that were never really addressed by the Soviet Union bore fruit. Because, for example, parental leave and childcare had been associated with women only, women were and are the ones most likely to be fired as workplaces have to cut costs. With gender roles at home never questioned, and with housework being so extraordinarily time-consuming in Russia (which does not have enough well-supplied, conveniently located shops or labor-saving devices), women, with no more "reserved seats" (few as they were) in government bodies, are at a disadvantage in trying to compete as political players. Old-fashioned male chauvinism also plays a part in keeping women out of politics, and out of business as well.

Not all of this is new; the Communist Party and other powerful institutions had long been affirmative action programs for sons of party leaders. But along with the new opportunities of the post-Soviet era have come new obstacles for Russian women.

Yet the women in this book seem equal to the challenge. The larger groups they founded or reorganized all have Soviet roots, in some cases quite strong ones. One of the best-known is the Center for Gender Studies, the Soviet Union's first center for research on women, and its sister umbrella group, the Independent Women's Forum, which organized the first countrywide, independent gathering for women's groups. The Center and the Forum have been very successful in publicizing their critiques of Russian society. They are less involved in politicking to get women into positions of power, although their members often serve as consultants to government bodies. Although the Center is associated with the venerable Academy of Sciences, it has been outspoken in its feminism, as has its founding director, Anastasia Posadskaya-Vanderbeck.

Posadskaya early on found the Soviet system to be sexist and hypocritical, once she saw underqualified but well-connected men getting into academic programs for which she was rejected although she had passed the exams. She comes across in this book as less comfortable being interviewed than being the interviewer; she calls herself a "reluctant activist," saying she would have preferred to be a full-time scholar, but felt impelled to fight for women to "have their own voice, to speak independently, to speak not from a position of class or of one-half the population, which has been rescued by somebody else, but to set up their own agenda." . . .

What, then, has women's activism accomplished? There is not a lot of information here on specific achievements, and those interested will have to do further research elsewhere. What clearly has been achieved, however, has been a revolution of consciousness. Although Women's Activism leaves us with questions about the future of feminism in Russia—indeed, the future of Russia itself is always a big question—it also leaves us with hope. While some women have chosen to become active in far-left or far-right splinter groups in the belief that resurrecting the old Stalinism or traditional patriarchalism will restore some imagined women's paradise (although it should be noted that it was the post-Soviet Communists who first organized around women's disproportionate unemployment), there is no going back for Russian women. Too many now know their history, or are being forced to acknowledge it.

The challenges are truly daunting, especially with regard to women's economic situation, to which the growth in sex trafficking of Russian and other women from the Newly Independent States provides eloquent testimony. But activists won't get fooled again; there will be no more "mobiliz[ing] women's support for men's political agendas," for women to be only "producers and reproducers" for the state. There may be few babas left, but "comradeship" will be defined on women's terms. And then women will truly have a revolution of their own. . . .

**LESLEY A. RIMMEL** is an associate professor in the department of history, School of International Studies at the Oklahoma State University in Stillwater, Oklahoma.

# EXPLORING THE ISSUE

## Did the Bolshevik Revolution Improve the Lives of Soviet Women?

## Critical Thinking and Reflection

1. Briefly describe the implications of associating women with the sickle of agriculture and men with the hammer of industry; critically examine the effects of this iconography.
2. Research and critically analyze Karl Marx's critique of the family under capitalism and his critique of the capitalist economic system as it affected the proletariat (or working class).
3. Based on this double critique, why did Marx believe that when women became workers, freed from household drudgery, they would be liberated? Was he correct? Critically discuss.
4. Despite the eventual outcomes of the Bolshevik Revolution, is it valuable to study what history professor Richard Stites, calls its "idealistic foreground"? Did the early vision raise the consciousness of women and men, as Stites claims? Critically discuss.
5. Critically examine the theory and historical reality of the Zhenotdel or Women's Department of the Communist Party, especially its purpose—to educate and mobilize Soviet women for full participation in the revolution.
6. Is something like Zhenotdel necessary to radically alter the lives and expectations of the people who must live the changes wrought by the revolution? Why were Zhenotdel's efforts ultimately doomed? Critically discuss.
7. Russian scholar Lesley Rimmel, contends that, although workers' rights were emphasized, gender roles remained firmly in place. Research and critically evaluate the meaning behind this claim.
8. Why, in your view, did this key part of the revolution (the gender role system) remain unchallenged? Critically discuss.

## Is There Common Ground?

If we were to read the YES and NO selections together, we might have a more complete and a more accurate picture of the Bolshevik Revolution's effect on women's lives. The theory of women's liberation was very clear, well-articulated, and radical. In practice, things were considerably more "messy." As the revolution progressed, it gradually became clear that the goals were decidedly socialist, rather than feminist. Women would be emancipated workers. However, their responsibilities at home would remain virtually unchanged.

Although Russian women gained the right to work alongside men, easy divorce often left them alone with children to raise. Even within marriage, factory work was often followed by full responsibility for housework and child care—the double shift that many Western women object to today. Women who had or wanted to have children looked for stability in the family and revolutionary patterns offered instability instead. Where we look will determine what we see.

As in the French Revolution, the earlier phase is the encouraging one. Idealism and expansion of rights inspire people to revolution. However, the hard practical realities that soon set in can lead to violence (in the French case) or to a conservative backlash (in the Russian case). In the long run, Zhenotdel failed in its ambitious plans to improve the lives of Soviet women. However, for 11 years, many dazzling possibilities existed.

*Question:* Are possibilities sufficient? What path into the future might the Zhenotdel have offered? How might women's lives be different if it had continued?

## Create Central

www.mhhe.com/createcentral

## Additional Resources

For essays on the lives of women during this period, students may want to see *Women in Soviet Society* edited by Gail Lapidus (University of California Press, 1978) and *Women in Russia,* edited by D. Atkinson, A. Dallin, G. Lapidus (Stanford University Press, 1977), which grew out of a 1975 conference that was held at Stanford University titled "Women in Russia." The fascinating character Alexandra Kollontai, who died at 80, may be explored through her own writings in *Selected Writings* (W.W. Norton, 1972), *The Autobiography of a Sexually Emancipated Communist Woman* (Schocken Books, 1975), *Red Love* (Hyperion Press, 1990), and *Love of Worker Bees* (Academy of Chicago Press, 1978). Books about Kollontai include *Bolshevik Feminist* by Barbara Clements (Indiana University Press, 1979).

# *Internet References . . .*

### Marxist Writers: Alexandra Kollontai (1872–1952)

Devoted to the early Soviet Union's most powerful women, this site contains a biographical sketch and more than 30 links to her most important writings and actions. Kollontai was a radical supporter of women's rights.

**www.marxists.org/archive/kollonta/**

Selected, Edited, and with Issue Framing Material by:
Helen Buss Mitchell, *Howard Community College*
and
Joseph R. Mitchell, *Howard Community College*

# ISSUE

# Was German "Eliminationist Anti-Semitism" Responsible for the Holocaust?

**YES: Daniel Jonah Goldhagen,** from "The Paradigm Challenged," *Tikkun: A Bimonthly Interfaith Critique of Politics, Culture & Society* (May/June 1998)

**NO: Christopher R. Browning,** from "Ordinary Germans or Ordinary Men? A Reply to the Critics," in Michael Berenbaum and Abraham J. Peck, eds., *The Holocaust and History: The Known, the Unknown, the Disputed, and the Reexamined* (Indiana University Press, 1998)

---

## Learning Outcomes

**After reading this issue you should be able to:**

- Describe the controversial roles played by ordinary German and non-German people as apparently willing participants in the Holocaust.
- Describe what political science professor Daniel Goldhagen, calls "German eliminationist anti-semitism," the theoretical basis for Hitler's "Final Solution."
- Summarize Holocaust historian Christopher Browning's, contention that non-German killing units behaved similarly to German ones, suggesting that claims of a particularly virulent German anti-Semitism must be questioned.

---

### ISSUE SUMMARY

**YES:** Political science professor Daniel Jonah Goldhagen argues that due to the nature of German society in the twentieth century—with its endemic, virulent anti-Semitism—thousands of ordinary German citizens became willing participants in the implementation of Holocaust horrors.

**NO:** Holocaust historian Christopher R. Browning argues that Goldhagen's thesis is too simplistic, and that a multicausal approach must be used to determine why ordinary German citizens willingly participated in the Holocaust.

Few historical events engender stronger emotional responses than the Nazi-directed Holocaust of World War II, in which millions of Jews were systematically exterminated as part of a ghastly plan for a diabolical new world order. Since its occurrence, many scholarly works have been written in an attempt to answer the questions that this "crime against humanity" has raised: What historical factors were responsible for it? How did people and nations allow it to roll toward its final destructive consequences? What lessons did it teach us about human nature? Could something like this happen again? Who bears the responsibility for it?

Much of Holocaust scholarship has concentrated on European anti-Semitism as a major factor in the cause of the event itself and as a major reason why little was done to stop it. Some scholars have emphasized the schizophrenic nature of post-World War I politics, which they say allowed demagogic madmen to weave their magic web around an unsuspecting public. Others have stressed the violent nature of the twentieth-century world (especially after the Great War), which created an immunity-against-brutality temperament that made the Holocaust possible. And, of course, the major blame has been placed on Adolf Hitler and his Nazi henchmen for the initiation, design, and implementation of the Holocaust.

But just how unsuspecting was this public? Most people have long ago dismissed (as did the Nuremberg War Crimes Tribunal) the "I was only following orders" argument that so many who actively participated in Holocaust horrors have used. Others who were not directly involved have cited the hopelessness of opposition and the fear of reprisal to explain their acquiescence. But, as we have been made witness to countless trials for war crimes in the last 50 years, some have wondered whether or not a larger segment of the population in those Nazi-controlled countries was involved in the Holocaust's worst aspects.

Both in the United States and Germany, the publicity engendered by Goldhagen's book has been overwhelming. Because of its seemingly anti-German message, the book has been surprisingly well received in Germany, and a book tour there was attended by largely enthusiastic audiences. However, when the book was translated into German, its title was translated as *Hitler's Willing Executors*, which gives quite a different slant to the book's thesis. Some have accused Goldhagen and his publisher of changing the German title in order to increase sales in Germany, adding their complaints to those who claimed that Goldhagen's original title was intentionally inflammatory.

Many critical articles and reviews of *Hitler's Willing Executioners* have appeared—and Goldhagen has rebutted many of them in print. A most important one appeared in *The New Republic* (December 23, 1996). As noted in the Introduction, Browning's responses to Goldhagen's criticisms appear in a new Afterword to his book *Ordinary Men* (HarperPerennial, 1998).

Daniel Jonah Goldhagen was not the first scholar to investigate this subject, but his book *Hitler's Willing Executioners: Ordinary Germans and the Holocaust* (Vintage Books, 1996) has raised the issue to a new level and has created a maelstrom of controversy within the historical profession. Using recently discovered sources of information first analyzed by Christopher Browning's *Ordinary Men*, published 4 years earlier, Goldhagen takes a fresh look at why and how the Holocaust occurred through an analysis of three related subjects: "the perpetrators of the Holocaust, German anti-Semitism, and the nature of German society during the Nazi period." Central to his thesis is the concept of "eliminationist anti-Semitism" (his own phrase), which turned "ordinary Germans" into "Hitler's willing executioners." Goldhagen's conclusions are a stinging indictment of large numbers of average German citizens, who he claims willingly participated in the Holocaust's worst aspects, including police battalion killing squads, work camps, and death marches.

Goldhagen's work has received much public praise, including a national book critic's nomination for nonfiction book of the year. But it has also had its share of critics,

many of them Holocaust scholars. Some have found his work to be one-sided, inflammatory, and too narrow in its focus. Goldhagen's criticism of Browning's work has engendered an extended debate. In the NO selection, Browning states that anti-Semitism may have been widespread in pre-Nazi Germany, but it was not the major ideology of most German citizens. According to Browning, there are a variety of factors that were responsible for making ordinary Germans into willing killers. Goldhagen is critical of Browning's conclusions and his critique can be found in "The Evil of Banality," *The New Republic* (July 13 and 20, 1992). Browning published a rejoinder to Goldhagen's critique as an afterword to the second edition of *Ordinary Men: Reserve Police Battalion and the Final Solution in Poland* (HarperPerennial, 1998).

It should be noted that Jews were not the only victims of the Nazi Holocaust. Gypsies, homosexuals, Jehovah Witnesses, high officials in the Polish government and armed forces, and others, also suffered from Nazi war crimes. It should also be clear that Jews were singled out as the Third Reich's most hated enemy. From the beginning, they were the main target of the Nazi propaganda machine whose ranting verbal attacks led to denial of rights, confinement and persecution, and eventually extermination. No European Jews under Hitler's control were spared. Also, when new areas came under Nazi control, the Germans found locals who willingly participated in the extermination process. Some of these accomplices were allowed to take control of the property and possessions of their victims.

Finally, it must be stated that after the war, when the world was forced to confront the horror of the Holocaust, there was condemnation, war crimes trials, and eventual executions and prison sentences for the perpetrators. It is an ongoing process. "Never Again" became the words of the day. However, recent actions in Cambodia in the 1970s and similar actions in the Balkans and the African country of Rwanda in the 1990s prove that the world's nations have short memories and a lack of courage in allowing Holocaust-like activities to occur. This volume explores genocidal actions in the latter two countries mentioned above.

# YES ↵

**Daniel Jonah Goldhagen**

## The Paradigm Challenged

Imagine a history of American slavery whose authors assert that the testimony of slaves should not be used and where the practice is not to use it, where there is no extensive investigation of whites' conceptions of the enslaved Africans, where it is said that the whites were unwilling slaveholders and that few non-slave owning southern whites supported the institutions of slavery, where it is said that those enslaving and routinely brutalizing the slaves were not at all influenced by their conceptions of the victims, where the precept and practice is not to describe the full extent and character of the slaveholders' brutality, where it is said furthermore that African American scholars today are suspect because they are African American and the motivation is imputed to them of writing about slavery solely for monetary or political gain or psychological gratification. Imagine what our understanding of American slavery would look like, how skewed it would be, if even only some of these positions prevailed. We would wonder how slavery ever could have existed.

When writing about the Holocaust, many scholars and commentators routinely adopt positions analogous to one or several of these examples. Indeed, some of these positions are a never justified, seemingly unquestioned norm among those who write about the Holocaust. These positions would seem curious—methodologically, substantively, and interpretively—even absurd, if put forward about slavery or about other genocides or mass slaughters such as those in Rwanda or Bosnia. Yet when asserted about the Holocaust, barely an eyebrow is raised. The question naturally arises as to why such manifestly false positions have been frequently adopted? Why until recently were almost no studies, especially no systematic studies, of the perpetrators—namely of those who killed Jews, guarded the camps and ghettos, and deported them to their deaths—to be found among the tens of thousands of books written about the Holocaust, despite the wealth of evidence that had long been available?

The heretofore hegemonic paradigm about the Holocaust has rendered them puppet-like actors, mere pawns whose inner world need not be investigated. It denies the moral agency and assent of the perpetrators and holds that they were compelled to act by forces external to them, such as terror, bureaucratic strictures and modes of behaving, the logic of the system, or social psychological pressure. For a long time, this paradigm diverted attention away from the perpetrators because its logic of external compulsion meant that the perpetrators' internal lives (their beliefs and values) and anything that was sociohistorically particular to them (that they were members of a deeply anti-Semitic political culture) did not influence their actions and that, therefore, the study of them would not contribute much to explaining the Holocaust. The problems with this view and its construction can be indicated by comparing it to the hypothetical, fanciful rendering of slavery above.

The perpetrators are finally being discussed extensively, even if the number of empirical studies remains small. Yet in the last couple of years, a phalanx of scholars and commentators have adopted positions which would make the perpetrators of the Holocaust the only perpetrators of genocide who believed that their victims did not deserve to die, indeed that their victims were innocent. This strange view seems still stranger given that many of the German perpetrators knew explicitly that they had a choice not to kill, and that no German perpetrator was ever killed, sent to a concentration camp, jailed, or punished in any serious way for refusing to kill Jews. That it was possible for many perpetrators to avoid killing Jews, and that some of them availed themselves of this possibility, became known already at the Nuremberg Trials. The related, stunning fact that not a single German perpetrator was ever seriously punished for refusing to kill Jews has been known since 1967 when the jurist Herbert Jager published his pioneering study, Crime Under Totalitarian Domination. (I treated both the general issue and presented the case of one man who refused to kill in "The 'Cowardly' Executioner: On Disobedience in the SS" in 1985). Yet this latter fact has remained unmentioned in virtually every work written on the perpetration of the Holocaust since Jager first established it.

Why would Martin Broszat, Raul Hilberg, Eberhard Jackel, Hans Mommsen, and other scholars who wish to explain the Holocaust not discuss these fundamental facts extensively or incorporate their significance into the explanations and interpretations which they put forward? Is it of so little importance—that men and women who knew that they could avoid killing children would choose to destroy them anyway—that it is not even worth mentioning this information? Acknowledging these facts would have shaken the foundations of the paradigm to which many scholars are wedded, namely that the perpetrators were compelled by external forces to act against their will. This crucial omission of evidence, for which no justification has been offered, has for decades skewed non-experts' and the public's understanding of the Holocaust.

Similarly, when these writers depict and analyze the events of the Holocaust and particularly, when they analyze the motives of the perpetrators, they rarely, if ever, use the testimony of the victims, neither their letters, diaries, memoirs, nor oral testimonies. That is not to say this testimony is never used; certainly, it is used by those writing about the lives and plight of the victims, and by scholars like Yehuda Bauer, Saul Friedlander, and Israel Gutman. But when constructing interpretations of the perpetrators of the Holocaust, it has been the unspoken practice of so many scholars to all but ignore, and certainly not to use systematically, victims' accounts of the perpetrators' actions and the victims' understanding of perpetrators' attitudes towards them. With the sometime exception of a quotation or two from Primo Levi (or some other particularly distinguished memoirist), one searches such authors' works in vain for the instances where they use such evidence seriously or even at all.

Some authors explicitly declare that victim testimony is of little value and an impediment to understanding. Raul Hilberg, who is one of the principal exponents of the conventional paradigm and practice and who often speaks authoritatively for those who are in his school, has written roughly seven pages on survivor testimony in his recent memoir, *The Politics of Memory,* which are highly distorting and almost thoroughly disparaging. He makes not a single positive statement about the victims' testimony as a historical source, except when it shows Jews in a bad light. Even though Hilberg acknowledges in passing, in a strikingly critical vein, that the survivors' "principal subjects are deportations, concentration camps, death camps, escapes, hiding, and partisan fighting"—precisely those themes relevant to learning about and analyzing the perpetrators—his practice and that of those who follow him suggests that they believe that there is little evidentiary or interpretive value in all this testimony.

This widespread devaluation of the testimony of the Jewish victims is peculiar. I know of no other historical or contemporary instance about which it is said that the victims of genocidal onslaughts, sustained violence, or brutality have little of value to tell us about those who victimized and brutalized them. I know of no other crime (e.g., assault, kidnapping), no instance of largescale brutal domination (e.g., slavery, serfdom), no genocide (e.g., Rwanda, Cambodia), nor any other historical instance in which the victims—in the case of the Holocaust a group of eyewitnesses numbering in the millions—are said, as a class, to have little or nothing to tell us about the deeds and attitudes of the men and women who victimized them and whose murderousness and brutalities against others they witnessed. And not only is their testimony silently ignored by many and explicitly devalued by some but it is also sometimes deprecated by writers like Istvan Deak,

who began a review of several books on the Holocaust in *The New York Review of Books* (June 26, 1997) by presenting a caricature of and an attack on survivors' memoirs. He goes so far as to say that "an accurate record of the Holocaust has been endangered, in my opinion, by the uncritical endorsement, often by well-known Jewish writers or public figures, of virtually any survivor's account or related writings." How have the survivors' writings "endangered . . . an accurate record of the Holocaust"? Except to say (correctly) that personal details may be inaccurate or embellished, Deak does not justify his sweeping condemnation.

The invaluable importance of survivor testimony is attested by the crucial, indeed, indispensable part that the survivors have played in the trials of thousands of perpetrators in the Federal Republic of Germany. Many of these trials could not have been held without survivor testimony. The judgment in the most famous of these trials, that of a contingent of guards and administrators of Auschwitz held in 1963, states: "Apart from scattered and not very informative documents, the court had to rely exclusively on witness testimony to help it reconstruct the acts of the defendants." One thousand three hundred witnesses (among them former guards) gave testimony for that trial.

The Germans' documentation of the killing institutions and operations never record the details of the hundreds or thousands of perpetrators' many actions. Typically, the documents contain, at most, the bare logistics and results of killing operations. So an entire killing operation that might have lasted a full day will appear in a document with nothing more than one line stating that on a given date, the German unit "resettled" (a euphemism) or "shot" some number of Jews.

The accounts of survivors afford a more transparent, more spacious window to the Nazi inferno than the often beclouded and distorting postwar testimonies of the perpetrators who, in order to escape punishment, frequently lie. (Still, some of the perpetrators are surprisingly forthcoming, especially about other perpetrators, and many unwittingly reveal a great deal. Such testimony is invaluable and should be used.) Who would expect to learn from the perpetrators or from contemporaneous German documents a full and accurate account of the texture and details of the Holocaust, of the daily living and dying, of the treatment of the prisoners by the German overlords, including their frequent gratuitous brutality, of the social life of the inmates, their thoughts and feelings, their suffering and their agony? Where can we more fully learn about the character of the perpetrators' actions—the degree to which the perpetrators tortured, brutalized, beat, degraded, and mocked the victims—about the perpetrators' demeanor and attitudes, about whether they acted zealously or reluctantly, about whether they expressed hatred for the victims, and gain insight into the perpetrators' willingness and motivation?

The answer is obvious: from the victims.

Could accurate histories of the Jewish ghettos and of the concentration camps be written without the accounts of the survivors contained in their depositions and memoirs? A perusal of three great books, H. G. Adler's *Theresienstadt, 1941–1945*, Israel Gutman's *The Jews of Warsaw 1939–1943*, and Hermann Langbein's panoramic analysis of Auschwitz, People in Auschwitz, shows that the authors have drawn heavily on the accounts of survivors. Are these historical works thereby vitiated? Do they imperil the accuracy of the historical record?

A comparison with the historiography of the Soviet Gulag is instructive. Its scholars do not cast aspersion on the memoirs and accounts of former inmates, whose narratives are indispensable. Aleksandr Solzhenitsyn writes in his Preface to The Gulag Archipelago: "This book could never have been created by one person alone. In addition to what I myself was able to take away from the Archipelago—on the skin of my back, and with my eyes and ears—material for this book was given me in reports, memoirs, and letters by 227 witnesses . . . this is our common, collective monument to all those who were tortured and murdered." Evidence of the kind that Hilberg, Deak, Christopher, Browning, and others dismiss, explicitly or tacitly, as unreliable and inessential forms the foundation of Solzhenitsyn's magisterial work. Would Deak argue that Solzhenitsyn has "endangered. . . . an accurate record" of the Gulag? Or are only survivors of the Holocaust and those who find great value in their testimony prone to such "endangerment"?

It is not because this witness testimony is meager, imprecise, or devoid of insight that it has been ignored. It includes hundreds of memorial volumes, each one containing compilations from survivors of one destroyed Jewish community after another detailing their fates; depositions of many thousands of survivors in the trials of the perpetrators from one camp, killing unit, and ghetto after another; vast amounts of oral testimony; and thousands of memoirs. It would be hard to imagine an instance of mass slaughter, violence, or brutality that would be documented by a greater abundance of rich, detailed, often highly literate testimony that contains penetrating analyses of the events and of the people who perpetrated them. This makes the disparagement of the victims' testimony and its paltry use that much more surprising and indefensible.

Victims' accounts belie the conventional paradigm and the attendant scholarly theories about the perpetrators that have held sway, namely that the perpetrators either explicitly disapproved or at least did not approve of the mass slaughter of Jews and of other victims. The victims know differently. They have testified so again and again. If the proponents of these explanations had incorporated the voices of the victims into their own writings, then they would have undercut immediately and devastatingly their own theories, and the conventional paradigm.

The omission of the survivors' accounts has obscured, among many other aspects of the Holocaust,

one of its constituent features. Scholars' failure to use victim accounts has thus, to use Deak's phraseology, "endangered" "an accurate record": the perpetrators' virtually boundless cruelty towards the Jews has been all but ignored by those who purport to explain the perpetrators' actions. If, as many authors do, one relies principally on highly partial and often unrevealing contemporaneous German documents, then, of course, one will not find frequent and detailed recitations of Germans' routine torturing of Jews. These authors construct a distorted portrait of the Holocaust in which the perpetrators' brutality—so frequent, inventive, and willful—is minimized, blurred, or absent. Consequently, it is not surprising that those few authors adhering to the conventional paradigm who do at least say something in passing about the sources of the German perpetrators' brutality to the Jews do not deem the perpetrators to have been moved by hatred of their victims.

Hilberg, for instance, in *Perpetrators, Vicitims, Bystanders,* puts forward the notion that the German perpetrators' brutality was "most often" an "expression of impatience" with the pace of killing operations. Browning's related view, in *Ordinary Men,* is that the perpetrators' brutality was utilitarian, the consequence of a pragmatic need to be brutal when they were under "pressure," "in terms of manpower . . . to get the job done," like rounding up Jews for deportation. When not under such pressure, in Browning's view, they were cruel when under the sway of cruel officers but seemingly not at other times. Hilberg and Browning have failed to present evidence which supports what are ultimately little more than speculations. (How does Hilberg know that they were impatient? He never says. And is the torture of defenseless people, including children, the invariable result of impatience, as Hilberg's quick and casual manner of presenting his speculation suggests?) But that is the least of their problems. Hilberg and Browning's empirical claims are falsified by evidence of the perpetrators' widespread, non-utilitarian cruelty in all manner of circumstances, even when they were not undermanned, even when they were not impatient, even when they were not undertaking killing operations at all.

For example: although the Germans of Police Battalion 101, during one of the ghetto roundups and deportations in Miedzyrzec, Poland, degraded and tortured Jews in the most gratuitous, willful manner, their deeds are entirely absent from their testimony and, therefore, also from Browning's analysis of the killing operation. The accounts of survivors tell a different, more accurate, and more revealing story. Survivors are adamant that the Germans' cruelty that day was anything but instrumental. It was wanton, at times turning into sadistic sport. At the marketplace the Jews, who had been forced to squat for hours, were "mocked" (khoyzek gemacht) and "kicked," and some of the Germans organized "a game" (shpil) of "tossing apples and whoever was struck by the apple was then killed." This sport was continued at the railway station, with empty liquor bottles. "Bottles were tossed over

Jewish heads and whoever was struck by a bottle was dragged out of the crowd and beaten murderously amid roaring laughter. Then some of those who were thus mangled (tseharget) were shot." Afterwards, the Germans loaded the dead together with the living onto freight cars bound for Treblinka. One photograph documenting the final stage of what may be this deportation has survived.

Small wonder that in the eyes of the victims—but not in the self-serving testimony of the perpetrators, in contemporaneous German documents, or in Browning's book—these ordinary Germans appeared not as mere murderers, certainly not as reluctant killers dragged to their task against their inner opposition to genocide, but as "two-legged beasts" filled with "bloodthirstiness." (Browning claims that from survivors "we learn nothing about" Police Battalion 101 or, for that matter, about itinerant units in general.) Germans' cruelty towards Jews, as the victims (and also some of the perpetrators after the war) reveal, was voluntary, widespread, sustained, inventive, and gleeful. Such gratuitous cruelty could have been produced only by people who approved of what they were doing.

The vast corpus of the victims' testimony substantiates the conclusion that ordinary Germans degraded, brutalized, and killed Jews willingly because of their hatred of Jews. So profound and near universal was the anti-Semitism during the Nazi period that to the Jewish victims it appeared as if its hold on Germans could be captured and conveyed only in organic terms. As Chaim Kaplan, the trenchant observer and diarist of the Warsaw ghetto, concluded: "A poison of diseased hatred permeates the blood of the Nazis." Once activated, the Germans' profound hatred of Jews, which had in the 1930s by necessity lain relatively dormant, so possessed them, that it appeared to have exuded from their every pore. Kaplan observed many Germans from September 1939 until March 1940, when he penned his evaluation derived from their actions and words:

The gigantic catastrophe which has descended on Polish Jewry has no parallel, even in the darkest periods of Jewish history. First, in the depth of hatred. This is not just hatred whose source is in a party platform, and which was invented for political purposes. It is a hatred of emotion, whose source is some psychopathic malady. In its outward manifestations it functions as physiological hatred, which imagines the object of hatred to be unclean in body, a leper who has no place within the camp.

The [German] masses have absorbed this sort of qualitative hatred. . . . They have absorbed their masters' teachings in a concrete, corporeal form. The Jew is filthy; the Jew is a swindler and an evildoer; the Jew is the enemy of Germany, who undermines its existence; the Jew was the prime mover in the Versailles Treaty, which reduced Germany to nothing; the Jew is Satan, who sows dissension between one nation and another, arousing them to bloodshed in order

to profit from their destruction. These are easily understood concepts whose effect in day-to-day life can be felt immediately.

Significantly, this characterization is based on the words and acts of Germans—of SS men, policemen, soldiers, administrators, and those working in the economy—before the formal genocidal program of systematic killing had begun. It is the masses, the ordinary Germans, not the Nazi ideologues and theoreticians, whom Kaplan exposes. The causal link between the Germans' beliefs and actions is palpable, so that the Jews feel the effect of their "concepts" "in day-to-day life." In the more than two-and-a-half years of subsequent concentrated observation of the Germans in Warsaw, Kaplan saw no reason to alter this evaluation, an evaluation confirmed by a German police official, who states plainly that those serving alongside him in the Cracow region of Poland "were, with a few exceptions, quite happy to take part in shootings of Jews. They had a ball!" Their killing was motivated by "great hatred against the Jews; it was revenge. . . ." The revenge was not for any real harm that the Jews had visited upon Germans, but for the figmental harms for which the perpetrators believed, in their anti-Semitically-inflamed minds, the Jews were responsible.

Effectively extinguishing the voices of the victims, and sometimes suggesting that they do little more than glorify themselves, is not only indefensible methodologically but also a deep affront to survivors. Most victims want to do nothing more than convey what the perpetrators did to them, their families, and to others. Victims of such crimes can never gain full restitution for their losses and suffering. What they generally seem to want is to have the truth be told, particularly so that the perpetrators will acknowledge their crimes. Survivors often express bewilderment that their experience has been generally ignored by the scholarship that treats the perpetration of the Holocaust. Many survivors have told me that they are thankful for my book, *Hitler's Willing Executioners,* and for its detailed analysis of the German perpetrators, including their gleeful cruelty and brutality, which the survivors attest was almost always voluntary. They say my interpretation of the Holocaust accords with what they and so many others witnessed and experienced.

A new way of approaching the study of the Holocaust is implicit in much of the unparalleled, widespread public discussion about various aspects of the Holocaust that has been taking place for the last two years. The old paradigm consists of abstract, faceless structures and institutions (bureaucracy, the greatly exaggerated "terror apparatus" that was supposedly directed at ordinary Germans, the SS, the Nazi Party, the gas chambers) and allegedly irresistible external forces (totalitarian terror, the exigencies of war, social psychological pressure). This paradigm effaces the human actors and their capacity to judge what they were doing and to make moral choices. It is ahistorical. All of this implies that any people from any era with any set of beliefs about Jews (even non-anti-Semites) would have acted in exactly the same manner as the perpetrators, with the same brutality, zeal, and Mephistophelean laughter. This is being challenged by a view that recognizes that the Holocaust was brought about by human beings who had beliefs about what they were doing, beliefs which they developed within a highly specific historical context, and who made many choices about how to act within the institutions in which they worked and which brought them to their tasks in the first place. The human beings are finally at the center of the discussion. The heretofore dominant question of "What compelled them to act against their will?" is being replaced by the question of "Why did these people choose to act in the ways that they did?"

As a result, powerful myths are crumbling: the myth that the Swiss or the Swedes acted as they did only because of the German threat; the myth that the peoples in different occupied countries did not do more to thwart the Germans or less to help in the killing of the Jews merely because of their fear of the occupying Germans; the official Allied governmental myths that they could not reasonably have attempted to do much more to save the victims; the myth that those who procured Jewish property, including art, generally did so innocently; the myth that the perpetrators, by and large, disapproved of what they were doing but were coerced, were being blindly obedient, or were pressured to act as they did; and the three related myths that the German people more broadly (all the exceptions notwithstanding) did not know that their countrymen were killing Jews en masse, did not support the Nazi regime even though its many brutal policies (forced sterilization, so-called "euthanasia," the violent persecution of the Jews and others, the reintroduction of slavery into the European continent) were widely known, and did not approve of the general eliminationist persecution of the Jews.

Not surprisingly, many people who have either been comforted by such views or whose careers have been made by adopting positions that buttress them, and who find the new, powerful challenges to these views to be politically undesirable or personally threatening, are extremely unhappy and have let that be known. The frequent response is to attack, often in the most vitriolic and unprincipled ways, the messengers—whether they be scholars, institutions like the Hamburg Institute for Social Research which produced the exhibit, "War of Extermination: The Crime of the Wehrmacht, 1941–1944" that has been traveling around Germany, the World Jewish Congress for forcing the issue of Swiss gold onto the agenda, or the witnesses, namely Jewish survivors, whose testimony has always been a devastating threat to many of the myths.

It would be beneficial if certain basics could become widely accepted which the crumbling paradigm has obscured. They include:

1. The discarding of the caricature of individual Germans as having had no views of their own about the rightness of what they or their countrymen were doing, which included slaughtering children. We need to know how these views were distributed among Germans, and how they, singly or in interaction with other factors, influenced Germans' actions during these years. The same applies to the peoples of other countries, those where the Germans found many willing helpers and those where the populace worked to thwart (sometimes successfully) the program of extermination.

2. The rejection of the myth that the large-scale, mass killing of Jews remained unknown to the broader German public. Germans themselves are becoming more candid: twenty-seven percent of those who were at least fourteen years old at the end of the war now admit that they knew of the extermination of the Jews when it was taking place. (The survey which determined this stunning new finding, which the chief pollster of the German wire service, dpa, says is still clearly a substantial underreporting of the real figure, was conducted for the German television network ZdF in September 1996. Yet in the flood of articles written about the Holocaust since then, I have seen no mention of this finding, perhaps because it explodes a central element of the conventional paradigm—even though the survey's results were announced and discussed on German national television during a panel discussion on the Holocaust and reported by the dpa.)

3. The acknowledgment that Germans who were not members of specifically targeted groups (Jews; Gays; the Sinti and Roma peoples, who are commonly known as gypsies; the mentally infirm; the Communist and Social Democratic leadership) were not so terrorized as the totalitarian terror model posits. The enormous amount of dissent and opposition that Germans expressed against so many policies of the regime and the regime's responsiveness to public sentiment and action makes this clear. So a new understanding of the relationship between state power, regime policy, and popular consent needs to be worked out. The comparative question of why Germans expressed different degrees of dissent and opposition to different policies, yet virtually no principled dissent against the eliminationist persecution of the Jews, becomes central. More generally, all models that posit that irresistible external forces compelled people—Germans, French, Poles, Swiss, or the Allies—to act as they did need to be replaced by views that acknowledge the existence of human agency. If the vast majority of the German people had genuinely been opposed to the radical eliminationist persecution of the Jews, then Hitler would never have been able to pursue it as he did.

4. The adoption of a comparative perspective on genocide, so that those who study the Holocaust do not adopt methodological practices or causal claims that are at odds with how we study and

what we know of other analogous phenomena. All available evidence (contemporaneous documents and the testimony of perpetrators, victims, and bystanders) that is not rendered suspect according to clearly articulated, standard social scientific principles is to be used. Regarding the use of the testimony of Jewish survivors, for example, the reasons given for excluding it must be defensible if one changed the word "Jews" to Tutsis, Bosnians, Cambodians, Armenians, the victims of the Gulag, or enslaved Blacks in the American South. The methods of the social sciences present rules regarding research design and the structure of inference, including when generalization is allowed and even required. A major research project might be undertaken using all available evidence to catalogue what is known of the backgrounds, actions, and attitudes of every perpetrator in every ghetto, camp, and other institution of killing—those who victimized Jews and non-Jews—so that a general portrait and systematic analysis of them can be composed.

5. The recognition that the Holocaust had both universal and particular elements. Its universal aspect is that all people have the capacity to dehumanize groups of others so intensely that their hatred can impel them to commit genocide. Its particular aspect is that such views do not come to exist in equal measure in every society about every group, and when they do, it is not every society that has a state which mobilizes those who hold such views in a program of mass annihilation. The universal capacity to hate does not mean that all people actually do hate and hate all others in the same way, or that all hatreds will motivate people to treat the object of their aggression similarly. Real existing hatreds, as opposed to the capacity to hate, are primarily socially constructed and historically particular.

The Holocaust is not "beyond human comprehension." In principle, it is as explicable as every other genocide. No one says that the Rwandan or Cambodian genocide cannot be explained. What so many people simply do not want to accept is that the victims of the Holocaust have a great deal to tell us about their victimizers (no less than do the victims in Rwanda and Bosnia); and that the German perpetrators were like the perpetrators of other mass slaughters: the vast majority of these Germans were also willing executioners. That people automatically accept these facts about non-Jewish victims of genocide and about African or Asian perpetrators but not about Jews and "civilized" white Christian Europeans respectively is disturbing. Does anyone think for a moment that the Turkish, Hutu, or Serbian perpetrators did not believe that slaughtering Armenians, Tutsis, or Muslims was right? Does anyone for a moment believe that the testimony of these genocides' victims should not be used extensively in order to learn about the texture of the genocides, including the attitudes of the perpetrators? Indeed, in the Armenian genocide, in Bosnia, Cambodia, Rwanda, and other instances of mass slaughter, such testimony is eagerly used by scholars and has provided the principal knowledge of the perpetrators' deeds and attitudes. . . .

**DANIEL JONAH GOLDHAGEN** is a professor of government and social studies at Harvard University. He has written articles and reviews on subjects related to the Holocaust.

**Christopher R. Browning**

 **NO**

# Ordinary Germans or Ordinary Men?
# A Reply to the Critics

In the spring of 1992, I published a book entitled *Ordinary Men,* the case study of a reserve police battalion from Hamburg that became the chief unit for killing Jews in the northern Lublin district of the General Government. In general, the book has been quite well-received, but it has not been without its critics in both the United States and Israel. While these critics have accepted the narrative presentation in the book that reveals the mode of operation and degree of choice within the battalion, they have objected to my use of sources, my portrayal of the perpetrators (particularly their motives and mindset) and, above all, the conclusions that I draw—the crux of which is summed up in the title *Ordinary Men.* As one friendly but critical letter-writer suggested, "Might not a preferable title . . . possibly have been Ordinary Germans?"

The argument of my critics for German singularity rests above all upon their assertion of a unique and particular German antisemitism. The letter-writer cited above argued that "cultural conditioning" shaped "specifically German behavioral modes." He continued, hypothesizing that "even many decidedly non-Nazi Germans . . . were so accustomed to the thought that Jews are less human than Germans, that they were capable of mass murder." Non-Germans in the same situation as the men of Reserve Police Battalion 101, he implies, would have behaved quite differently.

Daniel Goldhagen, the most severe critic of what he called my "essentially situational" explanation, put the matter more pointedly. The "Germans' singular and deeply rooted, racist anti-Semitism" was not "a common social psychological phenomenon" that can be analyzed in terms of "mere" negative racial stereotypes, as I had so "tepidly" done. "The men of Reserve Police Battalion 101 were not ordinary 'men,' but ordinary members of an extraordinary culture, the culture of Nazi Germany, which was possessed of a hallucinatory, lethal view of the Jews." Thus, ordinary Germans were "believers in the justice of the murder of the Jews." In their "inflamed imaginations," destruction of the Jews "was a redemptive act."

The issue raised here, namely the appropriate balance of situational, cultural, and ideological factors in explaining the behavior of Holocaust killers, is an important—indeed central—subject that merits further exploration. I would like to approach this issue along two lines of inquiry. First, what has the bulk of recent scholarship concluded about the nature, intensity, and alleged singularity of antisemitism within the German population at large? Second, what light can comparisons between German and non-German killers of Jews in the Holocaust shed on the issue of "specifically German behavioral modes"?

Let us turn to the first line of inquiry, namely the nature and intensity of antisemitism within Nazi Germany Perhaps the most ardent advocate of an interpretation emphasizing the singularity and centrality of German antisemitism was Lucy S. Dawidowicz. In her book *The War against the Jews,* she argued that

> generations of anti-Semitism had prepared the Germans to accept Hitler as their redeemer. . . . Of the conglomerate social, economic, and political appeals that the NSDAP [National Socialist German Workers Party] directed at the German people, its racial doctrine was the most attractive. . . . Out of the whole corpus of racial teachings, the anti-Jewish doctrine had the greatest dynamic potency. . . . The insecurities of post-World War I Germany and the anxieties they produced provided an emotional milieu in which irrationality and hysteria became routine and illusions became transformed into delusions. The delusional disorder assumed mass proportions. . . . In modern Germany the mass psychosis of anti-Semitism deranged a whole people.

A large number of other scholars, however, have not shared this view. Three scholars in particular—Ian Kershaw, Otto Dov Kulka, and David Bankier—have devoted a significant portion of their scholarly lives to examining German popular attitudes toward National Socialism, antisemitism, and the Holocaust. While there are differences of emphasis, tone, and interpretation among them, the degree of consensus on the basic issues is impressive.

While Kulka and Bankier do not pick up the story until 1933, Kershaw argues that prior to the *Machtergreifung,* antisemitism was not a major factor in attracting support for Hitler and the Nazis. He cites Peter Merkl's study of the "old fighters," in which only about one-seventh of Merkl's sample considered antisemitism their most salient concern and even fewer were classified by Merkl as "strong ideological antisemites." Moreover, in the electoral breakthrough phase of 1929–1933, and indeed up to 1939, Hitler rarely spoke in public about the Jewish question. This reticence stood in stark contrast to the Hitler speeches of the early 1920s, in which his obsession with and hatred of the Jews was vented openly and repeatedly. Kershaw concludes that "antisemitism cannot . . . be allocated a decisive role in bringing Hitler to power, though . . . it did not do anything to hinder his rapidly growing popularity."

For the 1933–1939 period, all three historians characterize German popular response to antisemitism by two dichotomies. The first is a distinction between a minority of party activists, for whom antisemitism was an urgent priority, and the bulk of the German population, for whom it was not. Party activists clamored and pressed, often in violent and rowdy ways, for intensified persecution. The antisemitic measures of the regime, though often criticized as too mild by the radicals, served an integrating function within Hitler's movement: they helped to keep the momentum and enthusiasm of the party activists alive. Despite Hitler's pragmatic caution in public, most of these radicals correctly sensed that he was with them in spirit.

The second dichotomy characterizes the reaction of the general population to the antisemitic clamor of the movement and the antisemitic measures of the regime. The vast majority accepted the legal measures of the regime, which ended emancipation and drove Jews from public positions in 1933, socially ostracized the Jews in 1935, and completed the expropriation of their property in 1938–1939. Yet this same majority was critical of the hooliganistic violence of party radicals toward the same German Jews whose legal persecution they approved. The boycott of 1933, the vandalistic out breaks of 1935, and above all the Kristallnacht pogrom of November 1938 produced a negative response among the German population. Bankier and Kulka emphasize the pragmatic concerns behind this negative response: destruction of property, foreign policy complications, damage to Germany's image, and general lawlessness offensive to societal notions of decorum. In Kershaw's opinion, the idea that the population discounted virtually any moral dimension is "a far too sweeping generalization." Nonetheless, these historians agree that a gulf had opened up between the Jewish minority and the general population. The latter, while they were not mobilized around strident and violent antisemitism, were increasingly "apathetic," "passive," and "indifferent" to the fate of the former. Antisemitic measures—if carried out in an orderly and legal manner—were widely accepted for two main reasons: such measures sustained the hope of curbing the violence most Germans found so distasteful, and most Germans ultimately agreed with the goal of limiting, and even ending, the role of Jews in German society.

The records of the war years upon which Kulka, Bankier, and Kershaw based their studies were sparser and more ambiguous. Accordingly, the difference in interpretation is greater. Kulka and Bankier deduce a more specific awareness of the Final Solution among the German people than does Kershaw. Kershaw and Bankier advocate a more critical and less literal reading of the SD [security service] reports than does Kulka. Kershaw sees a general "retreat into the private sphere" as the basis for widespread indifference and apathy toward Nazi Jewish policy. Kulka sees a greater internalization of Nazi antisemitism among the population at large, particularly concerning the acceptance of a solution to the Jewish Question through some unspecified kind of "elimination," and accordingly prefers the term "passive" or "objective complicity" over "indifference." Bankier emphasizes a greater sense of guilt and shame among Germans, widespread denial and repression, and a growing fear concerning the consequences of impending defeat and a commensurate rejection of the regime's antisemitic propaganda. But these differences are matters of nuance, degree, and diction. Fundamentally, the three scholars agree far more than they differ.

Above all, they agree that the fanatical antisemitism of the party "true believers" was not identical to the antisemitic attitudes of the general population and that the antisemitic priorities and genocidal commitment of the regime were not shared by ordinary Germans. Kershaw concludes that while

> the depersonalization of the Jew had been the real success story of Nazi propaganda and policy . . . the "Jewish question" was of no more than minimal interest to the vast majority of Germans during the war years. . . . Popular opinion, largely indifferent and infused with a latent anti-Jewish feeling . . . provided the climate within which spiralling Nazi aggression towards the Jews could take place unchallenged. But it did not provoke the radicalization in the first place.

Kershaw summarized his position in the memorable phrase that "the road to Auschwitz was built by hatred, but paved with indifference.". . .

The general conclusions of Kershaw, Kulka, and Bankier—based on years of research and a wide array of empirical evidence—stand in stark contrast to the Dawidowicz/Goldhagen image of the entire German population "deranged" by a delusional mass psychosis and in the grips of a "hallucinatory, lethal view of the Jews." If "ordinary Germans" shared the same "latent," "traditional," or even "deep-seated" antisemitism that was widespread in European society but not the "fanatical" or "radical" antisemitism of Hitler, the Nazi leadership, and the party "true believers," then the behavior of the "ordinary Germans" of Reserve Police Battalion 101 cannot be explained by a singular German antisemitism that makes them different from other "ordinary men."

My characterization of the depersonalizing and dehumanizing antisemitism of the men of Reserve Police Battalion 101, which Goldhagen finds too "tepid," places them in the mainstream of German society as described by Kershaw, Kulka, and Bankier, distinct from an ideologically driven Nazi leadership. The implications of my study are that the existence of widespread negative racial stereotyping in a society—in no way unique to Nazi Germany—can provide fanatical regimes not only the freedom of action to pursue genocide (as both Kershaw and Kulka conclude) but also an ample supply of executioners.

In regard to the centrality of antisemitic motivation, it should be noted that German executioners were capable of killing millions of non-Jews targeted by the Nazi regime. Beginning in 1939, systematic and large-scale mass murder was initiated against the German handicapped and Polish intelligentsia. More than three million Soviet prisoners of war perished from hunger, exposure, disease, and outright execution—two-thirds of them in the first nine months after the launching of Barbarossa but before the death camps of Operation Reinhard had even opened. Tens of thousands fell victim to horrendous reprisal measures. Additionally, the Nazi regime included Gypsies in their genocidal assault. Clearly, something more than singular German antisemitism is needed to explain perpetrator behavior when the regime could find executioners to murder millions of non-Jewish victims.

Let us follow another approach to this issue as well by examining the behavior of non-German killing units in the Ukraine and Belorussia, which carried out killing actions quite similar to those performed by Reserve Police Battalion 101. I will not be looking at those elements that enthusiastically carried out the initial murderous pogroms in the summer of 1941—often at German instigation—and were then frequently formed into full-time auxiliaries of the Einsatzgruppen for the subsequent large-scale systematic massacres. The zealous followers of Jonas Klimaitis in Lithuania or Viktors Arajs in Latvia, who eagerly rushed to help the invading Germans kill communists and Jews, are not appropriate counterparts of Reserve Police Battalion 101 for the purpose of cross-cultural comparison.

Instead, I will examine the rural police units in Belorussia and the Ukraine, which did not really take shape until 1942, when they participated in the "second wave" of killing on Soviet territory. Like the men of Reserve Police Battalion 101 in Poland, these policemen provided the essential manpower for the "mopping-up" killings of Jews in small towns and villages and for the "Jew hunts" that relentlessly tracked down escapees. . . .

In summary, the precinct-level Ukrainian police were first organized by the military administration in 1941. They were vastly expanded under the Order Police in 1942, whom they outnumbered in precinct service by at least a 10 to 1 ratio. The local police joined for numerous reasons, including pay, food for their families, release from POW camps, and especially a family exemption from deportation to forced labor in Germany. Although the Germans had difficulty recruiting as many Ukrainian police as they wanted, the Ukrainian police nonetheless numbered in the tens of thousands and constituted a major manpower source for the "second wave" of the Final Solution that swept through the Ukraine in 1942.

There is scant documentation from the precinct level on the day-to-day participation of the auxiliary police in the mass murder of Jews. From the Ukraine one series of police reports survives, from which we can see that the local Schutzmänner and their supervising German Gendarmerie performed precisely the same duties as Reserve Police Battalion 101 in Poland, with one exception—there were no deportations to death camps, only shooting actions. . . .

The Gendarmerie outpost in Mir, in Belorussia . . . reported the results of its killing activities to headquarters in Baranoviche. Its commander noted that "560 Jews were shot in the Jewish action carried out in Mir" on August 13, 1942. . . . Around Mir, the Jew hunt continued. On September 29, 1942, a "patrol of the Mir Schutzmannschaft" found in the forest six Jews, who "had fled the previous Jewish action." They were shot on the spot. Six weeks later a forest keeper discovered a Jewish bunker. He led a patrol of three German gendarmes and sixty Schutzmänner to the site. Five Jews, including the former head of the Judenrat of Mir, were hauled from the bunker and shot. "The food"—including 100 kilos of potatoes—"as well as the tattered clothing were given to the Mir Schutzmannschaft."

In short, the role in the Final Solution of the precinct-level police recruited on Soviet territory seems scarcely distinguishable from that of German reserve police in Poland. The precinct-level Schutzmänner were not the eager pogromists and collaborators of mid-summer 1941, just as the German reserve police were not career SS and policemen but post-1939 conscripts. The role and behavior of the Ukrainian and Belorussian auxiliary police in carrying out the Final Solution do not lend support to the notion of "specifically German behavioral modes."

I would like to look into the particular case of the German Gendarmerie in Mir and their Belorussian auxiliaries in greater detail because this case pertains to a further criticism of my book, my alleged misuse of German sources and nonuse of Jewish sources. It has been suggested on the one hand that I was much too gullible and methodologically uncritical in my acceptance of German testimony, particularly that which I cited in support of my portrayal of a differentiated reaction by the perpetrators and a dramatic transformation in character of many of the policemen over time. I argued that most of the men were upset by the initial killing action, and that over time a considerable minority of the men became enthusiastic and zealous volunteers for the firing squads and Jew hunts; that the largest group within the battalion did not seek opportunities to kill but nonetheless routinely contributed to the murder operations in many ways with increasing numbness and callousness; and that a not insignificant minority remained nonshooters while still participating in cordons and roundups. On the other hand, both Goldhagen and a number of my Israeli colleagues have chided me for not using Jewish sources. If I had been more critical of my German sources and more inclusive in my use of Jewish sources, a more reliable image of a uniform and pervasive bestiality, sadism, and even "jocularity," "boyish joy," and "relish" on the part of the perpetrators would have resulted, they suggest.

After working with these German court testimony records for more than twenty years, I would readily concede that the vast bulk of it is pervasively mendacious and apologetic, especially concerning the motivation and attitude of the perpetrators. It was precisely on the basis of my previous experience with German court testimony, however, that I judged the court testimonies of Reserve Police Battalion 101 to be qualitatively different. The roster of the unit survived, more than 40 percent of the battalion members (most of them rank and file reservists rather than officers) were interrogated, and two able and persistent investigating attorneys spent five years carefully questioning the witnesses.

The resulting testimony provides a unique body of evidence that permits us to answer important questions for which previous court records did not provide adequate information. A historian would be wrong to lump this body of evidence together indiscriminately with other court records. Admittedly, these are subjective judgments on my part, and other honest and able historians could reach other conclusions. My critics' dismissal of my use of this particular German testimony as gullible and methodologically unsound, without giving due attention to the special character of these records, ought to be noted, however.

As for the nonuse of Jewish sources, I would make several observations. First, Jewish testimony was indispensable to my study in establishing the chronology for the fall of 1942. What became a blur of events for the perpetrators remained quite distinct days of horror for the victims. Also, while survivor testimony may be extremely valuable in many regards, it does not illuminate the internal dynamics of an itinerant killing unit. It would be difficult for the victim of such a unit to provide testimony concerning the various levels of participation of different perpetrators and any change in their character over time. Where long-term contact between victims and perpetrators did occur, survivors are able to and in fact do differentiate on such issues. Such long-term contact did not occur in the situations that I examined, however. The testimony of survivors and even Polish bystanders of a massacre or ghetto-clearing action by a unit such as Reserve Police Battalion 101 would inevitably focus on the brutality sadism, and horror of the perpetrator unit, with little differentiation among its individual members. It would indeed support the conclusions of my critics concerning the uniform and enthusiastic behavior of the perpetrators, but that does not make those conclusions correct. . . .

A remarkable testimony has recently been published by Nechama Tec in her book about Oswald Rufeisen. It is especially valuable because Rufeisen observed the internal workings of the Mir Gendarmerie post as a translator for the German sergeant in charge. Since some of Rufeisen's testimony so strikingly confirms the dynamics within the reserve police that I portrayed based on perpetrator testimony, I will quote it at length. Tec reports that, according to Rufeisen, there was:

> a visible difference in the Germans' participation in anti-Jewish and anti-partisan moves. A selected few Germans, three out of thirteen, consistently abstained from becoming a part of all anti-Jewish expeditions. . . . No one seemed to bother them. No one talked about their absences. It was as if they had a right to abstain.

Among these middle-aged gendarmes too old to be sent to the front, Rufeisen noted the presence of enthusiastic and sadistic killers, including the second-in command, Karl Schultz, who was described as "a beast in the form of a man." "Not all the gendarmes, however, were as enthusiastic about murdering Jews as Schultz," Tec notes. Concerning the policemen's attitude toward killing Jews, she quotes Rufeisen directly:

> It was clear that there were differences in their outlooks. I think that the whole business of anti-Jewish moves, the business of Jewish extermination they considered unclean. The operations against the partisans were not in the same category. For them a confrontation with partisans was a battle, a military move. But a move against the Jews was something they might have experienced as "dirty." I have the impression that they felt that it would be better not to discuss the matter.

This is hardly the image of men uniformly possessed of a "lethal, hallucinatory view of the Jews" who viewed their killing of Jews as "a redemptive act."

Finally, I would like to look at a third example of cross-cultural omparison that is very suggestive: the Luxembourgers. Reserve Police Battalion 101 was composed almost entirely of Germans from the Hamburg region, including some men from Bremen, Bremerhaven, and Wilhelmshaven, as well as a few Holsteiners from Rendsburg who felt like relative outsiders. In addition, the battalion included a contingent of young men from Luxembourg, which had been annexed to the Third Reich in 1940. The presence of the Luxembourgers in Reserve Police Battalion 101 offers the historian the unusual opportunity for a "controlled experiment" to measure the impact of the same situational factors upon men of differing cultural and ethnic background.

The problem is the scarcity of testimony. Only one German witness described the participation of the Luxembourgers in the battalion's activities in any detail.

According to this witness, the Luxembourgers belonged to Lieutenant Buchmann's platoon in first company and were particularly active in the roundups before the first massacre at Jozéfow. This was a period in late June and early July 1942 when the trains were not running to Belzec, and Jews in the southern Lublin district were being concentrated temporarily in transit ghettos such as Piaski and Izbica. On the night before the initial massacre at Jozéfow, Lieutenant Buchmann was the sole officer who said he could not order his men to shoot unarmed women and children, and who asked for a different assignment. He was designated responsible for taking the work Jews to Lublin and, according to the witness, the Luxembourgers under his command provided the guard. Hence they did not participate in the massacre.

Thereafter Lieutenant Buchmann continued to refuse participation in any Jewish action. However, those in his platoon, including the Luxembourgers, were not exempted. Under the command of the first sergeant, who was a "110% Nazi" and a real "go-getter," the Luxembourgers in particular became quite involved. According to the witness, the company captain took considerable care in the selection of personnel for assignments. "In general the older men remained behind," he noted. In contrast, *the Luxembourgers were in fact present at every action* [emphasis mine]. With these people it was a matter of career police officials from the state of Luxembourg, who were all young men in their twenties." Despite their absence at Jozéfow, it would appear that the Luxembourgers became the shock-troops of first company simply because of their younger age and greater police experience and training, the absence of "specifically German

behavioral modes" and a singular German antisemitism notwithstanding. . . .

I will conclude briefly. If the studies of Kershaw, Kulka, and Bankier are valid and most Germans did not share the fanatical antisemitism of Adolf Hitler and the hardcore Nazis, then an argument based on a singular German antisemitism to explain the murderous actions of low-level perpetrators does not hold up. If the Nazi regime could find executioners for millions of non-Jewish victims, the centrality of antisemitism as the crucial motive of the German perpetrators is also called into question. If tens of thousands of local policemen in Belorussia and the Ukraine—taken as needed by the Germans, who were desperate for help and offered a variety of inducements—basically performed the same duties and behaved in the same way as their German counterparts in Poland, then the argument of "specifically German behavioral modes" likewise fails. Finally, if Luxembourgers in Reserve Police Battalion 101 did not behave differently from their German comrades, then the immediate situational factors to which I gave considerable attention in the conclusion of my book must be given even greater weight. The preponderance of evidence suggests that in trying to understand the vast majority of the perpetrators, we are dealing not with "ordinary Germans" but rather with "ordinary men."

---

**CHRISTOPHER R. BROWNING** is a professor of history at the University of North Carolina, Chapel Hill and a leading Holocaust historian. His most recent book is *Nazi Policy, Jewish Workers, German Killers* (Cambridge University Press, 2000).

# EXPLORING THE ISSUE

## Was German "Eliminationist Anti-Semitism" Responsible for the Holocaust?

### Critical Thinking and Reflection

1. Examine Professor Goldhagen's evidence for a particular German anti-Semitism. Do you find the evidence compelling? Critically discuss.
2. Examine historian Browning's claim that these willing participants were "ordinary men," not "ordinary Germans." What does he mean? Do you find his arguments compelling? Critically discuss.
3. Why, in your view, did so many people willingly participate in the widespread killing of Jews and non-Jews? Critically discuss.
4. What evidence from these two selections is most helpful to you in explaining the Holocaust? What is it particularly compelling? Critically discuss.
5. Do you accept the claim that attitudes in German society made Hitler's "Final Solution" possible? Critically discuss.
6. Christopher Browning seems to suggest that, under the right conditions, any of us might do what thousands did in the Holocaust. Critically discuss this suggestion.
7. Research the origin of the phrase "The banality of evil." If evil, itself, becomes banal, is anything possible? Critically discuss.

### Is There Common Ground?

These two scholars cite largely the same specific evidence. If this aberration in history was peculiar to German culture and a particularly powerful form of anti-Semitism, as Goldhagen claims, the rest of us can distance ourselves from these atrocities. On the other hand, if these were "ordinary men," as Browning asserts, the questions we must ask are much more complex. While the acts committed by these citizens are shocking, there does seem to be a significant issue that takes us beyond our initial shocked response and that resides at the heart of these atrocities.

*Question:* Were these "ordinary Germans," sharing a particular cultural worldview that normalized such behavior? Or, were they "ordinary men," doing what still seems unthinkable?

### Create Central

www.mhhe.com/createcentral

### Additional Resources

Needless to say, there have been so many books written about the Holocaust, that to single out a few for mention

can be a precarious operation. But a few general sources that should be consulted would be:

Raul Hilberg, *The Destruction of the European Jews* (Holmes & Meier, 1985); Yehuda Bauer, *A History of the Holocaust* (Franklin Watts, 1982); and Martin Gilbert, *The Holocaust: A History of the Jews of Europe During the Second World War* (Owl Books, 1987). Michael Marrus's *The Holocaust in History* (Meridian Books, 1987) serves as one of the Holocaust's most thoroughly historiographical studies.

Ron Rosenbaum's *Explaining Hitler* (Random House, 1998) provides an interesting and accessible look at Holocaust historiography, as the journalist/author interviews and writes about the world's leading Holocaust scholars and their works. For neophytes, this might be a good place to start. Also, the journal *Holocaust and Genocide Studies* always provides interesting and thought-provoking articles on the subject.

Lastly, a book of essays critiquing Goldhagen's work is: *Hyping the Holocaust: Scholars Answer Goldhagen* (Cummings and Hathaway, 1997), which provides ample criticism of Goldhagen's scholarship. Finally, *Unwilling Germans? The Goldhagen Debate*, Robert R. Shandley, editor (University of Minnesota Press, 1998), offers a large sampling of German reaction to *Hitler's Willing Executioners*.

## *Internet References . . .*

**Holocaust Learning Center**

This website, the creation of the Washington-based United States Holocaust Memorial Museum, provides

multi-linked connections to the subject, useful for both novice and experienced hands.

**www.ushmm.org**

Selected, Edited, and with Issue Framing Material by:
Helen Buss Mitchell, *Howard Community College*
and
Joseph R. Mitchell, *Howard Community College*

# ISSUE

# Was Stalin Responsible for the Korean War?

YES: **Paul Wingrove**, from "Who Started Korea?" *History Today* (July 2000)

NO: **Hugh Deane**, from "Korea, China, and the United States: A Look Back," *Monthly Review* (February 1995)

| Learning Outcomes |
|---|
| **After reading this issue you should be able to:** |
| • Recount the recent history of Korea, especially its strategic position and its role as the location of a proxy war between the United States and the U.S.S.R. |
| • What is a Cold War? In what specific ways does it differ from a "Hot War"? |
| • Describe the Cold War that arose between the two surviving powers (United States and U.S.S.R.) in the aftermath of the Hot War (World War II) in which they were allies. |
| • Detail the role of the United Nations in the undeclared Korean War (sometimes called a conflict because it was undeclared) between 1950 and 1953. |

## ISSUE SUMMARY

**YES:** Historian Paul Wingrove argues that Josef Stalin should be held primarily responsible for the Korean War.

**NO:** Historian Hugh Deane argues that the United States' support for Syngman Rhee's non-communist government was responsible for the Korean War.

**K**orea, a small peninsula jutting into the Sea of Japan and the East China Sea, has a history dating back to the Paleolithic Era. This culture's existence has been characterized by warring clans, creation of kingdoms, and threats from larger neighbors, especially Japan and China. Because of its strategic location, it should not be surprising that Korea would become a pawn in the Cold War struggle in the middle of the twentieth century.

After a long and bitter struggle, Korea was annexed by Japan in 1910. Despite fierce opposition from Korean nationalists, including armed conflict, that condition remained unchanged until the end of World War II. In 1945, the Potsdam Declaration proclaimed Korea to be an independent country.

The year 1945 marked the beginning of the Cold War. It became clear that former allies, the Soviet Union and the United States, the only major countries to survive with power after World War II, were fast becoming bitter rivals for world supremacy. Conflicts between the two were numerous, extending from Europe to Asia and touching many points between. Acquisition of territory became an important part of the power struggle. Eventually, the United States would adopt a policy of "containment," the

purpose of which was to limit communist conquests in the world. China had already been lost and the Soviet Union was quickly trying to add Eastern Europe to its sphere of influence. Korea would become one of "containment's" first test cases.

A the end of World War II, the Korean peninsula was divided between Soviet and United States occupation forces at the 38th parallel. In 1947, the newly created United Nations established a Temporary Commission on Korea to seek a solution to the two Korea situation. In the following year, UN-sponsored elections that were held in Korea produced predictable results. In the U.S.-controlled south, the Republic of Korea was created with Syngman Rhee as its president. In the Russian-dominated north, the Democratic People's Republic of Korea was established with Kim Il-sung as its Premier. Those who longed for a united Korea were bitterly disappointed.

One such person was Kim Gu, a Korean nationalist opposed to the formation of a separate South Korean state. In 1949, he was assassinated by Ahn Doo Whi, a lieutenant in the South Korean army and an employee of the U.S. Counter Intelligence Corps in Korea. Yum Dong Jin, an army officer with close ties to Syngman Rhee, was said to have ordered the assassination, the purpose of which was to silence an opponent of the creation of the Republic of Korea. The United States may have been complicit in this murder.

On June 25, 1950, North Korean troops invaded South Korea by crossing the 38th parallel. Within 3 days, they were in control of the South Korean capital of Seoul. The Korean War had begun. United Nations forces (mainly American servicemen) were sent to Korea under the command of General Douglas MacArthur. After some early setbacks, the UN forces gained the upper hand and drove the North Korean forces back across the 38th parallel, pursuing them to the Yalu River, the border between North Korea and Manchuria (a province of China). Predictably, this brought Chinese military forces into the war and eventually led to a stalemate between the two forces, which lasted until 1953, when a ceasefire ended the war. It remains in force today.

Responsibility for the Korean War has long been a contentious subject among historians. Some see Russian Premier Josef Stalin as being the prime instigator, claiming that Kim Il-sung would never had invaded the South without his approval. Also, some blame Mao Zedong, the premier of the newly created People's Republic of China, for prolonging the conflict. Others hold the long-standing U.S. support for Syngman Rhee's government, dating back to1945, as responsible. In this issue, Paul Wingrove takes the former position, while the late Hugh Deane argues for the latter one.

As a result of a student uprising in 1960, President Syngman Rhee was forced out of office. He resigned and went into exile. In the following year, military forces overthrew the existing regime and established a new government. Since that time, South Korea has experienced the trials and tribulations that beset many new, inexperienced democracies. But recent decades have brought a strong commitment to democratic government and a strong economic system, which had made it one of Asia's "economic tigers." In 1988, Seoul hosted the 24th Olympic Games; in 2002, Korea and Japan co-hosted the 17th World Cup Soccer Championships. Both attest to the respect that the world now holds for South Korea.

The conditions in North Korea offer a stark contrast. A strictly controlled centrist-run economic system has produced something lower than Third World status. Kim Il-sung's communist, one-man rule has been the only constant. When he died in 1994, he was succeeded by his son Kim Jong-Il. This has resulted in little economic or political progress. The contrast between the two Koreas couldn't be more striking.

In the last decade, several summit conferences have been held between the governments of North and South Korea. However, at this time, conditions remain the same.

Was the Korean War worth the price for the United States? South Korea was saved from communism's grasp, but at a heavy cost in American lives. Containment was achieved, but as the Korean War was ending, the United States was already getting entangled in another divided Asian nation—Vietnam. This time the results would be different.

# YES ↵

**Paul Wingrove**

## Who Started Korea?

**O**n June 25th, 1950, Communist North Korea launched an invasion across the 38th Parallel into South Korea. Initially taken aback, the West, under American leadership, quickly recovered and within days had obtained United Nations Security Council agreement to repel the attack. For President Truman this was a decisive encounter. As he saw it, North Korea's Communist leader Kim Il Sung was not acting independently, nor was the aim of this attack simply limited to reunification of the divided Korean peninsula. In this aggressive action he discerned the hand of the USSR, and possibly that of Communist China. In Truman's words: 'The Reds were probing for weaknesses in our armour; we had to meet their thrust without getting embroiled in a world-wide war'. His Secretary of State, Dean Acheson, also concluded that 'it seemed close to certain that the attack had been mounted, supplied and instigated by the Soviet Union . . .', and:

> To back away from this challenge . . . would be highly destructive of the power and prestige of the United States . . . we could not accept the conquest of this important area by a Soviet puppet under the very guns of our defensive perimeter with no more resistance than words and gestures in the Security Council.

Only recently, however, have the roles of Stalin and Mao in unleashing the Korean War become better known, thanks to the opening of the archives of former Communist bloc countries. Researchers have also benefited from President Yeltsin's personal decision in 1994 to present to the South Korean government hundreds of pages of high-level declassified documents relating to the origins of the war. Even so, the record is far from complete. In Russia many documents from the highly sensitive 'Presidential Archive' and from KGB and military archives are simply not available, while China's archives are effectively closed to outsiders.

Nonetheless, fifty years on we are much clearer about the war's origins. Who wanted the war, and why? The answer seems to be that it was primarily Kim Il Sung who sought reunification of Korea through military action, but as a client state of the USSR he needed, and was given, the support and encouragement of Stalin. Kim was driven by the cause of reunification, but was also perhaps, too easily impressed by Mao Zedong's successes in the Chinese civil war of 1946–49. Stalin came to see an attack on South Korea as a potentially cheap Cold War victory.

Reunification through war seems first to have been raised as a serious possibility in March 1949 when Kim travelled to Moscow to meet with Stalin. Their exchange of March 7th is recorded as follows:

**Kim Il Sung:** We believe that the situation makes it necessary and possible to liberate the whole country through military means. The reactionary forces of the South will never agree on a peaceful reunification and will perpetuate the division of the country until they feel themselves strong enough to attack the North. Now is the best opportunity for us to take the initiative into our own hands. Our armed forces are stronger, and in addition we have the support of a powerful guerrilla movement in the South. The population of the South, which despises the pro-American regime, will certainly help us as well.

**Stalin:** You should not advance to the South. First of all, the Korean People's Army does not have an overwhelming superiority over the troops of the South. Numerically, as I understand, you are even behind them. Second, there are still American troops in the South which will interfere in the case of hostilities. Third, one should not forget that the agreement on the 38th Parallel is in effect between the USSR and the United States. If the agreement is broken by our side, it is more of a reason to believe that the Americans will interfere.

**Kim Il Sung:** Does it mean that there is no chance to reunify Korea in the near future? Our people are very anxious to be together again and to cast off the yoke of the reactionary regime and their American masters.

**Stalin:** If the adversary has aggressive intentions, then sooner or later it will start the aggression. In response to the attack you will have a good opportunity to launch a counterattack. Then your move will be understood and supported by everyone.

Whatever his inclinations, Stalin was clear that this was not the time for military action. Indeed, for some time in 1949 his concern was the opposite—that the South might launch an early attack against the North. In a telegram of April 17th to Terentii Shtykov, Soviet ambassador to North Korea, Stalin suggested that:

> In April-May the Southerners will concentrate their troops near the 38th Parallel. In June the

Southerners will start a sudden attack on the North in order to finish off the total destruction of the Northern Army by August.

Kim was undeterred by Stalin's caution. Indeed he was spurred on by events such as the withdrawal of US troops from South Korea in mid-1949, and by Mao's victory in China. On September 3rd, 1949, Shtykov reported to Moscow that Kim had requested permission

> . . . to begin military operations against the South, with the goal of seizing 'the Ongjin peninsula and part of the territory of South Korea to the east of the Ongjin peninsula, approximately to Kaesong, so as to shorten the line of defense.' Kim Il Sung considers . . . that if the international situation permits, they are ready to move further to the south. Kim Il Sung is convinced that they are in a position to seize South Korea in the course of two weeks, maximum two months.

Shtykov prudently counselled Kim that this question was 'very large and serious', and not to do anything until Moscow had considered the matter. Moscow, in the person of Andrei Gromyko, replied a week later, with instructions to the ambassador to 'give your evaluation of the situation and of how real and advisable is the proposal of our friends', indicating some change in Stalin's policy following the US withdrawal. After consultations in Pyongyang the Soviet charge d'affaires, Tunkin, reported back to Moscow on September 14th, that Kim had again indicated that he planned only a 'partial' operation on the Ongjin peninsula, with the possibility of moving further south if this attack resulted in 'demoralisation' of the enemy forces. Irrespective of the scope of Kim's plans, Tunkin stated that he personally remained unconvinced of the ability of the north to carry out an invasion, or to contain the war:

> . . . the northern army is insufficiently strong to carry out successful and rapid operations against the south. Even taking into account the help which will be rendered to the northern army by the partisans and the population of South Korea it is impossible to count on a rapid victory. Moreover, a drawn out civil war is disadvantageous for the north, both militarily and politically. . . . After their lack of success in China, the Americans will probably intervene more decisively than they did in China . . .

Despite his over-optimistic expectations of the population of the south, Tunkin's assessment was sound. The message to Kim, formally delivered from the Soviet Politburo on September 24th, reflected this judgement:

> . . . it is impossible to acknowledge that a military attack on the south is now completely prepared for and therefore from the military point of view it is not allowed.

Yet Kim remained committed to his plans. In mid-January 1950, at a rather emotional lunchtime meeting, he told Shtykov:

> Lately, I do not sleep at night, thinking about how to resolve the question of the unification of the whole country. If the matter of the liberation of the people of the southern portion of Korea and the unification of the country is drawn out, then I can lose the trust of the people of Korea.

Kim then:

> . . . placed before me [Shtykov] the question, why don't I allow him to attack the Ongjin peninsula, which the People's Army could take in three days, and with a general attack the People's Army could be in Seoul in several days.

Shtykov replied that Kim should put such questions to Stalin personally, and reported this conversation to Moscow. In the event, an emboldened Stalin informed Shytkov in January 1950 that he agreed to a second meeting with Kim, now hinting at his new view of things:

> I understand the dissatisfaction of comrade Kim Il Sung, but he must understand that such a large matter in regard to South Korea as he wants to undertake needs large preparation. The matter must be organised so that there would not be too great a risk. If he wants to discuss this matter with me then I will always be ready to receive him. Transmit all this to Kim Il Sung and tell him that I am ready to help him in this matter.

From now until the outbreak of the war on June 25th, 1950, Stalin encouraged Kim and armed him in preparation for an attack on the South. Why this change of heart? Partly because US troops had departed, but also because the 'international situation' had changed in a number of ways advantageous to the Communist world. According to a document prepared by Soviet Communist Party officials which summarised the second Stalin–Kim talks, held in April 1950, Stalin reasoned that

> The Chinese Communist Party's victory over the Guomindang has improved the environment for actions in Korea . . . if necessary, China has at its disposal troops which can be utilised in Korea . . . the Chinese victory is also important psychologically . . . [and] now that China has signed a treaty of alliance with the USSR, Americans will be even more hesitant to challenge the Communists in Asia. . . . Such a mood is reinforced by the fact that the USSR now has the atomic bomb.

Having decided that US intervention was unlikely, Stalin now made clear what would happen if, against his expectations, the war should spread:

> Comrade Stalin added that the Koreans should not count on direct Soviet participation in the

war because the USSR had serious challenges elsewhere to cope with, especially in the West. He again urged Kim Il Sung to consult with Mao Zedong and mentioned that the Chinese leader had a good understanding of Oriental matters. Stalin repeated that the USSR was not ready to get involved in Korean affairs directly, especially if Americans did venture to send troops to Korea.

Kim's argument had always been that American intervention was unlikely and that the war would be short. From a more calculated perspective, Stalin had come to accept this view, while taking precautions against the event of a different outcome.

Given that China was to play such a crucial role in the war, it is surprising that these Moscow–Pyongyang interactions were largely hidden from Mao. While some writers suggest that Stalin and Mao may have discussed Korea during the latter's visit to Moscow from December 1949 to January 1950, this was almost certainly not the case. Indeed, in a telegram from Stalin to Shtykov sent in February 1950 Stalin commanded that:

> The question he [Kim] wants to discuss with me must be completely confidential. It should not be shared with anyone even in the North Korean leadership, as well as the Chinese comrades.

Although Mao was in Moscow until the signing of the Sino-Soviet Treaty of Friendship on February 14th, 1950, Stalin chose not to to talk to him about Korean affairs. Mao did not discover what was afoot until May, following Kim's month-long visit to Moscow in April. On Stalin's suggestion, Kim had travelled to Beijing to see Mao to lay out his plans. While Mao and Kim were in talks Vyshinsky, writing on May 14th, informed Mao that Stalin had already agreed to Kim's 'proposal', and hinted at a role for Beijing:

> In a conversation with the Korean comrades Filippov [Stalin] and his friends expressed the opinion that, in light of the changed international situation, they agree with the proposal of the Koreans to move toward reunification. . . . In this regard a qualification was made . . . that the question should be decided finally by the Chinese and Korean comrades together, and in case of disagreement by the Chinese comrades, the decision on the question should be postponed until a new discussion.

Thus, China was to be tied into the war, if only loosely. Mao gave a rather lukewarm agreement to Kim's plans, although for Kim this was sufficient. Stalin had proved himself generous in his support and Kim took the view that since 'all his requests were satisfied in Moscow' there was no need to bother Mao too much. This meeting, which ended with Mao's muted approval for the enterprise, cleared the way for the June 25th attack.

The North's invasion turned out to be spectacularly successful for the period that it took the West to recover, re-group and send troops to Korea. Stalin, taken aback by a United Nations intervention which confounded his calculations, initially pretended he was not involved in the war—a ploy that dismayed Kim and failed to deceive the West. MacArthur's bold execution of the landings at Inchon in September turned the tide, producing heavy defeats for the North Koreans. In a ciphered telegram of September 30th, Kim pleaded with Stalin:

> If the enemy does not give us time to implement the measures which we plan, and, making use of our extremely grave situation, steps up its offensive operations into North Korea, then we will not be able to stop the enemy troops solely with our own forces. Therefore, dear Josif Vissarionovich, we cannot help asking you to provide us with special assistance. In other words, at the moment when the enemy troops cross the 38th Parallel we will badly need direct military assistance from the Soviet Union.

This, of course, was at odds with Stalin's intentions. Fortunately, Kim went on to request the formation of 'volunteer units in China and other countries of people's democracy', a request Stalin was only too eager to assist with. He immediately fired off a message to Mao:

> If in the current situation you consider it possible to send troops to assist the Koreans, then you should move at least five-six divisions towards the 38th Parallel at once.

As Stalin had always intended, he was not going to pull North Korean chestnuts out of the fire; the Chinese would undertake that task. In later years Mao recalled that it was only when the Chinese had proved their mettle in combat in Korea that Stalin lost some of his earlier suspicion of them. But this was no comfort for Mao, for not only did the Korean war involve huge sacrifices for his country, it also put off indefinitely the higher priority—the conquest of Taiwan.

This was an unnecessary war, for which the responsibility lies mainly with Stalin. His miscalculation damaged the interests of the USSR and the Communist world in general, and it is not surprising that upon his death in 1953 his successors quickly sought a formal end to the conflict. Nor is it surprising that Mao Zedong held a rather jaundiced view of the man who had armed the North for this war, permitted it to be launched, then expected others to save the day.

---

PAUL WINGROVE is a senior lecturer in politics at the University of Greenwich, specializing in the politics of communist states, past and present.

**Hugh Deane**

# Korea, China, and the United States:
## A Look Back

The triumph of the Chinese revolution in 1949 secured the Manchurian rear of Kim Il Sung's Democratic People's Republic and brought it the bonanza of scores of thousands of battle-experienced troops. Koreans whom Kim had sent to fight in the Chinese People's Liberation Army against the Kuomintang came home, bringing much equipment, and were integrated into the new northern army.

That year North Korea responded defensively when South Korean troops provocatively crossed the 38th parallel on the Onjin peninsula. But when the south crossed again in the same area in 1950, as substantial evidence indicates, North Korea struck all along the parallel in what turned into an attempt to unite Korea by force. Yet the northern assault of June 25, 1950, did not begin the Korean war. The war started in 1945 and it was begun by the United States.

When the U.S. Twenty-fourth Corps, commanded by General John R. Hodge, landed in Inchon that September, it found in place a thriving Korean People's Republic organized and led by jubilant patriots with a sense of historic mission. The United States responded by allying itself with Korean collaborators, the Japanese trained police, youthful terrorist groups, the dominant landlord class, and returned rightist exiles like Syngman Rhee, to bring about the destruction of the People's Republic and its supportive new-born organizations—trade unions, peasant associations, the youth federation, and all sorts of cultural groups. Cruelties beyond count led to the establishment in 1948 of a separatist southern regime headed by Rhee, who began many trips to the podium with promises to invade the north and free its enslaved population.

The official rhetoric and most accounts in the media portrayed the Rhee dictatorship as a praiseworthy young democracy valiantly confronting a despotic Soviet puppet in the north. But the CIA told it broadly as it was in internal documents. It said that South Korean politics were dominated by rightists "who control most of the wealth" and exercise control through the National Police, which, allied with "rightist youth groups," are "ruthlessly brutal in suppressing disorder." The left had been driven underground.

Rhee's abuses and inflammatory rhetoric alarmed and troubled important U.S. officials, largely for pragmatic reasons. Moves to try to shift to a centrist regime were considered and debated. But, as elsewhere, the deterrent was a serious uncertainty, the possibility that centrism might slip over to a left success. The United States clung to Rhee and to the dictatorships that succeeded him.

Still in naval uniform, I was in Seoul briefly in October 1945. General Hodge had recently described Japanese and Koreans as "the same breed of cat." Syngman Rhee arrived on one of MacArthur's planes to be warmly welcomed at a ceremony organized by the United States and its Korean collaborator friends. Rhee was provided with quarters with the generals in the Chosen Hotel, with a huge slush fund and ready access to the radio. I returned for substantial stays in 1947 and 1948. In 1947 I feverishly reported on the destruction of the above-ground left and in 1948, with Pierre Doublet of Agence France Presse, I worked to get at the truth of the farcical election that elevated Rhee to power.

Left-oriented educated Koreans had been misled into believing that if U.S. correspondents were amply supplied with the facts, they would use them to get the truth out. The result was that hundreds of nocturnal hours were spent in preparing detailed papers on a score of subjects. The English was flawed (a scholar who became a friend spoke Shakespearean English) and some of the facts were hearsay, but they were a powerful, numbing recitation of the brutalities that frustrated the aspirations of a long-suffering people. My copies are among my Korean papers at the University of Chicago.

The left did not succumb easily. The Autumn Harvest Uprisings of 1946 were a surge of bitter anger, ill-organized by the local people's committees of the People's Republic, and savagely crushed. The villages on Cheju island rebelled unitedly in 1948 and killed many police and other tormentors before suppression. The brief Yosu rebellion began with the refusal of constabulary units to go to Cheju on a counter-insurgency mission. The United States commanded the subduing of the rebels—secret protocols gave them covert authority. Retribution was merciless, U.S. intelligence reported. But before the year was over much of the south was engulfed in a guerrilla war that continued diminished in some areas until it linked up with the assaulting northern divisions in 1950. Reporting on the guerrilla war in March 1950, Walter Sullivan of the New York Times, the best of the U.S. correspondents, wrote,

Large sections of South Korea are darkened today by a cloud of terror that is probably unparalleled in the world. . . . Nights in the hundreds of villages across the guerrilla areas are a long, cold vigil of listening.

The number of southern guerrillas killed during the first two months of the war (July and August) was double the number of soldiers from the United States killed in the entire war.

North Korea developed into an independent commandist state. Even in its formative stage it was not a satellite, but in many respects it was modelled on China. Kim Il Sung had been a member of the Chinese Communist Party in his youth and he waged a hard-bitten guerrilla war along the Korean–Manchurian border like that characteristic of the Chinese party's struggle for power. A number of Koreans studied under Zhou Enlai and Guo Morou at the Whampoa Academy in Guangzhou and at least one made the Long March. A Korean military–political school was organized at Yanan. As noted, many thousands of Koreans fought in the Chinese civil war, throughout which North Korea was a rest and recuperation area for Chinese troops. A study in late 1949 revealed that of 1,881 "cultural cadres" in North Korea, 422 had experience in China's Eighth Route Army.

But Kim was selective in his emulation of the Chinese. He borrowed heavily from Mao when he made speeches and organized a Koreanized, moderated, Great Leap Forward. But he stayed clear of the Cultural Revolution, which he saw as a threatening alienation of the people. The party he led was named the Workers' Party and in 1975 he took North Korea into the Non-Aligned Movement, in effect into the Third World. His cult matched Mao's (Mao was the Red Sun in Our Hearts, Kim was a Beautiful New Red Star in the Sky). He had Pak Hon-yong, leader of the southern Communists, who was perceived as a rival, executed following concocted charges. Like Chiang Kai-shek, he named his son (Kim Jong II) as successor.

But the demonization of North Korea is wide of the mark. The regime carried out an effective land reform and was successful in expanding literacy and education generally. It lavished money on cultural opportunities. Industrialization created many thousands of jobs. Many Koreans must have felt stifled by the top-downism and the adulation of the leader but no evidence points to a great loss of popular support.

Two critical differences separate the north and the U.S.–Rhee south. First, in contrast to the Chinese and Korean revolutionary experience of the military in the north, the southern army was commanded by Koreans who had been officers in the Imperial Japanese Army and were proud of it. Some had been in units trying to extirpate Kim's guerrilla force, some were guilty of war crimes in the Philippines and China. Secondly, guerrillas were both a historical legacy and a current North Korean asset in both the south and north. Late in 1950 U.S. intelligence counted some 60,000 guerrillas operating nearly as far south as Pusan. The U.S.–Rhee regime, on the other hand, had not the slightest hope of gaining a guerrilla auxiliary and never tried.

Early in the 1950 war MacArthur boasted that with a single division, the First Cavalry, he would quickly have the Reds skedaddling north, but he soon found that division after division had to be committed. After capturing Seoul, the North Korean forces fatally paused a week, apparently to resupply, which enabled MacArthur to reinforce and hold the Pusan perimeter in the southeast. Afterward, MacArthur skillfully executed his Inchon leapfrog. A huge armada (it secretly included a Japanese minesweeper flotilla manned by former Japanese navy personnel) landed a substantial military force at Seoul's port, bringing about the recapture of Seoul, the capital. The northern divisions to the south were more or less cut off and suffered heavy losses.

It was "MacArthur at his finest," many said and indeed it was a brilliant stroke. But overall MacArthur in Korea was at his worst, the victim of his ethnocentric bias, his ignorance of Chinese tactics and strategy, and his reliance on the intelligence provided by the bigoted General Charles Willoughby, "my little fascist," as MacArthur sometimes called him.

Inchon did not turn into a rout. Despite grievous losses in men and material, the Kim Il Sung leadership drew on Chinese experience for the planning of a largely realized strategic retreat to the northern mountains, the fastnesses where Kim's guerrillas had struggled years before. Surviving northern forces in the south, divided into small units with some in peasant clothes, they made their way north even as U.S. and South Korean troops crossed the parallel. The brief defense of Pyongyang permitted the exodus of key personnel and papers, and in the east an effective guerrilla resistance taught the United States that capture or destruction of cities did not assure control of the countryside. More returning Koreans from Manchuria joined the regrouping in the mountains.

Week after week Willoughby estimated the North Korean military as a scattered 20,000 incapable of organized resistance. MacArthur, with the acquiescence of the Truman administration, pressed on to the Yalu and "home by Christmas." MacArthur saw the triumph he was certain of as "Mars's last gift to an aged warrior." South Korean officers said they would soon bathe their sabers in the Yalu. The myth is that the force that struck at the U.S. and South Korean divisions in November, and inflicted a humiliating defeat on them, was entirely Chinese. In fact, it was a Sino-Korean force, the Korean divisions by then restored to a strength of about 160,000.

A stalemate developed more or less along the 38th parallel. The U.S. forces, commanded by General Matthew Ridgway after MacArthur's dismissal, were deterred from another drive to the Yalu by the expectation of heavy casualties—100,000 in Ridgway's judgment. And the Sino-Korean side knew that in the unlikely event of a successful deep drive south, the United States might well respond with nuclear bombs. Casualties continued as the wrangling over truce terms (I.F. Stone's account of this is superior) dragged on into 1953.

According to Bruce Cumings, the Chinese army was "the most disciplined and correct" in the war. But atrocities were general. Contrary to the easy assumptions of U.S. scholars and commentators, the U.S.–South Korean record is the worst. That followed from the fact that the north had popular support in the south and waged guerrilla war in both the south and north. Guerrillas are fish swimming in the water of the people, as the Chinese say, and their suppression requires the draining of the water. Both the Rhee regime and the United States emulated the "kill all, burn all" suppression tactics of the Japanese in China. They slaughtered villagers and torched villages, making torture a routine practice. The United States was guilty of an atrocity of its own—indiscriminate use of the then new weapon of napalm.

North Korean troops in the south in 1950 killed prisoners in repeated violation of stern high-level orders. In an internal command, not a propaganda concoction, the military leadership ordered that such killings cease. They issued a second reprimand when they did not. Several groups of thirty to forty U.S. prisoners were killed by bullets to the head, such killings taking place after the Inchon landing made taking prisoners north difficult. The northern record of treatment of Rhee officials, landlords, and police is a mix of mercy and extermination.

The northern tanks entering Seoul smashed the gates of the most notorious prison, freeing prisoners who had survived recent mass executions. Acts of vengeance followed but were quickly forbidden. But the north executed some on the eve of being driven from Seoul.

The South Korean handling of prisoners is described in a study by the U.S. Army as "a tendency to mistreat or kill prisoners at the slightest provocation." In one incident Captain Kim Sok-yun, called Tiger Kim, had fifty northern prisoners beheaded. The reaction of the U.S. Army when the Red Cross made inquiries was to worry that correspondents might find out about it.

The U.S. X Corps in eastern North Korea, beset by 20,000 guerrillas, turned sections of the countryside into a sea of fire, killing guerrillas and villagers, and turning others over to the South Koreans for swift dispatch. Estimates of the number of North Koreans executed or turned into roped work gangs by the Rhee forces during their brief stay range up to 150,000.

In one of the worst of the atrocities, women and children in a northern village area were kept in a shed for days without food or water while being interrogated. Then gasoline was poured on the shed and they were roasted. According to evidence gathered by the northern authorities, this was a joint South Korean–U.S. effort.

Both MacArthur and Ridgway requested consignments of nuclear bombs, and in 1951 in Operation Hudson Harbor raids with dummy bombs were carried out to determine if the real thing could be effective. The conclusion was that their use was impractical for technical reasons. Napalm became the weapon of choice. After the Chinese entered the war, MacArthur ordered that 1,000 square miles of the north be turned into wasteland. Ridgway directed that Pyongyang, the capital, be burned to the ground. From the air, the United States de-urbanized North Korea, making a major contribution to the 20 percent reduction of the northern population.

At a time when many GIs were fretting about the long delay in reaching a truce agreement at Panmunjom, Ridgway and an Eighth Army colonel made headlines with the charge that 6,000 or even 8,000 U.S. prisoners had been murdered by the Communists—many times the earlier estimate of about 400 victims. I.F. Stone devoted two feisty chapters to demolishing what he called "statistical slapstick," but, of course, many more read an editorial in the New York Times alleging that the Communists "butchered prisoners in cold blood."

Years later General Willoughby reacted scornfully to all the fuss being made of the Mylay massacre in Vietnam. "In Korea we had Mylay all the time," he said. He was wrong only in that he laid the burden of blame on North Korea.

When I was in Chonju, North Cholla, in August 1947, during a period of repression of leftists, a retired police chief from St. Louis serving in the U.S. Military Government told me that "Orientals are accustomed to brutality such as would disgust a white man." A British cabinet officer who visited the strife-torn prisoner of war camps on Koje explained that Koreans are "prone to violence." Such were the cliches that enabled the United States to feel less uncomfortable and remain silent about the horrors it could not help discovering. Bruce Cumings has conveniently gathered examples of racism current in high places: Hanson Baldwin, military editor of the New York Times, likened Koreans to "the hordes of Genghis Khan." He remarked that to the Korean "life is cheap. Behind him stand the hordes of Asia. Ahead of him lies the hope of loot." He hoped that "these simple, primitive and barbaric people" would be convinced that the United States was a friend.

MacArthur believed that the Oriental dies stoically because he thinks death is the beginning of life. Dying, he "folds his arms as a dove does its wings." He also said often that Asians respect nothing as much as demonstrations of authority. Ridgway, visiting a POW camp, commented that "these prisoners are in appearance but a shade above a beast." He called them "human canaille." Edgar Johnson, head of the Economic Cooperation Administration in Korea, called the North Koreans "half-crazed automatons" in the orbit of "a monolithic slave-and-master world."

A U.S. soldier who had served in the occupation wrote in the Far Eastern Economic Review that Korea was peopled by wild men, scoundrels, and semi-barbarians. He cited missionary opinion that too much inbreeding had led to "an arrested mental development."

General Willoughby thought that the worst aspect of the war was that "simple coolies," "half-men with blank faces" were killing highly civilized U.S. high school boys and college graduates.

The prisoner of war issue stalled the truce talks at Panmunjom. The United States decided not to respect

Article 118 of the Geneva Convention, which states that all prisoners were to be repatriated when hostilities ended. It had a valid argument. The war involved two Chinas as well as two Koreas and clashes in ideology. Some prisoners certainly had reason to fear repatriation. In April 1952 the Communists concurred, agreeing to screening of prisoners.

But the United States wanted much more. It wanted a substitute for the victory it had failed to get on the battle-field—a propaganda triumph in line with the roll-back doctrine that was prevailing over mere containment. An enormous number of prisoners were to refuse to go home to the Communist evils awaiting them. That was achieved. Of some 122,000 prisoners, only 31,000 chose repatriation. Including thousands who refused to be screened, the number wishing to be homeward bound reached only 70,000. The Communist negotiators were stunned and disbelieving.

The reality is a tale of U.S. criminality. Some eight of the compounds on Koje island were led or controlled by the Communists among the prisoners and refused screening. To gain defectors in the other Chinese compounds, the United States brought in seventy-five persuaders, about sixty of them from Chiang Kai-shek's equivalent of the Gestapo. They were given control of the food supplies. Nocturnal beatings and the killing of the stubborn led to a gratifying number who muttered "Taiwan, Taiwan, Taiwan" when screened. Similarly, to persuade Korean prisoners, the Rhee government sent in representatives of the terrorist youth groups that had battered the South Korean left.

Fragments of the truth about Koje got into the press (I.F. Stone was again helpful) and the United States responded with elaborations of its falsifications. Writers of its public statements, it was later revealed, were instructed not to mention the Taiwan role in the screening or the brutalities in the compounds. The British had misgivings but Winston Churchill said that they had to be "good comrades," both in the "field of action" and "at the council table." But Foreign Minister Anthony Eden joined Krishna Menon of India and Lester Pearson of Canada in an effort to find a somewhat more humane compromise, leaving Dean Acheson scornfully frustrated.

Convinced that any softening of the prisoner issue would mean an ignominious defeat and add to the ammunition of the Republicans, Truman and Acheson held firm. Eventually the Communists faced what amounted to a fait accompli.

The changes since the truce may be summed up as a number of reversals and continuities affecting the whole of Korea. The economic reversal has had broad implications. In the first peaceful years the north set the pace, swiftly repairing the ravaged cities and making record industrial gains. (Chinese troops stayed on for a period as work gangs.) But excessive self-reliance, exclusion from the global market, and more recently the breakup of the Soviet Union and the fading of Chinese aid, brought about continuing decline.

The south surged economically. The traditional landlord class was succeeded by, and in part transformed into, an aggressive business class allied with a financially generous government. The north helped that change by carrying out land reform during its brief occupation of much of the south that eliminated considerable landlordism. The World Bank advised southern business to heed Ricardo's comparative advantage and concentrate on textiles and the like. But the Korean conglomerates in the making, determined to get into the real game, quickly developed heavy industry and big ticket exports. The steel making complex at Pohang is the world's third largest and reportedly the most cost effective.

China has reversed its policy in part. The longtime ally of the north has turned eagerly to Seoul, developing trade and securing huge South Korean investment in the mainland across the Yellow Sea. Beijing has denied the north the substantial credit it needs to alleviate hardship but has opposed the imposition of sanctions on the north and continues to urge reunification.

A continuity is the continued U.S. military presence in South Korea, its prime mission now to keep the peninsula divided and the Seoul regime subordinate. That continuity reinforces another—nationalism, a nationalism deeply offended by a division imposed from abroad and preserved by U.S. intervention in the civil war.

Korea has a sad heritage of weak dynasties that tempted Japanese and Chinese interventions and thirty-five years of Japanese rule. Just when true liberation seemed at hand, Washington and Moscow drew the line along the 38th parallel. That deadly parallel divides some 5 million families and severely inhibits the rise of a strong nation that, in Kim Il Sung's words, "never again need be the plaything of foreign powers."

The north has always called for reunification. That is what drove its attempt to unite the country by force of arms. In the south, unification and Korea-for-the-Koreans have a history of fervent popular support. "If we Koreans are to prosper, let it be by our own efforts; if we are to suffer, let it be by our own hands," the Princeton-educated, moderate conservative Kim Kyu-sik said at a press conference in 1948, not long before he defected to the north.

Student demonstrations brought down the Rhee travesty in 1960, plaguing the succeeding dictatorships; all shouted for unification even as they denounced domestic injustice. The death of Kim Il Sung again brought demands in Seoul for participation in the memorial services and for real steps toward unity. As in the past the response of the regime was police truncheons.

---

**HUGH DEANE** (1916–2001) was a journalist and scholar of East Asia, as well as the author of several hundred books and pamphlets on a wide range of topics related to East Asia.

# EXPLORING THE ISSUE

## Was Stalin Responsible for the Korean War?

### Critical Thinking and Reflection

1. This issue permits us to examine new material, available in recently declassified documents. After studying this new material, what do you believe we now understand about the Korean War that we did not understand 60 years ago? Critically discuss the implications of these new findings.
2. Kim Il Sung is the grandfather of newly installed leader Kim Jung Un (and the father of recently deceased Kim Jung Il). If the young man, Kim Jung Un, who now controls North Korea were to read about the decisions made by his grandfather, what lessons might he learn? Critically discuss.
3. What does historian Paul Wingrove mean by writing "[Josef] Stalin came to see an attack on South Korea as a potentially cheap Cold War victory"? Critically discuss.
4. Historian Hugh Deane blames U.S. support for South Korea's Syngman Rhee: "The war started in 1945 and it was begun by the United States." This claim takes the origin of the Korean War all the way back to the end of World War II. Do you find this charge supportable? Critically discuss.
5. What do recently declassified documents reveal that permit Deane to make this claim? Critically examine this new material.
6. With a divided Korea still patrolled at the 38th parallel that divides North from South Korea, assess the current situation. To borrow a phrase from another issue in the book, was the Korean War worth its both human and financial costs? Critically discuss and respond to this question.
7. Many wars have been fought to stalemates. If hostilities have ended, might this be regarded as a positive outcome? Debate this premise after researching both possible responses.

### Is There Common Ground?

Both historians have relied on newly opened archives. Hugh Deane also relies on his personal, on-the-ground experience as a young naval officer. Professor Wingrove found the evidence of Stalin's involvement that he was expecting to find. So did historian Hugh Deane.

*Question:* Is it possible that both claims are correct? How would you go about answering this question?

### Create Central

www.mhhe.com/createcentral

### Additional Resources

For further information about Korea's history, consult Bruce Cumings, *Korea's Place in the Sun: A Modern History* (W.W. Norton, 2005). For books on the Korean War itself, see Michael Hickey, *The Korean War: The West*

*Confronts Communism* (The Overlook Press, 1999) and David Halberstam, *The Coldest Winter: America and the Korean War* (Hyperion, 2007). Halberstam, who was killed in an automobile accident in the same year this book was published, was also the author of the definitive work on how the United States became involved in the Vietnam War, entitled *The Best and the Brightest* (Fawcett Publications, 1969).

A book that speaks directly to the questions raised in this issue is Richad C. Thornton, *Odd Man Out: Truman, Stalin, Mao, and the Origins of the Korean War* (Brassey's, 2000). And, there are two particularly helpful video resources. The Great Books Video Series (www.discovery.com) on Sun-tzu's *The Art of War* ("To be certain to take what you attack attack the place the enemy does not defend," Chapter 6) uses the Korean War to illustrate both MacArthur's skill at Inchon and his strategic error at the Yalu River where Chinese forces secured the advantage. Finally, the History Channel has created a four-part DVD on the Korean War (ShopHistoryChannel.com/dvdlibrary).

## *Internet Reference . . .*

**The Korean War, 1950–1953**

This very inclusive, user-friendly site includes maps and their sources, cartoons, vocabulary, a timeline, and links for answering further questions. Helpful explanations of

the Domino Theory, the 38th parallel, and the TV series *M*A*S*H* are included.

**www.johndclare.net/cold_war10.htm**

# Unit 3

# UNIT

# The Contemporary World

*A*s the world moves through the second decade of a new millennium, it is difficult to predict what this first century will bring. The revival of ancient hatreds and the challenges new conflicts present to a stable world order make prognostication especially difficult. Examining the roots of these ongoing oppositions, however, does offer some possibilities for resolving them. As Rwanda unraveled into ethnic conflict, many were horrified to see ancient hatreds rekindled. Memories of the Holocaust remain very vivid.

The aftermath of World War II and the Holocaust included the formation of the state of Israel. Support from the United States was crucial, and Israel continues to consider the United States a key ally today. Another legacy of the two great wars was a decades-long standoff between the two remaining superpowers—the Soviet Union and the United States—that erupted into a "hot" conflict in the Korean War. Now that the Cold War has ended, is the world safer or more dangerous?

The first half of the twentieth century also witnessed struggles for national independence. In India, Mohandas K. Gandhi combined moral and political leadership to achieve the goal of home rule in India. Long independent, India today remains divided by provincial and religious strife. And, religious nationalism presents a challenge to India's secular democracy. Gandhi's vision might again have relevance as Hindus and Muslims clash over disputed religious sites and questions of parity for religious minorities remain unresolved.

Islamic revivalism can be seen as both a threat and a force for change. The United States has spent more than a decade in Afghanistan after the attacks on the World Trade Center in 2001. There, the goal was to disrupt terrorist training camps and prevent the launching of additional attacks. More than a decade later, however, Islamic revivalism has, at least in part, fueled the overthrow of longtime dictators in North Africa and the Arabian Peninsula in the so-called Arab Spring. As in all revolutions, we wonder whether the forces of disruption will lead to a more stable order in the long term.

As the European Union has become an economic and political force in the contemporary world, we are examining its use of "soft power" in exerting influence. Diplomacy, rather than militarism, can be a powerful tool in resolving conflicts and preventing some of the horrors of the last century. The recent debt crisis has hobbled the European Union, which must redefine its economic union, even as it seeks to expand and consolidate its political union.

Selected, Edited, and with Issue Framing Material by:
Helen Buss Mitchell, *Howard Community College*
and
Joseph R. Mitchell, *Howard Community College*

# ISSUE

## Are Chinese Confucianism and Western Capitalism Compatible?

YES: A.T. Nuyen, from "Chinese Philosophy and Western Capitalism," *Asian Philosophy* (March 1999)

NO: Jack Scarborough, from "Comparing Chinese and Western Cultural Roots: Why 'East Is East and . . .'," *Business Horizons* (November/December 1998)

---

### Learning Outcomes

After reading this issue you should be able to:

- Outline the basic tenets of both Chinese Confucianism and Western capitalism.
- Describe the values that flow from each of these systems, in their classical formulations, as well as in their present, twenty-first century forms.
- Understand the connections among Adam Smith, Francois Quesnay, and the concept of Wu-wei.
- Describe the contrast Professor Scarborough finds between present-day capitalism and traditional Chinese values.

---

### ISSUE SUMMARY

YES: Philosophy professor A.T. Nuyen argues that the basic tenets of classical capitalism are perfectly compatible with the key elements of Chinese philosophy.

NO: Management professor Jack Scarborough argues that the Confucian values of harmony, filial loyalty, and legalism are incompatible with the Western heritage of democracy, rationality, individualism, and capitalism.

**W**hy do Western nations play such a dominant role in the world economy? Are scientific materialism and aggressive individualism responsible for the West's economic prosperity? And, does the East need to abandon the conservative values of Confucianism and Taoism if it wishes to compete economically in the twenty-first century? There is widespread agreement that capitalism has been a successful economic ideology. What the authors of the YES and NO selections disagree about is whether classical capitalism, as articulated more than 200 years ago, or a more modern form of capitalism should receive the credit. The resolution of this question will help us understand whether or not Confucianism and capitalism are compatible.

Both Confucianism and capitalism can be confusing concepts. Confucian values, as they made their way eastward, contributed significantly to the formation of the Japanese worldview. Any good translation of the *Analects* will introduce the teachings of Confucius, a Chinese master from the sixth century B.C.E., and allow him to speak for himself. A very complete resource for Chinese thought in general is *Sources of Chinese Tradition*, compiled by William Theodore de Bary and Irene Bloom (Columbia University Press, 1999). The first volume extends from earliest times to 1600 C.E.

Capitalism can be equally daunting. A good backup source for terms is John Black's *Oxford Dictionary of Economics* (Oxford University Press, 1997). And, the first issue in this volume provides a context for the modern world by looking at the role of capitalism in launching the Industrial Revolution during the eighteenth century in Europe. Adam Smith's classic *The Wealth of Nations* is available from the University of Chicago Press, 1976 and in a Modern Library edition (Random House, 1994). A good, straightforward introduction to the field, using simple engaging prose, is *Economics Explained* by Robert Heilbruner and Lester Thurow (Simon & Schuster, 1998). This book makes a fascinating connection between Adam Smith, the French physiocrat, Francois Quesnay, and the Chinese concept of *Wu-wei* ("no action").

When Adam Smith published *An Inquiry into the Nature and Causes of the Wealth of Nations* in 1776, the same year as the Declaration of Independence, he inspired the Western economic system that came to be known as capitalism. Smith, himself, was profoundly influenced by the ideas of the French physiocrats, especially a medical doctor, Francois Quesnay. As the name suggests, these thinkers supported physiocracy, "the rule of nature"— letting natural laws prevail in human society. This is also the central tenet of the Chinese worldview. The Tao moves the natural system with effortless, ego-free action. We would be wise to follow its wisdom.

Classical capitalism urges a hands-off approach, adopting a French term *laissez-faire* (meaning to leave alone) as the best method of creating economic prosperity. Left unmolested, so the theory goes, economic forces will be self-regulating, guided by what Smith called "the invisible hand" of the marketplace. Too much of a product would drive prices down, discouraging further production; scarcity would increase prices, stimulating production. Supply and demand would naturally regulate the economy, if government stayed out of the process.

We now know that Adam Smith first encountered the ideas of Francois Quesnay on a trip to Europe around 1760. Quesnay was a brilliant French physician who originated the ideas of physiocracy after a long and thoughtful investigation into the functioning of the economic system. Smith, who had previously written on morals, turned his attention to his own inquiry into what causes "the wealth of nations." He would have dedicated his masterpiece to Quesnay had Quesnay not died. Some scholars believe that Quesnay may have been inspired by the Chinese philosophy of *wu-wei* (literally "no action"), which encourages individuals to allow the Tao to regulate everything with perfect efficiency, benefiting all. One historian has even suggested that the French term *laissez-faire* is a translation of the Chinese *wu-wei*.

Without pressing this point, A.T. Nuyen traces Quesnay's admiration of Confucius as a model human being and establishes Quesnay's view that the Chinese system of government was an appropriate model for European nations to emulate. The Emperor might have to enact "despotic laws," aimed at ensuring the smooth functioning of the natural laws regulating the economy. But, these laws would function simply to remove impediments and allow natural forces to operate freely. Nuyen cites antitrust laws in the United States as just such a modern application of "legal despotism" in the service of natural laws. For him, classical capitalism arose from the same virtues that inspired the ancient Chinese philosophical systems of Confucianism and Taoism.

Jack Scarborough, by contrast, uses a couplet from a Rudyard Kipling poem about India and the West ("East is east and west is west and never the twain shall meet") to explain the "enormous gulf" he sees separating Asia from Western capitalist economies. While the East (especially "once-great China") was reduced, through imperial repression and Confucian discipline, to "unrelenting poverty and hardship," the West would go on to nearly conquer the world—first politically and later economically. Scarborough's article is aimed at communicating the "cultural differences" that must be taken into account if one hopes to do business in China.

Scarborough has in mind present-day capitalism, which presumes an aggressive individualism that would have been equally foreign to both Confucius and Adam Smith. He attributes China's economic weakness in the modern world—a weakness that seems to be turning to strength in our own time—to centuries of self-imposed isolation as well as a cultural appreciation of harmony, communal loyalty, and an acknowledgment that nature acts with a superior wisdom. Nuyen, having demonstrated the compatibility between Chinese philosophy and classical capitalism, argues that the economic gap between the West and Asia cannot be attributed to the "cultural factor." Instead, he suggests colonialism and postcolonial ideologies as more likely factors.

# YES ↵

A. T. Nuyen

## Chinese Philosophy and Western Capitalism

As we stand now at the end of the 20th century, many nations in the East are well on their way along the path of economic growth and development. To be sure, the East, with the exception of Japan, still has a great deal of catching up to do before it can become the equal of the West in terms of economic prosperity. Also, progress has been uneven. On this score, economic commentators seem to agree that the nations that have done well are those that have adopted the capitalist model that has served the West well over the last hundred years. For instance, W. J. F. Jenner points out that, apart from Japan, "all the East Asian countries that have prospered in recent decades were colonies of either Britain or of Japan for generations before the Second World War," and as such inherited the capitalist structure of the West. Japan itself, Jenner contends, could not have prospered without "external conditions needed for rapid industrial growth," such as Western technology, capital and export markets.

Despite the fact that one can point to many obvious exceptions to Jenner's observations, there is fairly widespread support for his view. Thus, it is often enough said that what is holding back economic progress in the East is the "cultural" factor. Commentators frequently suggest that peoples of the East, particularly the ethnic Chinese, subscribe to values which are not conducive to economic progress, values that place the family and the community above individual interests, and spirituality above material well-being. By contrast, the West is said to subscribe to the kind of individualism and materialism that give its peoples a competitive edge. To do well in the economic arena, the suggestion goes, the East needs to embrace the Western capitalist model wholeheartedly by making fundamental changes in their cultural and philosophical outlook. If Asian, particularly Chinese, values had anything to do with economic success, they would have to be thoroughly cleansed through Western values and beliefs. Pace those commentators who credit the success in many Asian countries to Confucianism, Jenner insists that for Confucianism, or any other Chinese philosophical system, to work, "it needs dynamic, alien, Western institutions and forms of economic organization." Thus, in Jenner's view, only when "alien, Western factors came into play were certain elements within some inherited East Asian value systems able to bring about successful capitalist development." By themselves, such value systems are an obstacle to growth.

Behind views such as Jenner's is the supposition that capitalism is wholly a product of the West, that it is inherently an alien system from the point of view of the East, that it does not sit well with the traditions of the East and that the capitalist model cannot be successfully embraced without some violence being done to those traditions. The aim of this [selection] is to challenge such a notion. My thesis is that it is classical capitalism that first set the West on its course towards economic prosperity, and that the fundamental tenets of classical capitalism are perfectly compatible with the key elements of Chinese philosophy. Indeed, as we shall see, many historians of ideas have traced the origins of classical capitalism all the way back to Chinese thought. Setting aside whether anything can be made of the historical link, I shall attempt to show how classical capitalism could have developed from the fundamentals of Chinese philosophy. If I am right, the economic gap between the West and Asia has to be accounted for in terms other than the "cultural" factors, such as, perhaps, colonialism and post-colonialist ideologies.

By classical capitalism I mean an economic system based on unfettered competition, the unrestricted availability of productive technologies, the free movement of labour and other factors of production, and the smooth flow of information within both the producer and consumer groups. It is a system based on what economists call "perfect competition." Such a system would result in commodities being produced at the lowest possible costs and made available to consumers at the lowest possible prices. Under ideal conditions, the system would result in what economists call "Pareto efficiency," a state of affairs in which it is not possible to make someone better off, in the economic sense, without making someone else worse off. It is important to note that anti-competitive behaviour is an obstacle in the attainment of the economic benefits of the system. The most common form of anti-competitive behaviour is monopoly. This could result from the monopolisation of factors of production, or productive technologies, or the distribution of commodities. It is for this reason that anti-competitive behaviour has been outlawed in many capitalist nations. The USA, for instance, enforces its anti-trust law fairly vigorously, albeit with varying degrees of success. The other factor that tends to

From Nuyen, A. T. "Chinese Philosophy and Western Capitalism," *Asian Philosophy* (March 1999), vol. 9, no. 1. Copyright © 1999 by Asian Philosophy. Reprinted by permission of Taylor & Francis Ltd., www.tandf.co.uk/journals, and the author. Notes omitted.

restrict competition is government intervention through burdensome rules and regulations, and the involvement of the state in the economy itself through state-owned companies. This is why capitalist nations such as the USA tend to make laws aimed at giving all economic agents a free reign and to minimize public ownership (in a process known as "privatisation"). The term "free enterprise," or the French equivalent, namely, laissez-faire, can be used as a name for the capitalist system I have described, provided that by "free" we mean free from anti-competitive forces, not free to engage in restrictive practices, and certainly not free to indulge in any kind of behaviour whatsoever in the pursuit of profit.

Classical capitalism, as I have described it, has evolved from the works of classical thinkers such as Francois Quesnay and the physiocrats, Bernard Mandeville and Adam Smith. It was Quesnay and his fellow physiocrats who persuaded the French government to overturn the interventionist policy of the mercantalists and to free up the market. It is true that Quesnay supported a governmental system known as "legal despotism," interpreted by some commentators as a model for absolute monarchy and thus might be taken as being against the spirit of free enterprise. However, Quesnay's intention in advocating legal despotism really was to set up the legal framework for free enterprise. The "despotic" laws were meant to ensure the smooth functioning of economic laws which were for the physiocrats, as we shall see later, identical with natural laws. The laws that Quesnay advocated have to be compared with the laws aimed at promoting free enterprise in modern capitalist nations, such as anti-trust laws in the USA. It is for this reason that Quesnay is regarded by many commentators as undoubtedly the founder of modern capitalism. For instance, according to Weulerrse, Quesnay's doctrine expresses "the scientific principles of capitalism, pure and simple, of complete capitalism"; it represents "the triumph of the spirit of capitalism." At any rate, Quesnay's advocacy for free enterprise found a powerful support in Adam Smith in whose hands his economic/natural laws became the laws of the "invisible hand." I take for granted that Smith's doctrine of the wealth of nations is directly responsible for the wealth of modern capitalist nations. Given the theoretical connection between Smith and Quesnay, I shall restrict myself to Quesnay.

The brief excursion into economic history above may serve to confirm the impression that the intellectual roots of modern capitalism lie buried wholly in Western soil and that the East needs to make drastic internal changes if it is to adapt the alien capitalist model successfully. However, many historians have claimed that, at the philosophical level, Quesnay's ideas came directly from the East, from Chinese philosophy to be more precise. It is not altogether clear whether and to what extent Quesnay was influenced by Chinese thoughts, or whether he borrowed anything from the East. However, it is worth pursuing the historical link before turning to the more straightforward comparative reading of Quesnay and Chinese philosophers.

What we do know is that Quesnay himself acknowledged his debt to Chinese philosophy, especially to Confucianism. His book, *Le Despotism de la Chine*, is not a critique of the Chinese system of government; rather, it is a description of a system on which he based his concept of legal despotism, mentioned [earlier]. According to J. J. Clarke, Quesnay

> regarded China as an ideal society that provided a model for Europe to follow, and in discussing Chinese despotism he wrote that 'I have concluded from the reports about China that the Chinese constitution is founded upon wise and irrevocable laws which the Emperor enforces and which he carefully observes himself'.

While the Chinese system of government was for Quesnay a model that Europe should follow, Confucius himself was for him a model of the perfect person. According to one historian, Quesnay modelled himself on Confucius, so much so that his disciples called him "The Confucius of Europe": "His manuscript for *Le Despotism de la Chine* contains a few pages on the life of Confucius which were deleted from the published version, but which provide a disarmingly close approximation to an autobiographical assessment and statement of personal purpose". In the manuscript, Quesnay expressed his admiration for Confucius's "grave, modest and serious air," his "most profound knowledge" and his "intent of spreading his doctrine and working for the reformation of men." Above all, Quesnay admired Confucius for the fact that by "his gravity, his modesty, his sweetness and his frugality, by his scorn of terrestrial pleasures, and by a continual vigilance on his own conduct, he was himself, an example of the precepts he advanced in his writings and his discourses. . . . "

Given what we know about Quesnay's respect and admiration for Confucius as a person, it is not surprising that historians go on to speculate that Quesnay freely made use of Confucius's philosophy and derived from it many useful ideas. What is evident is that he interpreted that philosophy as advocating the observance of the laws of nature and the adoption of nature's guiding principle, having in mind no doubt the notion of the tao. As Quesnay saw it, nature's guiding principle, in the philosophy of Confucius, is a force that commands "the respect, the fear [and] the recognition" in all of us, a force that "knows all, . . . even the most secret recesses of the heart. . . . " Furthermore, this force of nature, if allowed to operate unhindered, will result in the best for all, including human beings. From this it is but a small step to the conclusion that Quesnay either borrowed or was influenced by this view of Chinese philosophy, given his own doctrine that in economic affairs, it is best to follow the laws of nature, a doctrine for which Pierre-Samuel du Pont de Nemours aptly coined the term "physiocracy" in 1767, meaning literally "the rule of nature." It is certainly true that Quesnay thought that the laws of nature should not be interfered with, that nature should be left alone to operate, that in the economic sphere, we should let nature be, laissez-faire. Interestingly, one historian has speculated that the term "laissez-faire" is the French translation of the Chinese wu-wei: "Both lawmaker and law had to recognize the principle of . . . natural order, and in doing so conform to the Chinese ideal of wu-wei, which has ever inspired their theories of government."

It may be said that the historical evidence above is consistent with the thesis that Quesnay was influenced by Chinese philosophy as it is with a quite different thesis, namely, that Quesnay merely saw a parallel between his own doctrine and what he took to be the philosophy of Confucius. It is not my intention in this [selection] to settle this issue. My interest is confined to the question of whether capitalism is really so alien to the East, that the East could not assimilate it without making some profound changes in its fundamental beliefs. However we interpret the historical evidence connecting physiocracy with Confucianism, or Quesnay with Confucius, the fact remains that the historical discussion above opens up the possibility for arguing that Chinese philosophy, and in particular Confucianism, provides a hospitable background for, rather than thwarting, the development of the kind of capitalism that has brought economic prosperity to the West. If the argument is successful then, as pointed out above, we have to look elsewhere for an explanation as to why such development failed to take place early enough in the East, thus resulting in the current economic gap between the East and the West. With this in mind, we can now take a closer look at Quesnay's doctrine of free enterprise, or the physiocrats' idea of laissez-faire, in order to see whether it could have grown out of Chinese philosophy.

From Quesnay's writings, it is clear that he saw the world as a self-regulating machine governed by a set of immutable laws ordained by God, its Creator. He also saw that the economy and its economic agents were part of that world and subject to the same laws. The economic part of the world in turn could be seen as a whole consisting of interdependent parts, such as production, consumption, exchange, etc. That part of the world, the economy, would function well if its component parts were to function in harmony with each other. As is well known, Quesnay constructed the Tableau economique to model the interdependencies in the economy, thus allowing a greater understanding, better prediction and more effective regulation of economic activities. The key to it all is the harmony of the various component parts comprising the whole, a harmony that depends on the balancing of the oppo-sitional forces exercised by the component parts. As Quesnay puts it in the essay "Hommes," in the case of the state, good government depends on "the balance of the bodies of the state, each restrained in turn by the other." What is true about the state is also true about the economy, indeed true generally. Thus, the general aim in human affairs is to achieve and maintain the "balance of bodies" comprising the whole. Since the whole is a self-regulating mechanism governed by natural

laws, this is the same as saying that we should aim at restoring the natural order. Indeed, being a self-regulating mechanism, the economy possesses self-adjusting forces that tend to return it to the natural order and so in the usual course of events, the best policy turns out to be one of letting such forces operate unhindered, of letting nature be, of laissez-faire. Intervention is necessary only to restore the natural order.

Breaking down the component parts of the economy, we get to the ultimate economic unit, the individual person. The person too is a natural entity subject to natural laws. Quesnay knew this only too well, being a medical practitioner, a renown surgeon, for most of his life. Since the aim of the economy is, as Quesnay put it, the "perpetual reproduction of those goods necessary for the subsistence, conservation and convenience of men," it is important to understand the nature of "men." Influenced by the rationalist philosophy of Descartes, Quesnay saw the individual person as a rational creature who, naturally endowed with the capacity to reason, knew what he or she wanted and knew the best way to obtain it. It follows that the best economic policy is to allow the individual the freedom to pursue his or her own interests. However, it would be wrong to say that Quesnay advocated economic individualism. For Quesnay, the pursuit of self-interest was never an end in itself; it was rather the means towards the goal of social harmony, and ultimately the harmony of the whole of nature. It is natural to let people engage in activities aimed at the satisfaction of natural needs and wants. To let people be, laissez-faire, is to follow the rule of nature, to be physiocratic. Self-interested economic activity should be permitted and assisted to take place unhindered, enterprise at the individual level should be free, only because it would lead to a good outcome at the social level, and a good society in turn would result in the well-being of the world. As is well known, this doctrine is foreshadowed by Mandeville's *Fable of the Bees* and later received theoretical backing in Adam Smith, who turned it into the doctrine of the "invisible hand."

I have outlined the fundamental tenets of classical capitalism, or laissez-faire capitalism, as formulated by its founder, Francois Quesnay. By the time of Adam Smith, the economy of Western Europe, particularly that of Great Britain, had begun to reorganize itself along the lines of free enterprise, aided along in the process by Enlightenment ideas that emphasise personal freedom. In the case of France, the transition was facilitated by the presence of physiocrats in the government itself. Indeed, a well-known promoter of physiocracy, Anne Robert Turgot, became a finance minister of Louis XVI. The foundation stone was set for the economic prosperity of Western Europe. Why similar developments did not take place in Asia is a matter I happily leave to the historians. My purpose here is to show that it is not because the laissez-faire doctrine is philosophically alien to the East. Indeed, as pointed out [earlier], some historians even claim that

Western thinkers responsible for the laissez-faire doctrine were influenced by Chinese philosophy—Turgot himself was described by Martin Bernal as a "promoter of Chinese economic ideas." Whatever can be made of this historical claim, we can certainly show that the fundamental tenets of classical capitalism could have grown out of Chinese philosophy, out of Confucianism in particular. I turn now to this task.

That the world is governed by a universal and natural force is a fundamental belief in Chinese philosophy. It is a part of most Chinese philosophical systems. This force is the tao. While Taoism and Confucianism draw different implications from the belief in the tao, both subscribe to the view that the tao is a creative force causally responsible for the existence of the world. The process of creation is described in the well-known chapter 42 of the Tao Te Ching. The tao is not only a creative force; it is also a regulative principle that maintains its own creation. Indeed, the tao permeates all aspects of the world and so can properly be equated with nature itself. Thus, the tao is God, nature and natural laws rolled into one. Where the laws of the tao operate unhindered, there is established the natural order and there is harmony. Where there are acts in defiance of the laws of the tao, the natural order is upset and there is chaos. Thus, for there to be harmony, all actions must comply with the laws of the tao, or with the rule of nature. To act in accordance with the tao is to let nature rule, to subscribe to physiocracy in the literal sense. Clearly then, the Chinese cosmology translates easily into the physiocratic belief in a natural order which regulates all aspects of life, including all human experiences.

As we saw [earlier], the French physiocrats considered the society and all the social units within it down to the individual persons as parts of the natural order subject to the same rule of nature. However, unlike other animals, humans have the capacity to reason and so can choose to act in ways that are contrary to the rule of nature. This gives rise to the physiocratic belief that the harmony of the world rests squarely on the individual person, that to establish the order of nature we have to start with the individual person. This idea could have grown out of Chinese philosophy. In both Taoism and Confucianism, the natural law, or the law of the tao, should be observed by all component parts of the natural whole, by all societies, groups of individuals, families and finally the individual people themselves. Given that the individual person has the power of choice, on his or her shoulders alone rests the responsibility to realise the law of the tao. Thus, as recorded in *The Analects,* Confucius said that "It is man that can make the Way [Tao] great, and not the Way that can make man great." This is echoed in the last few lines of chapter 25 of the Tao Te Ching: "Man models himself on earth, Earth on heaven, Heaven on the way, And the way on that which is naturally so." Clearly then, the focus of Chinese philosophy is on the individual, no less than is the case in physiocracy or in the Western tradition

generally. If we understand "individualism" in this sense, there is no reason to think that Quesnay's "economic individualism" is alien to the Chinese tradition.

If it rests on the individual to "make the Way great" then, it follows, the individual should be left alone, if not encouraged, to do so. To interfere with the individual in his or her natural pursuits, particularly in the pursuits to secure the goods "necessary for their subsistence, conservation and convenience" (to borrow Quesnay's words), is to interfere with the way of nature itself. Thus, not only that the individual should let nature be if he or she is to follow the tao, or to "model himself on the earth," the government too should follow the tao by letting the individuals be. To let be is to take no action, or rather to do by not doing, wu-wei. This policy can be found advocated in many diverse philosophical systems. It is, as we would expect, most prominent in Taoism. Thus,

The way never acts yet nothing is left undone.
Should lords and princes be able to hold fast to it,
The myriad creatures will be transformed of their
own accord.

—(Tao Te Ching, chapter 37)

Wu-wei is the way of the tao. For lords and princes to follow the way of the tao is for them to take no action, to let the people be. Lords and princes can "win the empire by not being meddlesome", and when they are "not meddlesome . . . the people prosper of themselves" (Tao Te Ching, chapter 57). This policy is endorsed by Confucius, who praised Shun for governing his empire well by taking "no [unnatural] action." Even the Legalists, who were well known for their advocacy of a strong government, subscribed to the policy of wu-wei. As Wing-Tsit Chan puts it, the "Taoist ideal of taking no action (wu-wei) had a strong appeal to the Legalists because if laws worked effectively at all times, there would be no need for any actual government." Given the widespread philosophical support for the idea that "people prosper of themselves" if the government lets them be, it is surely perverse to suggest that any economic doctrine that advocates letting people be to pursue their economic interests, or laissez-faire, is alien to the East.

It may be said that the Chinese doctrine of wu-wei encourages passivity which is contrary to the qualities of drive and determination required for economic success. However, it should be noted that translating "wu-wei" as "taking no action" or "doing nothing" is highly misleading. Even within Taoism, wu-wei does not mean total passivity. Taking no action is not an end in itself but rather a means to achieving something positive. Thus, chapter 10 of the Tao Te Ching speaks of not "resorting to action" in order to "govern the state," and chapter 51 speaks of taking no action to "give(s) [the myriad creatures] life," to "benefit(s) them." That positive things result from the non-action of the tao is due to its te, its "mysterious virtue," or "its "Dark Potency" as A. C. Graham has put it. It is true, though, that the Taoists, particularly Chuang Tzu, believe in the potency of the tao, and believe that nature will have its own way in the end and does not need much from humans to assert its own order. The Confucianists, by contrast, attribute to humans a greater capacity for departing from the order of nature. For them, wu-wei amounts to taking action to emulate the no-action way of nature itself. For this reason, some commentators describe the Confucian policy as wei-wu-wei, active inaction, rather than simply wu-wei. What this means is that the individual should be vigilant to correct his or her behaviour, and the government should take action to help the individual "make the way great." Clearly then, wu-wei does not translate into a lack of drive and determination. On the contrary, it entails the utmost determination to embrace the tao, and requires the constant drive to improve oneself by following the way of nature. The same thing applies to the state. Wu-wei does not mean inaction on the part of the government. Since humans have the capacity to act contrary to nature, to let nature be, wu-wei, is to intervene to keep recalcitrant humans in line. If restrictive behaviour in economic affairs is contrary to the way of nature then wu-wei calls for a positive action against it. Quesnay's advocacy for "despotic laws" to preserve and restore the natural order could have grown out of the Chinese doctrine of wu-wei. As we saw earlier, some historians are convinced that it did. Whether laissez-faire was in fact the physiocrats' translation of wu-wei, it could easily have been.

It may be said further that many different economic systems could have grown out of the Chinese metaphysics of the tao. What remains to be shown is how such metaphysics could have engendered classical capitalism described earlier. The key feature of classical capitalism is competition. However, this is not to be taken as a destructive relationship in which each economic agent is out to dominate others, to drive them out of business. Rather, it is a mutually dependent relationship in which each economic unit acts to check and to balance the actions of all other units. For instance, prices are kept at the lowest possible level because the action of raising the price by any one producer will be neutralised by the actions of other producers who will take the advantage of selling more of their own products by undercutting their rivals. Classical capitalism is a system of checks and balances, resulting in a state of equilibrium among the opposing forces. This is what Quesnay had in mind when he spoke of the "balance of the bodies." Such balance exists in nature. This is why, for Quesnay, there should be the same natural checks and balances in the economy. To let it be, laissez-faire, is to let the natural checks and balances operate to produce harmony, or equilibrium. Could this doctrine have grown out of Chinese philosophy? The answer is, once again, yes. It could have grown out of many Chinese philosophical systems, but more specifically, out of the Confucian doctrine of Chung Yung.

As Chung-ying Cheng has pointed out, the idea of harmony is embraced by all the major schools of Chinese philosophy. This idea is encapsulated in the I Ching diagram of yin and yang forming a harmonious unity. The harmony in any unity rests on the balance of the forces exercised by the component parts, or the "bodies" of the whole. There is harmony if the force of one "body" is balanced by that of another. There is harmony in nature because

> . . . Something and Nothing produce each other;
> The difficult and the easy complement each other;
> The long and the short off-set each other;
>
> —(Tao Te Ching, chapter 2)

The idea of harmony as the balance of oppositional forces is also endorsed in the book of Chung Yung. For instance, taking a person's psychology as a unified whole, Chung Yung declares that when the "passions awaken and each and all attain due measure and degree, that is harmony." There is harmony in nature because "the seasons succeed each other and the sun and the moon appear with the alternations of night and day." The human society is capable of attaining harmony insofar as its laws "form the same system" with the laws of nature. Harmony in society will be attained if laws are enacted to preserve the balance of opposing forces. This means in turn to keep to the middle path, the mean, between the extremes. Mapping all this onto the economy, we can draw the conclusion that economic harmony will be attained if the opposing forces in the economy are kept in a balance, if no one economic unit is allowed to dominate the others. Thus, only a competitive economic system is consistent with the Chinese idea of harmony. A system consisting of monopolies, state or private, lacks the checks and balances necessary for harmony. Such a system may be stable in the sense of producing a technical equilibrium with predictable and non-fluctuating outputs and prices, but it is not harmonious and is contrary to the order of nature, contrary to the tao. The Chinese notion of harmony entails that the state should make laws to ensure the balance of economic forces, laws that prevent anti-competitive behaviour, laws that strengthen the mutual dependencies of all economic units on each other. Such laws would be continuous with the laws of nature, the laws by which "the seasons succeed each other and the sun and the moon appear with the alternations of day and night."

I have argued that laissez-faire or free-enterprise capitalism is not alien to the Chinese way of thinking insofar as that way is informed by philosophical beliefs in the way of nature. What is certainly alien is an economic system that is driven by greed, ruthless individualism and the desire for absolute power. What is alien is a system of cut-throat competition without checks and balances, a system that allows extremes to develop rather than stays in the middle path, a system that encourages monstrous monopolies having the power to take over the laws of the market, to upset the order of nature. To be sure, the popular image of capitalism is closer to cut-throat competition than to free-enterprise in the classical sense. However, it is doubtful that the former has had anything to do with the economic prosperity of the West. If this is alien to the East then it is a reason to celebrate, not a cause of despair. Indeed, future historians could well attribute the economic crisis occurring in Asia at the end of the 20th century to Asia's attempt to embrace the greed-is-good mentality of cut-throat competition. I have argued that Asia need not sacrifice its philosophical soul at the altar of economic progress. On the contrary, if I am right in my reading of Chinese philosophy and if classical thinkers such as Quesnay and Smith are right about the causes of the wealth of nations, now that Asia has regained its power to determine its own destiny, economic prosperity depends on Asia's returning to its philosophical roots, maintaining the path of Chung Yung and embracing the way of the tao.

---

**A.T. NUYEN** is a member of the department of philosophy at the University of Queensland in Brisbane, Australia.

**Jack Scarborough**

 **NO**

# Comparing Chinese and Western Cultural Roots: Why "East Is East and . . ."

*"Oh, East is East, and West is West, and never the twain shall meet."*

—Rudyard Kipling, The Ballad of East and West (1889)

**W**ell, we meet now. As China accelerates into its inevitable place among the world's most important states and markets, the world is paying close attention. And as Westerners scrutinize China's pronouncements and actions, they become more aware of the great differences in how we think, what we believe, and how we behave. Although Kipling's familiar words applied to India, the thought expressed applies at least as well to China. Some might expect to see some convergence as trade, travel, and education bring us closer. But an enormous gulf remains because these differences have very deep and substantial roots that have produced highly divergent value systems.

The attitudes and behavior of a cohesive or otherwise unified group of people are shaped by the prevailing value system that defines for them what is good and bad, acceptable and unacceptable, desirable and undesirable, important and unimportant. We call this collectively shared value system that establishes behavioral norms a "culture": an artifact of a common experience and history, the dominant religion, political, social, and economic conditions, geographic, climatic, and topographic factors, and resource endowments. The ability to resist the tendency to judge another culture according to one's own values—the trap of ethnocentrism—can be strengthened by an understanding of how those differences came to be.

A brief review of the more salient differences between China and the West, as seen through Western eyes, is a good place to begin. Students of this topic, particularly those interested in Chinese ways of business and management practices, are familiar with such notions as "face," guanxi, and guo qing. "Face" generally is a matter of maintaining one's public dignity and standing. For the Chinese, there are two components of face: lien and mianzi. The former concerns one's reputation for integrity and morality; the latter is prestige attached to professional reputation, knowledge, wealth, and success.

A large component of lien is people's ability to live up to their obligations within the framework of Confucian hierarchy, social harmony, and strict behavioral ritual (li). The surest way to lose face is to act in a way that causes another to lose it. To avoid such uncivilized, disharmonious behavior, the Chinese practice a form of indirect speech that, to Westerners, seems overly modest and even self-effacing. The practice is sometimes so extreme as to appear disingenuous or even deliberately deceitful, as in overly optimistic promises and commitments. Another by-product of face-saving (or harmony-preserving) behavior is shaming, the ploy of getting one's way in negotiation by appealing to one's counterpart's obligation to conform to li. A common example is related to the Confucian ideal of the doting, overly solicitous parent and the resulting asymmetrical relationship of obligation whereby the parent expects much less from the child than the parent gives. A Chinese negotiator might attempt to portray a counterpart representing a large, accomplished company or developed country in the role of parent. Thus, an ostensibly weaker or technologically less advanced Chinese firm or governmental body assumes the role of the needy child to extract asymmetrical concessions.

Guanxi is the now well-known custom of relying on a network of fully committed personal relationships when conducting business or other affairs. A by-product is the need for go-betweens to establish a new business relationship. Another is that, unlike in Japan, personal loyalties and commitments take precedence over all others except family—including company ties. These asymmetrical relationships also favor the weaker party and must be cultivated assiduously. The obligations embodied in Confucian values and guanxi take the place of laws and contracts relied upon by Westerners to regulate business relationships.

Guo qing is a 2,000-year-old term meaning that China is special and the way things are done there are unique and, presumably, superior. This implies that outsiders (long considered barbarians) must learn these ways and adapt if they are to become functional in China. Such an attitude is to be expected from a people who constitute the world's oldest culture, the Middle Kingdom, and who lived for thousands of years largely in self-imposed isolation but who, nevertheless, accomplished much artistically, scientifically, and socially. Fan Xing sums up the

*Table 1*

| Chinese | American |
| --- | --- |
| Intuitive | Rational |
| Aesthetic | Scientific |
| Introverted | Extroverted |
| Self-restrained | Aggressive |
| Dependent | Independent |
| Procrastinating | Active |
| Implicit | Explicit |
| Synthetic | Analytical |
| Patient | Impatient |
| Group-oriented | Individualistic |
| Desire for eternity (i.e., continuity) | Eager to change |

observations and views of many with [a] comparison of common traits [in Table 1].

Hence, the Chinese lean toward a more holistic, systemic, nonlinear, fatalistic worldview. Their attitude toward time is more relaxed; they tend to be humble and modest; and their culture is one of high-context communication and collectivism. . . .

## Chinese and Western Cultural Roots Compared

. . . Confucian disdain for science and commerce has been an enormous constraint on economic development. Nevertheless, according to Paul Kennedy's 1987 *The Rise and Fall of the Great Powers*, in the Middle Ages the Chinese invented paper, printing by movable type, gunpowder, a mechanical clock, and the magnetic compass. And they were producing more iron than Great Britain did in the early years of the Industrial Revolution. With the exception of iron, used for arms, these technological advances were developed by Taoist alchemy, primarily for religious and ceremonial purposes.

Chinese ships were trading as far as the Indian Ocean a century before the Portuguese rounded the Cape of Good Hope. However, as the Ming dynasty sought to reestablish the ancient order after the Mongols were finally subdued at the end of the fourteenth century, the Mandarins put an end to foreign adventures and turned inward once again. In keeping with its relative isolation and highly ethnocentric self-concept as the Middle Kingdom, China has a strong tradition of xenophobia. Westerners have long been called yang gui zi, or "foreign devils" (gui lao in Cantonese). Even China's cultural progeny, the Japanese, are called "devils of the Eastern Sea." When Western adventurers, priests, and merchants finally arrived in some force in the nineteenth century, they were confined to a few coastal enclaves, and the Mandarins limited intercourse to the minimum necessary to sustain a tidy stream of tax revenue from trade.

This reaction to the West stands in stark contrast to Japan's. Once finally opened to the West after the Meiji Restoration in 1868, the Japanese aggressively sought Western expertise in industry, technology, and administration—a practice that still continues. One consequence was that relatively tiny Japan was able to invade and occupy much of China in the 1930s, the first nation to do so successfully since the Mongols.

As is typical of agrarian, subsistence economies, the large and extended family—essential to eke out an existence from the land—was and remains the primary social and economic unit. The ultimate source of security and refuge, the family was responsible for the debts and conduct of its members. Individual wrongdoing caused great loss of face (lien) for the entire family. The Confucian emphasis on social harmony was intended largely to maintain the family's central role and extend its organization to society as a whole. Many Chinese still feel very strong ties to their home villages, including those now living in urban, industrial environments. Typical Chinese enterprises remain relatively small, with simple functional structures built around the founding family.

Europeans had a very different experience that would be replicated in North America. A much more heterogeneous people, they are comprised of numerous indigenous tribes and many others that made their way into Europe primarily from Central Asia. Europe's topography and extensive river systems allowed great internal mobility, and its location and many ports made it a crossroads between Asia and Africa. Temperate climate and ample arable land supported surplus agriculture, which enabled the early development of towns and the attendant specialization of labor that impelled acceleration of trade and foreign exploration. These adventures made Europeans aware of new products and brought riches that stimulated still more exploration and, ultimately, mercantilism. Thus was made possible the accumulation of wealth that financed the artistic, technological, and political advances of the Renaissance. After the fall of the Roman Empire, there was no monolithic, centralized authority capable of enforcing an inward focus, as the imperial Mandarins did in China. The Roman's extensive financial, legal, and transportational infrastructure supported internal intercourse and opened the door to the external world.

## Government

In the sixth century B.C., when the Greeks were contemplating protection of individual rights and the rule of law as the best means for rendering order and peace from chaos and oppression, Confucius was pondering the same problem. But although his intentions were equally benign, his solution was quite different. He concluded that social harmony would best be served not by a system of citizens' rights protected by law, but by a rigidly hierarchical system of reciprocal duties and highly regulated and ritualized behavior built around the principle of filial loyalty. This was the origin of guanxi, li, and face. Taught and perpetuated by the family, Confucianism established and enforced behavioral norms. Confucius believed leaders should earn their authority through a demonstration of learning, wisdom, and the virtues of humanity—benevolence, righteousness, propriety, and trustworthiness—in the way a good father commanded the respect of his children. In return, people would owe their leaders total loyalty and support. Analogous relationships could be established throughout society in a hierarchical cascade, thereby rendering it peaceful, harmonious, and productive.

Confucius believed leadership was too important to leave the accidents of heredity; the opportunity to lead should be open to all so that the most meritorious would rise to the top. He believed people were essentially good and that they required only education in the ways of a harmonious society. Education, then—including setting a proper example—was the most fundamental responsibility of leadership. Wisdom, along with character, was an important measure of merit. This is why knowledge and accomplishment are a major source of face (mianzi).

Leaders were expected to conduct themselves with placid reserve, modesty, and self-restraint, much like the Greek stoic ideal. The people had the right to question leaders who failed these tests, but not to question the fundamental order of society. However, no consideration was given to individual rights or due process. Rule was a matter of personality and preparation, not law.

Eventually, Confucius's views came to permeate China's culture and constitute the essence of its value system and that of all East Asia. One institution that did not adopt Confucian thinking, at least with respect to merit being the primary qualification for power, were the imperial dynasties that ruled China until Sun Yat-Sen's nationalist revolution in the early twentieth century. Nevertheless, the governmental structure that evolved was clearly Confucian, an elaborate bureaucracy replete with ministries, many hierarchical layers extending down to the local level, and a professional civil service with its own examination system and training academy (many centuries before Max Weber introduced merit-based bureaucracy to the West). It was much more elaborate than the Romans' administrative structure and more similar to that of the medieval Church. Portuguese traders labeled the top bureaucrats Mandarins, from the Latin mandare, "to command." Confucius's views were traditional and conservative, and the Confucian bureaucracy did what bureaucracies do best: preserve them.

Within the context of imperial rivalries and internal and external strife, the administrative decisions of the Mandarins have controlled day-to-day life in China for more than 2,000 years. Even under the most benign of rulers, Confucianism was applied as a kind of state orthodoxy. Under its rubric, China's highly centralized rule routinely confiscated and redistributed wealth, established state monopolies, price controls, and collective landownership, and conscripted unwilling soldiers and forced labor (used in building the Great Wall).

Confucius saw commerce as a pursuit of low status, an attitude that would persist in China except for the small entrepreneurial class that emerged around the European enclaves in the late nineteenth century. These entrepreneurs became the "Overseas Chinese," the foundation of expatriate communities in Hong Kong, Singapore, Vietnam, and elsewhere after the communist victory in 1949. Of course, the long-standing, statist tradition had made China fertile ground for communism, which differed from the state orthodoxy more in name than in substance.

Many man-made hardships combined with frequent natural disasters made life miserable for the ordinary Chinese. According to LaTourette, average life expectancy remained below 30 years of age even as China entered the twentieth century. The depredations of Mao, including his purges and artificial famines (when, for example, during the "Great Leap Forward" every village was to manufacture steel regardless of the consequences of fields left untended) were but a recent example.

A stream of thought that emerged concurrently with Confucianism was legalism, offering a very different prescription for maintaining order. Unlike Confucius, the legalists held that people were inherently bad and that a firm hand was needed to keep them in line. They believed that the primary responsibility of government (the king, and later the emperor) toward its subjects was to maximize their martial skills to help preserve and expand the state. Indeed, legalism was instrumental in first unifying the empire in the third century B.C. Although it soon dissipated as a philosophical discipline, the precedent it set cast China's emperors from that point forward with a much harder edge than Confucius would have envisioned or preferred.

The Romans applied Greek ideals to a large empire. Whereas Greek democracy, limited to the city-state and the upper class, took the form of a simple plebiscite or referendum, the Roman solution was representative democracy. The Romans elaborated and expanded the protection of law to more classes of citizens and developed the notion of checks and balances. All this may have come to naught after the Empire fell but for the towns that emerged during the Pax Romana, created by surplus agriculture and its handmaiden, specialized labor. The vitality of trade centered in these towns eventually produced sufficient wealth to finance the revival of classical art, science, and thinking known as the Renaissance and the great period of European exploration and empire-building. The ensuring Enlightenment refined classical political ideas, generated new ones (such as the social contract and the right of all people to own private property), and produced the philosophical rationale and impetus that led to the institutional arrangements governing Western democracies today.

It is an interesting coincidence that the sixth century B.C. witnessed the origins of the divergent value systems of East and West: Confucius's harmony and filial loyalty combined with legalism and Taoist fatalism on one hand, and Greek democracy, rationality, and individualism on the other. Thenceforth, imperial repression continued in once-great China, abetted by Confucian discipline, Taoist passivity, Buddhist introspection, and unrelenting poverty and hardship. But the West would go on to nearly conquer the world, at least for a time, first politically and then economically.

## Cosmology

Taoism (pronounced "dowism") filled a spiritual void in the pragmatic Confucian world. It advocated simplicity, detachment from the concerns of everyday life, and harmony with nature as the means of establishing social unity and harmony. Like other agrarian societies perpetually struggling to eke out an existence and accustomed to frequent hardship, the Chinese felt dependent upon and subservient to nature and sought the protection of their ancestors. (In Chinese art, one never sees flower arrangements or a still life of fruit in a bowl representing an attempt to improve on nature.) Natural disasters were believed to be an expression of nature's wrath over human misdeeds.

According to the Tao (the "Way") taken from the ancient I. Ching, people must seek harmony with nature and accommodate its whims. This cosmology is embodied in the notion of yin and yang, the arrangement of nature into opposing but complementary and oscillating forces such as day and night, high and low tide, male and female. Time has no beginning or end; it does not lapse or expire; it is cyclical rather than linear. Time and phenomena simply happen; hence, they are to be sensed or experienced, not conserved or measured. Everything is related to everything else—what Trompenaars called a diffuse view of the world rather than a specific or compartmentalized view. A perception of interrelatedness promotes holistic thinking and a systemic view. Cyclical patterns of yin and yang, like a spinning gyroscope, create a sense of stability, whereas a more linear path trails off into the unknowable.

The application of accumulated wisdom and intuition rather than rationality is the normal way of thinking for the traditional Confucianist. The scientific method would be an alien and dangerous notion because, in the Taoist world view, it would tend to polarize rather than harmonize. Excessive knowledge was thought to make people ungovernable. The fatalism inherent in Taoist cosmology renders superfluous any search for cause-and-effect relationships—the essence of scientific inquiry. Moreover, science would be tantamount to tampering with nature and its natural rhythms. It would also present the risk of departure from the tradition and stability dear to Confucian bureaucrats. Many of China's technological advances were driven not by a search for understanding but by the efforts of Taoist priests to achieve immortality on earth—efforts the Confucianists considered frivolous and superstitious.

The contrast between Chinese and Western cosmology is stark. For the Westerner, there is no greater truth than what can be objectively measured and tested. The opposite of that shown to be true must be false. In other words, Western logic cannot accommodate the simultaneous validity of contradictory circumstances embodied in the Tao. Westerners tend to think in logical, linear patterns. For the Chinese, intuition, emotion, and the need to maintain harmonious relationships constitute truth; objective information is less important. Westerners assume they can employ and shape nature to their own ends. It is difficult to imagine the Chinese deciding, as did the medieval Dutch, that it was not only desirable but quite possible to push back the North Sea, reclaim much of its bottom, and convert it to cities and fertile farmland.

All of this, of course, traces back to a very different cosmological view with roots in ancient Greece. Aristotle thought that by observation and experimentation, man could begin to understand how nature worked. Once that understanding began to accumulate, it was quite natural for the Greeks and their heirs to find ways to employ this knowledge. Early success gave Westerners confidence that they could harness nature and its resources rather than submit to it.

## Religion and Ethical Standards

By Western standards, China is a secular society; most Chinese do not "belong" to a faith in the sense of being a Christian, a Jew, or a Muslim. Little thought is given to supreme beings, other than venerated ancestors, or to such matters as holiness or life after death. There is a dearth of universal ethical principles or moral absolutes other than maintaining the security and well-being of the family and living up to one's Confucian obligations. These remain the primary normative prescriptions for correct behavior. Because maintaining social harmony and order is the highest ideal, minimization of conflict is essential and absolutes are seen as sources of conflict.

Like the ancient Greeks, Confucius advocated a "golden mean," a moderation and balance in all things. But unlike the Greeks, Confucius and his followers believed this meant being reasonable rather than relying on reason. They held no relentless quest for the "truth," which many Westerners search for in the spiritual realm as diligently as they do in the scientific. Such a search would be futile, for when and where the yang prevails, its opposite yin will follow, and so on.

Behavior that maintained one's system of relationships was expected, rather than adherence to abstract principles. The "right" decision was the one that best served the present circumstances, not some code of temporal or religious law. Ethics were largely relative or situational, particularistic rather than universal. In any given circumstances, one might invoke Confucius, Buddha, the Tao, a venerated ancestor, or an animistic spirit, depending on whatever seemed to provide the most appropriate guidance. Europeans found this lack of "principle" barbarian. On the other hand, the Chinese considered barbarian the Europeans' aggressive, disharmonious behavior and ignorance of li.

Confucianism makes no pretense as a religion. Rather, it is a system of values that govern interpersonal behavior with an eye toward building a civil society. It does not speak to humanity's relationship with any supreme being. Taoism and Buddhism are more concerned with obtaining release from worldly cares and woe than with holiness or heavenly aspirations. The asceticism and mendicancy of Buddhist monks is not consistent with Confucian humanism and its ideals of hard work, order, and propriety. Celibacy attacks the bedrock of the Chinese society, the family.

Nevertheless, even as Buddhism declined in its home on the Indian subcontinent, it spread rapidly throughout East Asia. Buddha's first principle, that life is pain, certainly rang true with the vast majority of Chinese, who lived largely miserable lives. His prescription for escape into a state of enlightenment had great appeal. Accordingly, the more inclusive Mahayana form of Buddhism was more welcome in China because it held that a good Buddhist in any walk of life could reach an enlightened state, nirvana, and freedom from the needs and desires that made life so painful. In contrast, the more rigorous Theravada form held the pursuit of enlightenment to be a full-time pursuit and thus possible only for cloistered monks. In practice, the Chinese tended to set aside the search for enlightenment and settled for abiding by the behavioral standards embodied in Buddha's prescriptive "Eightfold Path"—standards that were consistent with those of Confucius. Buddhism's most significant impact on the Chinese value system lay in teaching that life is in a state of constant flux and a sorrow-free life of serenity and peace means accepting rather than resisting change. Any sense of individuality, self, ego, or soul was made transient and meaningless by this flux. Thus, Buddhism served to amplify the importance of Confucian behavioral norms and collectivism and Taoist receptivity to change.

Chinese religion has evolved in ways that support and advance the maintenance of social harmony. In contrast, Judaism and Christianity (and Islam as well) prescribe behavioral and ethical standards intended to allow the faithful an opportunity to please and prove their worthiness to their Creator and Supreme Being. While banning behavior detrimental to maintaining a civil society (though perhaps one not quite as well-mannered as China's), these religions also prescribe how the Supreme Being should be worshipped and require followers to hold certain beliefs, make certain expressions of faith, and participate in various rituals.

Secular authorities in the West, particularly the Romans building on the precedent set by the ancient Greeks, extended ecclesiastical law into a natural law that dealt with practices, abstract principles, and beliefs beyond the spiritual domain. From natural law, greatly elaborated during the Enlightenment, were derived such notions as liberty, justice, equity, fairness, the binding contact, and, ultimately, the social contract between people and their governments. These important social and political virtues, binding governments as well as citizens, acquired the force of principle as important to many—and perhaps more so to some—as the tenets of sacred scripture. Though Westerners might disagree on what is "fair" in any set of circumstances, few would argue against the worth of "fairness."

The Chinese, like most human beings, will recognize the evil of a wanton crime, but they will have trouble responding to the invocation of abstractions such as "fair trade." What is fair to the Chinese is whatever works, whatever action or manner of speech is necessary to execute a transaction satisfactorily for both parties. Westerners are taught to place the principle of honesty above the nicety of harmony; for them, constructive criticism is the "right" thing to do, even if painful. For the Chinese, this threat to harmony is antisocial. Likewise, most Westerners would be appalled that a manager could be so unprincipled as to show favoritism in hiring a relative. A Chinese would be equally appalled by any reluctance to do so.

## Managerial Implications

The Chinese are not necessarily better or worse than Westerners, only different. As we have seen, this is the result of a very different set of traditions, not of inherent flaws in the Asian or national character or even of communism. An appreciation of these actual attitudinal and behavioral differences is obviously of great interest to those who would negotiate with the Chinese, teach or learn from them, do business in China, or find themselves working with them in any capacity. Table 2 encapsulates some of these differences and the ways in which they may affect working relationships. . . .

The Chinese mind is accustomed to coping comfortably with dichotomies and accepting both poles as valid. Such bipolar conundrums as effectiveness and efficiency, high quality and low cost, short-term and long-term, profit and growth, stability and progress, may come easier to the Chinese. They intuit a holistic and mutually complementary, dependent, or symbiotic relationship among all things. Accordingly, they may be better strategic thinkers than Westerners because they can come to terms with the attendant multiplicity of variables and mental trade-offs, recognize and adapt to what "nature" gives them (recall the strategic lessons of the Vietnam War), be comfortable with flux, and stay less encumbered by the urge to find the "truth" before acting.

Another manifestation of holistic thinking is the Chinese sense that the relationship among the parties to a business transaction is part of that transaction, not preliminary to it. When you want to get beyond the social niceties and relationship-building and get down to business, you must step back and recognize that the social interaction is an essential part of the process. All Chinese seek to cement such relationships into their guanxi networks,

*Table 2*

### A Summary of Western and Chinese Cultural Differences and the Implications for Management

Comparing pertinent features of the history of the West with that of China, we can make the following distinctions:

| The West | China |
| --- | --- |
| Individual rights | Individual duty and collective obligations |
| Rule by law | Rule by personality and imperial authority |
| The collective right to grant, question, and reject political authority | Unquestioning submission to hereditary authority backed by force |
| Political and ethnic pluralism | Monolithic power and homogeneity |
| Cultural interaction | Cultural isolation |
| Sufficient resources to support early urbanization, specialization of labor, and large-scale trade | An agrarian, subsistence economy and endless hardship, both natural and imposed |
| An external orientation | An internal orientation |
| Physical and social mobility | Permanence in situ |
| Reliance on reason and the scientific method | Reliance on precedent, intuition, and wisdom |
| An aggressive, active approach to nature, technology, and progress | Passive, fatalistic submission |

building a system of reciprocal, mutual obligation and dependency (renqing).

The Chinese will respect and appreciate a Westerner's knowledge of their culture. However, it is probably better to act with good manners and a sincere respect for Chinese culture than as an expert if, as a result, one comes across as self-assured to the point of arrogance. Remember that, like the Japanese, the Chinese tend to think of themselves as so unique that foreigners cannot comprehend them and their ways completely. It is probably wise to accept that proposition and, accordingly, be open-minded and meticulously well-mannered, listen more and speak less, learn at least as much as you try to teach, and avoid any form of aggressiveness, arrogance, individual competitiveness, self-promotion, or ostentation.

It is worth repeating here that interpersonal relationships, rather than the content and practice of business, are affected most by these cultural differences. Your domestic success can be replicated in China if you learn and adapt to Chinese ways of building and maintaining relationships. You can introduce Western practices successfully, but you must first build trust. This is best done by demonstrating your sincerity in working for some common good that accrues to your Chinese counterparts, to their enterprise, and to the Chinese people.

JACK SCARBOROUGH *is a management educator at Barry University in Florida and a retired U.S. Coast Guard commander.*

# EXPLORING THE ISSUE

## Are Chinese Confucianism and Western Capitalism Compatible?

### Critical Thinking and Reflection

1. Critically examine Professor A.T. Nuyen's opposition to modern "cutthroat" capitalism. His embrace of Adam Smith's version of capitalism permits him to find capitalism and Confucianism compatible.
2. How do you think Adam Smith would respond to today's version of capitalism, with multinational corporations controlling more wealth than many national states? Which features of Smith's original capitalism have been compromised by today's world economies? Critically discuss.
3. Critically examine professor Jack Scarborough's contrast between modern capitalism and traditional Chinese values. What are the characteristics of classical Confucianism that Scarborough finds incompatible with modern capitalism? Critically discuss.
4. Which version, in your view, is the "real" capitalism—Adam Smith's original formulation of principles or the current version, which presumes an aggressive individualism? Research and critically debate this question.
5. Would it be possible to return to the "original" form of capitalism? What structures and assumptions would have to be changed in order to do this? And, would China be able to return to the form of Confucian values that existed in a world before capitalism? Critically discuss.
6. Is there a way in which the values of an older worldview can inform a current one? Can you find an example from history in which people looked to the past and consciously imitated what they found there? Perhaps the clearest example is the European Renaissance that looked back to classical Greece and Rome for inspiration and gave what they found there a "rebirth."
7. How much influence do capitalism and Confucianism, respectively, have on Western and Chinese cultures? Are most people today more influenced by the wider worldviews they learned as children or are they acting more as solitary individuals? Thoughtfully and critically discuss this question.

### Is There Common Ground?

The clue to this question for this issue lies in the origins of classical capitalism. The common ground these two authors share is a nod to Taoism and its rootedness in nature, as well as the cohesive values of Confucianism. The Pacific Rim nations, all strongly influenced by Confucian values, are among the most successful economically today. At first glance it seems logical that the Western rational and empirical approach would be better suited to addressing modern problems. However, the intuitive Chinese approach that professor Scarborough compares unfavorably with the Western view appears to be working more effectively over the past few decades.

If we do some research into the "styles" of Asian and Western businesspeople, we might meet the philosophy of Sun-tzu, a rough contemporary of Confucius. Quotes from his work made their way into the film "Wall Street," where a greedy sleaze named Gordon Gecko mined Sun-tzu for business strategies. Perhaps the most famous piece of advice Sun-tzu offered to the princes on war was this. Know your enemy/opponent. Know yourself. If you know both deeply, you will be successful 100 percent of the time. If you know one, but not the other, the odds are 50/50. If you know neither, you will lose every contest.

*Question:* Is this advice compatible with Chinese Confucianism? With Western capitalism?

### Create Central

www.mhhe.com/createcentral

### Additional Resources

For greater depth, see *The Physiocrats: Six Lectures on the French Economistes of the 18th Century*, originally delivered at the London School of Economics in 1897 and reprinted by Augustus M. Kelley, Publishers in 1989. Elizabeth Fox-Genovese's *The Origins of Physiocracy* (Cornell University Press, 1976) provides a modern historical account of the works of Francois Quesnay and his unacknowledged collaborator Victor Riqueti, marquis de Mirabeau. Gianni Vaggi's *The Economics of Francois Quesnay* (Duke University Press, 1987) offers a reconsideration of Quesnay's theories in the light of contemporary economic theory. *Francois Quesnay (1694–1774)*, Mark Blaug, ed. (Edward Elgar Publishing Limited, 1991) is Volume II of the *Pioneers in Economics* series, which presents "critical appraisals of influential economists." And, finally, *Quesnay's Tableau Economique*, Marguerite

Kuczynski and Ronald L. Meek, eds. (Augustus M. Kelley Publishers, 1972), explores the history of the several editions of Quesnay's conceptual construct—the *tableau* *economique*—which lays out the ideas on which classical capitalism will be constructed.

# Internet Reference . . .

### Confucian Tradition(s)

This site covers the pre-Confucian texts, the core concepts of Confucianism, its history and spread throughout China, and some current debates about Confucianism. The sections on the Confucian virtues are particularly helpful.

**www.ibiblio.org/chinesehistory/contents/ 02cul/c04s04.html**

Selected, Edited, and with Issue Framing Material by:
**Helen Buss Mitchell,** *Howard Community College*
and
**Joseph R. Mitchell,** *Howard Community College*

# ISSUE

# Was Ethnic Hatred Primarily Responsible for the Rwandan Genocide of 1994?

**YES: Alison Des Forges**, from "The Ideology of Genocide," *Issue: A Journal of Opinion* (1995)

**NO: René Lemarchand**, from "Rwanda: The Rationality of Genocide," *Issue: A Journal of Opinion* (1994)

---

## Learning Outcomes

**After reading this issue you should be able to:**

- Describe key elements in the history of Rwanda, especially as they relate to the relations between the majority Hutus and the minority Tutsis.
- Understand the implications of colonial powers—Germans, then Belgians—favoring Tutsis over Hutus.
- Understand and explain the myths of ethnic superiority/inferiority in Rwanda.
- Understand and explain the role of worldwide apathy and lack of response as 800,000 Tutsis were slaughtered over a three-month period.

---

### ISSUE SUMMARY

**YES:** Alison Des Forges argues that ethnic hatred between Hutus and Tutsis in Rwanda was primarily responsible for the Rwandan genocide of 1994.

**NO:** René Lemarchand, while admitting that ethnic rivalries played a role in the catastrophe, argues that the ability of the Hutus to engage in "planned annihilation" free of any local or international restraint was a more important factor.

**O**n April 6, 1994, Rwanda's President Juvenal Habyarimana and Burundi's President Cyprien Ntaryamira were killed when their plane was shot down near the Kingali, Rwanda airport. Both men were working to bring peace to their countries, which had been ripped apart by ethnic rivalries and resultant violence, which had plagued their countries and the entire central African Lake District for decades. It was thought that extremists in Rwanda, who did not want these peace negotiations to succeed, were responsible for this act.

In the 3 months that followed, 800,000 Tutsis were slaughtered by the Hutu-dominated Rwandan government while the world's nations stood by and did nothing to stop it. By all accounts the genocide was not a spontaneous eruption of bloodlust; rather, it was rationally and methodically carried out, beginning with roadblocks and barricades an hour after the plane crash that killed President Habyarimana. Local officials and government-sponsored radio urged people to murder their Tutsi and moderate Hutu neighbors. What circumstances could have combined to make this blatant act of genocide possible?

Throughout the twentieth century, Rwanda experienced periods of ethnic violence involving the rival Hutu and Tutsi tribes. The former, native to the region, represented more than 80 percent of the country's people, while the latter, who emigrated to the area from another part of Africa centuries ago, numbered 15 percent. This violence began during the colonial period when first the Germans, and then the Belgians, favored the Tutsi over the Hutu during their colonial rule; the latter even used the Tutsi to enforce their colonial rule. This created resentment among the Hutu who waited for an opportunity to assert their majority power. This occurred in the 1960s when many European countries were pulled out of Africa.

In 1961–1962, when the Belgians withdrew from the area and the two nations of Rwanda and Burundi were formed, massacres of the Tutsi ensued. Peace was finally restored when General Juvenal Habyarimana, a Hutu, seized power and restored a semblance of order to the country in 1973. Under his rule, which would last for more than 20 years, Hutus were given preferential treatment in practically all aspects of Rwandan life. This was opposed by Tutsi exiles in the region, who ultimately formed the Rwanda Patriotic Front (RPT) to defend Tutsi rights in the country. Both sides waged war throughout the 1980s.

In 1990, under pressure from Western nations, Habyarimana agreed in principle to establish a true democratic government based on ethnic rights, which led to peace and stability in the area. When his plane was shot down on April 6, 1994, many thought peace was close at hand. In fact, his assassination is blamed on extremists from his own party who did not want the peace plan to succeed. The slaughter of Tutsis—and moderate Hutus who spoke against it—began immediately and lasted until July. While the world watched and its nations did nothing, more than three-quarters of a million people were slaughtered, most by machete-wielding paramilitary troops. Many women who survived the ordeal told stories of wholesale rape, which ultimately resulted in pregnancies and children that no one wanted. Furthermore, these deeds exacerbated Africa's AIDS crisis due to its wholesale perpetration of unsafe sex.

What factors created the Rwandan genocide of 1994? According to Alison Des Forges, the long-standing differences between Hutu and Tutsi created in the Hutu extremists an "ideology of genocide," which they used to maintain their political control over the country by annihilating their Tutsi rivals. René Lemarchand states that a more important factor was the Hutu's ability to launch a genocidal campaign free of any local or international restraint.

The Holocaust, in which six million Jews were murdered by Nazi Germany, was supposed to have taught valuable lessons to the world, namely that it did happen, and could happen again if steps were not taken to prevent it. In 1948, the United Nations defined and condemned genocide, and many expected that lessons were indeed learned and genocidal acts would never again occur. Fifty years later, political annihilation in Cambodia, "ethnic cleansing" in the former Yugoslavia, and the slaughter in Rwanda have demonstrated the apparent naïveté of such thinking. Why did we fail—again?

A lesson we should have learned from Rwanda is that words are important, but actions are better suited to prevent acts of genocide. In the case of Rwanda, no one—not the UN, the United States, European nations, or African nations—stepped forward until it was too late. Comparisons have been made to the "ethnic cleansing" that took place in the former Yugoslavia. In the aftermath of the Rwandan genocide, U.N. Secretary General Boutros Boutros-Ghali told the PBS news show *Frontline:* "The failure of Rwanda is 10 times greater than the failure of Yugoslavia. Because in Yugoslavia the international community was interested, was involved. In Rwanda, nobody was interested."

In October 1994, the International Criminal Tribunal for Rwanda (meeting in neighboring Tanzania), an extension of the International Criminal Tribunal for Yugoslavia (meeting in The Hague) undertook the process of bringing perpetrators to justice. This was the first set of criminal tribunals since the better known one in Nuremberg, Germany, that met in the aftermath of World War II from 1945 to 1946. As in the Nazi Holocaust, the Rwandan genocide had been rationally planned and carried out. And, there were clearly ethnic stereotypes, including the so-called Hamitic Myth, which labeled the Tutsis genetically superior, which were reminiscent of Hitler's Nuremberg Laws that labeled Jews inferior and non-Aryan.

Although some of those most responsible for the Rwandan genocide had left the country, a decade of indictments and trials targeted a number of high-ranking people for their war crimes. And, in 2008, three former senior Rwandan defense and military officials were indicted for organizing the genocide. A myriad of world leaders, including U.S. President William Clinton and UN Secretary Kofi Annan, have expressed remorse for what they didn't do in regards to the Rwandan genocide. Have lessons finally been learned? We'll have to wait for that answer.

# YES ↵

**Alison Des Forges**

## The Ideology of Genocide

**M**obilizing thousands of Rwandans to slaughter tens of thousands of others required effective organization. Far from the "Failed State" syndrome that appears to plague some parts of Africa, Rwanda was too successful as a state. Extremists used its administrative apparatus, its military, and its party organizations to carry out a "cottage-industry" genocide that reached out to all levels of the population and produced between five hundred thousand and one million victims. Those with state power used their authority to force action from those reluctant to kill. They also offered attractive incentives to people who are very poor, giving license to loot, and promising them the land and businesses of the victims. In some cases, local officials even decided ahead of time the disposition of the most attractive items of movable property. Everyone knew who had a refrigerator, a plush sofa, a radio, and assailants were guaranteed their rewards before attacking. But even with the powerful levers of threat and bribe, officials could not have succeeded so well had people not been prepared to hate and fear the Tutsi. Extremists who were ready to use slaughter to hold on to political power constructed an ideology of genocide from a faulty history that had long been accepted by both Hutu and Tutsi. Like the identity cards that had guaranteed privileges to the Tutsi during the colonial period and then served to identify them as victims for the genocide, the history that had once legitimated their rule was ultimately turned against them to justify their massacre.

Before the arrival of the Europeans, the ruling elite had a sense of its own superiority. (Has there ever been an elite that did not?) In the late eighteenth and early nineteenth centuries, when Rwanda was located in regions best suited for pastoralism, members of the elite prided themselves on their knowledge about and control of cattle and looked down on cultivators lacking in both. Later in the nineteenth century, the central state expanded into regions dominated by cultivators and the elite increasingly made alliances with local leaders, whether *abahinza*, persons with ritual importance, or *abakuru*, heads of important lineage groups. In the same period, the ruler Rwabugiri took into his service significant numbers of men from outside the elite in order to increase his control over the old aristocratic lineages. Keeping pace with these political changes, aristocrats adjusted their attitudes to stress military skills and scorned masses who fell short in martial ability and experience.

This sense of superiority appears to have been linked to the aristocrats' sense of what they owned and what they could do, than to any emphasis on racial characteristics. Indeed, the elite that we now call Tutsi encompassed a number of competing lineages who had arrived in Rwanda at different times over a period of centuries and who had different interests as well as varied backgrounds. In the same way, the masses that are now known as Hutu included both peoples long residing within Rwanda and those who had just arrived from Zaire or Uganda. Given the complex variables in the situation, the categories of Hutu and Tutsi remained flexible and individuals could and did move from one to the other.

While the Tutsi sense of superiority to Hutu appears more elitism than racism, the attitudes of both groups towards the Twa were clearly racist. They scorned this small part of the population, in recent times less than one percent of the total, and refused not just intermarriage but even the normal courtesies of sharing food and drink with them.

When the Europeans arrived at the start of the twentieth century, they brought their own kind of racism, which would have enormous impact upon Rwandan ideas and practices. They assumed their own superiority and valued others in relation to their perceived nearness—physically and geographically—to themselves. Translating their racism into the African context, they formulated the "hamitic hypothesis," according to which "white Africans" from the northeast had brought civilization to the rest of the benighted continent. Colonialists found the Tutsi of Rwanda the ideal Hamites: tall, elegant, narrow-featured. Tutsi even wore togas, surely proof of a remote connection with Roman colonies of North Africa. Determined to validate their own prejudices, Europeans explained as unfortunate aberrations those Tutsi who did not conform to their image of what a Tutsi should look like, that is, like a dark-skinned European. They paid little attention to the distinctions among "Hutu" of different regions and origins. Accustomed to viewing Tutsi and Hutu as homogeneous groups, they ascribed stereotyped intellectual and moral qualities to the people of each category. With little hesitation, they decided that the Tutsi were more intelligent—and perhaps more devious—and so born to rule, while the Hutu, dumb but good-natured, could never be other than productive, loyal subjects. They put these ideas into practice by limiting posts in the administration, as well as the higher education needed

Des Forges, Alison. From *Issue: A Journal of Opinion*, January 20, 1995, vol. xxiii/2, pp. 44–47. Copyright © 1995 by African Studies Association Secretariat. Reprinted by permission.

for these jobs, to Tutsi. And to ensure that only Tutsi had access to these benefits, they instituted a system of population registration, labeling each person at birth as Hutu, Tutsi or Twa.

The Tutsi, politically astute by training not by birth, readily understood the prejudices of the Europeans and exploited them fully to their own benefit. Not only did they use European backing to extend and intensify their control over the Hutu—whose faults they exaggerated to the gullible Europeans—they also joined with the Europeans to create the ideological justification for this exploitation.

In a great and unsung collaborative enterprise over a period of decades, Europeans and Rwandan intellectuals created a history of Rwanda that fit European assumptions and accorded with Tutsi interests. The Europeans provided a theoretical, teleological framework and the Rwandans provided the supporting data to describe the progress of Rwanda to the height of its power at the end of the nineteenth century. The first and most "primitive" inhabitants were the Twa, the hunters and gatherers. Next the trusty Hutu lumbered upon the scene to cut the forests and create some fledging political organizations. Then in swooped the conquering Tutsi from Ethiopia, a minority that subjugated the far more numerous mass through their martial skill and superior intelligence—and, some said, through offering the grant of their cattle. The final and still uncompleted chapter in this steady climb upward, was, of course, the arrival of that even lighter-skinned and more clever minority, still fewer in numbers but more powerful in organization, the Europeans, who established their control over all the others. The determined onward thrust of the narrative allowed for no pauses or deviations from this simple and substantially distorted account of the growth of the nation. Ignoring the fundamentally "Hutu" nature of much of the ritual and many of the institutions of the central state, and neglecting the role played by leading Hutu in the late nineteenth and early twentieth centuries, these mutually supportive historians created a mythic history to buttress a colonial social order. The Europeans who participated in this enterprise included administrators, scholars, and missionaries. The Rwandans were chiefs, poets, and historians attached to the court, although the most outstanding of them, Alexis Kagame, was also identified with the church. The sophisticated and convincing canon they produced, backed as it was by extensive data, served as the accepted description of the Rwandan past until Jan Vansina challenged some of its basic assumptions in 1962.

The joint product was shaped in Rwanda and packaged in Europe, and then delivered back into the schoolrooms of Rwanda by European or European-educated teachers. In addition, the results of the collaborative enterprise were accepted by intellectuals in the circles around the court, even those without European-style schooling—and integrated into their oral histories. It was not surprising that Tutsi were pleased with this version of history. But even the majority of Hutu swallowed this distorted account of the past, so great was their respect for European-style education. Thus people of both groups learned to think of the Tutsi as winners and the Hutu as losers in every great contest of the Rwandan past.

Faulty history was complicated by inadequate anthropology: the categories "Bantu" and "Ethiopoid," drawn from terms purporting to describe language groups, were applied to Hutu and Tutsi, reinforcing the idea that they were two distinct and internally coherent groups of people who had originated in different parts of Africa.

Extremist Tutsi, encouraged by European admiration and influenced by the amalgam of myth and pseudoanthropology, moved from elitism to racism. They transformed the dividing line between themselves and Hutu into the same kind of line that had once separated them and the Hutu from the Twa. The majority of Tutsi apparently did not accept this racism and continued to interact with Hutu much as they had in the past. But the formulation of the extreme position altered the terms of discourse and opened the way to a corresponding and equally virulent formulation on the part of extremist Hutu.

When Hutu overthrew the Tutsi in a revolution beginning in 1959, they did not question the basic elements of the myth—the arrival of a Tutsi minority and its subjugation of the Hutu majority. Although in the years immediately after, Rwandan and foreign scholars began presenting a different version of the past, one in which the Hutu played a more important role in shaping the growth of the state, these new ideas did not make their way into either political discourse or popular consciousness. Indeed, some politicians continued to stress the completeness of Tutsi control as a way to heighten feeling against them and to increase solidarity among the Hutu. They did not openly subscribe to the idea of Tutsi superiority as such, but by offering no explanation of how a small number could have conquered a much larger population, they perpetuated the belief that the Tutsi had capacities greater than those of the Hutu.

Ordinary people, who had no way to evaluate how truthfully the distant past was presented, did have their own experience to draw on, the experience of the colonial period. They knew that in that time Tutsi domination had been repressive, so they not surprisingly concluded that Tutsi control in earlier periods had been similarly intense.

In the early days of the revolution, Hutu had attacked mostly Tutsi who had some link with official power; they had left their ordinary Tutsi neighbors in peace. Then in the early 1960s Tutsi refugee groups, who had fled into exile at the start of the revolution, launched a series of attacks into Rwanda. After each, Hutu attacked Tutsi who still lived within the country, steadily widening the circle of victims until even Tutsi who had had no connection with previous power-holders were at risk. Local politicians and officials were responsible for this gradual enlarging of the pool of potential victims, whom they accused of aiding the invaders. They whipped up feeling against Tutsi to increase their own power, to consolidate the community behind them in unifying it against the minority. They profited from encouraging attacks on the Tutsi both directly, by showing they were strong enough to get people killed, and indirectly, by confiscating and then redistributing the property of victims who had been killed or driven away.

Then after more than twenty years of inaction, the refugee community attacked Rwanda on October 1, 1990, President Juvenal Habyarimana and his supporters saw the chance to exploit the invasion to consolidate Habyarimana's power base, which had been slipping after his long years in power. Like authorities in the 1960s, they attempted to do this by targeting Tutsi within the country as "accomplices" of the invading Rwandan Patriotic Front (RPF). They had at hand all the elements needed to construct an ideology of hate against the minority:

- the identification of all Tutsi with those who once ruled, an identification developed during the attacks of the 1960s;
- the link, real for a few but supposed for all, with the RPF who had invaded the country;
- the belief that in the past Tutsi had ruled repressively and that, through the RPF, they intended to re-establish the same exploitative regime;
- the belief that Tutsi were a separate and alien people, not part of the "Bantu" group, but from somewhere outside Rwanda and hence with no right to live in Rwanda;
- the conviction that the Tutsi had been able in the past to subjugate far larger numbers of Hutu because of superior intelligence or deviousness and still possessed the capacity to do so.

From the early days after the invasion, the extremists began to exploit these elements. According to one Rwandan army officer he was directed almost immediately after the invasion to spread the word throughout northeastern Rwanda that the RPF had attacked to restore the Tutsi monarch. Over the months that followed two other elements were added to transform the ideology of hate into the ideology of genocide:

- the belief that previous measures to end Tutsi control—killing some and driving away others—had failed and that the only way to ensure they would never take power again was to eliminate them completely; and
- the fear that Tutsi themselves intended to slaughter vast numbers of Hutu and would so do unless the Hutu struck first.

The moment when hatred became a determination to extirpate no doubt occurred at different times for different people, but certainly was widespread among the Habyarimana circle by November 1992. At the end of that month, Leon Mugesera, a Canadian-educated linguist who was a favorite of Habyarimana, delivered an inflammatory speech in northwestern Rwanda urging the Hutu to unite to send all the Tutsi back where they came from, that is, to Ethiopia, by "the river route," by killing them and throwing them in the rivers that eventually feed into the Nile. This solution, appealing in its simplicity and completeness, was never challenged, far less disavowed, by Habyarimana or others of his MRND party.

But some months before Habyarimana had been obliged to open up his single-party state to other parties and had enlarged his government to include representatives of opposition groups. The Minister of Justice, Stanislas Mbonampeka, represented the Liberal Party, a party then opposed to Habyarimana. He issued a warrant for the arrest of Mugesera, but was unable to carry out the warrant because Mugesera fled to a military camp where he remained hidden until he escaped from the country. (He turned up eventually in Canada where he is at the time of present writing.)

There is no better indication of the spread of the cancer of genocidal ideas than the positions of Mbonampeka. Ready to arrest Mugesera for incitement to violence in December 1992, he had himself been won to the merits of genocide by the spring of 1994. At the meeting of the United Nations Human Rights Commission held in Geneva, in late May 1994, Mbonampeka appeared as part of the Rwandan government delegation to defend its actions. At that time, he told a small group of participants in the meeting, including the writer, that the killing taking place in Rwanda was "normal." After the RPF victory, Mbonampeka fled to Zaire where, in November 1994, he was named to the rump government, once again, as Minister of Justice.

As the war continued and the RPF gained ground both militarily and through its diplomacy, the ideology of genocide was taken up by growing numbers of people. Two events were key in pushing many to this extreme position. First, the Arusha accords signed in August 1994 consolidated so many RPF gains that they seemed proof to many that once again the Tutsi were to be the winners. Second, in October 1993, Melchior Ndadaye, the recently elected President of Burundi and a Hutu, was assassinated by officers of the Tutsi-dominated army. The violence, and the suddenness by which the apparently successful transition to majority Hutu rule in Burundi was disrupted, demonstrated to many in Rwanda that no Tutsi could be trusted. It was then easy to argue that Tutsi/RPF in Rwanda, like Tutsi in Burundi, would inevitably overturn any power-sharing arrangement.

By April, the ideology was fully developed. When President Habyarimana's plane was shot down, those who assumed control of the government had no trouble integrating the assassination into the already-existing framework. Who was actually responsible was irrelevant to the use they could make of the killing. Without hesitation or doubt, they proclaimed that the RFP, with usual Tutsi deviousness and ruthlessness, had struck down the national leader who had wanted to make peace with them. Well prepared by exposure to the ideology of hate, most Hutu believed them. This assassination provided yet another reason to hate and fear the Tutsi.

A theme which had been present from the early days of the revolution but which had only limited importance in the ideology of genocide was the extent to which Tutsi had depended on outside support for their success. Most Hutu recognized that the support of the colonialists had been a fundamental element of the Tutsi repression, but they placed little stress upon this, particularly once the Belgian administration had switched its support to them. After the 1990 invasion, the Habyarimana government did exploit the link between the RPF and Ugandan President Museveni and attempted to discredit the RPF as the tool of a foreign government. A substantial number of RPF leaders had served in the army that brought Museveni to power, many of the troops who first invaded Rwanda had deserted from the Ugandan army, and Uganda had served as a channel for RPF supplies. The Rwandan government even charged that the RPF invasion was the start of a campaign to re-establish a grand Tutsi empire of the Great Lakes region. (Within this argument, Museveni was described as Tutsi, an exaggeration of the fact that apparently one of his grandmothers was Tutsi.)

In more recent propaganda efforts, the Belgians, the United Nations, and the Americans have displaced the Ugandans as prime supporters of the RPF. A pamphlet entitled "Le Peuple Rwandais Accuse . . . ," circulated since September 1994 over the signature of then Minister of Justice Agnès Ntamabyaliro, names these outsiders as responsible for backing the RPF success. This pamphlet seems to represent a slight modification in the ideology of hate concerning Tutsi. No longer are they strong enough to conquer the Hutu masses alone; now, they must instead use their skills to attract the foreign support that then allows them to triumph. In other respects, this pamphlet continues the old themes and even states explicitly that the Tutsi were guilty of genocide against the Hutu, surely the most extraordinary of the distortions yet introduced into the description of events in the region. The assertion now heard among leaders of the rump government is that the Tutsi themselves were guilty of genocide and that, if there were in fact a Hutu genocide of the Tutsi, it was justified by the need for defense against the Tutsi plan. This latest addition to the ideology of genocide suggests that the killing is far from over.

In late October 1994, a varied group of Rwandans met at a seminar sponsored by the Fondation pour le Progrès de l'Homme to discuss how to rebuild the country. Given its location in Kigali, the seminar did not attract any representatives from Rwandans who were in exile in surrounding countries, but it did include Hutu and Tutsi with very different interests and point of view from within Rwanda. One day of discussion was devoted to the theme of "History," giving the participants ample opportunity to voice their versions of the past. At the end, all agreed that the history of Rwanda must be rewritten. Indeed, provided it is done not by attempting to "unwrite" the faulty version of the past, but rather by preserving it, examining its distortions, understanding them and—one hopes—learning from them.

---

**ALISON DES FORGES (1942–2009)** was a board member and researcher at The Human Rights Watch and is the author of *Leave None to Tell the Story: Genocide in Rwanda* (Human Rights Watch, 1999).

René Lemarchand

# Rwanda: The Rationality of Genocide

The image of Rwanda conveyed by the media is that of a society gone amok. How else to explain the collective insanity that led to the butchering of half a million civilians, men, women, and children? As much as the scale of the killings, the visual impact of the atrocities numbs the mind and makes the quest for rational motives singularly irrelevant. Tribal savagery suggests itself as the most plausible subtext for the scenes of apocalypse captured by television crews and photojournalists.

Ironically, just as "tribalism" is being reaffirmed by the media as the bane of the continent, Rwanda's descent into hell makes it a society not unlike others in Europe and Asia where genocide has been intrinsic to their recent historical experience. Seen in the broader context of 20th-century genocides, the Rwanda tragedy underscores the universality—one might say the normality—of African phenomena. The logic that set in motion the infernal machine of the Rwanda killings is no less "rational" than that which presided over the extermination of millions of human beings in Hitler's Germany or Pol Pot's Cambodia. The implication, lucidly stated by Helen Fein in a recent publication of the Institute for the Study of Genocide, is worth bearing in mind: "Genocide is preventable because it is usually a rational act: that is, the perpetrators calculate the likelihood of success, given their values and objectives."

The Rwanda genocide is neither reducible to a tribal meltdown rooted in atavistic hatreds nor to a spontaneous outburst of blind fury set off by the shooting down of the presidential plane on April 6, as officials of the Habyarimana regime have repeatedly claimed. However widespread, both views are travesties of reality. What they mask is the political manipulation that lies behind the systematic massacre of civilian populations. Planned annihilation, not the sudden eruption of long-simmering hatreds, is the key to the tragedy of Rwanda.

It is not my intention to dispose of one myth by promulgating another, the fantasy of a pre-colonial society where Hutu and Tutsi lived in an eternally blissful harmony. That Rwandan society was one of the most centralized and rigidly stratified anywhere in Africa cannot be denied, any more than the use of force in the conquest of peripheral Hutu kingdoms. But this does not mean that conflict was necessarily more intense or frequent between Hutu and Tutsi than between Tutsi and Tutsi. Much of the historical evidence suggests precisely the opposite.

## The Legacy of Revolution

While there is general agreement among Rwanda specialists that the roots of conflict lie in the transformation of ethnic identities that has accompanied the advent of colonial rule, the chain of events leading to the killings begins with the Hutu revolution of 1959–62—a revolution, I might add, which would have quickly fizzled had it not been for the sustained political, moral, and logistical assistance which the Catholic Church and the *tutelle* authorities provided the insurgents. The result was a radical shift of power from Tutsi to Hutu and the exodus of thousands of Tutsi families to neighboring territories.

Few would have imagined that thirty years later the sons of the refugee diaspora in Uganda would form the nucleus of a Tutsi-dominated politico-military organization, the Rwanda Patriotic Front (RPF), that would successfully fight its way into the capital city and defeat an army three times its size.

Fewer still could have anticipated the price of their victory. On the eve of the October 1, 1990 invasion, no one within the RPF had the slightest idea of the scale of the cataclysm they were about to unleash. The assumption, fed through rumor and self-induced optimism, was that the Habyarimana regime was a pushover, and would quickly collapse in the wake of the invasion. While grossly overestimating the strength of the internal opposition, the RPF did not anticipate the massive military support that President Juvénal Habyarimana was about to receive from the French. Nor did they foresee the catalytic effect of the invasion on Hutu solidarities, and the growing determination of hard-liners within the government to manipulate ethnic hatreds for political advantage. The perceptions that the RPF leaders had of themselves—that of liberators, dedicated to the overthrow of a thoroughly corrupt and oppressive dictatorship—turned out to be sadly out of sync with the image that a great many Hutu had of their would-be "liberators."

## Counter-Revolutionaries as Hamites

Different levels of meaning can be read into the invasion of Rwanda by the RPF, each corresponding to a distinctive set of actors. What the French saw as an intolerable Anglo-Saxon threat to their *chasse gardée*—"the Fashoda syndrome"—the hard-liners in the Habyanmana camp did not hesitate to denounce as a brazen attempt by externally supported counter-revolutionaries to turn the clock back to the pre-revolutionary era, when Tutsi hegemony was the order of the day.

The "Hamitic" frame of reference added yet another ominous dimension to the counter-revolutionary image projected by the invaders. This is where the legacy of missionary historiography, evolving from speculation about cultural affinities between Hamites and Coptic Christianity to politicized dogma about the Ethiopian origins of the Tutsi, now referred to as "féodo-Hamites," contributed a distinctively racist edge to the discourse of Hutu politicians. Already the ideological stock-in-trade of Hutu revolutionaries in the fifties (who saw in "Hamitization" a Tutsi plot to exclude them from positions of responsibility), official references to the Hamitic peril gained renewed salience in the wake of the invasion. Thus Leon Mugesera, the Hutu "boss" from Gisenyi, who, in a much quoted statement, urged his followers to send the Tutsi back to their country of origins, Ethiopia, through the quickest route, via the Akanyaru river (known to have disgorged countless Tutsi corpses into Lake Victoria).

What emerges from the urgings of a Leon Mugesera, and the incitements to violence distilled by "Radio Libre des Mille Collines," the extremist outlet, is an image of the Tutsi as both alien and clever, not unlike the image of the Jew in Nazi propaganda. His alienness disqualifies him as a member of the national community; his cleverness turns him into a permanent threat to the unsuspecting Hutu. Nothing short of physical liquidation can properly deal with such danger.

## The Regional Dimension of Hutu Rule: North vs. South

Acceptance of the Hamitic myth by Hutu politicians was not limited to any particular region or locality, yet it was among the northern Hutu that it found its most receptive echo. The reason, in part, is historical. Unlike the Hutu of the southern and central regions, their northern kinsmen were incorporated rather late into the fold of the monarchy, and with considerable assistance from the German Schutztruppe. To this day, the northerners, also known as Kiga, form a distinctive subculture. Their contacts with the Tutsi monarchy, and Tutsi culture in general, were few and far between; very few northerners married Tutsi women; for their awareness of a pre-Tutsi past, inhabited by kinglets (*abahinza*) and lineage heads (*kaburi b'imiryango*), landowners (*aba-konde*) and clients (*abagererwa*), sorcerers and prophetesses, there is no equivalent among southern Hutu. No wonder the thrust of their "revolutionary" efforts in the 1950s aimed at turning the clock back to the golden age of pre-Tutsi days.

Nor is it too surprising if the army coup that brought Habyarimana to power in 1973 had as its key political objective to take power away from the southern Hutu (led by the late President Grégoire Kayibanda) and place it

firmly into northern hands. And to make sure that power and privilege would remain a monopoly of the north, what was more natural, in Habyarimana's mind, than to order the massacre of anywhere from 40 to 50 incarcerated Hutu politicians from the central and southern regions, thus eliminating at one fell swoop his regional enemies, the "révolutionnaires de la première heure"? (From this deed Habyarimana derived an additional benefit, when, some years later he turned against Major Théoneste Lizinde, at the time his chief of security and now a key RPF personality, and accused him of having personally engineered the assassination of the southern politicians in Ruhengeri!)

It was this critically important regional dimension in the distribution of power that inspired in the minds of the northerners, a nightmarish vision of the RPF as a potential ally of Hutu politicians from the south. To the image of the Hamite as an essentially alien and predatory creature was added the frightening possibility that they might join hands with the Hutu opposition and undo everything that had been accomplished since the 1973 coup.

Since June 1991, when the legitimacy of multi-party democracy was finally recognized, the ruling Mouvement National pour la Révolution et le Développement (MNRD) had to reckon with several opposition groups, most notably the ethnically mixed Parti Liberal (PL), the Parti Social Démocrate (PSD), and the Mouvement Démocratique Républicain (MDR). All three parties could conceivably be viewed as potential allies of the RPF, but because of its substantial support among the Hutu masses of Butare and Gitarama, in the south, and because of its unique pedigree, traceable to the historic, southern-led Parti de l'Emancipation du Peuple Hutu (Parmehutu), the spearhead of the Hutu revolution until dissolved by Habyarimana in 1973, the MDR became the object of intense suspicion by northerners. This perhaps explains their determined and largely successful efforts to split it down the middle. The result was a growing rift between moderates and hard-liners (the latter also known as "Hutu power"), the former led by Faustin Twagiramungu (now Prime Minister), the latter by Dismas Nsengiyaremye, Frodouald Karamira and Donat Murego. That all three were once among Habyarimana's bitterest opponents, only to emerge as his staunchest supporters, is illustrative of how appropriate rewards, or thinly veiled threats, could bring about spectacular shifts of loyalty.

## The Scuttling of Arusha

Whether as counter-revolutionary threat, vector of Hamitic hegemony, or potential ally of the Hutu opposition, the RPF, in the minds of the Habyarimana clique, had to be destroyed as a political force. This meant the rejection of any kind of political compromise with the RPF, including ad hoc alliances with its representatives during the transition to multiparty democracy.

Yet the concept of compromise was at the very heart of the Arusha accords, signed on August 4, 1993, after a year of off-and-on negotiations. In the power-sharing arrangement hammered out at Arusha the RPF would have a total of five cabinet seats out of a total of 21, and eleven seats in the transitional national assembly out of a total of 70, putting it on par with the ruling MNRD. Compromise, likewise, was the name of the game in the restructuring of the armed forces: 40 per cent of the troops and 50 per cent of the officer corps would consist of RPF elements. Agreement of sorts was also reached on the repatriation of refugees, the demobilization of troops and on multi-party elections 22 months after the signature of the accords.

By instigating ethnic violence on a substantial scale the MNRD, assisted by its faithful ally, the crypto-fascist, rabidly anti-Tutsi Coalition pour la Défense de la République (CDR), knew that they could effectively derail the peace process. The killing of some 300 Tutsi in the Gisenyi prefecture in February 1993 was designed to do just that. It is surely not a matter of coincidence that the killings occurred shortly after the signature of one of the key power-sharing agreements (technically known as "protocol of agreement with the RPF on the sharing of power within the context of a broadly based transitional government") on January 9, 1993.

The wanton killing of Tutsi civilians thus became the quickest and most "rational" way of eliminating all basis for compromise with the RPF: the reassertion of Hutu solidarities would soon transcend regional differences and make it virtually unthinkable for Hutu and Tutsi to agree on anything.

The pattern was set long before the Arusha talks got under way. In the weeks immediately following the October 1990 invasion an estimated 300 Tutsi were massacred in cold blood in Kibilira. Then in retaliation for the RPF raid on Ruhengeri, in January 1991, came the physical elimination of at least a thousand Bugogwe cattle herders and their families, a Tutsi subgroup. In 1992 hundreds of Tutsi were killed in the Bugesera region when government-sponsored rumors warned the Hutu that they were about to be massacred by the RPF and their civilian collaborators.

The persistent indifference of the international community in the face of organized murder, coupled with France's rising levels of military assistance to the murderers, was a powerful inducement for the regime to further strengthen its organizational capacities. By 1992 the institutional apparatus of genocide was already in place. It involved four distinctive levels of activity or sets of actors: (a) the akazu ("little house" in Kinyarwanda), that is the core group, consisting of Habyarimana's immediate entourage, i.e., his wife (Agathe), his three brothers-in-law (Protée Zigiranyirazo, Seraphin Rwabukumba, and Elie Sagatwa), and a sprinkling of trusted advisers (most notably Joseph Nzirorera, Laurent Serubuga, and Ildephonse Gashumba); (b) the rural organizers, numbering anywhere from two to three hundred, drawn from the communal and prefectoral cadres (préfets, sous-préfets, conseilleurs communaux, etc.); (c) the militias (interhamwe), estimated at 30,000, forming the ground-level operatives in charge of doing the actual killing; (d) the presidential guard,

recruited exclusively among northerners, and trained with a view to providing auxiliary slaughterhouse support to civilian death squads. Thus came into being an organizational structure ideally suited to the task at hand.

## Ndadaye's Assassination

With the assassination of President Melchior Ndadaye of Burundi on October 21, 1993, genocide came to be seen increasingly by MNRD politicians as the only rational option, and compromise, along the lines of Arusha, as synonymous with political suicide. As the first Hutu president in the history of Burundi, Ndadaye's election brought to a close 28 years of Tutsi hegemony. His death at the hands of an all-Tutsi army carried an immediate and powerful demonstration effect to the Hutu of Rwanda. As ethnic violence swept across the country, causing some 200,000 panic-stricken Hutu to seek refuge in Rwanda, the message conveyed by Ndadaye's assassination came through clear and loud: "Never trust the Tutsi!"

With Ndadaye's death vanished what few glimmers of hope remained that Arusha might provide a viable formula for a political compromise with the RPF. Though formally committed to implement the accords, Habyarimana was fast losing his grip on the situation. Meanwhile, and as if to further bolster the posture of MNRD hard-liners, tens of thousands of Hutu refugees from Burundi, and highly politicized by the events there, were now available for political mobilization precisely where they were most needed, in the south-central regions, seen by the akazu as the least "reliable."

Compounding the divisive effects of Ndadaye's assassination, the selection of candidates to the transitional organs of government unleashed a frenzy of competition for the spoils of office both within and among parties. Some opposition parties, such as the Parti Liberal (PL), or the Parti Social Démocrate (PSD), found themselves overnight in the throes of bitter ethnic struggles; others seemed almost to disintegrate in factional squabbles between extremists and moderates. Political assassinations sometimes disposed of both, in tit-for-tat fashion.

Nonetheless, orchestrating a transition that would meet the expectations of "Hutu power" (the phrase that came to designate the extremist fringe among opposition parties) and effectively reduce the influence of RPF elements in government seemed utterly illusory as long as Arusha provided the basic constitutional frame of reference for institutionalizing a compromise.

## The Shooting Down of the Presidential Plane: A Rational Plot?

This is where the shooting down of Habyarimana's plane, on April 6, seems entirely consistent with the overall strategy of MNRD extremists. Despite the absence of solid evidence in support of an akazu-sponsored plot, it is easy to see the logic that might have prompted such a move. Not only did Habyarimana's death remove once and for all the specter of Arusha (even at the cost of losing in the process a key member of the "akazu," Elie Sagatwa), but by making it unmistakably clear that "it was the RPF that did it" the same extremists could now point to their "dastardly crime" as a moral justification for genocide. Who actually fired the missile that brought down Habyarimana's plane may never be known, any more than who ordered the missile to be fired. But if the circumstantial evidence is any index, there is every reason to view the shooting of the plane as an eminently rational act from the standpoint of the immediate goals of Hutu extremists.

In Kigali, the killing of opposition figures, Hutu and Tutsi, began moments after the crash, on the basis of pre-established lists. Two categories of potential allies of RPF were targeted: (a) moderate (as distinct from "Hutu power") Hutu politicians from the south/central regions, most of them affiliated to the Mouvement Démocratique Républicain (MDR), and (b) opposition leaders (Hutu and Tutsi) identified with the Parti Liberal (PL) or Parti Social Démocrate (PSD). So far from being selected on the basis of ethnic criteria, the victims were generally seen as animated by a sense of compromise and conciliation towards the RPF, in short as potential traitors. Those two categories were disposed of in a matter of hours. Doing away with Tutsi civilians proved a more difficult undertaking, yet the scale and swiftness of the carnage leaves no doubt the efficiency of the machete-wielding death squads. If we are to believe the testimony of eye witnesses, there was a macabre rationality to the methods employed by the killers: as one survivor told this writer, "where large numbers of people had to be killed, as happened where dozens or hundreds had sought refuge in churches, the death squads went about it methodically: phase one involved breaking the ankles so as to prevent the victims from running away; once the victims were immobilized, they worked on the wrists and arms, to prevent them from fighting back; the killers could then turn to the last phase, using clubs, sticks and machetes to break the skulls and necks." Horribly "rational" as well was the systematic slaughter of infants: after all, many of the RPF soldiers were toddlers when their parents fled their homeland during the 1959 revolution; why make the same mistake twice?

That a carnage of this magnitude could have been going on day after day, week after week, without interference from the international community speaks volumes for its lack of resolve in dealing with massive human rights violations. That they could literally get away with murder must have been a major consideration in the minds of the organizers of the killings. Given the extent of French backing, military, logistical, political, and economic, they correctly assumed that they could act with impunity. They knew that the Fashoda syndrome would work to their advantage; they knew that the French Embassy would look the other way each time it was confronted with irrefutable evidence of massive human rights violations; and they knew, when the circumstances required, how to capitalize upon the close ties of friendship between President Mitterrand's son, Jean-Christophe, and his "buddy," Juvénal Habyarimana.

It is difficult to believe that the French were not aware of the potential for genocide created by the systematic manipulation of ethnic identities, by the mob killings of Tutsi over a period of years, and by the incitements to violence broadcast by Radio Mille Collines. If so, it defies Cartesian logic to comprehend how the self-styled "patrie des droits de l'homme" could shove under the rug such massive human rights violations in the name of the threats posed to its higher geopolitical interests by the Trojan horse of Anglo-Saxon imperialism. It only took a logic of calculated risks for the authors of the genocide to grasp the implications of this paradox. The lesson to be drawn is nowhere more clearly articulated than by Helen Fein: "Abusive powers will continue to abuse as long as it works: the movement to change the taken-for-granted assumption that sovereignty implies indifference to our neighbors' crimes (like respect for family implied by overlooking child abuse next door) is still to emerge from gestation in images of mass flight, chaos, blood and death."

---

**René Lemarchand** is a professor emeritus at the University of Florida and has written about and worked extensively in South Africa.

# EXPLORING THE ISSUE

## Was Ethnic Hatred Primarily Responsible for the Rwandan Genocide of 1994?

### Critical Thinking and Reflection

1. Analyze the claim made by Alison Des Forges, that extremists used the administrative apparatus, military, and party organization of the state to carry out what she calls a "cottage industry" genocide. What support and/or acquiescence would be required for this kind of co-opting to succeed? Critically discuss.
2. Analyze the claim of René Lemarchand that "Genocide is preventable because it is usually a rational act." Do you agree with this claim? Critically discuss.
3. As in the Holocaust, when later analysis revealed the extent of the horror, the aftermath of the Rwandan genocide uncovered massacre on a very large scale. Speculate as to why the full extent of a genocide remains hidden for so long. Is complicity required? Critically analyze and discuss.
4. In both the Holocaust and Rwanda, people later wondered why nobody tried to stop it. Why, in your view, did the international community not intervene in Rwanda? Could neighboring countries have done something to stop or lessen the killing? Critically discuss this lack of intervention.
5. Defend or attack the proposition that ethnic hatreds are a necessary but not a sufficient cause for genocide. What else might be required, in addition to ethnic hatreds? Critically analyze and discuss.
6. Does the fact that this massacre was so carefully planned make it more or less understandable? The Holocaust was also very well planned. Critically analyze and discuss.

## Is There Common Ground?

There appears to be a lot of common ground in these two selections. Both authors recount the ethnic rivalries, the Colonia history, and the precipitating event of the president's assassination. Alison Des Farges concludes the YES selection with Hutus and Tutsis agreeing to rewrite the history of Rwanda. René Lemarchand concludes with an indictment of "indifference to our own neighbors' 'crimes'."

*Question:* Would a rewriting of Rwanda's history require a full and deep understanding of what was done and not done to make this massacre possible? Perhaps we need both selections to give us a full picture of causes and possible cures.

## Create Central

www.mhhe.com/createcentral

## Additional Resources

The literature regarding the Rwandan genocide is substantial and cannot be repeated here. A few important sources are: Bill Berkeley, *The Graves Are Not Yet Full: Race, Tribe,* *and Power in the Heart of Africa* (Basic Books, 2001); Alison Des Forges, *Leave None to Tell the Story: Genocide in Rwanda* (Human Rights Watch, 1999); Alain Destexhe, *Rwanda and Genocide in the Twentieth Century* (New York University Press, 1999); Philip Gourevitch, *We Wish to Inform You That Tomorrow We Will Be Killed with Our Families: Stories from Rwanda* (Farrar, Straus, and Giroux, 1998); Fergal Keane, *Season of Blood: A Rwanda Journey* (Viking, 1995); Mahmood Mamdami, *When Victims Became Killers: Colonial Nativism, and the Genocide* in Rwanda (Princeton University Press, 2001); Linda Melvern, *A People Betrayed: The Role of the West in Rwanda's Genocide* (Zed Books, 2000); and Gerard Prunier, *The Rwanda Crisis: History of a Genocide* (Columbia University Press, 1995).

Finally, an important source on the subject of genocide in the modern era is: Samantha Power, *A Problem from Hell: America in the Age of Genocide* (Basic Books, 2002), with chapters devoted to each of the era's major acts of genocide. And, *Duhozanye* is a film about a Rwandan village of widows. After the massacres, the surviving women of both tribes came together in their sorrow to form a community based on loss and resilience. Most survived rape and are HIV positive. The village began with a few dozen and now includes widows and orphans in the thousands, supported by cottage industries financed by micro-credit.

# *Internet Reference . . .*

### Rwanda Genocide: Ten Years Later (BBC News)

Site includes the story of the "One Hundred Days" in audio and images, the return of survivors, how the West failed to intervene, ceremonies to honor the victims, movies on the subject, and the challenge of deep divisions that remain.

**http://news.bbc.co.uk/1/hi/in_depth/africa/2004/ rwanda/default.stm**

Selected, Edited, and with Issue Framing Material by:
Helen Buss Mitchell, *Howard Community College*
and
Joseph R. Mitchell, *Howard Community College*

# ISSUE

# Does Islamic Revivalism Challenge a Stable World Order?

YES: John L. Esposito, from *The Islamic Threat: Myth or Reality*, 2nd ed. (Oxford University Press 1995)

NO: Sharif Shuja, from "Islam and the West: From Discord to Understanding," *Contemporary Review* (May 2001)

---

## Learning Outcomes

**After reading this issue you should be able to:**

- Define and describe Islamic revivalism.
- Understand the response of Muslims to Western secularism.
- Explain the dilemma of modernizing for Muslims—how to become "modern" without giving up their core values and embracing those of the West.

---

### ISSUE SUMMARY

**YES:** Professor of Middle East studies John L. Esposito argues that the Iranian Revolution against Western-inspired modernization and Egypt's "holy war" against Israel are examples of the Islamic quest for a more authentic society and culture, which challenges a stable world order.

**NO:** Professor of international relations Sharif Shuja argues that the rise of Islamic movements represents resistance to Western domination rather than a threat to the West as such and traces Western fears of a monolithic Islamic entity to the errors of an Orientalist mindset.

For many Westerners the adjective *Islamic* seems to be linked inexorably with either *fundamentalist* or *terrorist*. Particularly since the Islamic Revolution of 1978–1979 in Iran, images of Western hostages and calls for a *jihad* or holy war have created a climate of fear and mistrust between the West and Islam. Are the two on a collision course, rooted in history, and driven by an absolute incompatibility of beliefs and lifestyles? Or, can Islam play a role in a stable world order that affirms Islam's own tradition while accommodating secularism and pluralism. The YES and NO selections acknowledge the flash points and conclude by placing the emphasis at different places.

Because Islam sees itself as the fulfillment of both Judaism and Christianity—as the final word of God for human beings—it has from the beginning sought to spread its truth throughout the world. In the tradition of jihad, those who died in the attempt to bring Islam to nonbelievers had ensured a place in paradise. Early successes came during Europe's so-called Dark Ages. Muslim learning and culture were more advanced, and it was only natural for conquering armies to assume their religion enjoyed a comparable superiority. Unlike Christianity, Islam gained secular power within the founder Muhammad's lifetime (c. 570–632) and the rulers that followed him, known as caliphs, combined secular and religious powers. There could be no conflict between church and state because the church and the state were one.

For many Muslims in the modern world, the political and military domination of the West has brought a secularism that is repugnant to all they hold sacred. It seems to them that Westerners—with their lack of respect for traditional authority, their emancipated and exploited women, and their shallow and materialistic values—have won. Becoming modern is generally equated with embracing the consumer culture and values of the West. When the Shah of Iran Muhammad Reza Pahlavi imposed a Western revolution on his country in the 1970s, he disregarded Muslim leaders and repressed all resistance. The result was an Islamic backlash that deposed the Shah and installed in his place the Ayatollah Ruholla Khomeini, a rigid religious authority who demanded obedience to the strictest interpretation of the teachings of the Prophet Muhammad. The question seems to be whether or not Islamic countries can modernize without giving up their core values and embracing those of the West.

Both the YES and NO selections point out that people in the West must begin by understanding the history and idea systems of modern Islam, whose believers constitute one fifth of the world's population. In the YES selection, John L. Esposito notes that the clout provided by oil has brought the Islamic Middle East into the world economy and given it the power to be a significant player in either supporting or destabilizing a peaceful world order. Traditional Islam sees itself as governing all of life and its system of law, or *shari'a*, as binding on all who share its culture—the entire community of believers, and others who live under its authority. From this perspective, the Western concept of religion as a system of belief and worship that forms one compartment of an individual's or a society's existence and remains separate from most of the rest of secular life is incomprehensible. Believing that Islam has superseded both Judaism and Christianity calls Muslims to impose the law of God on the entire world. In the search for an authentic Islamic culture, Esposito concludes, Muslims present a strong challenge to the political and cultural values of the West.

In the NO selection Professor Sharif Shuja acknowledges the points of potential conflict between Islam and the West but insists that the rise of Islamic movements signals resistance to Western domination and control over Muslim territories and resources and does not necessarily pose a threat to the West as such. He describes the Westernization that colonized more than two-thirds of the Muslim world during the first half of the twentieth century as one major globalizing force. There is now underway another globalizing force, which he calls the demographic Islamization of the Western world, represented by dramatic increases in the Muslim populations of Europe and the United States. Shuja counters Samuel P. Huntington's contention that the Islamic threat, of which the Gulf War of 1990 is only the most recent example, has been going on for 1300 years. What is wrong with Huntington's thesis, according to Shuja, is the depiction of Islamic countries as "part of a wider pan-Islamic movement, united in their hostility to the West and the United States." This kind of phobia can arise out of an "Orientalist" mindset that glosses over the diversity within Islam in favor of a conveniently simple explanation. We must get beyond

such distortions, Shuja suggests, if we are to understand Islamic revivalism as a successor to failed nationalist programs that in their own way tried to chart a third alternative between the undesirable poles of capitalism and communism. The best way to reduce extremism, Shuja contends, is through gradual democratization. He points to hopeful signs, such as the voices of moderate Muslims who joined a worldwide outcry against the Islamist regime in Afghanistan's decision to blow up centuries-old statues of the Buddha during the early months of 2001.

Understanding how Islam sees itself and its place in the world might make us fearful or hopeful. If Islam cannot accommodate to Western, secular values, as Esposito points out, does it challenge a stable world order? Shuja is more hopeful, believing that through a process of political maturation Islamic states may become more fully integrated into an increasingly globalized world civilization. One key is a fuller understanding among Western nations of the goals of Islamic revivalism. Furthermore, the West must understand its own image in the Muslim world and not expect a commitment to secularism that would appear to Muslims as blasphemy. Whether deeper dialogue will bring Islam and the West closer together or push them further apart is not yet clear.

A fascinating survey of how people have perceived God from the time of Abraham to the present can be found in Karen Armstrong's *A History of God* (Ballantine Books, 1993). Since Judaism exists in its own right and is the foundation for both Christianity and Islam, this "4,000-year quest" provides insight into key similarities and points of difference. Any good text on world religions will provide an introduction to Islam; particularly accessible is Huston Smith's *Illustrated World's Religions: A Guide to Our Wisdom Traditions* (HarperSanFrancisco, 1994), which is also available on video. Students who have not read the Qur'an might like to explore the scriptures that are available in English translation in paperback.

The dilemma of becoming modern without becoming Western is addressed by Bernard Lewis in "The West and the Middle East," *Foreign Affairs* (January/February 1997). Other books by Lewis include *Islam and the West* (Oxford University Press, 1993) and *The Middle East: A Brief History of the Last 2,000 Years* (Scribner, 1995).

# YES ↵

**John L. Esposito**

## The Islamic Threat: Myth or Reality?

Are Islam and the West on an inevitable collision course? Are Islamic fundamentalists medieval fanatics? Are Islam and democracy incompatible? Is Islamic fundamentalism a threat to stability in the Muslim world and to American interests in the region? These are critical questions for our times that come from a history of mutual distrust and condemnation.

From the Ayatollah Khomeini to Saddam Hussein, for more than a decade the vision of Islamic fundamentalism or militant Islam as a threat to the West has gripped the imaginations of Western governments and the media. Khomeini's denunciation of America as the "Great Satan," chants of "Death to America," the condemnation of Salman Rushdie and his *Satanic Verses*, and Saddam Hussein's call for a jihad against foreign infidels have reinforced images of Islam as a militant, expansionist religion, rabidly anti-American and intent upon war with the West.

Despite many common theological roots and beliefs, throughout history Muslim–Christian relations have often been overshadowed by conflict as the armies and missionaries of Islam and Christendom have struggled for power and for souls. This confrontation has involved such events as the defeat of the early Byzantine (eastern Roman) empire by Islam in the seventh century; the fierce battles and polemics of the Crusades during the eleventh and twelfth centuries; the expulsion of the Moors from Spain and the Inquisition; the Ottoman threat to Europe; European (Christian) colonial expansion and domination in the eighteenth and nineteenth centuries; the political and cultural challenge of the superpowers (America and the Soviet Union) in the latter half of the twentieth century; the creation of the state of Israel; the competition of Christian and Muslim missionaries for converts in Africa today; and the contemporary reassertion of Islam in politics.

"Islamic fundamentalism" has often been regarded as a major threat to the regional stability of the Middle East and to Western interests in the broader Muslim world. The Iranian Revolution, attacks on Western embassies, hijackings and hostage taking, and violent acts by groups with names like the Army of God (Jund Allah), Holy War (al-Jihad), the Party of God (Hizbullah), and Salvation from Hell have all signaled a militant Islam on a collision course with the West. Uprisings in the Muslim republics of the Soviet Union, in Kosovo in Yugoslavia, in Indian Kashmir, in Sinkiang in China, and on the West Bank and in Gaza, and more recently, Saddam Hussein's attempted annexation of Kuwait, have reinforced images of an expansive and potentially explosive Islam in global politics.

With the triumph of the democratization movement in Eastern Europe and the breakup of the Soviet empire, Islam constitutes the most pervasive and powerful transnational force in the world, with one billion adherents spread out across the globe. Muslims are a majority in some forty-five countries ranging from Africa to Southeast Asia, and they exist in growing and significant numbers in the United States, the Soviet Union, and Europe. For a Western world long accustomed to a global vision and foreign policy predicated upon superpower rivalry for global influence if not dominance—a U.S.–Soviet conflict often portrayed as a struggle between good and evil, capitalism and communism—it is all too tempting to identify another global ideological menace to fill the "threat vacuum" created by the demise of communism.

However diverse in reality, the existence of Islam as a worldwide religion and ideological force embracing one fifth of the world's population, and its continued vitality and power in a Muslim world stretching from Africa to Southeast Asia, will continue to raise the specter of an Islamic threat. . . .

As Western leaders attempt to forge the New World Order, transnational Islam may increasingly come to be regarded as the new global monolithic enemy of the West: "To some Americans, searching for a new enemy against whom to test our mettle and power, after the death of communism, Islam is the preferred antagonist. But, to declare Islam an enemy of the United States is to declare a second Cold War that is unlikely to end in the same resounding victory as the first." Fear of the Green Menace (green being the color of Islam) may well replace that of the Red Menace of world communism.

Islam and Islamic movements constitute a religious and ideological alternative or challenge and in some instances a potential danger to Christianity and the West. However, distinguishing between a religious or ideological alternative or challenge and a direct political threat requires walking the fine line between myth and reality, between the unity of Islam and the diversity of its multiple and complex manifestations in the world today, between the violent actions of the few and the legitimate aspirations and policies of the many. Unfortunately,

American policymakers, like the media, have too often proved surprisingly myopic, viewing the Muslim world and Islamic movements as a monolith and seeing them solely in terms of extremism and terrorism. While this is understandable in light of events in Iran and Lebanon and the Gulf crisis of 1990–91, it fails to do justice to the complex realities of the Muslim world and can undermine relations between the West and Islam. . . .

## The Islamic Resurgence

Islam reemerged as a potent global force in Muslim politics during the 1970s and 1980s. The scope of the Islamic resurgence has been worldwide, embracing much of the Muslim world from the Sudan to Indonesia. Heads of Muslim governments as well as opposition groups increasingly appealed to religion for legitimacy and to mobilize popular support. Islamic activists have held cabinet-level positions in Jordan, the Sudan, Iran, Malaysia, and Pakistan. Islamic organizations constitute the leading opposition parties and organizations in Egypt, Tunisia, Algeria, Morocco, the West Bank and Gaza, and Indonesia. Where permitted, they have participated in elections and served in parliament and in city government. Islam has been a significant ingredient in nationalist struggles and resistance movements in Afghanistan, the Muslim republics of the former Soviet Central Asia, and Kashmir, and in the communal politics of Lebanon, India, Thailand, China, and the Philippines.

Islamically oriented governments have been counted among America's staunchest allies (Saudi Arabia and Pakistan) and most vitriolic enemies (Libya and Iran). Islamic activist organizations have run the spectrum from those who work within the system—such as the Muslim Brotherhoods in Egypt, Jordan, and the Sudan—to radical revolutionaries like Egypt's Society of Muslims (known more popularly as Takfir wal-Hijra, Excommunication and Flight) and al-Jihad (Holy War), or Lebanon's Hizbullah (Party of God) and Islamic Jihad, which have resorted to violence in their attempts to overthrow prevailing political systems.

Yet to speak of a contemporary Islamic revival can be deceptive, if this implies that Islam had somehow disappeared or been absent from the Muslim world. It is more correct to view Islamic revivalism as having led to a higher profile of Islam in Muslim politics and society. Thus what had previously seemed to be an increasingly marginalized force in Muslim public life reemerged in the seventies—often dramatically—as a vibrant sociopolitical reality. Islam's resurgence in Muslim politics reflected a growing religious revivalism in both personal and public life that would sweep across much of the Muslim world and have a substantial impact on the West in world politics.

The indices of an Islamic reawakening in personal life are many: increased attention to religious observances (mosque attendance, prayer, fasting), proliferation of religious programming and publications, more emphasis upon Islamic dress and values, the revitalization of Sufism (mysticism). This broader-based renewal has also been accompanied by Islam's reassertion in public life: an increase in Islamically oriented governments, organizations, laws, banks, social welfare services, and educational institutions. Both governments and opposition movements have turned to Islam to enhance their authority and muster popular support. Governmental use of Islam has been illustrated by a great spectrum of leaders in the Middle East and Asia: Libya's Muammar al-Gaddafi, Sudan's Gaafar Muhammad Nimeiri, Egypt's Anwar Sadat, Iran's Ayatollah Khomeini, Pakistan's Zia ul-Haq, Bangladesh's Muhammad Ershad, Malaysia's Muhammad Mahathir. Most rulers and governments, including more secular states such as Turkey and Tunisia, becoming aware of the potential strength of Islam, have shown increased sensitivity to and anxiety about Islamic issues. The Iranian Revolution of 1978–79 focused attention on "Islamic fundamentalism" and with it the spread and vitality of political Islam in other parts of the Muslim world. However, the contemporary revival has its origins and roots in the late sixties and early seventies, when events in such disparate areas as Egypt and Libya as well as Pakistan and Malaysia contributed to experiences of crisis and failure, as well as power and success, which served as catalysts for a more visible reassertion of Islam in both public and private life.

## The Experience of Failure and the Quest for Identity

Several conflicts (e.g., the 1967 Arab–Israeli war, Chinese–Malay riots in Malaysia in 1969, the Pakistan–Bangladesh civil war of 1971, and the Lebanese civil war of the mid-seventies) illustrate the breadth and diversity of these turning points or catalysts for change. For many in the Arab and broader Muslim world, 1967 proved to be a year of catastrophe as well as a historic turning point. Israel's quick and decisive defeat of Arab forces in what was remembered as the Six-Day War, the Israeli capture and occupation of the Golan Heights, Sinai, Gaza, the West Bank, and East Jerusalem, constituted a devastating blow to Arab/Muslim pride, identity, and self-esteem. Most important, the loss of Jerusalem, the third holiest city of Islam, assured that Palestine and the liberation of Jerusalem would not be regarded as a regional (Arab) issue but rather as an Islamic cause throughout the Muslim world. The defense of Israel is dear to many Jews throughout the world. Likewise, for Muslims who retain a sense of membership in a transnational community of believers (the *ummah*), Palestine and the liberation of Jerusalem are strongly seen as issues of Islamic solidarity. As anyone who works in the Muslim world can attest, Israeli control of the West Bank, Gaza, and Jerusalem as well as U.S.–Israeli relations are topics of concern and bitter debate among Muslims from Nigeria and the Sudan to Pakistan and Malaysia, as well as among the Muslims of Europe and the United States.

The aftermath of the 1967 war, remembered in Arab literature as the "disaster," witnessed a sense of disillusionment and soul-searching that gripped both Western-oriented secular elites as well as the more Islamically committed, striking at their sense of pride, identity, and history. Where had they gone wrong? Both the secular and the Islamically oriented sectors of society now questioned the effectiveness of nationalist ideologies, Western models of development, and Western allies who had persisted in supporting Israel. Despite several decades of independence and modernization, Arab forces (consisting of the combined military might of Egypt, Jordan, and Syria) had proved impotent. A common critique of the military, political, and sociocultural failures of Western-oriented development and a quest for a more authentic society and culture emerged—an Arab identity less dependent upon the West and rooted more indigenously in an Arab/Islamic heritage and values. Examples from Malaysia, Pakistan, and Lebanon reflect the turmoil and soul-searching that occurred in many parts of the Muslim world. . . .

## From Failure to Success

During the seventies Islamic politics seemed to explode on the scene, as events in the Middle East (the Egyptian–Israeli war and the Arab oil embargo of 1973, as well as the Iranian Revolution of 1978–79) shocked many into recognition of a powerful new force that threatened Western interests. Heads of state and opposition movements appealed to Islam to enhance their legitimacy and popular support; Islamic organizations and institutions proliferated. In 1973 Egypt's Anwar Sadat initiated a "holy war" against Israel. In contrast to the 1967 Arab–Israeli war which was fought by Gamal Abdel Nasser in the name of Arab nationalism/socialism, this war was fought under the banner of Islam. Sadat generously employed Islamic symbols and history to rally his forces. Despite their loss of the war, the relative success of Egyptian forces led many Muslims to regard it as a moral victory, since most had believed that a U.S.-backed Israel could not be beaten.

Military vindication in the Middle East was accompanied by economic muscle, the power of the Arab oil boycott. For the first time since the dawn of colonialism, the West had to contend with and acknowledge, however begrudgingly, its dependence on the Middle East. For many in the Muslim world the new wealth, success, and power of the oil-rich countries seemed to indicate a return of the power of Islam to a community whose centuries-long political and cultural ascendence had been shattered by European colonialism and, despite independence, by second-class status in a superpower-dominated world. A number of factors enhanced the Islamic character of oil power. Most of the oil wealth was located in the Arab heartland, where Muhammad had received the revelation of the Quran and established the first Islamic community-state. The largest deposits were found in Saudi

Arabia, a self-styled Islamic state which had asserted its role as keeper of the holy cities of Mecca and Medina, protector of the annual pilgrimage (*hajj*), and leader and benefactor of the Islamic world. The House of Saud used its oil wealth to establish numerous international Islamic organizations, promote the preaching and spread of Islam, support Islamic causes, and subsidize Islamic activities undertaken by Muslim governments.

No event demonstrated more dramatically the power of a resurgent Islam than the Iranian Revolution of 1978–79. For many in the West and the Muslim world, the unthinkable became a reality. The powerful, modernizing, and Western-oriented regime of the Shah came crashing down. This was an oil-rich Iran whose wealth had been used to build the best-equipped military in the Middle East (next to Israel's) and to support an ambitious modernization program, the Shah's White Revolution. Assisted by Western-trained elites and advisers, the Shah had governed a state which the United States regarded as its most stable ally in the Muslim world. The fact that a revolution against him and against the West was effectively mounted in the name of Islam, organizing disparate groups and relying upon the mullah–mosque network for support, generated euphoria among many in the Muslim world and convinced Islamic activists that these were lessons for success to be emulated. Strength and victory would belong to those who pursued change in the name of Islam, whatever the odds and however formidable the regime.

For many in the broader Muslim world, the successes of the seventies resonated with an idealized perception of early Islam, the Islamic paradigm to be found in the time of the Prophet Muhammad, the Golden Age of Islam. Muhammad's successful union of disparate tribal forces under the banner of Islam, his creation of an Islamic state and society in which social justice prevailed, and the extraordinary early expansion of Islam were primal events to be remembered and, as the example of the Iranian Revolution seemingly verified, to be successfully emulated by those who adhered to Islam. Herein lies the initial attraction of the Iranian Revolution for many Muslims, Sunni, and Shii alike. Iran provided the first example of a modern Islamic revolution, a revolt against impiety, oppression, and injustice. The call of the Ayatollah Khomeini for an Islamic revolution struck a chord among many who identified with his message of anti-imperialism, his condemnation of failed, unjust, and oppressive regimes, and his vision of a morally just society.

By contrast, the West stood incredulous before this challenge to the Shah's "enlightened" development of his seemingly backward nation, and the resurrection of an anachronistic, irrational medieval force that threatened to hurtle modern Iran back to the Middle Ages. Nothing symbolized this belief more than the black-robed, bearded mullahs and the dour countenance of their leader, the Ayatollah Khomeini, who dominated the media, reinforcing in Western minds the irrational nature of the entire movement.

## The Ideological Worldview of Islamic Revivalism

At the heart of the revivalist worldview is the belief that the Muslim world is in a state of decline. Its cause is departure from the straight path of Islam; its cure, a return to Islam in personal and public life which will ensure the restoration of Islamic identity, values, and power. For Islamic political activists Islam is a total or comprehensive way of life as stipulated in the Quran, God's revelation, mirrored in the example of Muhammad and the nature of the first Muslim community-state, and embodied in the comprehensive nature of the Sharia, God's revealed law. Thus the revitalization of Muslim governments and societies requires the reimplementation of Islamic law, the blueprint for an Islamically guided and socially just state and society.

While Westernization and secularization of society are condemned, modernization as such is not. Science and technology are accepted, but the pace, direction, and extent of change are to be subordinated to Islamic belief and values in order to guard against the penetration of Western values and excessive dependence on them.

Radical movements go beyond these principles and often operate according to two basic assumptions. [First,] they assume that Islam and the West are locked in an ongoing battle, dating back to the early days of Islam, which is heavily influenced by the legacy of the Crusades and European colonialism, and which today is the product of a Judaeo-Christian conspiracy. This conspiracy is the result of superpower neocolonialism and the power of Zionism. The West (Britain, France, and especially the United States) is blamed for its support of un-Islamic or unjust regimes (Egypt, Iran, Lebanon) and also for its biased support for Israel in the face of Palestinian displacement. Violence against such governments and their representatives as well as Western multinationals is legitimate self-defense.

Second, these radical movements assume that Islam is not simply an ideological alternative for Muslim societies but a theological and political imperative. Since Islam is God's command, implementation must be immediate, not gradual, and the obligation to do so is incumbent on all true Muslims. Therefore individuals and governments who hesitate, remain apolitical, or resist are no longer to be regarded as Muslim. They are atheists or unbelievers, enemies of God against whom all true Muslims must wage jihad (holy war). . . .

As some dream of the creation of a New World Order, and many millions in North Africa, the Middle East, Central Asia, and southern and Southeast Asia aspire to greater political liberalization and democratization, the continued vitality of Islam and Islamic movements need not be a threat but a challenge. For many Muslims, Islamic revivalism is a social rather than a political movement whose goal is a more Islamically minded and oriented society, but not necessarily the creation of an Islamic state. For others, the establishment of an Islamic order requires the creation of an Islamic state. In either case, Islam and most Islamic movements are not necessarily anti-Western, anti-American, or anti-democratic. While they are a challenge to the outdated assumptions of the established order and to autocratic regimes, they do not necessarily threaten American interests. Our challenge is to better understand the history and realities of the Muslim world. Recognizing the diversity and many faces of Islam counters our image of a unified Islamic threat. It lessens the risk of creating self-fulfilling prophecies about the battle of the West against a radical Islam. Guided by our stated ideals and goals of freedom and self-determination, the West has an ideal vantage point for appreciating the aspirations of many in the Muslim world as they seek to define new paths for their future.

**JOHN L. ESPOSITO** is a professor of religion and international affairs at Georgetown University in Washington, D.C., and director of the Center for Muslim Understanding at Georgetown's Edmund A. Walsh School of Foreign Service. His publications include *Islam and Democracy* (Oxford University Press, 1996).

Sharif Shuja

# Islam and the West: From Discord to Understanding

The spread of Islam has had an impact on the globalisation of culture. Islam has spread not only as a religion but has also helped to give birth to languages which are spoken by many more non-Muslims than Muslims. Kiswahili in Africa is today the most important indigenous language to have emerged out of Africa—but its origins lie in the interaction between Islam and African culture. Islam and the Arabic language have bequeathed the Arabic alphabet for languages like Farsi, Urdu, Old Hausa and others. The Arabs have given the world the so-called Arabic numerals through which the twentieth century has computerized the human experience. Today the Quran (Koran) is the most widely read book in its original language in human history. Muslims are expected to read the Quran in the original Arabic and not a translation that may change the intended meaning. The Bible is the most widely read book in translation.

As the twenty-first century begins, almost one out of every five human beings is a Muslim. In the course of the 21st century a quarter of the human race will probably be Muslim. The new demographic presence of Islam within the Western world is indicative that Islamisation is now a major globalising force.

## Perspectives on Islamisation/Westernisation

In the second half of the twentieth century both Muslim migration to the West and conversions to Islam within the West consolidated a new Islamic presence. In Europe, as a whole, there are now 20 million Muslims, eight million of whom are in Western Europe. These figures exclude the Muslims of the Republic of Turkey, who number some 50 million. There are new mosques from Munich to Marseilles.

Also as a manifestation of the demographic Islamisation of the Western world, there are now over a thousand mosques and Islamic centres in the United States alone. And the country has professional associations for Muslim engineers, Muslim social scientists, and Muslim educators. There are some six million American muslims—and the number is rising impressively. Indeed, the American society in general is now coping with this issue, which creates cultural tensions between Islam and the West, as some observers have noted.

Currently Islam is the fastest growing religion in Central Asia. After the collapse of the U.S.S.R., all five states of Central Asia—Kazakhastan, Kyrghystan, Uzbekistan, Turkemenistan, and Tajikistan—made an official place for Islam as the dominant religion. In France, Islam is becoming the second most important religion numerically after Catholicism. In Britain, Muslims have been demanding state subsidies for Muslim denominational schools. In Germany it has been belatedly realised that the importation of Turkish workers in the 1970s was also an invitation to the muezzin and the minaret to establish themselves in German cities. Australia has discovered that it is a neighbour to the largest Muslim country in the world in terms of population (Indonesia). There are new mosques, Islamic schools, and Quranic centres from Brisbane to Perth.

Westernisation, on the other hand, is also a major globalising force. In the first half of the twentieth century, the West had colonised more than two-thirds of the Muslim world, from Africa to Asia. The first half of the twentieth century also witnessed the collapse of the Ottoman Empire and the complete de-Islamisation of the European state-system. The aftermath included the abolition of the caliphate as the symbolic centre of Islamic authority. The ummah (Islamic community) became more fragmented than ever and became even more receptive to Western cultural penetration. Other forces which facilitated the cultural Westernisation of the Muslim world included the replacement of Islamic and Quranic schools with Western style schools; the increasing use of European languages in major Muslim countries; and the impact of the Western media upon the distribution of news, information and entertainment. In other words, the West has in turn spread not only its technology and market ideology but also its languages (especially English, French and Spanish), its educational systems, consumer culture, including the dress code for men world-wide, and its mass media. The net result has indeed been a form of globalisation of aspects of Western culture. But at what cost?

In almost every liberal country in the West, crime is escalating, violence sometimes quadrupling, street mugging is on the rise, and the culture of the fortress city is developing. Suicide is now the second leading cause of death among American adolescents, the causes including the decline of family values and a more general national malaise. By comparison, suicide is a rare form of violence in the Muslim world.

There are scholars who feel that there is another way of looking at globalisation—and that is to focus on the three techno-systemic revolutions of all human history. There was first the agricultural revolution which started before Islamic and Western civilisations and transformed the relationship between man and plants. Millennia later there was the industrial revolution for which Islamic science helped to prepare the ground but which was essentially led by the West. This transformed the relationship between man and all material resources.

And now there is the emerging information revolution which leaves the West both triumphant and vulnerable—but is also leaving Islam marginalised. This is the revolution which is transforming the relationship between man and knowledge itself. But the question arises: can the Muslim world enter the positive sphere of globalisation without risking the negative aspects of Westernisation?

One of the remarkable things about the twentieth century is that it combined the cultural Westernisation of the Muslim world, on the one hand, and the more recent demographic Islamisation in the Western world, on the other. The foundations for the cultural Westernisation of the Muslim world were laid mainly in the first half of the twentieth century. The foundations for the demographic Islamisation in the Western world were laid in the second half of the twentieth century. The cultural Westernisation of Muslims contributed to the brain drain of Muslim professionals and experts from their homes in Muslim countries to jobs and educational institutions in North America and Europe. It is in this sense that the cultural Westernisation of the Muslim world in the first half of the twentieth century was part of the preparation for the demographic Islamisation in the West in the last fifty years.

## Islamic Revivalism in Context

There are scholars and policymakers in the West who are concerned with recent Islamic revivalism and face tensions about how Islam is to be treated in Western textbooks and the media, especially as Islam becomes a more integral part of Western society. As one observer (Ali Mazrui) put it:

> Judaism, Christianity and Islam are the three Abrahamic creeds of world history. In the twentieth century the Western world has often been described as a 'Judeo-Christian civilisation', thus linking the West to two of those Abrahamic faiths. But if in countries like the US Muslims will soon outnumber Jews, is Islam becoming the second most important Abrahamic religion after Christianity? Numerically Islam may overshadow Judaism in much of the West, regardless of future immigration policies.

The question has therefore arisen about how Islam is to be treated in Western classrooms. In the Muslim world, 'education has become substantially Westernised. Is it now the turn of education in the West to become partly Islamised?' Can the Western world enter the positive sphere of globalisation and draw on the traditional wisdom of cultures such as Islam which point towards a more integrated society with drastically decreased levels of crime and violence?

The rise of Islamic movements in different parts of the world, aimed at resisting Western domination and control over Muslim territories and resources, Muslim cultures and communities, has provoked a new wave of aggressive emotions against the religion and its practitioners. That it is resistance to Western domination and control—and not some threat to the West as such—which is taking place within the Muslim world is a reality that is concealed from the general public. What Islamic movements are opposed to is the annexation and occupation of their lands as in the case of Palestine and Lebanon, the usurpation of their rights over their own natural resources as in the case of the Gulf Sheikhdoms, and the denigration of their religion as often happens in the Western media, sometimes abetted by local elites and writers.

Salman Rushdie's *The Satanic Verses* is a case in point. The results were terrifying. A holy man called for the author's death. Thousands were engaged in riots, dozens were killed, and normally brave defenders of free expression hunkered down or bent with the wind. Undoubtedly, the book is offensive to many Muslims. But books are published, plays are written, and movies produced throughout the year that are deemed offensive by some group or other. And civilised people have learned not to murder the librarian or bomb the theatre to express their distaste. In this case, the intolerant reach of the Ayatollah has touched us all. Islamic groups and some individuals have expressed strong resentment and anger over Rushdie, the publisher of the book, and Western media, and demanded the immediate ban of this book. Broadly speaking, they see their struggle as part of the still unfulfilled quest for self-determination and for genuine sovereignty. Such Muslim resistance is portrayed as an 'Islamic threat' by some Western academics, including Samuel P. Huntington. Conflict between Western and Islamic civilisations, Huntington in his article 'The Clash of Civilizations' points out, 'has been going on for 1300 years. The Gulf War is only the most recent important example'. His argument has been the centre of controversy for the last decade.

At the turn of the Western millennium, it is crucial to consider whether Islam is a monolithic force; whether the clash between Islam and the West is inevitable; and whether the so-called Islamic civilisation poses a credible threat to the West.

Huntington depicts the Islamic countries as part of a wider pan-Islamic movement, united in their hostility to the West and the United States. So convinced is Huntington of the 'kin-country' syndrome that even the

Gulf War of 1990 becomes clear evidence of the brewing clash between Islam and the West.

The depiction of Islam and the Islamic countries as a monolithic entity may reflect the errors of the Orientalist mind-set, which refuses to understand the diversity within Islam for the convenience of a simple explanation. The assumed identity, through segregation and confinement of the Islamic civilisation, is a product of the Western imagination and sustains a deep phobia because the simple explanation, ironically, renders Islam both 'unknown' and mysterious.

It is orientalist scholarship that has invested Islam both with internal unity and an external political ambition. Orientalists have reconstructed Islam as a political religion despite the fact that there is little in original Islamic sources on how to form states or run governments. It also produced a particular reading of the 'orient' that was at odds with reality. Edward Said, in his article 'Orientalism Reconsidered' argued that 'designations like Islam and the Arabs . . . represented interests, claims, projects, ambitions, and rhetorics that were not only in violent disagreement, but were in situation of open warfare'. These diversions, however, were quickly glossed over and the myth that the Islamic countries possessed a fundamental unity of purpose that transcended national boundaries became the accepted consensus. The myth has, so far, refused to adapt itself to reason.

If the notion of a political and monolithic Islam should be taken with some scepticism, it is still true that a fundamentalist movement has emerged with the specific political task of reforming Muslim societies. This, however, is essentially a reaction to Westernisation, though not modernisation, and constitutes an attempt to check a perceived social drift and weakening of morals. In the West, modernisation is synonymous with Westernisation, but Muslim 'fundamentalists' clearly dissociate the two. This discordant understanding of modernisation has given Western analysts the impression that a rejection of Westernisation is the equivalent of a battle-cry against the West.

It should also be mentioned that the fundamentalist movement, most active in the Shi'ite countries of Iran, Iraq, and Lebanon, is diverse and a minority movement in most Islamic countries. Even assuming Islamic fundamentalism would spread significantly, it is not inevitable that it will inexorably lead to a clash with the West. After all, the West, and particularly the United States, has maintained a very special relationship with Saudi Arabia, one of the most fundamentalist Arab States.

Therefore, even if we grant that Islam forms a united movement in comparison to Western culture, it is not certain whether the Islamic civilisations will constitute a true adversary to the West. However, it would be helpful if commentators in the West recognised that the pursuit of modernisation need not be accompanied by Westernisation, and that a rejection of Westernisation is not an inevitable call to do battle with the West.

It is helpful here to recognise that Islamic revivalism is in many ways the successor to failed nationalist programmes and offers an Islamic alternative or solution, a third way distinct from capitalism and communism. Islamists argue that Islam is not just a collection of beliefs and ritual actions, but rather a comprehensive ideology embracing public as well as personal life. It is important to understand that Islamic activism in some countries is a cause of concern but not for alarm. It is not a challenge to any civilisation. Like radicals throughout history, Islamic radicals become moderate once accommodated and incorporated into the socio-political mainstream. If they do not, they perish or become sociologically irrelevant cults. Therefore, extremism can best be reduced through gradual democratisation, a process and a system of governance which the West is not actively encouraging in the Muslim world, and particularly not in the Middle East.

So far the reality is that Islamic revivalism is neither a product of the Iranian revolution nor a result of Libyan extremist policies. The depth of frustration and anger is a reaction against European colonial rule, support for unpopular regimes and the internal weaknesses of the Muslim governments. Although some scholars argue that the present awakening in the Muslim world is a response to the decline of power and the loss of divine favour, in fact, the current revolt is a product of the weak economies of the Muslim countries, illiteracy and high unemployment, especially among the younger generation. The lack of political institutions, absence of democracies and good governments in the Muslim world is also an immediate cause of extremism. In this context, the Muslim demands for change are no different from the demands in Eastern Europe.

In many Muslim countries the secular nationalists and Islamists are united in the common cause of popular democracy. They are demanding the right to gain legitimate power with ballots rather than bullets. These forces are also cooperating with each other to topple monarchies, military dictators and authoritarian governments. They blamed their governments for their countries' backwardness and failure to achieve economic self-sufficiency and development. In addition to these internal reasons, there are also some external factors which push the Islamists to struggle for the rights and protection of Muslims which are under the siege of oppressive rule. Muslims are worried about the people of Palestine and they cannot ignore the inhuman massacres of Muslims in Bosnia, Chechnya and Kashmir. Such experiences tend to make Muslims think that the West is against them.

This author believes that the conflicts in Bosnia, Chechnya, and Kashmir are political in nature. Others could say that the current conflict is either directly based on religious differences or at least involves an element of religion which contributes to the conflict. Military means, however, is not a solution. Devising appropriate mechanisms for their resolution continues to require the application of scientific method, rational inquiry, and balanced argument. Because you dislike war does not mean you should not study it. And because we don't like the behaviour of politicians does not mean we can ignore them.

## The Road Ahead

We should start from the premise that there is a need for all members of our global village to work towards harmony, cohesion, and a peaceful world. We need to emphasise that the expressed goal of all religions is to achieve peace in the world. Conflict often arises in the way in which representatives of religions interpret these principles and the way they should be applied.

In this context one needs to be clear about the teachings of Islam. Some analysts in the West take the view that the rapidly growing Muslim population in Europe and the United States, and Islamic revivalism generally, are potential threats to Western culture. The study of Islam demonstrates that this is not a violent doctrine. Islam, like other world religions, is a faith of peace and social justice. In fact, Islam is as universalist as Christianity, and offers generous consolation when it comes to finding purpose and guiding the soul in a confusing world. It does not turn to fundamentalist militancy, because it has always been a tolerant religion and dislikes extremism and killing. Islam does not encourage terrorism and threatening behaviour. These violent concepts do not originate in Islam as a faith. Those groups who practise terror under the flag of Islam are a small minority, rejected by the great majority of Muslims. In relation to aggressive attitudes, the key message to Western scholars is to oppose the extremist Muslims but not blame all Islam.

Today's tensions would lead to tomorrow's aspirations. What we need now is the culture of peace that would help broaden cross-cultural understanding between Islam and the West. With proper knowledge of the culture of the Arab and Muslim worlds, this understanding would help foster tolerance and resolve conflict. We need to 'sustain a diversity of cultures, not a diversity of imagined clashes and conflicts.'

Now that the Muslim world, through Pakistan, has an 'Islamic nuclear bomb', Muslim leadership matters more than ever. There is every likelihood of other Muslim nations joining Pakistan in the near future. The West should not ignore the danger. The world will become an even more dangerous and unstable place.

President [Bill] Clinton predicted that the events of 1998 (when Pakistan/India exploded nuclear devices) were a foretaste of things to come, that this is the way that the wars of the future will be fought. He may be right. But the response of the Muslim world will depend on whether the militancy model prevails, or that of moderation. Therefore, the need for the West to understand Islam and to actively encourage moderation and democratisation in the Muslim world has again arisen.

Indeed, extremism can best be reduced through gradual democratisation. Efforts should be directed to expedite the transition to democracy in the Muslim world. They should be made to feel that the West is on their side, particularly if the movements that precisely champion the values of democracy arise there.

The New Millennium brings fresh challenges and opportunities in relations between Islam and the West. Religious leaders now must re-establish the will to implement the true essence of their religion and to find those factors which provide common ground with other religions. It is then required for them to initiate dialogue with other religious leaders with the purpose of finding commonalities and joining forces in setting standards for dealing with the wider issues of cultural diversity. It is pointed out that governments must have a strong interest in supporting such moves. Moderate Muslims showed a good example of this recently when they joined in world-wide protests against the action of the Islamicist regime in Afganistan's decision to blow up statues of the Buddha.

This process has to be ongoing because as conditions in our world change, so does the need to find new responses. Now we are thinking in terms of 'cultural diversity'. The message is that people are not all the same, but that their differences are of mutual interest; their societies and cultures are often historically interdependent in surprising ways; and that seeking to understand one another is an intrinsically enlightening process whose fruits are material, political, and cultural.

---

**SHARIF SHUJA** is an adjunct assistant professor of international relations at Bond University, Australia and research associate in the Global Terrorism Unit at Monash University, Australia. He has contributed numerous articles to professional journals that specialize in Asian affairs.

# EXPLORING THE ISSUE

## Does Islamic Revivalism Challenge a Stable World Order?

## Critical Thinking and Reflection

1. Analyze Professor Esposito's assertion that oil revenues have given the Islamic Middle East the power to support or destabilize a peaceful world order? Do you agree? Critically discuss.
2. Analyze Professor Shuja's claim that an "Orientalist" mindset glosses over the diversity in Islam. Research the meaning of "Orientalist." Then, critically discuss this claim.
3. Do you agree with Professor Shuja's claim that the best way to reduce extremism is through gradual democratization. What does he mean by this? Analyze and critically discuss.
4. Do you agree with Professor Esposito's claim that, "for many Muslims, Islamic Revivalism is a social rather than a political movement"? What would be the significance for the West if this is the case? Critically analyze and discuss.
5. The recent revolutions of the so-called Arab Spring raise questions about how Islamist new constitutions in Tunisia and Egypt will be. Will research into this evolving narrative continue to inform the question of this issue? Critically analyze and discuss how this might contribute to our understanding.

## Is There Common Ground?

The meaning of Islamic revivalism seems to be undergoing change as revolutions in the Arab and non-Arab Middle East offer the possibility of political power to millions. As the world order evolves, the role of Islam and the role of the West are both evolving, too.

*Question:* Is there at least the possibility of a greater rapprochement between Islam and the West? What role will Islamic revivalism play in the shaping of the modern world?

## Create Central

www.mhhe.com/createcentral

## Additional Resources

Director of Columbia University's Middle East Institute Richard Bulliet has written an account of Islam's success among people who lived far from the political center, such as those in Iran. In *Islam: The View from the Edge* (Columbia University Press, 1994), Bulliet argues that the origins of today's Islamic resurgence are to be found in the eleventh century. Other books of note are *Orientalism* by Edward Said (Pantheon, 1978) and *Islam and the Cultural Accommodation to Social Change* by Bassam Tibi (Westview Press, 1991). In Francis Fukuyama's influential book *The End of History and the Last Man* (Free Press, 1992), the chapter titled "The Worldwide Liberal Revolution" considers Islam as an alternative to liberalism and communism. Finally, *The Turban and the Crown: The Islamic Revolution in Iran* by Said Amir Arjomand (Oxford University Press, 1988) explores the conflicts between the authority structures in Shi'a (minority branch of Islam) institutions and the mechanisms of the modern bureaucratic state.

## Internet Reference . . .

### Islam, the Modern World, and the West

Site is divided into four major sections: General Considerations; Islam in the U.S.; Islam, the Muslim World, and Contemporary Issues; and Islam Today in Various

Regions of the Muslim World. Many links are contained in each to a wide variety of information sources.

**www.arches.uga.edu/~godlas/islamwest.html**

Selected, Edited, and with Issue Framing Material by:
**Helen Buss Mitchell,** *Howard Community College*
and
**Joseph R. Mitchell,** *Howard Community College*

# ISSUE

# Have Afghan Women Been Liberated from Oppression?

**YES: Sima Wali,** from "Afghan Women: Recovering, Rebuilding," *Ethics and International Affairs* (October 2002)

**NO: Norwan, Mariam, and Nasima,** from "Afghanistan in Three voices: Three Afghan Women Talk About Violence and Shelter, the Taliban, and Getting to Vote," *The Wilson Quarterly* (vol. 37, no. 1, Winter 2013)

---

### Learning Outcomes

**After reading this issue you should be able to:**

- Describe the modern history of Afghanistan.
- Define the challenges faced by Afghan women.
- Identify markers of progress for women in Afghanistan.
- Evaluate the role of the NATO-led, U.S. military operation in maintaining stability.

---

### ISSUE SUMMARY

**YES:** International Afghan advocate for refugee women Sima Wali documents the pivotal roles Afghan women have played in rebuilding their communities, praises their courage in denouncing warlords, and calls for their full participation in the newly formed constitutional government.

**NO:** Norwan, Mariam, and Nasima, three Afghan women, argue that, despite some progress, many challenges remain for Afghan women as they seek liberation from oppression.

---

The modern history of Afghanistan began in 1979, with the Soviet invasion and subsequent occupation. The powerful jihad that ultimately expelled the Soviets also fortified indigenous tribal codes that treat women as property and encouraged the fundamentalism that brought the Taliban to power in 1996. During the 1990s, Western journalists began reporting on the draconian measures decreed by the Taliban that barred women from education, health care, work, and freedom of movement. In this oppressive environment, RAWA (Revolutionary Association of the Women of Afghanistan) opened clandestine schools and hospitals for Afghan women and girls, provided international journalists with secret film footage of Taliban atrocities (including public executions of women for adultery), and offered ferociously anti-fundamentalist rhetoric that was repeated in news media around the world. Founded in 1977, this organization seeks to involve more women in social and political actions. Its ultimate goal is to secure a government, based on "democratic and secular values" in Afghanistan.

Likening the situation of rigid separation of the sexes in Afghanistan to rigid separation of the races in South Africa, human rights organizations in the West began to use the term "gender apartheid" to describe the plight of Afghan women. Following the September 11, 2001, attacks, the United States launched a bombing campaign targeting Taliban and Al-Qaeda bases in Afghanistan. After the Taliban regime fell, the United Nations held peace talks in Bonn, Germany, that brought various political parties together in conversation and sketched out the parameters of an interim government with Hamid Karzai, a unifying political figure, as president. In January 2002, Interim President Karzai signed a "Declaration of Essential Rights of Afghan Women," which guaranteed legal equality between women and men, equal protection under the law, equal rights to both education and political participation, and the freedoms of movement, speech, and dress (to wear or not wear the *burqa* or any form of head covering). The following June a *loya jirga* or grand assembly met to elect a transitional government; women delegates participated.

Months of intense negotiations led to a constitution that was agreed to in January 2004 by a *loya jirga* of regional representatives. Hamid Karzai, president of the transitional government, signed the constitution later that month. In 12 chapters and 161 articles, the Afghan constitution mandates a strong presidency and provides for upper and lower legislative houses, secures equal legal rights for women and men, and establishes Islam as the country's sacred religion, but guarantees protection for other faiths. Women have been guaranteed a percentage of the seats in both upper and lower legislative houses. On October 9, 2004 the first presidential election was held in Afghanistan, with extraordinarily high turnout, including large numbers of women who stood in line for hours. Although Hamid Karzai was elected in a landslide, Massouda Jalal, a female physician, was also a candidate for the post of president. She gave campaign speeches inside mosques and rallies in villages where women still needed their husband's permission to register to vote. Many women, if fact, were instructed by their husbands how to vote. In preparation for parliamentary elections on September 18, 2005, a census—the first since 1979—was conducted in spring 2005. The lower house would have 249 seats (68, at minimum, allocated to women), with provinces sharing them on the basis of population, very much like the U.S. House of Representatives.

There are clear signs of hope. Roads and schools have been rebuilt, women will have a voice in the government. The first woman-managed radio station in Kabul came on the air November 13, 2001 with the words, "The Taliban are gone," and Voice of Afghan Women received the first Reflections of Hope Award from Oklahoma City, on the 10th anniversary of the bombing of the Murrah Federal Building. A second round of parliamentary elections was held in 2010; some women were elected, and the parliament now has a women's commission.

But, the Taliban are resurgent, people do not feel safe, narcotic trafficking and the flow of arms continue unabated, and warlordism and violence against women persist. In the villages far from the capital city of Kabul, women are not allowed to speak with men outside their immediate families, and fathers can still force their daughters into arranged marriages, even treating them as commodities to settle debts. Once married, a woman has no protection from an abusive husband. If a woman runs away from her husband (threatening his honor and dignity), she can be beaten or even jailed and prosecuted. A woman who is kidnapped or raped brings shame upon her household and, typically, will not be accepted back. An increasing number opt for suicide. In May 2013 Afghanistan's parliament failed to pass a law banning violence against women. There were objections to establishing shelters for abused women and for keeping the marriage age for girls as high as 16. Throughout Afghanistan, maternal and infant mortality ratios are the highest in the world, 300,000 children die each year from preventable diseases, and 85 percent of women are illiterate. Clearly, some Afghan women have been liberated from oppression, but others have not.

Afghanistan was rapidly eclipsed by Iraq as the focus for international media attention. Today, even when a story is reported from inside Afghanistan, it almost always reflects life in the capital city of Kabul. President Hamid Karzai lives and works in a heavily fortified area in Kabul and rarely ventures outside the capital. For most women (and men) in Afghanistan, village life proceeds as it always has. The Strategic Partnership Agreement, signed by Presidents Karzai and Obama in 2012, outlines a plan for U.S. troop withdrawal, beginning in 2014. What will happen, as this plan unfolds, remains uncertain.

A good place to begin exploring this issue might be with the Amnesty International Report *Afghanistan: Women Under Attack*. Published in May 2005, the report compiled by Nazia Hussein reflects interviews she conducted with women across the country. It details the persistence of feudal customs, in which men treat women as property with no fear of punishment or social disapproval. Afghan women, the report concludes, are murdered, raped, and imprisoned with impunity.

*Women for Afghan Women*, Sunita Mehta, ed., (Palgrave Macmillan, 2002), is a collection of essays, poems, and photographs from the organization named in the title. An introduction by Sima Wali, author of the YES selection, defines the Afghan people as historically and ethnically distinct from both Arabs and Iranians, describes the languages they speak—chiefly Dari and Pashto—and strongly asserts their lack of connection with Osama bin Laden and Al-Qaeda. Selections dispel the stereotype of Afghan men as "women-haters" and explore both the *loya jirga* and United Nations policies as they affect Afghan women. The YES selection argues that progress has been made. The NO selection offers textured personal testimony about the unevenness of change.

# YES ↵

Sima Wali

## Afghan Women: Recovering, Rebuilding

The United States' foreign policy in Afghanistan has a long history of misguided plans and misplaced trust—a fact that has contributed to the destruction of the social and physical infrastructure of Afghan society. Afghans contend that after having fought as U.S. allies against the Soviet Union—with the price of more than two million dead—the United States swiftly walked away at the end of that bloody, twenty-three-year conflict. The toll of the war on Afghan society reflected in current statistics is so staggering as to be practically unimaginable: 12 million women living in abject poverty, 1 million people handicapped from land mine explosions, an average life expectancy of forty years (lower for women), a mortality rate of 25.7 percent for children under five years old, and an illiteracy rate of 64 percent. These horrific indicators place Afghanistan among the most destitute countries in the world in terms of human development.

In 1996, the Taliban walked into this breach, immediately issuing edicts banning Afghan women from the public domain. The harshness of the terms of segregation evoked comparisons with South Africa's apartheid regime-leading human rights organizations in the West to call it "gender apartheid." Women were prohibited from working outside their homes, attending school, or appearing in public without a close male relative. They were forced to ride on "women only" public buses, were forbidden to wear brightly colored clothes, and had to have the windows in their houses painted so that they could not be seen from outside. Initially, they could only be treated by female doctors; later, they could be examined—but not seen or touched—by male doctors, in the presence of a male relative. The standard punishment for theft and adultery was public stoning, or even execution; yet a woman had no right to petition a court directly.

These ultraconservative policies and the hardships they imposed are by now quite well known—thanks in part to work done before the war in Afghanistan by women's groups in the United States. In 1998, for example, an alliance of women's rights groups protested the U.S. oil company Unocal's collaboration with the Taliban regime in a project to build a natural gas pipeline through Afghanistan. This grassroots campaign, much like the 1980s' anti-apartheid movement for South Africa, publicized the plight of Afghan women and provided a new set of interlocutors in U.S. foreign policy. In essence, the message of this movement was that the conditions of life for Afghan women symbolized the total devastation of Afghan society.

## The Status of Women

From the beginning of the war, the status of women denied even the most basic human rights under the Taliban regime was a significant part of the moral justification for the antiterrorism campaign in Afghanistan. The Taliban's introduction of draconian measures against Afghan women left them exceedingly poor, unhealthy, and uneducated. In Afghan society, women constitute the most underprivileged group: the vast majority of the 22 million Afghans who rely on international assistance for survival have been women. Globally, they represent the most extreme example of what is known as the "feminization of poverty": for years their health care and nutritional needs have been ignored; their labor has gone unrecognized and unpaid; they have lacked access to education; they have been denied land ownership or inheritance rights; and they have had no decision-making power in the community. That is, they have had none of the resources they would need to escape the cycle of poverty.

Contributing to this near-total lack of capabilities, women in particular have to adequately take care of themselves and their families is the fact that the Afghan crisis is currently the most serious and complex human emergency in the world. There are 1.1 million internally displaced people in Afghanistan and almost 3.6 million living in neighboring countries. The majority of them are women. Because of the disproportionate death toll in men during the war against the Soviet Union, it is women who are now charged with taking care of the approximately one million orphaned children, the elderly, and the handicapped—though they are, themselves, traumatized, malnourished, and undersupported.

How can the status of women in Afghanistan improve given these daunting challenges? The first thing to realize is that despite these appalling statistics, Afghan women are resources for development, not just victims. I can testify to their resilience and courage and to the contributions they have made in the past two decades of war. While men took up arms, Afghan women and their male supporters were busy rebuilding their communities by providing critically needed human services. Thus, the

Wali, Sima. From *Ethics & International Affairs*, vol. 16, no. 2, October 2002, pp. 15–20. Copyright © 2001 by Carnegie Council on Ethics & International Affairs. Reprinted by permission. Notes omitted.

success of rapid development schemes hinges on the formal rehabilitation and active protection of women's equal status in Afghan society.

The implications of gender inequality for the future of Afghanistan are significant given that women represent more than half of the population. Without their participation in political and economic life, it will be impossible for the country to develop and integrate successfully into a global society. What is needed to start the process is an up-to-date, accurate analysis of gender inequality. Reliable basic data—such as the percentage of women in the total population, family size, the number of households headed by women—and human development indicators for health, education, and income were last published in 1996.

Only after the appropriate data is collected can the government create responsible policies for gender mainstreaming—that is, for alleviating the segregation of women and their effective social, economic, and political margin-alization. Women must be integrated into all sectors of Afghan society, including public life as paid government employees. For gender inequality to be addressed seriously, women need to participate more proportionately in government (currently, they hold only 11 percent of seats in the *loya jirga* council). They should also hold posts in all ministries, not just in the Ministry of Women's Affairs.

## The War on Terrorism and Its Aftermath

Following a long lapse in U.S. interest in Afghanistan, this war-ravaged nation stood at the epicenter of world attention almost immediately after the September 11 attacks on U.S. soil. Afghanistan, which had been denied the credit it was due for having helped free the world of communism, now grabbed headlines for all the wrong reasons. Suddenly made famous as the homeland of the Taliban and host to Osama bin Laden and his mercenaries, Afghanistan was excoriated as a country that waged war against its women. The Western world did not need any more justifications than these to launch its offensive. For the first time in world history, a major war was being linked—however tenuously—to the freedom of women.

Initially, the people of Afghanistan—and women in particular—welcomed U.S. and international forces, publicly rejoicing in the streets of Kabul. As the euphoria wore off, however, the burqa-clad women were increasingly unwilling to emerge from their shroud-like coverings, alleging a lack of security, rampant rape, ethnic witch-hunting campaigns against the Pashtun tribe, generalized violence, and widespread abuse by various factions of the Northern Alliance forces. Women in refugee camps spoke of becoming the targets of recently disarmed men—whose new weapons were harassment and rape. Without the protection of security forces, refugee and internally displaced women from neighboring countries who had fled the war fear returning to their home areas in Afghanistan, while others fear leaving their homes to participate in public life as teachers, health workers, entrepreneurs, and government officials.

Given these dangers, women demonstrated remarkable courage during the recent *loya jirga*—the council that met in Kabul June 10–16 to elect a transitional government by articulating their long-held grievances against warlords and their armed supporters. Giving testimony was not without its risks, particularly for those who came from outside Kabul and whose safe return to their provinces and respectful treatment by local warlords could not be assured. As the campaign to bring down al-Qaeda progressed, both Afghan women and men had to be wary of the increased power of these warlords, whom the U.S.-led forces hoped to win over to the war on terrorism through gifts of weapons and money. Indeed, Afghan women cite this empowerment of warlords as one of the gravest threats to the establishment and the maintenance of a secure environment. For these reasons, multinational peacekeeping forces must be expanded beyond Kabul to provide security for women and all Afghans, and to train Afghan security forces which should themselves accept women recruits.

In addition to serious questions about basic security for women, there are deep socioeconomic issues for all Afghans such as the lack of adequate employment, education, income, and housing—coupled with a new nepotism among certain forces in power. Under these circumstances, the needs of Afghan women have once again been deferred. However, as the cases of intimidation against Sima Samar, the former minister of women's affairs, and other female *loya jirga* delegates indicate, women's issues concern everyone—not just women. Samar was alleged to have said that she did not believe in *sharia* (Islamic law), and was charged in court with blasphemy. Warlords invoked the allegation to threaten her repeatedly, and it became the basis for the Supreme Court chief justice's claim that she was not fit to hold a government office. It took the intervention of then-chairman Karzai to abolish all charges against her and subsequently reassign her to head the Human Rights Commission. By undermining the legitimate representation of all Afghan people, gender-inspired threats to current or former government officials directly imperil the prospects for Afghanistan's success in building a state governed by the rule of law and the respect for human rights.

It is thus important that international nongovernmental organizations and other interlocutors pressure national governments to place conditionalities on reconstruction aid that are predicated on gender sensitivity. . . . Only a fraction of the funds may be used to address the social and civil institutions ravaged by the war. It is here, then, that the international community should reorient some of its priorities toward these latter institutions, and thereby show its commitment to helping build a peaceful, tolerant, and democratic Afghan society.

## Looking Ahead

The era when states might commit grave human rights abuses against their own citizens with impunity is past. The U.S. public has, as a result of September 11, broad access to images of and news stories about human beings who are experiencing inordinate suffering. Will they reach out to help? That depends. First, Americans should reconsider the origins of the war in Afghanistan, and come to terms with the United States' own role in it. Second—and consequentially—they should understand that events in Afghanistan directly affect their lives in the United States.

As tragic as the attacks on September 11 were, one of their unintended outcomes was to produce renewed thinking about the need to address the inhumane conditions to which the Afghan people have long been subject. The most striking aspect of this effect is that rhetoric decrying the indecency and criminality of Taliban treatment of Afghan women actually passed from rhetoric to action. This may have simply been a by-product of the U.S.-led war on terrorism, but it should not distract us from accepting and building on these opportunities for the Afghan people and, especially, for Afghan women.

**SIMA WALI** is the president of Refugee Women in Development and vice president and treasurer of the Sisterhood Is Global Institute. A native of Afghanistan, she is an international advocate for the rights of refugee and internally displaced women.

**Norwan, Mariam, and Nasima**

 **NO**

# Afghanistan in Three Voices: Three Afghan Women Talk About Violence and Shelter, the Taliban, and Getting to Vote

**I**t's one thing to theorize about the transition to democracy, another to live it. Here, three Afghan women, Norwan, Mariam, and Nasima, describe life in a country that, after 30 years of war, has vowed to become more liberal.

They all know refugee life, as part of an immense Afghan diaspora that grew following the 1979 Soviet invasion (in the 1980s, one of every two refugees in the world was Afghan), the 1996 Taliban takeover, and the U.S.-led invasion in 2001. The chaos kept school out of reach for many children, especially girls. Today, Afghanistan has one of the lowest literacy rates in the world, at 43 percent for males and less than 13 percent for females. A recent survey by Trust-Law, a legal news service, named Afghanistan the most dangerous country in the world for women. In becoming educated women who could write their own stories, Norwan, Mariam, and Nasima really have all but walked uphill both ways to school.

The three women contribute regularly to the Afghan Women's Writing Project, an online workshop and magazine that publishes several dozen writers, and where, as a volunteer editor, I first encountered their work. Animated with anger, hope, and sweet humor, the poems and essays tell the story of a people who will never reconcile themselves to tents and funerals. Children, families, friendships—they're all important, but the writers refuse to be confined only to domestic concerns. Facing the looming withdrawal of U.S. combat troops next year and the prospect of peace negotiations with the Taliban, the writers were eager to talk about the future of democracy in their homeland.

While they've written here in English, it is not, of course, their first language, nor even their second—among the other languages they speak are Dari, Pashto, and Urdu. For their own security, they use only their first names, and have omitted identifying details.

—Darcy Courteau

## A Way of Good Thinking

In the cold winter nights when I was a child and my father talked about the meaning of freedom and democracy, I could not really understand those words, even though I thought they were the names of my dreams.

Then the Taliban took power when I was 15 years old. Six years after that, democracy came together with B-52 bombers following 9/11. We had a small, old radio running on dying batteries, and we listened to the news. That is how I learned about the war against terrorism.

I'd grown up in war and had heard rockets and bombs. When the Mujahedeen were fighting in Kabul, I understood which kind of rockets they shot, but the bombs from the United States' B-52s made sounds that I still can't forget, as if the mountains above had become angry and suddenly crashed down. Sometimes I went deaf for hours and could not hear anything. For the first time I experienced the fear of being dead. When one of the bombs blasted very close to our house, I cried and hugged my father and looked at his eyes. He told me that the war would be over and we would experience freedom soon.

I told myself to wait for the end of the war, and for the day to come that I could go to school. At that time nothing was important for me but to be out of the blue cage, my stupid burqa, and to go to school.

I heartily welcomed democracy. With it I changed from an uneducated Afghan girl to a proud, educated woman—a golden achievement. After six years of being locked in the house, I could go to school with a pen and paper in my school bag. At school, however, some of my teachers said that democracy is a bad word, and that anybody who likes democracy is against Allah. In my class I learned that democracy is not for Afghans; it only belongs to Western people.

At that time, everybody had a special definition for democracy. A woman imprisoned for killing her husband said that she killed him because he was not a good man, and she could do it because now we had democracy in Afghanistan.

Other women understood they had civil rights. Women who had been forced into marriages, having their first child at age 13—some did not want their daughters to be child brides, too, and started to fight against oppression. Other women ended their lives by burning themselves. Now that they knew their rights, they could not tolerate the wrong decisions of men in their family. In Kabul, I went to the hospital to talk with burned girls and women. They all told me they did it because there was no other option to release them from their family's decision to stop their education, or force them into arranged marriage.

Other families showed that if they could not make big changes, at least they could say no to barbarism. Some families that were not educated sent their daughters to schools, even in unsecured and remote provinces such as Kandahar, Paktiya, Logar, Bamyan, and Badghis. Families believed that we needed educated women, especially women doctors. Even old women could go to literacy courses and get a job outside the house. And now, Afghan women could join the military.

A good telecommunications system meant that people from a shopkeeper to a help man with his donkey could own a mobile phone. Telephone companies held midnight specials, and young boys called their girlfriends secretly and could not sleep until morning. (I pity this misuse of the energy of our young generation.)

We had freedom of speech. Anyone could own a radio station or TV channel. We had about 10 TV channels that all broadcasted dance clips and music. Most of the young boys and girls wanted to be singers! Ariana Sayed and Muzhda Jamalzada, who'd led the country as children and became pop stars abroad, returned to give concerts.

I got to vote in the second parliamentary election, in September 2010. My father had died by then, and none of my family members had decided whether or not to vote. If they did not, then I didn't have permission to go out on Election Day. It was almost the end of the day when my brother came and told my mom and me, "We are going to vote!"

In the car my brother said that both of us should vote for Mullah Abdul Salam Rocketi, a warlord during the Mujahedeen time who had killed a lot of innocent Afghans. My brother supported him because Rocketi was paying $100 to each person who voted for him. I was shocked, and thought that it is better to commit suicide than vote for Rocketi. My brother gave us a camera so that we could take a picture of our ballots to show we'd voted for the right person. When I went to the polling station and mom took the camera, my hands were shaking as if somebody stood beside me with a knife. I selected my favorite person who I thought could do something for Afghans.

But my hope for having a democratic country was like a paper boat in the water.

Now I feel ashamed of myself when I remember that when the world introduced Hamid Karzai as president of Afghanistan, and the U.S. government and international community hugged him and kissed him, while watching him on TV I was clapping for him and welcomed him with tears.

We trusted Karzai and thought that because he was selected by the international community, we would experience big changes. The world paid special attention to the situation in Afghanistan, and money rained down from everywhere.

But it went to Karzai and his family, his corrupt, lazy cabinet, and people around him. Throwing away their turbans and wearing ties and suits, they were very successful in pretending to support democracy while they filled their pockets with money. The international community would give money to build highways, for example, but because in Afghanistan there is no transparency, a contractor would keep the money and use mud for the roads instead of concrete.

Afghans were disappointed in Karzai's misgovernment, and some thought that the Taliban would be better. Now, when people have problems with corrupt courts, some turn to the Taliban and ask them to help solve their most important issues.

The past 12 years have not brought changes to the lives of poor, ordinary Afghans. Women still suffer violence at home. Children as young as seven are in the streets begging, and they are the supporters of the house.

We had presidential and parliamentary elections again, and all went well according to media announcements. The Afghan people selected a president for themselves, Afghanistan had a parliament, and, by the way, again the world congratulated our failures!

But it was not only Afghanistan's government that did not understand the meaning of democracy. Some people really considered it a bad word, while they expected the United States and other countries to rebuild Afghanistan! Many Afghan people really counted on Obama to bring democracy and stability to Afghanistan. But with the bombing of women and children in the villages, and then, worst of all, talking about making peace with the Taliban, the U.S. government showed that their efforts to bring democracy to Afghanistan were a commercial—it looks so attractive in the newspaper, but if we go and buy it, it isn't worth a penny. It is still a puzzle for Afghans that the United States is thinking about making peace with the Taliban. I feel pity for those Americans who paid the high cost of losing their lives in 9/11, for American soldiers who died in Afghanistan's war, and for Afghans who died in wars against the Taliban and Al Qaeda. Making peace with the Taliban means that, yes, we forgive you! And who can guarantee that Afghanistan will not become a nest of terrorists that will bring up other bin Ladens?

Democracy is a way of thinking, good thinking. It doesn't mean that whatever your heart wants to do, do it. I think that democracy cannot go together with war. As long as we Afghan people ourselves don't work for real change and freedom, and as long as we put the Quran in the high shelves of our houses and instead respect ignorant mullahs as leaders, we can never experience democracy in Afghanistan.

—Norwan

## Why Am I Remembering Sad Stories?

I was a teacher in a primary school, with a university degree, when the Taliban captured Afghanistan in 1996. The Taliban did not allow women to go outside their homes unless they were sick, and then they were not allowed to go alone to see a doctor. Outside, they had to wear burqas. But one day I went out without wearing one. I had to accompany my mother-in-law to a doctor's appointment, and my family owned just one burqa. I covered my body with a big shawl and I covered my face. At a crossroads, we ran into some members of the Taliban. I looked away with my eyes, but the Taliban began beating me. There was no law to defend my rights as an Afghan woman. I thought that there was not any other choice for me but to leave my country.

I migrated to Pakistan with my husband, three sons, and my daughter (I now have two more children, a daughter, eight years old, born in Pakistan, and a son, two years old). Most Afghan refugees in Pakistan made carpets, and they had to work very hard for 16 hours a day to make rent money, and to cover their huge daily expenses. They could not afford to send their children to school. I decided to work as a servant in a Pakistani house to earn money for my children to go to school rather than weave carpets. But every day when I started to sweep the Pakistani house, I started to cry. I not only felt my life's pain—I felt all of our homeland's hardships. Finally, I was able to start a school for immigrant children with funds from the International Rescue Committee, and I established some classes for young girls and women.

After the United Nations and United States helped create an Islamic republic in Afghanistan, we returned to our country. I started a job in a different nongovernmental organization that helps provide opportunities for rural women in order to raise their income and their awareness about their role and rights. Women have the right to education, work, and legal support. According to Afghanistan's constitution, every citizen who is at least 18 years old, male or female, has the right to vote. We are evidence of a big change.

Today, women can go everywhere, with permission from family. As an Afghan woman, I have the permission of my husband to go alone outside of our country to attend events and programs related to my job. We are in a Muslim country, and it is a basic requirement of our religion to get this permission. I am very happy with my rights. Currently, I am very happy with my life and my job.

But even while I talk about democracy, I think of all the crimes that I hear about on the news every day. For example, there was 15-year-old Sahar Gul, rescued from the home of her in-laws after being tortured for months. She had refused to be forced into prostitution. And there are thousands of similar stories of Afghan women and girls, gloomy tales. But why I am remembering such sad stories while I am talking of democracy and freedom?

Some of our people face problems because of security issues. Many of our problems are caused by ignorance, misconceptions, and illiteracy. In city centers the problems are fewer, but in remote areas there are a huge number of violent attacks against women. My concern is that the Taliban will destroy our security and deprive women of their rights. I think we need to work more through various programs and projects to provide awareness about law.

We tolerated a lot of problems caused by decades of war in our country. Today there are gains in education, construction, and civil rights, especially women's. There are scholarship opportunities, employment opportunities, and so on. I don't want the United Nations or the U.S. Army to leave Afghanistan after 2014. Please provide support for Afghanistan in the upcoming election and for the establishment of a good policy to bring peace and democracy in our country.

—Mariam

## A Message of Peace

I was born in a refugee camp in Iran, but my family had a bad time as immigrants there, so in June 2001 my father decided to move us back to our country, Afghanistan. He said that we should destroy all of our photos, books, mementos, notes, and music CDs, because the Taliban don't let people have these things. He warned us that women must have burqas for hiding their faces, and being a woman means not having rights to make choices or go to school, or to have rights of expression. We just had the right to listen to men and do what they wanted us to do.

It was very hard for me to accept these laws because at that time I was a 16-year-old and had so many wishes as a woman. I wanted to continue my education and travel to other countries to learn about different cultures.

When we put feet to our country's ground, instead of there being leaves and fruits on trees, there were pieces of cassette tapes and CDs. There were rough men with soiled faces, high turbans, long beards, and guns full of bullets. They were Taliban soldiers.

Everywhere was dirt and dust. There was no sign of peace or friendship or prosperity. War was hungry and thirsty children sitting on the streets to beg rather than going to school.

We arrived in our city. Frightened people ran toward us to watch; they knew that we had come back from living in Iran. They were good people, and their wish was that we would be OK. Their hearts burned to us; their faces told us, "God will save you from this situation."

Four months later, we heard on the radio news that the tyrants had been pushed out. It was a free country. Children could go to school, and both men and women could go to jobs according to their experience and education. Even the sky knew that this country needed rain, and it poured that night. This rain was the sign and message of peace and friendship and for the people of Afghanistan to flourish.

I married in 2003 and became a teacher, and when the government had an election for president the next year, I got a voting card. I saw an old woman, about 90 years old, crying from delight. She said, "My God, I arrived to my wishes!" and kissed her voting card.

The promised day arrived. I wanted to go to the voting site; it was my school where I was a teacher. But I faced some problems from my husband. He was a fan of Yunus Qanooni, one of the candidates. I didn't like Qanooni, but so I could participate in the voting process, I lied to my husband and said, "Fine and OK, I will vote for Yunus Qanooni." Five minutes before the polls closed, I was the last person to vote. I got a pen and with pleasure voted for Hamid Karzai, and I was so happy for completing my duty as one human, an Afghan woman.

Now I am divorced, and I am living with my mother and my young son, whose name means "my hope and wishes." Sometimes I feel like my ex-husband is a shadow in back of me, and I feel like he wants to kill me or beat me again. I always try to travel by car, not as a pedestrian, because I am afraid. Most painful for me is when I think he will come and take my son away.

Now I am not a teacher. I work for an organization that supports fair elections. Elections face serious challenges. If we don't pay attention to them, we will endanger the achievements of 12 years. Lack of security, lack of awareness among people in villages, and election rigging are all problems.

What I see in Afghanistan is not true democracy. The Islamic republic countries cannot accept components of democracy; for example, there is not freedom of opinion and expression. The culture of the people cannot understand it, because a lot of people speaking on the radio and TV are against the government or public authority or are fans of one person of one political group based on ethnic prejudice.

Democracy can be realized in a society where people have knowledge about the word "democracy," and people have experienced peace in the country for several years. But years of war in Afghanistan have caused a backward mentality in people. Now it is not that easy for people to accept democracy.

Finally, I want to share with you some of my search for the meaning of democracy:

If I asked some children, "What is democracy?" they would answer me: "To follow the ball and kite, to play and build snowmen in winter and wait for the coming of spring."

If I asked a farmer, he would say: "To plow land in the spring and harvest in the summer and have a slice of bread in winter."

If I asked a woman, she would say: "Having life without violence."

If I asked a mother, she would say: "To foster children and give them kindness."

If I asked a shoemaker on our street, he would say: "For a moment I can warm my frozen hands in winter."

If I asked street children, they would say: "Going to school to be a doctor or engineer or manager."

If I asked students in schools: "To turn the pages of books and color on our hands with pens."

If I asked some birds: "Soaring in the sky and not in a cage."

Fishes of seas: "Clean seawater."

The blind: "To see the light of day and sun, and not always see the dark of night."

The deaf: "Hearing the beating of mother's heart and the sound of friends."

If asked a patriot, the patriot would say: "I love my beautiful country, and I want to fall in it and feel the roses and smell the plains and mountains, not the reek of war and blood."

—Nasima

Afghan painter Hangama Amiri's "Girl Under the Taliban" depicts a burqa, the full-body covering that the militants forced women to wear. The artist fled to Canada with her family in 1996 when she was six years old. A 2010 visit to Afghanistan inspired her series The Wind-Up Dolls of Kabul.

"Raining Stones" by Hangama Amiri. In areas under their control, the Taliban still orders executions of women accused of social crimes such as adultery. Some are stoned to death.

War has plagued Kabul since the Soviet invasion in 1979, leaving street after street lying in destruction. Families still manage to live in the hollowed remains of homes.

---

**Norwan, Mariam, and Nasima** are the first names of three Afghani women who tell their textured, personal stories of life in Afghanistan today.

# EXPLORING THE ISSUE

## Have Afghan Women Been Liberated from Oppression?

## Critical Thinking and Reflection

1. Afghanistan has been called "the most dangerous country in the world for women." Research the conditions and dangers faced by Afghan women and critically discuss the ways in which this claim is justified or not justified.
2. On what basis does Sima Wali write: "Afghan women are resources for development, not just victims"? Critically discuss what she means and the ways in which this might be an accurate assessment.
3. After a 10-year battle, the Soviet military was forced to withdraw from Afghanistan in 1989. The United States, which had assisted the Afghanis, also withdrew. The ensuing chaos left many yearning for some order and stability. In 1996, the Taliban stepped into the void, issuing harsh orders separating women and men and denying women access to public spaces. Critically evaluate the charge that these policies, many of which continue today, constitute "gender apartheid." Critically debate the meaning and applicability of this term.
4. Why does Norwan describe the *burqa* she was required to wear "the blue cage"? Try to imagine being covered from head to toe, with only a small screen for your eyes remaining open. Research other testimony from women forced to wear the burqa and critically discuss the effect this requirement would have on a society seeking to enter the modern world.
5. In the mid-nineteenth century, the British occupied Afghanistan. In addition to keeping out the Russians, they had humanitarian aims—to champion social reform by banning the stoning of adulterous women and to establish a government based on Western-style political ideas. The British were forced to withdraw from Afghanistan in 1842, defeated by Wazir Akbar Khan, who is regarded as a national hero for ridding the country of "foreigners." Critically examine the parallels between the British and U.S. experiences in Afghanistan. Are there characteristics of Afghan society that will remain resistant to Western influence, no matter how well intentioned?
6. Why does Nasima think that an Afghan woman's fondest wish for democracy in her country would mean "a life without violence"? What is and is not possible if half a country fears violence on a daily basis? Critically discuss the implications.
7. The website of RAWA, the Revolutionary Association of the Women of Afghanistan, charges that the U.S. War on Terrorism in 2001 removed the Taliban, but has not removed "fundamentalism, which is the main cause of all our miseries." In what sense can ideology be a more fear-producing force? Critically discuss historical parallels in which an ideology has brought about violence and death for targeted groups.
8. Speculate about what is likely to happen if substantial numbers of U.S. troops withdraw from Afghanistan, beginning in 2014. Research the conditions under which this is likely to happen; then debate whether the final outcome would likely leave the country better or worse than when U.S. troops arrived in 2001.

## Is There Common Ground?

One way to approach this question is to acknowledge that Afghanistan is not a homogeneous society. In the capital city of Kabul, some things that are possible are totally impossible in the more rural areas that remain under the control of reinstated warlords. As in many issues, where we look determines what we see. If we grant that all the progress outlined in the YES selection is accurately depicted and also acknowledge that the fears of Norwan, Mariam, and Nasima, outlined in the NO selection, are as real as their hopes and dreams, we may find the common ground in this issue.

*Question:* How much of the progress is dependent on NATO-led forces?

## Create Central

www.mhhe.com/createcentral

## Additional Resources

Cheryl Benard's *Veiled Courage: Inside the Afghan Women's Resistance* (Broadway Books, 2002) explores the resistance of Afghan women to oppression. She provides a history of RAWA, beginning with its founding in the late 1970s by a charismatic woman known as Meena, who was killed by Pakistani police with ties to the Afghan secret police. Her courageous leadership continues to inspire RAWA members today, especially the 11 elected women who comprise leadership. RAWA members serve as role models for others who face demoralizing conditions and engage both supporters and challengers in dialogue. Resisting the current project of nation building that accepts ethnic identity as the most important factor, RAWA seeks to alter the culture of female inferiority by altering patterns of male socialization and ideals of masculinity.

*My Forbidden Face: Growing Up Under the Taliban, a Young Woman's Story by Latifa* (Talk Miramax, 2002) offers a true account of Kabul life from 1996 to 2001, by a young author using a pseudonym. Educated during the Soviet occupation and ready to begin her university education as a journalist in 1996, "Latifa" describes how her life was "confiscated" by the Taliban. Her narrative concludes as the American bombing begins in October 2001—". . . who speaks for Afghanistan? I don't know anymore." *Prisoners of Hope: The Story of Our Captivity and Freedom in Afghanistan* (Doubleday, 2002), by Dayna Curry and Heather Mercer, describes the imprisonment, trial by the Taliban, and rescue by U.S. special forces of two Christian missionaries from Waco, Texas. And, *Behind the Burqa: Our Life in Afghanistan and How We Escaped to Freedom* by "Sulima" and "Hala" as told to Batya Swift Yasgur (John Wiley & Sons, 2002), is the story of two sisters, sixteen years apart in age. "Sulima," the elder, fled the Communist regime in 1979 and "Hala," the younger fled persecution by the Taliban in 1997. Both were working to educate women. Finally, the first novel in English about Afghanistan is *The Kite Runner* (Penguin, 2003) by Khaled Hosseini, an Afghani physician now living in the United States. It is especially helpful in illustrating the power of tribal differences (majority Pashtun and minority Hazara) as well as sectarian ones (majority Sunni and minority Shi'a). It evokes life before the 1979 Soviet invasion and confronts the repressive Taliban regime as well. A popular film by the same name is also available.

## Internet Reference . . .

**RAWA—the Revolutionary Association of the Women of Afghanistan**

The association hosts a website that provides history, ongoing projects, current challenges, and plans for political and social actions.

**www.rawa.org/rawa.html**

Selected, Edited, and with Issue Framing Material by:
Helen Buss Mitchell, *Howard Community College*
and
Joseph R. Mitchell, *Howard Community College*

# ISSUE

# Is the Influence of the European Union in World Affairs Increasing?

YES: Mitchell P. Smith, from "Soft Power Rising," *World Literature Today* (January/February 2006)

NO: Efstathios T. Fakiolas, from "The European Union's Problems of Cohesion," *New Zealand International Review* (March/April 2007)

---

### Learning Outcomes

After reading this issue, you should be able to:

- Explain the meaning and application of "soft power."
- Give a brief history of the European Union, from its origin in a 1951 Common Market, through the adoption of a common currency (the Euro) in 2000, to the present.
- Evaluate the progress or lack of progress toward unity within the European Union.

---

### ISSUE SUMMARY

**YES:** Political science and international studies professor Mitchell P. Smith argues that the European Union excels in the use of soft power to achieve desired outcomes at minimal cost, by avoiding the use of military force and sharing the burden of enforcement with others.

**NO:** Efstathios T. Fakiolas, strategy and Southeast European affairs analyst, argues that Europe's failure to achieve European "Union-hood" seriously hampers its effectiveness in the global community.

The European Union (EU) celebrated its 50th anniversary in 2007. From the early common market forged by the European Coal and Steel Community in 1951, through the 1957 Treaty of Rome that created the European Economic Community, to the so-called Maastricht Treaty that created the EU in May 1993, Europe has been on a path toward great cohesiveness. Almost a half billion people from 27 member nations share unfettered economic and commercial exchange. Of the 27 member nations, 13 share a common currency, the Euro, as do four nations not currently members of the EU—Andorra, the Holy See, Monaco, and San Marino. There is a flag, with a circle of 12 gold stars against a deep blue background, and an anthem, based on "Ode to Joy" from Beethoven's Ninth Symphony.

Some of the member nations might not fit the traditional image of Europe. These include Bulgaria, Estonia, Finland, Latvia, Lithuania, Romania, and Slovenia. And two unequivocally European nations—Norway and Switzerland—are not members of the EU and have no wish to be. There is no common language or shared media. In fact, the European Parliament in Brussels, Belgium, conducts its business in 20 official languages and can seem distant and impersonal. A proposed constitution, drafted by former French President Valerie Giscard d'Estang and 104 colleagues comprising a Convention on Europe's Future, though signed amid great celebration in Rome in 2004 by all member nations and three candidate countries, has failed to be ratified. When France and the Netherlands voted no, this effectively brought the ratification process to a standstill.

There is significant tension over the question of how much of a federation Europe should be. This debate has been brought to a head during the current debt crisis, as economically stable nations, such as Germany, are increasingly called upon to "bail out" financially troubled nations, such as Greece. Should there be a banking union, with authority to regulate and intervene in policy decisions, at the level of national banks? Some member nations are wondering whether there is too much sovereignty at the local level and not enough Europe-wide banking supervision in the EU.

At the same time there is a strong commitment to shared values among citizens of the EU, which favors diplomacy and internationalism to resolve global disputes and is formally committed to peace, opposition to the death penalty, and support of climate initiatives to resist or reverse global warming. There is also substantial shared opposition to what is often perceived as hegemony on the part of the United States. In current flash points, such as Afghanistan and Iran, Europe favors talking and holding out carrots rather than brandishing sticks.

This issue focuses on the contrast between hard and soft power. Clearly, the United States is the master of hard power, with its military might and sophisticated weapons systems. Europe trades in soft power, defined by Joseph Nye as the ability to get others to follow, through attraction rather than coercion. The YES selection argues that Europe's soft power is on the rise. The NO selection cites Europe's lack of cohesion and "union-al" identity as serious barriers to its influence on the world stage.

The EU faces some compelling challenges beyond the resolution of the debt crisis. One concerns the question of the geographical limits of Europe. Turkey, now a candidate country, lies mostly in Asia. Its largest city, Istanbul, straddles the Bosporus Strait, giving it one foot in Europe and another in Asia. However, Ankara, its capital city, is fully outside Europe. Its membership would push the limits of the EU all the way to the borders of Iran and Iraq. Further, its population of 70 million rivals Germany's population in size and is 99.8 percent Muslim. The former Pope John Paul II lobbied strenuously and unsuccessfully for over 2 years for acknowledgment of Europe's "Christian roots." Most Europeans are comfortable with Turkey's secular government. However, its accession to the EU will rest in part on substantially improved respect for the rights of non-Muslim communities as well as on Turkey's recognition of Cyprus, an EU member since 2004.

A more philosophical question asks whether there will ever be a United States of Europe. How strong a federation will be possible, how much pooling of sovereignty? France and Germany, historic enemies, now form a core of the EU and continent-wide war is now unthinkable—a clear gain. But, how deep is European identity? Is "Europe" a source of emotional attachment for most Europeans? A recent survey in the French daily *Le Figaro* found that 71 percent of French respondents took some pride in their European identity. But, for countries that remain peripheral, such as Britain, Europe, may remain "a convenience rather than a concept," in the words of German ministry official Karsten Vogt.

The most intriguing question might be whether living in one European country and working in another will ever be as routine as living in New Jersey and working in New York. Will a common currency and increasingly common economic and political interests forge a European supernation that does not need the military power of the United States to resolve its internal conflicts and does not want either American culture or American pressure to marginalize rogue nations such as Iran? Would the emergence of an economically powerful Euroland bring an end to the asymmetrical advantages the dollar has enjoyed as the world's only truly global currency?

The Socrates-Erasmus Program has brought 1.5 million Europeans to study for a year in a university outside their own country. The film *L'Auberge Espagnole* (The Spanish Inn) chronicles this jumbling of cultures and explorations of all kinds, as students develop new identities during their year of mingling.

Robert Kagan, in a much-quoted 2002 *Policy Review* article, contended that Europe has the luxury of its peace-loving, environmentally conscious society only because the United States and its military might are standing watch over the world. Kagan fleshes out this thesis in *Paradise and Power: America and Europe in the New World Order* (Alfred A. Knopf, 2003). America is like the sheriff in the movie "High Noon," according to Kagan, forced to face the outlaw alone, because the townspeople don't see the outlaw as a direct threat to themselves.

A book much more supportive of the EU is *Protecting Our Environment: Lessons from the European Union* by Janet R. Hunter and Zachary A. Smith (SUNY Albany, 2005), which praises the EU for including sustainability in its core objectives and integrating environmental and economic policies. The authors conclude that "international environmental regimes"—transnational systems of norms, rules, and structures that guide environmental action—will be necessary to solve worldwide environmental problems and, using case studies, find the EU a good model to follow.

# YES ↵

**Mitchell P. Smith**

## Soft Power Rising

Few successful international organizations can claim romantic as well as practical origins. In fact, the European Union (EU) is unique in its blending of (1) romantic aspirations for transcendence of the ills of the nation-state in the aftermath of two world wars and (2) practical objectives of enhancing the political stability and economic prosperity of its members.

The preamble to the Treaty of Rome that created the European Economic Community in 1957 embodies both elements of the European integration project. The romantic dimension finds expression in the call for "ever closer union among the peoples of Europe," and reference to the pooling of resources "to preserve and strengthen peace and liberty." Elsewhere in the preamble, the quest for removal of obstacles to "steady expansion, balanced trade, and fair competition" and "the progressive abolition of restrictions on international trade" gives voice to practical Europe. A half-century later, have practical considerations overwhelmed the romantic, or has the romantic longing for unity proven an obstacle to practical achievement? Arguably, as the European Union seeks a renewed sense of purpose and direction after conjuring a single currency and expanding to twenty-five member states, concrete objectives are attainable only as long as the romantic notion of constructing a better world finds resonance on the European continent and beyond.

The contemporary juxtaposition of a United States that appears to have shed the romance and idealism of its founding and the apogee of Europe's romantic dimension have prompted widespread interest in the EU as a meaningful global entity. Several recent accounts emerging from this tension portray the European Union as an anti-America: an increasingly unified world of low inequality, concern for the cohesiveness of society, respect for the environment, and commitment to a peaceful world order and resolution of conflicts through engagement and diplomacy. This romantic Europe is a magnetic pole of attraction, both to aspiring member states (the region of aspirants stretches increasingly further eastward, initially into the central European states of Poland, the Czech Republic, and Hungary, and now to Ukraine and Georgia as well as northward to the Baltics and southward to the Balkans) and to poorer countries outside the European continent that seek a reliable provider of development assistance and access to important markets.

More cynical observers—hardheaded realists in the language of international-relations theory, such as Robert Kagan, who in his much-debated 2002 *Policy Review* article contrasted Europe's weakness with America's strength—suggest that this postconflict semi-utopia is possible only with the military security provided by the United States. For these analysts, Europe must be judged by its practical self, and, from this perspective, it is a troubled entity. The large European Union economies—especially Germany and Italy, but France as well—characterized by sluggish growth, population aging, and persistent mass unemployment, appear to be spent forces relative to the dynamism of the United States. The European Union has proven ineffectual in responding to recent episodes of conflict and instability on the European continent. Such a Europe offers little as a model for emerging capitalist democracies and remains inconsequential as a global actor.

The coexistence of triumph and failure in the European Union during the past two years has added to the ambiguity of Europe's trajectory and to the apparent tension between the romantic and the practical. At midnight on April 1, 2004, fireworks lit the skies across central and eastern European capitals as countries from the former Soviet bloc (along with Malta and Greek Cyprus) celebrated their official accession to the European Union. With the expansion to twenty-five members, the European Union became a single market in goods, services, and capital for 455 million citizens, consumers, and businesspeople. Referendums on joining the EU were endorsed with enthusiasm by central and eastern European publics. As the world's largest market for goods and services, the EU appeared to be on the rise as a border-free region with a single currency of increasing heft in the international economy.

The proposed EU constitution—negotiated in 2002–3 and ultimately signed and sealed in December 2004—promised to codify the stunning achievements of the EU and create a foundation for effective decision making in a body of twenty-five members and more. Once in effect in 2006, the constitution would create the framework for more powerful global projection of the EU's voice. The organization sought to accomplish this by codifying the aspirations of the European Union and especially by increasing the continuity of the leadership of EU institutions and creating a single ministry for European Union foreign affairs.

As the first ten EU member states ratified the constitutional treaty, the EU appeared in spring 2005 to be well on the way to fulfilling its potential as a global power. Then, the fragility of the entire apparatus was ostensibly revealed by the French electorate's rejection of the constitution and an even more resounding "no" from a Dutch citizenry historically supportive of the integration project. More profound than the "no" votes themselves was the sense of uncertainty that emerged across Europe. Directionlessness prevailed. In Italy, a government minister (granted, from a right-wing populist party) called for abandonment of the European currency, the euro, and the return of the historically flimsy Italian lira. Confidence in the euro slipped, and EU political leaders expressed uncertainty about how to proceed. "Crisis" became a mantra.

In fact, Europe's current malaise preceded the French and Dutch referendum results. Given the size of the single European market and the large share of the EU in global trade, the EU has established parity with the United States in its ability to set the terms of global economic exchange. Speaking with one voice in the World Trade Organization, the EU is a pivotal actor in the setting of the global trade agenda and establishment of rules governing international finance and trade in goods and services. Building on this accomplishment and the introduction of the euro in 1999, leaders of EU member states meeting at a summit in Lisbon in 2000 articulated the lofty goal of becoming "the world's most dynamic, knowledge-based economy" by the end of the decade. Surpassing the dynamism of the U.S. economy was the aim. Progress toward this objective has proven elusive, however. Efforts to develop new mechanisms for job creation and intensified investment have yielded few results. The course of the Lisbon project bears little resemblance to the earlier project of establishing a single European market by 1992. In that endeavor—beginning in the mid-1980s, when the Europeans set their sights on a rising Japan as well as the United States, and so brilliantly crafted under the leadership of European Commission president Jacques Delors, a former French finance minister—the goals and means to the single market were firmly established, as were the costs of not acting. A decade later, the Lisbon objectives were nebulous and the means to attain them unclear and contested. In fact, between 2000 and 2006, the EU has by most measures lost ground relative to the United States. More than midway through the decade, the Europeans find themselves farther from their goal than when they began their quest for economic supremacy.

Nevertheless, there is a looming gap in global leadership that the EU, at least in part, may be positioned to fill. A United States mired in Iraq faces intense international unpopularity, if not outright hostility. This unpopularity is not limited to French impatience with American hyperpuissance but in fact emanates from numerous corners, ranging from those antagonized by pronounced American unilateralism and antiglobalization activists around the world to actors in developing countries opposed to U.S. overconsumption of global resources. The ability of the United States to set the agenda for global affairs, and the extent to which people across the globe look to the United States for leadership in solving international problems, appears to be waning in the opening years of the twenty-first century.

Critics of U.S. foreign policy warn that policymakers have lost sight of the crucial significance of "soft" power. As articulated by international-relations scholar Joseph Nye, soft power is the ability to get others to follow, by virtue of attraction rather than coercion. Soft power enables the possessor to achieve desired outcomes at minimal cost by avoiding the use of military force and sharing the burden of enforcement with allies. Whereas hard power remains relatively concentrated (with annual U.S. military expenditures exceeding those for all EU member states combined), there has been a geographical diffusion of other forms of power. This is especially true of economic power, which is increasingly shared not only by the EU and the United States, but also by China and such rising regional economic powers as Brazil, South Africa, and India. In this environment, the EU, as a leader in global humanitarian aid and development assistance, appears ascendant in the global hierarchy by virtue of its soft power. If the romantic longing to knit nations and peoples together in peace and prosperity represents a European vision, soft power is a means to its realization. Romantic Europe, it seems, is bearing fruit in the form of increased attraction as a locus of global problem solving and a system of values and institutions worthy of emulation.

The most compelling evidence of EU soft-power ascendance is the transformation undertaken by numerous governments in response to the lure of EU membership. The foremost examples are in eastern and central Europe, where dramatic transitions toward democracy and market economies occurred in the space of a decade. The behavior of other governments, including Turkey and Ukraine, with a combined population of more than 100 million, also has been altered by the attraction of eventual EU membership. Furthermore, the new member states have extended outward the geographical embrace of the European integration project. The Slovenian government has become a leading advocate for Croatian membership in the EU. Poland champions the Ukrainian cause. The European Union has been a touchstone for Ukraine in the aftermath of the Orange Revolution, helping define the path toward more efficient and less corrupt administration, reforming relations between state and society, and pursuing Ukrainian membership in the World Trade Organization.

Indeed, in his February 2005 speech before the European Parliament, Ukrainian president Viktor Yuschenko announced that "the new president and government of Ukraine have clearly defined the ingredients and forms for future decisions. These are the norms and standards of the European Union, its legislation, legal, political, economic, and social culture. European integration is the most effective and, in fact, the only programme of reforms for contemporary Ukraine."

Although its ultimate place in Europe remains highly contested, the Turkish government, under pressure from the EU institutions in which it seeks full participation, has during the past five years adopted an impressive array of reforms. Most significant of these is a serious effort to curtail the powers of the Turkish military. The National Security Council, formerly a vehicle for the military's exercise of power over the executive, has been transformed into an advisory body with a civilian majority. Parliament has been granted greater powers of oversight over the defense budget. The government even has pursued corruption charges against senior officers, a departure from the untouchable status of the officer corps in the recent past. In a set of constitutional reforms passed in 2001, Turkey abolished the death penalty except in times of war and for terrorist crimes, eased conditions for the broadcast and publication of materials in the Kurdish language, and broadened rights of political parties, trade unions, and other intermediary associations. The EU has been a catalyst for revival of the Turkish government's privatization program in the face of a reluctant state bureaucracy, entailing the withdrawal of government ownership from a wide range of state economic enterprises in industries from telecommunications to cigarettes, steel, and cement and from seaports to thermal power plants. The EU continues to press Ankara for additional reforms in the areas of women's rights and the rights of non-Muslim minorities.

Consonant with its rising soft power, the EU has captured a certain moral authority yielded by the United States. The conflict in Chechnya illustrates this point. Although the Russian government was by many accounts responsible for widespread human-rights abuses in its war in Chechnya, U.S. criticism of Russia was muted in the face of the Russian government's claim to be fighting the global war on terror alongside the United States. The EU, in contrast, submitted draft resolutions condemning Russian human-rights abuses in Chechnya to the UN Human Rights Commission in 2002, 2003, and 2004. The European Parliament was vocal in its criticism of the Russian human-rights violations. The credibility of EU institutions was elevated by virtue of their central role as advocates for the rights of Russian minorities in the Baltic states prior to their accession to the EU in 2004. Moreover, the European Union is now taking a leading role in the reconstruction of Chechnya following a decade of war. This includes such citizen initiatives as the French-based student group Etudes sans Frontieres, modeled after the Paris-based Medecins sans Frontieres, which has brought a small group of students from the University of Grozny to study in the French university system.

In the realm of humanitarian aid, the EU and its member states are by far the global leaders. Assailed for its inability to wield hard power in Bosnia and Kosovo, the EU led the humanitarian relief effort. In recent months, the EU has devoted substantial resources to famine relief in Ethiopia and Eritrea, drought relief in Afghanistan, natural-disaster preparation in the Central Asian republics, food aid in Niger and Mali, and promotion of regional economic integration in the Common Market for Eastern and Southern Africa. U.S. development and humanitarian aid has fallen steadily as a share of gross domestic product for more than four decades (to less than one-tenth of 1 percent, far lower than the poorest of the older fifteen EU member states, Greece and Portugal); levels in EU member states remain closer to those sustained by the United States at the peak of its soft power in the 1960s. The European Union seeks to reach an aid level of 0.56 percent of GDP by 2010. EU member states lead the effort on behalf of global poverty alleviation. Many development economists insist that aid does not foster autonomous economic growth; nevertheless, as the U.S. military learned in Indonesia in the wake of the 2004 tsunami, deployment of national resources for benign aims generates enhanced esteem around the globe.

Consistent with its predilection for the exercise of soft power, a Europe that rivals the United States economically wishes to equal the United States as a diplomatic power, even while leaving U.S. military supremacy uncontested. Iran offers a first test of whether this will be possible. The European Union, with the British, French, and German governments acting in the name of the entire organization, has led the way in nuclear diplomacy in Iran. Iran has resisted EU inducements, moving forward with its nuclear program, and the outcome remains undetermined. However, it is clear that, for the Iranian government, the EU is the only possible interlocutor. The United States hulks in the background, casting a shadow over negotiations with periodic threats to use force if necessary; with the United States mired in Iraq, such threats bear little credibility.

So how do we assess the rising soft power of the European Union in comparison, say, with the supreme military power of the United States? Above all, it must be kept in mind that in terms of trade, flows of capital, and international rule-making, the United States—EU relationship is the most densely interdependent on the globe. The United States and EU, in other words, are in fact more partners than rivals. An economically weak European Union is not in the interest of the United States, nor is it helpful for the global economy. The same may be said for a diplomatically weak EU. Pressing global problems cannot be resolved without international leadership, and mounting evidence indicates the United States can no longer lead alone.

How should we conceptualize soft power? Does it have a long half-life? Is it as easily created as destroyed? Experience suggests that, because soft power is largely a product of how others perceive the motives of a nation's policies, a concept closely related to trust, soft power tends to reproduce itself. Soft power begets soft power, just as mistrust begets misperception and further mistrust. In contrast, the U.S. experience in Iraq suggests that hard power, when used without a patina of soft power, can degrade if it does not swiftly produce the desired result. Prophets of international politics have incorrectly predicted the demise of military power as a source of international influence in the past. But soft power has long been a necessary complement to hard power, a dimension of power that enhances and renders more durable hard-power resources. Are we perhaps witnessing a growing disjuncture in the distribution of hard- and soft-power resources?

Ultimately, the EU's soft-power ascendance does not mean the EU will achieve all its economic and diplomatic objectives in the coming decade. Scholars generally agree that in order to enhance its global role, the EU will need to balance its stock of soft power with a modicum of hard power-something it has attempted to do through creation of a 60,000-strong European Rapid Reaction Force designed to address tasks of peacekeeping and emergency intervention on the European continent and beyond. The EU also must transcend its current malaise wrought of uncertainty and internal conflict and develop a renewed sense of purpose. Sustaining soft power demands resources; reviving economic growth is not a simple matter for countries with adverse ratios of active to retired persons and heavy public-pension burdens. Plans to increase global development aid will meet popular resistance without an improvement in domestic economic conditions. In the wake of the negative referendum outcomes in France and the Netherlands, European publics seem reluctant to countenance membership enlargement beyond Bulgaria and Romania, both slated for membership next year. If Turkey is rebuffed in the wake of heroic efforts to secure democracy, the EU pole may lose some of its magnetic pull.

In other words, practical achievements in European integration and the romantic longing for unity are interdependent. In the absence of sufficient material resources, the yearning for deeper union will falter; without a vibrant romantic Europe, the EU will struggle to transcend its internal languor. Similarly, only the vitality of romantic Europe can ensure the continued accumulation of soft power by the European Union and kindle the promise of a more influential EU in the world. A European Union with burgeoning soft-power resources would hardly emerge as a global hegemon. However, such an EU may well be an essential purveyor of global stability as the wedge between concentrated hard-power and diffuse soft-power resources deepens.

**MITCHELL P. SMITH** is an associate professor of political science and international and area studies, as well as codirector of the European Union Center at the University of Oklahoma. His latest book is *States of Liberalization: Redefining the Public Sector in Integrated Europe* (State University of New York Press, 2005).

**Efstathios T. Fakiolas**

 **NO**

# The European Union's Problems of Cohesion

The end of the war in 1945 left Germany entirely humiliated and Britain's and France's erstwhile mastery in world politics in ruins. Yet, while throughout Europe proper democracies might be counted only on the fingers of one hand, a course of building an Iron Curtain partitioning the continent into two rival camps was set in train. This occurred because most of Europe's governments and peoples had been dragged into the vortex of the Second World War. And they had war because as Robert Schuman, one of the founding fathers of today's European Union, put it: 'Europe was not united'.

However, the experience of decline, along with the direct threat posed by the Soviet Union and its Central and East European satellites, stimulated elites in Western Europe to set off, under the guidance of the United States, a process of integration by establishing the European Coal and Steel Community in 1952 and the European Economic Community in 1958. Nearly fifty years later, the process of enlarging and deepening integration in Europe, coupled with the end of the Cold War and the collapse of the Soviet Union and Yugoslavia, has led not only to the creation of a European common market and monetary union with a single currency but also to the incorporation of eight Central and East European countries (Hungary, Czech Republic, Poland, Slovakia, Slovenia, Lithuania, Latvia, Estonia) into the European Union. Today, most of Europe's peoples (450 million out of more than 820 million) and countries (25 out of 48, including the five so-called 'Lilliputians': Andorra, Monaco, Liechtenstein, Holy See and San Marino), stretching from the Atlantic coasts of Portugal and Ireland to the outer borders of mainland Russia and Turkey, are full members of a common economic and political space, of an increasingly integrated Union marked out by inter-governmental bargains and supranational dynamics in which, closing ranks as Europeans, they enjoy security and prosperity. What is more, in their collective capacity as a Union, they are able to perform a leading, though not yet determining, role in world politics.

## Secondary Status

Notwithstanding the European Union's global economic power, to date Europe has not restored its erstwhile hegemony on the world stage. It is still being relegated to the rank of a great power plagued by 'capability-expectations gap' weaknesses. This owes much to what Henry Kissinger points out: 'United Europe will continue as a Great Power; divided into national states, it will slide into secondary status.' A case in point, in that regard, has been the US-led war in Iraq, which has left Europe bitterly divided and its prestige severely raped. Incompatible leadership and national pursuits undeniably bear much of the blame for this development. The roots of the division, one might venture, lie in what Valery Giscard d'Estaing—the influential former French President, who chaired the Convention on the Future of Europe, which on 18 July 2003 submitted to the EU member states the 'Draft Treaty Establishing a Constitution for Europe'—asserts: 'you can't build a society purely on interests; you need a sense of belonging'.

In reality, contrary to Giscard d'Estaing's view, in terms of international distinctiveness and European commonality a shared sense of belonging to Europe among EU elites and publics exists, and with every passing day it grows. But the sense of belonging to the same 'European family' is technocratic, based on functional utility and common foundations of Europe's national identities and virtues, rather than sentimental, grounded on community attachment and allegiance. This sense in itself can hardly serve as a powerful intellectual and cultural force for much closer integration, as a constructive belief tool of binding and underpinning a full-fledged Union. At the core of the problem, therefore, is the question of the conceptualisation of an evolving EU identity. Something more is needed than a mere feeling of externally and internally recognisable legal-institutional identification and political and economic togetherness.

## Loosened Ties

Indeed, the war in Iraq has resulted in loosening the ties of the European Union. Early in 2003, on the one hand, France took the lead, backed as it was by Germany and Russia, to campaign against the war and ultimately succeeded in building up a blocking coalition in the Security Council, which denied US plans the legitimacy of a UN resolution. On the other, the leaders of five member states (United Kingdom, Italy, Spain, Portugal and Denmark) and three then candidate countries (Poland, Hungary and Czech Republic) of the European Union issued a public statement

Fakiolas, Efstathios T. From *New Zealand Review*, March–April 2007, vol. 32, no. 2, pp. 19–23. Copyright © 2007 by New Zealand Institute of International Affairs. Reprinted by permission.

laying down the reasons for their determination to help Washington in its efforts to overthrow Saddam Hussein. To this was added a declaration of a similar commitment of support by governments of ten states of the former Soviet bloc, of which seven were accession or potential candidate countries (Estonia, Latvia, Lithuania, Slovakia, Slovenia, Romania, Bulgaria, Albania, Croatia, and Macedonia).

Despite the opposition of the French-German axis and Russia, the United States succeeded in forming a coalition of the willing, rallying forces from 35 countries round the flag. Of those states, six originated from the EU-15 and thirteen from the EU-25, while nine were European but not EU member states. Against France and Germany, three out of the five great powers of the EU-15, that is United Kingdom, Italy and Spain, supported the Bush administration's moves. To a certain degree, it was the decision of the eight Central and East European states out of the ten new member states of the European Union to throw in their lot with the United States that tipped the scales against those member states who were pledged to stand up to American designs. Hence, no matter how marginal in number and in terms of population and economic might, the majority of the European Union and Europe sided with Washington in waging war on Iraq. This in turn set the stage for a dramatic split between two polar opposites, the 'old' and the 'new' Europes, as Donald Rumsfeld, the then US Secretary of Defense, characteristically labelled them. Natural as it was, this division led to the paralysis of EU foreign policy, thereby preventing it from playing a constructive, if any, resolution part in the conflict.

## United Opposition

Interestingly, the division of Europe over Iraq has had to do with its governments, not with its peoples. Unlike their leadership, the overwhelming majority of European citizens were united in their peace-loving attitude. This fact was not merely under-appreciated. More important still, it eroded the European public support for the war. On 15 February 2003, massive anti-war demonstrations swept most European capitals. Of the five largest peace protests, three were held in London, Madrid and Rome, the capitals of the United States' staunchest EU allies. In light of the growing gap between European political leaderships and publics, it is not by chance that Giscard d'Estaing named this day as the birthday of European consciousness, while Romano Prodi, the then President of the European Commission, was said to have declared that the governments of the EU countries had no choice but to follow their peoples.

It is true that the Central and East European member states of the European Union have found themselves in confusion with regard to the shape the Union they have recently joined should finally take. This basically relates to a split inside the European Union itself between those who advocate that European integration should go wider without expropriating more power from national governments and those who favour much stronger federalist impulses. At the same time, the Central and East European newcomers are determined not simply to preserve national sovereignties and identities retrieved after decades of Soviet rule but also to establish their right not to be treated as second-class fellows of the club. As they are convinced that Washington has historically been the most reliable defender of liberal democracy, they deem the anti-hegemonic actions of Paris and Berlin as biased against the United States. This may result in the eruption of an irreversible rift between the European Union and the United States and, by extension, in the breakdown of the trans-Atlantic security regime. From this angle, they appear to distrust French President Jacques Chirac, who has both warned them against their quite benevolent attitude towards the United States over the use of force in Iraq and berated them for pursuing an influence that their capabilities barely warrant.

## Core Axis

All in all, the opinion widely held at that time that European countries were once more as deadly divided as they had so often been in the past is a matter of taste and ephemeral impression, not of real substance. Notwithstanding several rivalries caused by specific national interests and the circumstances of the time, the French–German axis or strategic partnership remains the cornerstone of EU politics, though without being the predominant force within the Union. Nothing proceeds in the latter without prior consultation and agreement between France and Germany. Unless these two countries reach a compromise and take the lead in advancing new policies, the European Union is most often driven into stagnation. Attempts at isolating or breaking up this partnership are doomed to failure. Thoughts of bringing London, Madrid and Rome together into an alternative leadership coalition intended to line up with the Central and East European newcomers in a US-learning 'new' European bloc have been, if not shattered with the recent fall of the pro-American Jose Maria Aznar government in Spain, relegated to the realm of planning and rhetoric.

Rather, the consensus on the need for unity and solidarity has been restored in the European Union. In December 2003, EU heads of government decided to put Giscard d'Estaing's constitutional treaty to a ratification process. This treaty was expected both to forge the commonality among the member states and to enhance European Union's international standing, democratic accountability, functional coherence and policy effectiveness. Recent resounding French and Dutch No votes have cast doubts on whether the EU Constitution has any hope of being implemented, but it is notable that among the first member states to ratify it were Lithuania, Hungary and Slovenia. The Central and East European newcomers appreciate the positive effects of accession and see themselves as integral parts of the Union. They realise they must work with the European Union, which represents a dynamic process of integration over which they have a unique privilege of say and possibility of control. It is no coincidence that Slovenia has since the first days of 2007 become the thirteenth member-state of the European Monetary Union, while Estonia, Lithuania, Poland, Hungary and the Czech Republic are intent on meeting the criteria and joining the Euro-zone by 2010 at latest.

## Full Circle

Despite controversies and numerous setbacks, to come full circle, the European Union has within the span of half a century evolved into a growing and increasingly integrated union of nation-states. A clear sign of the attractiveness of EU membership is the fact that two Southeast European countries, Bulgaria and Romania, joined the Union in January 2007, three more have been conferred the status of candidacy (Croatia, Macedonia, Turkey) and four have been formally placed as potential candidates in queue (Albania, Montenegro, Bosnia-Herzegovina and Serbia with Kosovo). Today, the European Union has first-tier great power attributes and a considerable pool of human and material resources; as well as supranational administrative capabilities, and an acquis communautaire detailed in about 80,000 pages of regulations, directives and decisions covering almost everything from monetary affairs and the environment through safety rules in workplaces to foreign, security and defence policy. Still, it aspires to carve out its own sphere of influence through particular region-building and boundary-drawing policies in Southeast Europe and the Mediterranean. Last but not least, it proves able to transform border conflicts and, thereby, provide security within and outside its region.

All this progress is boosting the dynamics of EU integration, above all mirrored in the fact that the political, economic and social future of Europe and most European states is being affected more by decisions taken in Brussels than in the capitals of the great European or non-European powers of our day. Europe's security, growth and development are all the more dependent on the fate of the European Union. The result is that the European Union's institutional and legal apparatus of ruling, along with its firm commitment to democratic decision-making procedures, confer on its citizens a broader if somewhat loose sense of belonging to a common European grouping. Put differently, EU institutions, law, norms, policies and funding mechanisms serve as a solid, functional basis for constituting and reproducing a legal, political entity and an ensuing notion of togetherness, where not only international and domestic politics and economics are closely linked to the European Union's fortunes but also the status of membership is synonymous with the privilege of being part of Europe.

## Shared Memories

The sense of belonging originates in shared historical memories of lasting national divisions and murderous wars, a heritage of common civilisation in the areas of classic music and arts and a common tradition of respect for human and democratic values. It denotes a mutual awareness of the fact that national interests are becoming all the more functionally inter-related, and that without further political and defence integration the European Union will hardly be able to play for high stakes to the benefit of its people and the world's peace. Also, it points to a widespread conviction that European distinctiveness in itself is denoted by the European Union's ethnic diversity, cultural heterogeneity and linguistic pluralism. But does this sense entail a predisposition of EU citizens to feel, think and behave as having a solely EU identity at the European level regardless of nationality, language, religious conviction, local loyalties, ideology and party affiliation?

No one doubts that, say, the Euro and European citizenship are powerful cements of the sense of belonging between EU citizens. However, few people have convincingly argued that these elements can reshape national beliefs and value orientations of each member state's society in a way that will produce and foster popular identification with the European Union. They can hardly act alone as identity symbols destined to create the self-image of a post-national community and an ideal of 'union-alist' consciousness, and thereby to inculcate in the European Union's elites and peoples the idea of European 'Union-hood'.

## National Sense

Nationhood, nationalism and statehood remain alive across Europe. For EU citizens they are the primary sources not merely of authority and legitimacy, but also of felt identity. In as much as it does little to construct a standard of European 'Union-hood' and 'Union-al-ism' and substitute them for 'nationhood' and 'national-ism', the sense of belonging is not powerful enough to keep the European Union on the path towards further integration. It proves to be a sufficient but not the necessary cement of an evolving EU identity.

The problem is that it is not clear yet what the European Union means to its leadership and peoples. Despite the stunning success of its expansion to the east, the Union still needs to discover its purpose and inject new breath to the European project of integration. Does the European Union aim at building an inter-governmental, a supranational or a post-national Union? The mistake that some integrationists often commit is to identify the future of the European Union exclusively with the creation of a traditional federal state. Having in mind the case of the United States, they suggest that the EU countries should dissolve their national structures and build federal bodies. Yet they overlook the fact that the United States, or Italy and Germany, were formed through violence or civil strife, and that in general the federal state is a product of the historical development of the nation state, and reflects nothing less than a different conception of national identity, statehood and sovereignty.

## Peaceful Process

By contrast, the process of EU integration can in no way fall into line with a linear or pre-ordained course towards taking the shape and substance of a full-fledged European federation. Rather, it has resulted in the construction of several post-state institutions through the transfer of authority from the national to the supranational level, but without eliminating the legacy of the nation state's machinery of ruling and legitimacy at all. More important still, EU integration has been launched and so far carried on by peaceful means and mutually beneficial compromises, not through war and coercion. In effect, EU identity could be normally conceived as 'union-al' rather than purely inter-governmental or supranational. It is not merely intertwined with such commonly held values in Europe as liberty, the rule of law, justice, respect for human rights, tolerance, moderation and non-discrimination as to sex, race, religion and nationality. It is also tied to the European Union's integration dialectic of inter-governmentalism and supranationalism. Therefore, EU leadership and citizens need to look for their felt identity in European 'Union-hood' and 'Union-al-ism'.

What is badly lacking, in short, is a predominant frame of reference for the Union. It is this shortage that pushes European citizens apart. Ideally, the frame could be made of a legitimising ideology, a discourse, symbols and images, all designed to establish the historical time, depict the political and cultural space of the Union and articulate a vision of common mission. This is the necessary cement for the European Union's elites to tie its institutions together with its citizens into an integrated 'union-hood'. But that frame is striking by its absence. Alongside it goes the lack of a resolute leadership able to devise a 'union-ally' tailor-made model of democratic governance. With all those elements of identity construction missing, EU public opinion is unlikely to be swayed. That is the primary lesson to learn from the rejection of the EU Constitution in France and the Netherlands. The European Union must win the hearts and minds of its peoples. On that count, it displays a poor record. This is the Achilles heel of European integration. The idea of European 'Unionhood' and 'Union-al-ism' still remains to be constructed and deployed. This is the critical arena in which the future of the European Union will be decided in its long march towards fuller union.

---

**EFSTATHIOS T. FAKIOLAS**, a graduate of the department of war studies, King's College, London, is strategy and Southeast European affairs analyst in the Department of Strategic Planning, ATE bank (Agricultural Bank of Greece).

# EXPLORING THE ISSUE

## Is the Influence of the European Union in World Affairs Increasing?

## Critical Thinking and Reflection

1. How much of a federation should the European Union be: Will there ever be a United States of Europe? Should there be? Critically research and debate.
2. How far geographically can the European Union extend? If Turkey joins the EU, the Union will spread into Asia. Critically analyze and discuss.
3. Critically evaluate the claim of Professor Mitchell P. Smith that the European Union excels in the use of soft power to achieve desired outcomes at minimal cost.
4. Critically evaluate the claim of Efstathios T. Fakiolas that Europe's failure to achieve "Unionhood" seriously hampers its effectiveness in the global economy.
5. Do you agree or disagree with Robert Kagan's contention that Europe has the luxury of its peaceloving, environmentally conscious society only because the United States and its military might are standing watch over the world? Critically analyze this claim and debate it.
6. What effect will the financial downturn that began in 2008 have on fiscally weaker nations in the European Union? Speculate on Greece, Portugal, Spain, Italy, or Ireland.
7. What will happen if Greece secedes from the European Union? Critically discuss.

## Is There Common Ground?

The most urgent question about the European Union is whether the worldwide financial crisis will create greater unity within the European Union or whether the need to "bail out" debt-ridden members will cause the collapse of the European Union. Germany, with its strong economy and well-capitalized central bank, is becoming banker to the EU.

*Question:* How long can this continue?

## Create Central

www.mhhe.com/createcentral

## Additional Resources

*Ever Closer Union: An Introduction to European Integration*, 3rd ed., by Desmond Dinan (Lynne Rienner, 2005), offers a neutral and balanced view of the European Union that includes an excellent introduction, a map and list of abbreviations and acronyms, plus three sections of text: History, Institutions, and Policies. A general introduction may be found in the American Chamber of Commerce's *The EU Made Simple* (Amcham EU, Brussels, 2006). Every nation gets a thumbnail profile and there is a concise Who's Who in the EU. See *Statistical Yearbook of the EU Region* (available for free download at: http://ec.europa.eu) and Captain Euro at: www.captaineuro.com (for kids). Adam Andros, only child of a European ambassador and a professor of paleontology took on the identity of Captain Euro, after an event perpetrated by Dr. D. Vider.

## Internet Reference . . .

**Europa: The Official Website of the European Union**

The homepage contains portals in many languages. After clicking on the English portal, one finds history, policy areas, health care, work and business, consumer rights, blogs, video links, official documents, legislation and treaties, and an extensive archive. Quick links include quizzes, games, and competitions for kids.

**http://europa.eu/index_en.htm**

Selected, Edited, and with Issue Framing Material by:
Helen Buss Mitchell, *Howard Community College*
and
Joseph R. Mitchell, *Howard Community College*

# ISSUE

# Is India's Secular Democracy Severely Threatened by Religious Nationalism?

**YES: Sharif Shuja,** from "Indian Secularism: Image and Reality," *Contemporary Review* (July 2005)

**NO: Martha C. Nussbaum,** from "Fears for Democracy in India," *The Chronicle of Higher Education* (May 18, 2007)

| Learning Outcomes |
| --- |
| **After reading this issue you should be able to:** |
| • Define and describe "secular democracy." |
| • Define and describe "Hindutva." |
| • Understand the religious significance of Ayodhya, for Hindus and for Muslims. |
| • Explain the goals of the Bharatiya Janata Party (BJP). |

## ISSUE SUMMARY

**YES:** Sharif Shuja, research associate in the Global Terrorism Research Unit at Monash University in Australia, asserts that the goal of the Hindu Nationalist Party (BJP) to convert India into a Hindu nation threatens both the secular democracy and the unity of India itself.

**NO:** Professor in the philosophy department, law school, divinity school, and the college at the University of Chicago, Martha C. Nussbaum argues that, despite internal divisions, India's institutional and legal structure functioned well even after the Ayodhya riots, and within 2 years free national elections made a Sikh prime minister.

India, a nation of a billion people and the world's largest democracy, is also the second largest Muslim nation. Currently more Muslims live in India than in all the Middle Eastern countries combined. They constitute 12–15 percent of the population. Hindus are more than 80 percent and there are single-digit percentages of Christians, Buddhists, Jains, Sikhs, and others. Beginning in 1940, the Muslim League, concerned about how tolerant a majority-Hindu free India would be, demanded a separate homeland for Muslims. As a result of the inability of Hindus and Muslims to find common ground, India was partitioned when it achieved independence from Great Britain in 1947. The new state of Pakistan that was created flirted briefly with secularism but quickly declared itself an Islamic Republic.

Free India incorporated secular tenets into both its principles and practices of governing. Jawaharlal Nehru, India's first prime minister, was a secular socialist and a religious agnostic. However, his mentor, Mohandas Gandhi, was religious. So, the posture of the new government became one of neutrality toward religion (regarding it as a private affair) and tolerance for all faiths. The Indian National Congress, later and currently the Congress Party, assumed leadership in independent India by proclaiming its faith in secularism and its support for politics free of religion.

Though the constitution avoided the words "secular" and "secularism," it guaranteed all citizens equality before the law, equal opportunity in public employment, and freedom of conscience, as well as the freedoms to profess, practice, and promulgate any religion. Unlike the Middle Eastern monotheisms—Judaism, Christianity, and Islam—Hinduism has no unitary administrative structure, no central temple, and no universally acknowledged, authoritative, scriptural canon. So, for more than 30 years, Hindus seemed content to be in the majority and religious minorities were not unduly threatened.

All of this began to change during the 1980s and 1990s, as a dormant thread of Hindu exceptionalism was inflamed by Muslim and Sikh assertions of greater independence. Questions were raised: Was Hinduism one religion among many or was it a way of life? And, who is a Hindu? Did one give up one's caste position or forfeit eligibility for government-run affirmative action programs designed to help disadvantaged and lower caste citizens by converting to Buddhism, Christianity, or Islam?

Hindutva, a radical ideological assertion of Hindu uniqueness, unity, and pride, was buttressed by a paramilitary national volunteers' association, the RSS (Rashtriya Swayamsevak Sang). And, in 1992, religious tensions came to a boil in Ayodhya, the site of a sixteenth-century mosque built by the Mughal Emperor Babar. Though historians are not in agreement, some claimed that the mosque had been built where a temple to the god Ram, incarnation of the god Vishnu, had once stood and where Hindus believe the god Ram was born. Some 200,000 militants used sledgehammers to destroy the mosque, and in the aftermath, nearly 1,500 people (mostly Muslims) were killed. There were claims that the (mostly Hindu) police looked the other way.

By 1998, the political wing of religious nationalism had won a majority of seats in the parliament. Between 1998 and 2004, India was ruled by the Bharatiya Janata Party (BJP), which overturned the constitutional prohibition on religious instruction in public schools and rewrote the educational curriculum to assert a thousand-year history of India as a cultural and religious unity. Hinduism was to be the basic identity of all Indians, Hindu and non-Hindu alike, and Hindu gods and heroes were, similarly, to dominate Indian education and popular culture. Prime Minister Atal Bihari Vajpayee made a lot of people nervous when he declared India's nuclear capability in 1998.

India's current prime minister, Manmohan Singh, is a Sikh. Trained as an economist, he served as finance minister from 1991 to 1996 and is generally credited with saving India's economy by transforming it from socialism to capitalism and bringing it into the free market world of technological sophistication. When the Congress Party regained a parliamentary majority in 2004, Sonia Gandhi (Italian-born widow of Indira Gandhi's son Rajiv), the titular head of the Congress Party in Opposition, asked Dr. Singh to take over as prime minister. Dr. Singh was reelected in 2009 and the Singhs were guests of President and Mrs. Obama, at their first state dinner in November 2009. In September 2010, a three-judge court in Uttar Pradesh,

in a historic ruling, granted part of the land at Ayodhya to Hindus and another part to Muslims.

British rule in India gradually transferred loyalty to family, clan, and religion into a sense of common identity that was achieved by centralizing government, public education, and a network of railroads. Under the British Raj, Indians of all castes, classes, and religions throughout the vast subcontinent were encouraged to think of themselves as one nation. For a look at the last days of the Raj, see Paul Scott's *The Jewel in the Crown*, Book I of the Raj Quartet series (University of Chicago Press, 1966). Granada Television in Great Britain also produced a stunning television series, *The Jewel in the Crown* (1984), which is still available on DVD.

Independence crystallized the uneasiness of religious minorities. Many Muslims stayed in the newly created Pakistan, while others remained in India. The migration of millions of Hindus and Muslims across newly created borders is captured in Bapsi Sidhwa's novel, *Cracking India*. Virtually all the world's religions are present in modern India. The 17 annual holidays include Christmas, Easter (Christian), Eid, Muharram (Muslim Holy Days), Divali (Hindu), and the birthdays of the Buddha, Mahavira (founder of Jainism), Nanak (First Guru of Sikhism), and Muhammad (Prophet of Islam).

For a look at the many religions that have found a foothold in India, Fred Clothey's *Religion in India: A Historical Introduction* (Routledge, 2006) takes the reader on a journey from the Indo-European migration to the modern period. As India is home to all the major religions, it is also "host to every type of fanatic." This is the thesis of *Holy Warriors: A Journey into the Heart of Indian Fundamentalism* by Edna Fernandes, a British-Indian reporter for the *Financial Times*. Fernandes gives us the voices of Islamic, Christian, Sikh, and Hindu fundamentalism—each clinging to its own historical grievances and each seeking its sense of identity in a glorious past, now lost.

In the YES selection from Sharif Shuja, we see the excesses of the BJP and Hindu nationalism detailed. The NO selection from Martha Nussbaum looks to India's long history for reassurance that, despite internal tensions, a commitment to tolerance and pluralism will reassert itself.

# YES ↵

**Sharif Shuja**

## Indian Secularism: Image and Reality

In recent years, religious militancy and communal strife have become the biggest danger to India's secular fabric. Had the Bharatiya Janata Party (BJP) won last year's election, power would probably have gradually shifted into the hands of Hindutva fanatics, who were careful to play down the communal card. The term 'Hindutva' is derived from the two terms *Hindu Tattva,* which literally mean Hindu Principles, aimed at promoting Hindu unity. But there is a distinction between Hinduism and Hindutva. Such a distinction is important because the latter, Hindutva, has a history of blood letting—from the murder of Mahatma Gandhi (killed by a Hindutva ideologue, Nathuram Godse) to the more than 20,000 lives claimed in communal violence in India since 1950.

Hindutva is a nationalist ideology, based on a modern-day version of centralised intolerant Hinduism. Such a centralised and chauvinistic Hinduism—Hindutva—has been brought to the fore-front today by a group of political organisations called the 'Sangh Parivar' (Sangh family)—consisting of the Rashtriya Swayamsevak Sangh (RSS), the Bharatiya Janata Party (BJP), the Vishwa Hindu Parishad (VHP) and the Shiv Sena (the fascist front). Hindutva did not go down well with the voters in the 2004 Indian elections. Explanations for the BJP debacle vary; but one thing is clear—its effort to mould a national ethos that would reflect the ideology of Hindutva has failed miserably.

A defining element of Indian politics since independence has been a commitment to secularism. India, although predominantly Hindu, is a secular state, but it has to deal with the 'problem of Islam' and the Muslims. Muslims in India are persecuted every now and then. The cultural clash is not between the traditional, rural Hindus and Muslims, but the modern, urban ones. The 'modern Hindu' likes to distinguish himself from the Muslim, who is often blamed, along with his heritage and history, for being a problem in society. Such a trend is more visible in the conservative factions of Hindu society than among followers of the BJP. The BJP is a nationalist party which equates Indian national identity with Hindu religious identity. The country's radical nationalists view the secular political system as a threat to Hindu identity, largely because of the power it allows to India's 140 million Muslims. Weakening, or even abolishing, the secular state has therefore become part of the radical nationalist agenda.

This may force Indian Muslims—traditionally moderate and supportive of the secular state, even on the sensitive matter of Kashmir—to shift their allegiance from the state to some sort of large international Islamic movement, as many Muslims have done in Indonesia, Malaysia, and Singapore. Such a radicalisation of religious identities is a matter of serious concern in a nation of a billion people that possesses a nuclear arsenal and has had troubled relations with its populous and nuclear-armed Muslim neighbour, Pakistan.

Radical Hindu nationalism is a dominant form in mainstream Indian politics. The BJP is a nationalist party whose goal is to convert India into a Hindu nation. The Hindus are profoundly religious, but this religiosity has become more active and aggressive with the injection of nationalism. The ideology of the BJP threatens not only democracy but the unity of India itself. Its most violent elements were responsible for destroying the historic 430-year-old Babri mosque in the small city of Ayodhya in the northern Indian state of Uttar Pradesh. On December 6, 1992, a mob of 300,000 fanatics, brought together by the BJP and other extreme right-wing groups, demolished the mosque and promptly built a shrine dedicated to Rama. Hindus believed the site to be the birthplace of Ram, an incarnation of the god Vishnu. But the Muslim place of worship was a nationally recognised symbol of the secularism guaranteed by India's democratic constitution. The result was a series of riots in which more than 1,500 people, largely Muslims, died.

Similarly the BJP turned a blind eye to attacks on the Gujarat Muslim minority that killed about 2,000 people in March 2002. An Indian tribunal investigating the massacres found that Hindu nationalist groups had methodically targeted Muslim homes and shops. Local and national security forces failed to respond adequately to the crisis as it unfolded. Initially the state police did not intervene, and the central government only belatedly sent troops to Gujarat to restore order.

On the whole, the Gujarat episode left Indian Muslims feeling neglected by the government. It also destabilised the Vajpayee-led coalition government whose hard-line policies became increasingly unpopular with the 21 coalition partners, the media and civil organisations. The communal riots in Gujarat alone cost the nation millions of dollars not only in property damage, but also in lost productive time (grief, injury and stress causing underproduction), recovery costs (treatment, loss

Shuja, Sharif. From *Contemporary Review,* July 2005. Copyright © 2005 by Contemporary Review Company Limited. Reprinted by permission.

of experience, retraining of new incumbents) and other costs (legal, administrative and social). It was a horrendous crime committed on a mass scale. Its perpetrators must be punished because crimes unpunished generate more criminals.

The ascendancy of the Hindutva ideology and of BJP politics is partly attributable to the upward mobility of the middle-class, and to an extent, the property-owning middle-castes. Its ascendancy has led to a burgeoning middle-class with rising consumption, which is seriously alienated from the people, and secondarily, to a business elite that is highly predatory. This middle-class ascendancy occurred in particular circumstances—the rise of ethnic-religious identity politics in India's neighbourhood, and intensified India-Pakistan rivalry. Therefore, it came with a heavy baggage of chauvinist-nationalism and militarism. The BJP was the greatest beneficiary of this nationalism.

Militants associated with the larger Hindu movement, such as the *Rashtriya Swayamsevak Sangh* (RSS), are intolerant of members of lower castes and non-Hindus. They are opposed to Indian secularism and make no secret of wanting a common culture called Hindutva that all Indians, whatever their religion or background, would be required to accept. To appease them, the BJP-led government changed text books and courses in schools and colleges to emphasise the past glories of Hinduism.

The former BJP-led government made the writing of history a high-profile political issue. The BJP's initiative was to change history. Hence, the paradigm was relentlessly shifted from the secular to the communal—Murli Manohar Joshi being the chief architect of the enterprise. Murli was Minister for Human Resources and Development. One of his main acts was to reconstitute the Indian Council of Historical Research (ICHR), filling it with Sangh sympathisers. Secondly, the Council was required to review documents from the national archives for the years running up to 1947. Among the documents suppressed by the ICHR were statements by Hindu nationalists indicating ambivalence in their support for the freedom movement—a part of the historical record that might undermine the Sangh's patriotic credentials.

This attack is essentially rooted in a fear of history, and that fear arises from the fact that these volumes present a documentary record which cannot be denied. In 2000, Joshi's ministry issued a new National Curriculum Framework for School Education calling for greater emphasis on ancient India's achievements and 'sustaining and emphasising the indigenous knowledge ingrained in the Indian tradition'.

Following guidance from Joshi's ministry the National Council for Educational Research and Training (NCERT) ordered deletions in a number of history text books. The deleted passages included references to beef-eating among ancient Indians, the textual evolution over centuries of Sanskrit epics, the *Mahabharata* and the *Ramayana*, Brahmin antipathy to the Buddhist king, Asoka, and the origins and development of caste society.

This was followed by the commissioning, and in 2002 the publication, of a new range of history texts. To the dismay of many in the profession, these volumes were littered with errors and infused with a strong Hindutva slant. A report on the textbooks issued by the Indian History Congress, South Asia's largest forum of professional historians, catalogues hundreds of factual errors and examples of distortion.

The new texts adhere to the Hindutva insistence that the Aryans (and by implication their upper-caste Hindu descendants) were the original Indians and that their Vedic culture was entirely indigenous to India. The text equates the Indus Valley or Harappan civilisation with the Vedic—a claim which is strongly contested by most scholars in the field . Ancient India is also described as the original home of mathematics, astronomy and medicine.

On the subject of the medieval period , the new text emphasises the destruction of temples by Muslim rulers, but largely omits the atrocities committed by Hindu rulers. Any regime headed by Muslims is portrayed as an example of 'foreign domination'. The mutual influence of Hindu and Islamic art and thought is denied. In the account of the Mughal Emperor Akbar, there is no mention of his liberal social policies, his prohibition of the slave trade and of involuntary *sati* (widow burning). Similarly, when it comes to the modern era, the new text praises the leaders of the Hindu Mahasabha—predecessors of the BJP—but presents the resolutely secular Nehru in an unfavourable light. The great Indian social reform movements that challenged the status of women and lower-caste people are not mentioned, nor is the fact that Nathuram Godse. Gandhi's assassin, was an RSS associate.

Is it the function of history to ignore all unpleasant facts and become a collection of fables or happy tales? Why did the BJP government want to rewrite history? 'History of a particular kind is vital for the Sangh Parivar to consolidate its claim to be the sole spokesman of the Hindus, who have to be convinced that their interests and emotions are, and have always been, unitary and inevitably opposed to those of Muslims or Christians, regardless of differences of caste, gender, class, immense regional variation', said Sumit Sarkar, a former professor of history at Delhi University, 'and BJP'S doctoring of history is an attempt to turn the clock back and if possible do away with history altogether'.

In January 2004, mobs wreaked havoc at Pune's Bhandarkar Oriental Research Institute because a scholar working there had been acknowledged in a book (*Shivaji: Hindu King in Islamic India*) by James W. Laine, an American academic who allegedly defamed their hero, Shivaji, the seventeenth-century warrior-king who took on the Mughal empire and founded the Maratha Confederacy.

The book is a study of the legends and traditions surrounding the preeminent Maratha hero. The book caused outrage among Hindu nationalists and was later banned by the Maharashtra state government. While the Pune incident seems to have been prompted by a local caste-based group, its context is a national one—a public battle over the interpretation of Indian history and the historical method itself. This happened during the BJP-led government.

It is noted that, though the BJP suffered an unexpected defeat in the 2004 elections, they were quick to mount a counter-offensive against the victor, the Italian-born Congress leader Sonia Gandhi, claiming that her 'foreign origins' made her unacceptable as India's prime minister. The foundations for this aggressive campaign had been well laid by the Sangh's version of Indian history, in which Hindutva definitions of indigenous and alien were promoted as absolute.

Many conservatives, especially BJP sympathisers, believe Indian Muslims are backward, illiterate, overly religious, bigoted and resistant to change, especially in matters of dress, customs, and personal laws. in their view, Muslims are somewhat inferior, under-socialised human beings who deserve pity or sympathy, not equal treatment or respect. The Hindu-nationalist as well as the middleclass pseudo-liberal is deeply uncomfortable with the modern, liberal, educated, well-informed Muslim who has an open mind and cosmopolitan outlook. The discomfort is all the greater if the person is a woman.

Sania Mirza represents all of those modern attributes. The eighteen-year-old tennis player became well known when she entered the third round of the Australian Open but went down to Serena Williams. She is an Indian equivalent of Tiger Woods. Mohammed Azharuddin, Irfan Pathan, Mohammed Kaif and Zaheer Khan are too well-known in cricket to need recounting. Remarkably, to be recognised, these stars don't have to hide their Muslim religion or wear their patriotism on their sleeve.

Similarly, in the field of entertainment, the Three Khans (Shah Rukh Khan, Salman Khan, Amir Khan) hold unchallenged sway over Bollywood. Other Muslims have distinguished themselves in this field: Shabana Azmi, Tabu, Saif Alikhan, Saeed Mirza and Javed Akhtar. In modern art, it is impossible to ignore the pivotal importance of M.F. Hussain, S.H. Raza and Ghulam Muhammed Sheikh. In business, the richest Indian is Azim Premji, chairman of Wipro Ltd, who happens to be a Muslim.

The list can be greatly expanded. The point is simple. A significant modern Muslim intelligentsia has crystallised in varying fields, including academics (examples, Irfan Habib, Mushirul Hasan), literature and journalism (Faiz Ahmed Faiz, Kaifi Azmi, M.J. Akbar). 'This intelligentsia is qualitatively different from the old Muslim aristocracy. It is an accomplished group of self-made liberal middle-class professionals with a secular and universalist outlook. These are not Muslim intellectuals, as such. They are intellectuals first, Muslims second, by birth', said Praful Bidwai, a prominent Indian commentator, 'and the winds of modernisation and secularisation are sweeping through the larger Indian Muslim community to a far greater extent than is recognised'.

There is a lesson here for the larger society. It should respect and strengthen the pro-reform trend, not just among Muslim high achievers and stars, but among ordinary Muslims too. The future of India lies in modernisation, and reform based on the values of the Enlightenment. These values should be promoted in personal as well as public life. Only thus can India become tolerant of, and comfortable with, differences—a society that's truly pluralist and secular.

The new United Progressive Alliance (UPA) government's priority is to uphold and strengthen the secular principles embodied in the Indian Constitution. As India has always been a multicultural, multi-ethnic, multi-religious society, secular government is not an option but an absolute necessity. Only secularism, with its emphasis on equality and universal citizenship rights, can build a minimally civilised, inclusive, democratic society and ensure equal rights for all citizens, regardless of religion, ethnicity or culture. Secularism must be practised and advocated vigorously.

**SHARIF SHUJA** is an adjunct assistant professor of international relations at Bond University, Australia and research associate in the Global Terrorism Unit at Monash University, Australia. He has contributed numerous articles to professional journals that specialize in Asian affairs.

**Martha C. Nussbaum**

# Fears for Democracy in India

On February 27, 2002, the Sabarmati express train arrived in the station of Godhra, in the state of Gujarat, bearing a large group of Hindu pilgrims who were returning from a trip to the purported birthplace of the god Rama at Ayodhya (where, some years earlier, angry Hindu mobs had destroyed the Babri mosque, which they claimed was on top of the remains of Rama's birthplace). The pilgrimage, like many others in recent times, aimed at forcibly constructing a temple over the disputed site, and the mood of the returning passengers, frustrated in their aims by the government and the courts, was angrily emotional. When the train stopped at the station, the Hindu passengers got into arguments with Muslim passengers and vendors. At least one Muslim vendor was beaten up when he refused to say Jai Sri Ram ("Hail Rama"). As the train left the station, stones were thrown at it, apparently by Muslims.

Fifteen minutes later, one car of the train erupted in flames. Fifty-eight men, women, and children died in the fire. Most of the dead were Hindus. Because the area adjacent to the tracks was made up of Muslim dwellings, and because a Muslim mob had gathered in the region to protest the treatment of Muslims on the train platform, blame was immediately put on Muslims. Many people were arrested, and some of those are still in detention without charge—despite the fact that two independent inquiries have established through careful sifting of the forensic evidence that the fire was most probably a tragic accident, caused by combustion from cook stoves carried on by the passengers and stored under the seats of the train.

In the days that followed the incident, wave upon wave of violence swept through the state. The attackers were Hindus, many of them highly politicized, shouting slogans of the Hindu right, along with "Kill! Destroy!" and "Slaughter!" There is copious evidence that the violent retaliation was planned before the precipitating event by Hindu extremist organizations that had been waiting for an occasion. No one was spared: Young children were thrown into fires along with their families, fetuses ripped from the bellies of pregnant women. Particularly striking was the number of women who were raped, mutilated, in some cases tortured with large metal objects, and then set on fire. Over the course of several weeks, about 2,000 Muslims were killed.

Most alarming was the total breakdown in the rule of law—not only at the local level but also at that of the state and national governments. Police were ordered not to stop the violence. Some egged it on. Gujarat's chief minister, Narendra Modi, rationalized and even encouraged the murders. He was later re-elected on a platform that focused on religious hatred. Meanwhile the national government showed a culpable indifference. Prime Minister Atal Behari Vajpayee suggested that religious riots were inevitable wherever Muslims lived alongside Hindus, and that troublemaking Muslims were to blame.

While Americans have focused on President Bush's "war on terror," Iraq, and the Middle East, democracy has been under siege in another part of the world. India—the most populous of all democracies and a country who's Constitution protects human rights even more comprehensively than our own—has been in crisis. Until the spring of 2004, its parliamentary government was increasingly controlled by right-wing Hindu extremists who condoned and in some cases actively supported violence against minority groups, especially Muslims.

What has been happening in India is a serious threat to the future of democracy in the world. The fact that it has yet to make it onto the radar screen of most Americans is evidence of the way in which terrorism and the war on Iraq have distracted us from events and issues of fundamental significance. If we really want to understand the impact of religious nationalism on democratic values, India currently provides a deeply troubling example, and one without which any understanding of the more general phenomenon is dangerously incomplete. It also provides an example of how democracy can survive the assault of religious extremism.

In May 2004, the voters of India went to the polls in large numbers. Contrary to all predictions, they gave the Hindu right a resounding defeat. Many right-wing political groups and the social organizations allied with them remain extremely powerful, however. The rule of law and democracy has shown impressive strength and resilience, but the future is unclear.

The case of Gujarat is a lens through which to conduct a critical examination of the influential thesis of the "clash of civilizations," made famous by the political scientist Samuel P. Huntington. His picture of the world as riven between democratic Western values and an aggressive Muslim monolith does nothing to help us understand today's India, where, I shall argue, the violent values of the Hindu right are imports from European fascism of the 1930s, and where the third-largest Muslim population in the world lives as peaceful democratic citizens, despite severe poverty and other inequalities.

The real "clash of civilizations" is not between "Islam" and "the West," but instead within virtually all modern nations—between people who are prepared to live on terms of equal respect with others who are different, and those who seek the protection of homogeneity and the domination of a single "pure" religious and ethnic tradition. At a deeper level, as Gandhi claimed, it is a clash within the individual self, between the urge to dominate and defile the other and a willingness to live respectfully on terms of compassion and equality, with all the vulnerability that such a life entails.

This argument about India suggests a way to see America, which is also torn between two different pictures of itself. One shows the country as good and pure, its enemies as an external "axis of evil." The other picture, the fruit of internal self-criticism, shows America as complex and flawed, torn between forces bent on control and hierarchy and forces that promote democratic equality. At what I've called the Gandhian level, the argument about India shows Americans to themselves as individuals, each of whom is capable of both respect and aggression, both democratic mutuality and anxious domination. Americans have a great deal to gain by learning more about India and pondering the ideas of some of her most significant political thinkers, such as Sir Rabindranath Tagore and Mohandas Gandhi, whose ruminations about nationalism and the roots of violence are intensely pertinent to today's conflicts.

According to the Huntington thesis, each "civilization" has its own distinctive view of life, and Hinduism counts as a distinct "civilization." If we investigate the history of the Hindu right, however, we will see a very different story. Traditional Hinduism was decentralized, plural, and highly tolerant, so much so that the vision of a unitary, "pure" Hinduism that could provide the new nation, following independence from Britain in 1947, with an aggressive ideology of homogeneity could not be found in India: The founders of the Hindu right had to import it from Europe.

The Hindu right's view of history is a simple one. Like all simple tales, it is largely a fabrication, but its importance to the movement may be seen by the intensity with which its members go after scholars who present a more nuanced and accurate view: not only by strident public critiques, but by organized campaigns of threat and intimidation, culminating in some cases in physical violence. Here's how the story goes:

Once there lived in the Indus Valley a pure and peaceful people. They spoke Vedic Sanskrit, the language of the gods. They had a rich material culture and a peaceful temper, although they were prepared for war. Their realm was vast, stretching from Kashmir in the north to Sri Lanka (Ceylon) in the south. And yet they saw unity and solidarity in their shared ways of life, calling themselves Hindus and their land Hindustan. No class divisions troubled them, nor was caste a painful source of division. The condition of women was excellent.

That peaceful condition went on for centuries. Although from time to time marauders made their appearance (for example, the Huns), they were quickly dispatched. Suddenly, rudely, unprovoked, invading Muslims put an end to all that. Early in the 16th century, Babur, founder of the Mughal dynasty, swept through the north of Hindustan, vandalizing Hindu temples, stealing sacred objects, building mosques over temple ruins. For 200 years, Hindus lived at the mercy of the marauders, until the Maharashtrian hero Shivaji rose up and restored the Hindu kingdom. His success was all too brief. Soon the British took up where Babur and his progeny had left off, imposing tyranny upon Hindustan and her people. They can recover their pride only by concerted aggression against alien elements in their midst.

What is wrong with that picture? Well, for a start, the people who spoke Sanskrit almost certainly migrated into the subcontinent from outside, finding indigenous people there, probably the ancestors of the Dravidian peoples of South India. Hindus are no more indigenous than Muslims. Second, it leaves out problems in Hindu society: the problem of caste, which both Gandhi and Tagore took to be the central social issue facing India, and obvious problems of class and gender inequality. (When historians point to evidence of these things, the Hindu right calls them Marxists, as if that, by itself, invalidated their arguments.) Third, it leaves out the tremendous regional differences within Hinduism, and hostilities and aggressions sometimes associated with those. Fourth, it omits the evidence of peaceful coexistence and syncretism between Hindus and Muslims for a good deal of the Mughal Empire, including the well-known policies of religious pluralism of Akbar (1542–1605).

In the Hindu-right version of history, a persistent theme is that of humiliated masculinity: Hindus have been subordinate for centuries, and their masculinity insulted, in part because they have not been aggressive and violent enough. The two leading ideologues of the Hindu right responded to the call for a warlike Hindu masculinity in different ways. V.D. Savarkar (1883–1966) was a freedom fighter who spent years in a British prison in the Andaman Islands, and who may have been a co-conspirator in the assassination of Gandhi. M.S. Golwalkar (1906–73), a gurulike figure who was not involved in the independence struggle, quietly helped build up the organization known as RSS (Rashtriya Swayamsevak Sangh, or National Volunteers Association), now the leading social organization of the Hindu right. Savarkar's "Hindutva: Who Is a Hindu?" first published in 1923, undertook to define the essence of Hinduness for the new nation; his definition was exclusionary, emphasizing cultural homogeneity and the need to use force to ensure the supremacy of Hindus.

Golwalkar's *We, or Our Nationhood Defined* was published in 1939. Writing during the independence struggle, Golwalkar saw his task as describing the unity of the new nation. To do that, he looked to Western political theory, and particularly to Germany, where what he called "race pride" helped bring "under one sway the whole of the territory" that was originally held by the Germani. By purging itself of Jews, he wrote, "Germany has also shown how well nigh impossible it is for Races and cultures, having differences going to the root, to be assimilated into one united whole, a good lesson for us in Hindusthan to learn and profit by."

In the end, Golwalkar's vision of national unity was not exactly that of Nazi Germany. He was not very concerned with purity of blood, but rather with whether Muslim and Christian groups were willing to "abandon their differences, and completely merge themselves in the National Race." He was firmly against the civic equality of any people who retained their religious and ethnic distinctiveness.

At the time of independence, such ideas of Hindu supremacy did not prevail. Nehru and Gandhi insisted not only on equal rights for all citizens, but also on stringent protections for religious freedom of expression in the new Constitution. Gandhi always pointedly included Muslims at the very heart of his movement. He felt that respect for human equality lay at the heart of all genuine religions, and provided Hindus with strong reasons both for repudiating the caste hierarchy and for seeking relationships of respect and harmony with Christians and Muslims. A devout Muslim, Maulana Abdul Kalam Azad, was one of his and Nehru's most trusted advisers, and it was to him that Gandhi turned to accept food when he broke his fast unto death, a very pointed assault on sectarian ideas of purity and pollution. Gandhi's pluralistic ideas, however, were always contested.

On January 30, 1948, Gandhi was shot at point-blank range by Nathuram Godse, a member of the Hindu political party Mahasabha and former member of the RSS, who had long had a close, reverential relationship with Savarkar. At his sentencing on November 8, 1949, Godse read a book-length statement of self-explanation. Although it was not permitted publication at the time, it gradually leaked out. Today it is widely available on the Internet, where Godse is revered as a hero on Hindu-right Web sites.

Godse's self-justification, like the historical accounts of both Savarkar and Golwalkar, saw contemporary events against the backdrop of centuries of "Muslim tyranny" in India, punctuated by the heroic resistance of Shivaji in the 18th century. Like Savarkar, Godse described his goal as that of creating a strong, proud India that could throw off the centuries of domination. He was appalled by Gandhi's rejection of the warlike heroes of classical Hindu epics and his inclusion of Muslims as full equals in the new nation, and argued that Gandhi exposed Indians to subordination and humiliation. Nehru believed that the murder of Gandhi was part of a "fairly widespread conspiracy" on the part of the Hindu right to seize power; he saw the situation as analogous to that in Europe on the eve of the

fascist takeovers. And he believed that the RSS was the power behind this conspiracy.

Fast-forward now to recent years. Although illegal for a time, the RSS eventually re-emerged and quietly went to work building a vast social network, consisting largely of groups for young boyscalled shakha, or "branches"which, through clever use of games and songs, indoctrinate the young into the confrontational and Hindu-supremacist ideology of the organization. The idea of total obedience and the abnegation of critical faculties is at the core of the solidaristic movement. Each day, as members raise the saffron flag of the warlike hero Shivaji, which the movement prefers to the tricolor flag of the Indian nation (with its Buddhist wheel of law reminding citizens of the emperor Ashoka's devotion to religious toleration), they recite a pledge that begins: "I take the oath that I will always protect the purity of Hindu religion, and the purity of Hindu culture, for the supreme progress of the Hindu nation." The organization also makes clever use of modern media: A nationally televised serial version of the classic epic Ramayana in the late 1980s fascinated viewers all over India with its concocted tale of a unitary Hinduism dedicated to the single-minded worship of the god Rama. In 1992 Hindu mobs, with the evident connivance of the modern political wing of the RSS, the party known as the BJP (Bharatiya Janata Party, or National People's Party), destroyed a mosque in the city of Ayodhya that they say covers the remains of a Hindu temple marking Rama's birthplace.

Politically, the BJP began to gather strength in the late 1980s, drawing on widespread public dissatisfaction with the economic policies of the post-Nehru Congress Party (although it was actually Congress, under Rajiv Gandhi, that began economic reforms), and playing, always, the cards of hatred and fear. It was during its ascendancy, in a coalition government that prevented it from carrying out all its goals, that the destruction of the Ayodyha mosque took place. The violence in Gujarat was the culmination of a series of increasingly angry pilgrimages to the Ayodyha site, where the Hindu right has attempted to construct a Hindu temple over the ruins, but has been frustrated by the courts. Although the elections of 2004 gave a negative verdict on the BJP government, it remains the major opposition party and controls governments in some key states, including Gujarat.

For several years, I have studied the Gujarat violence, its basis and its aftermath, looking for implications for how we should view religious violence around the world. One obvious conclusion is that each case must be studied on its own merits, with close attention to specific historical and regional factors. The idea that all conflicts are explained by a simple hypothesis of the "clash of civilizations" proves utterly inadequate in Gujarat, where European ideas were borrowed to address a perceived humiliation and to create an ideology that has led to a great deal of violence against peaceful Muslims. Indeed, the "clash of civilizations" thesis is the best friend of the perpetrators because it shields them and their ideology from scrutiny. Repeatedly in interviews with leading members of the Hindu right, I was informed that no doubt, as an American, I was already on their side, knowing that Muslims cause trouble wherever they are.

What we see in Gujarat is not a simplistic, comforting thesis, but something more disturbing: the fact that in a thriving democracy, many individuals are unable to live with others who are different, on terms of mutual respect and amity. They seek total domination as the only road to security and pride. That is a phenomenon well known in democracies around the world, and it has nothing to do with an alleged Muslim monolith, and, really, very little to do with religion as such.

This case, then, informs us that we must look within, asking whether in our own society similar forces are at work, and, if so, how we may counteract them. Beyond that general insight, my study of the riots has suggested four very specific lessons.

**The rule of law:** One of the most appalling aspects of the events in Gujarat was the complicity of officers of the law. The police sat on their hands, the highest officials of state government egged on the killing, and the national government gave aid and comfort to the state government.

However, the institutional and legal structure of the Indian democracy ultimately proved robust, playing a key role in securing justice for the victims. The Supreme Court and the Election Commission of India played constructive roles in postponing new elections while Muslims were encouraged to return home, and in ordering changes of venue in key trials arising out of the violence. Above all, free national elections were held in 2004, and those elections, in which the participation of poor rural voters was decisive, delivered a strongly negative verdict on the policies of fear and hate, as well as on the BJP's economic policies. The current government, headed by Manmohan Singh a Sikh and India's first minority prime minister has announced a firm commitment to end sectarian violence and has done a great deal to focus attention on the unequal economic and political situation of Muslims in the nation, as well as appointing Muslims to key offices. On balance, then, the pluralistic democracy envisaged by Gandhi and Nehru seems to be winning, in part because the framers of the Indian state bequeathed to India a wise institutional and constitutional structure, and traditions of commitment to the key political values that structure embodies.

It should be mentioned that one of the key aspects of the founders' commitments, which so far has survived the Hindu-right challenge, is the general conception of the nation as a unity around political ideals and values, particularly the value of equal entitlement, rather than around ethnic or religious or linguistic identity. India, like the United States, but unlike most of the nations of Europe, has rejected such exclusionary ways of characterizing the nation, adopting in its Constitution, in public ceremonies, and in key public symbols the political conception of its unity. Political structure is not everything, but it can supply a great deal in times of stress.

**The news media and the role of intellectuals:** One of the heartening aspects of the Gujarat events was the performance of the national news media and of the community of intellectuals. Both print media and television kept up unceasing pressure to document and investigate events. At the same time, many scholars, lawyers, and leaders of nongovernmental organizations converged on Gujarat to take down the testimony of witnesses, help them file complaints, and prepare a public record that would stand up in court. The only reason I felt the need to write about these events further is that their analyses have, by and large, not reached the American audience.

We can see here documentation of something long ago observed by the Indian economist and philosopher Amartya Sen in the context of famines: the crucial role of a free press in supporting democratic institutions. (Sen pointed out that there has not been a famine in recent times in a nation where a free press brings essential information to the public; in China, by contrast, in the late 1950s and early 60s, famine was allowed to continue unabated, because news of what was happening in rural areas did not leak out.) And we can study here what a free press really means: I would argue that it requires a certain absence of top-down corporate control and an easy access to the major news media for intellectual voices from a wide range of backgrounds.

**Education and the importance of critical thinking and imagination:** So far I have mentioned factors that have helped the Indian democracy survive the threat of quasi-fascist takeover. But there are warning signs for the future. The public schools in Gujarat are famous for their complete lack of critical thinking, their exclusive emphasis on rote learning and the uncritical learning of marketable skills, and the elements of fascist propaganda that easily creep in when critical thinking is not cultivated. It is well known that Hitler is presented as a hero in history textbooks in the state, and nationwide public protest has not yet led to any change. To some extent, the rest of the nation is better off: National-level textbooks have been rewritten to take out the Hindu right's false ideological view of history and to substitute a more nuanced view. Nonetheless, the emphasis on rote learning and on regurgitation of facts for national examinations is distressing everywhere, and things are only becoming worse with the immense pressure to produce economically productive graduates.

The educational culture of India used to contain progressive voices, such as that of the great Tagore, who emphasized that all the skills in the world were useless, even baneful, if not wielded by a cultivated imagination and refined critical faculties. Such voices have now been silenced by the sheer demand for profitability in the global market. Parents want their children to learn marketable skills, and their great pride is the admission of a child to the Indian Institutes of Technology or the India Institutes of Management. They have contempt for the humanities and the arts. I fear for democracy down the road, when it is run, as it increasingly will be, by docile engineers in the Gujarat mold, unable to criticize the propaganda of politicians and unable to imagine the pain of another human being.

In the United States, by some estimates fully 40 percent of Indian-Americans hail from Gujarat, where a large proportion belong to the Swaminarayan sect of Hinduism, distinctive for its emphasis on uncritical obedience to the utterances of the current leader of the sect, whose title is Pramukh Swami Maharaj. On a visit to the elaborate multimillion-dollar Swaminarayan temple in Bartlett, Ill., I was given a tour by a young man recently arrived from Gujarat, who delighted in telling me the simplistic Hindu-right story of India's history, and who emphatically told me that whenever Pramukh Swami speaks, one is to regard it as the direct voice of God and obey without question. At that point, with a beatific smile, the young man pointed up to the elaborate marble ceiling and asked, "Do you know why this ceiling glows the way it does?" I said I didn't, and I confidently expected an explanation invoking the spiritual powers of Pramukh Swami. My guide smiled even more broadly. "Fiber-optic cables," he told me. "We are the first ones to put this technology into a temple." There you see what can easily wreck democracy: a combination of technological sophistication with utter docility. I fear that many democracies around the world, including our own, are going down that road, through a lack of emphasis on the humanities and arts and an unbalanced emphasis on profitable skills.

The creation of a liberal public culture: How did fascism take such hold in India? Hindu traditions emphasize tolerance and pluralism, and daily life tends to emphasize the ferment and vigor of difference, as people from so many ethnic, linguistic, and regional backgrounds encounter one another. But as I've noted, the traditions contain a wound, a locus of vulnerability, in the area of humiliated masculinity. For centuries, some Hindu males think, they were subordinated by a sequence of conquerors, and Hindus have come to identify the sexual playfulness and sensuousness of their traditions, scorned by the masters of the Raj, with their own weakness and subjection. So a repudiation of the sensuous and the cultivation of the masculine came to seem the best way out of subjection. One reason why the RSS attracts such a following is the widespread sense of masculine failure.

At the same time, the RSS filled a void, organizing at the grass-roots level with great discipline and selflessness. The RSS is not just about fascist ideology; it also provides needed social services, and it provides fun, luring boys in with the promise of a group life that has both more solidarity and more imagination than the tedious world of government schools.

So what is needed is some counterforce, which would supply a public culture of pluralism with equally efficient grass-roots organization, and a public culture of

masculinity that would contend against the appeal of the warlike and rapacious masculinity purveyed by the Hindu right. The "clash within" is not so much a clash between two groups in a nation that are different from birth; it is, at bottom, a clash within each person, in which the ability to live with others on terms of mutual respect and equality contends anxiously against the sense of being humiliated.

Gandhi understood that. He taught his followers that life's real struggle was a struggle within the self, against one's own need to dominate and one's fear of being vulnerable. He deliberately focused attention on sexuality as an arena in which domination plays itself out with pernicious effect, and he deliberately cultivated an androgynous maternal persona. More significantly still, he showed his followers that being a "real man" is not a matter of being aggressive and bashing others; it is a matter of controlling one's own instincts to aggression and standing up to provocation with only one's human dignity to defend oneself. I think that in some respects, he went off the tracks, in his suggestion that sexual relations are inherently scenes of domination and in his recommendation of asceticism as the only route to non-domination. Nonetheless, he saw the problem at its root, and he proposed a public culture that, while he lived, was sufficient to address it.

In a quite different way, Tagore also created a counter image of the Indian self, an image that was more sensuous, more joyful than that of Gandhi, but equally bent on renouncing the domination that Tagore saw as inherent in European traditions. In works such as Nationalism and The Religion of Man, Tagore described a type of joyful cosmopolitanism, underwritten by poetry and the arts, that he also made real in his pioneering progressive school in Santiniketan.

After Gandhi, however, that part of the pluralist program has languished. Though he much loved and admired both Gandhi and Tagore, Nehru had contempt for religion, and out of his contempt he neglected the cultivation of what the radical religions of both men had supplied: images of who we are as citizens, symbolic connections to the roots of human vulnerability and openness, and the creation of a grass-roots public culture around those symbols. Nehru was a great institution builder, but in thinking about the public culture of the new nation, his focus was always on economic, not cultural, issues. Because he firmly expected that raising the economic level of the poor would cause them to lose the need for religion and, in general, for emotional nourishment, he saw no need to provide a counterforce to the powerful emotional propaganda of the Hindu right.

Today's young people in India, therefore, tend to think of religion, and the creation of symbolic culture in general, as forces that are in their very nature fascist and reactionary because that is what they have seen in their experience. When one tells them the story of the American civil-rights movement, and the role of both liberal religion and powerful pluralist rhetoric in forging an anti-racist civic culture, they are quite surprised. Meanwhile, the RSS goes to work unopposed in every state and region, skill-fully plucking the strings of hate and fear. By now plural-ists generally realize that a mistake was made in leaving grass-roots organization to the right, but it is very difficult to jump-start a pluralist movement. The salient exception has been the women's movement, which has built at the grass roots very skillfully.

It is comforting for Americans to talk about a clash of civilizations. That thesis tells us that evil is outside, dis-tant, other, and that we are perfectly all right as we are. All we need do is to remain ourselves and fight the good fight. But the case of Gujarat shows us that the world is very different. The forces that assail democracy are inter-nal to many, if not most, democratic nations, and they are not foreign: They are our own ideas and voices, meaning the voices of aggressive European nationalism, refracted back against the original aggressor with the extra bile of resentment born of a long experience of domination and humiliation.

The implication is that all nations, Western and non-Western, need to examine themselves with the most fear-less exercise of critical capacities, looking for the roots of domination within and devising effective institutional and educational countermeasures. At a deeper level, the case of Gujarat shows us what Gandhi and Tagore, in their different ways, knew: that the real root of domination lies deep in the human personality. It would be so convenient if Americans were pure and free from flaw, but that fantasy is yet another form that the resourceful narcissism of the human personality takes on the way to bad behavior.

---

MARTHA C. NUSSBAUM is a professor in the philosophy department, law school, divinity school, and the college at the University of Chicago. Her most recent book on this subject is *The Clash Within: Democracy, Religious Violence, and India's Future* (Belknap Press of Harvard University Press, 2012).

# EXPLORING THE ISSUE

## Is India's Secular Democracy Severely Threatened by Religious Nationalism?

### Critical Thinking and Reflection

1. Briefly describe the incident at Ayodhya, in which 1,500 people were killed. What happened and why? Research and critically discuss.
2. What does Sharif Shuja mean by writing: "The BJP is a nationalist party which equates Indian national identity with Hindu religious identity"? Critically analyze and discuss the implications of this claim—for Hindus and for Muslims and other religious minorities.
3. Why is the claim that "the Aryans (and by implication their upper caste Hindu descendants) were the original Indians and that their Vedic culture was entirely indigenous to India" so inflammatory to non-Hindus? Critically discuss.
4. Martha Nussbaum rejects Samuel P. Huntington's "Clash of Civilizations" thesis—in this case, democratic Western values versus an aggressive Muslim minority. Where does she find the roots of the violent values of the Hindu right? Critically analyze and discuss both her claim and its implications for other cultures/nations.
5. Nussbaum sees India's experience with the religious right as a cautionary tale for all democracies: the lesson is that "the real root of domination lies deep in the human personality." Critically analyze and discuss the implications of this claim.
6. Based on your reading of this issue, what are the key threats to and the key safeguards of a secular democracy? Critically discuss.
7. What elements of Indian civil society does Nussbaum list that make her more optimistic about India's secular democracy surviving? Critically analyze and discuss this topic.

### Is There Common Ground?

Both selections admire India's secular democracy, and both see the religious right as a threat to it. Both are concerned about the rights of religious minorities in India. And, both find the incident at Ayodhya to be both disturbing in itself and emblematic of larger issues of concern. The difference lies in the degree of comfort they take from some of the responses to this incident. Shuja focuses on the threat, finding much to support his concerns about the future of India's secular democracy. Nussbaum is encouraged by the solidity of several elements in Indian civil society and, therefore, more optimistic about the future of India's secular democracy.

*Question:* Are there more reasons to be concerned or more reasons to feel hopeful about India's continuing commitment to a secular democracy?

### Additional Resources

It is useful to remember that Gandhi, a devout Hindu, was assassinated by a Hindu fanatic, who objected to Gandhi's nonviolence and tolerance of Muslims. As we have seen in this debate, tensions remain between those committed to the promise of pluralism and those who believe a powerful India must aggressively assert its own Hindu identity. Thomas Blom Hansen's *The Saffron Wave* (Princeton University Press, 1999) explores the lure of the Bharatiya Janata Party's harkening back to an "ancient" Hindu culture. The party's use of television, in the form of a1987 series *The Ramayana* to celebrate Lord Ram and embrace a former golden age, violated a longstanding taboo on religious partisanship. Arvind Rajagopal's *Politics after Television: Hindu Nationalism and the Reshaping of the Public in India* (Cambridge University Press, 2001) analyzes this phenomenon.

Modern India has many faces. For a broad survey of its postcolonial history, its opportunities and challenges, see *Reinventing India: Liberalization, Hindu Nationalism, and Popular Democracy* by Stuart Corbridge and John Harriss (Polity Press, Cambridge, 2000). The authors assert that the promise of modern India as a secular, federal, democratic Republic, committed to an ideology of development, has never been fully realized. The challenges of economic liberalization and Hindu nationalism, as well as those from India's "Backward Classes," have proved daunting. Yet, India is in the process of reinventing itself.

### Create Central

www.mhhe.com/createcentral

# *Internet Reference . . .*

### India—The Bharatiya Janata Party

This site is the homepage for the party of religious nationalism in India. It offers history, philosophy, press releases, and speeches.

**www.bjp.org/**

Selected, Edited, and with Issue Framing Material by:
Helen Buss Mitchell, *Howard Community College*
and
Joseph R. Mitchell, *Howard Community College*

# ISSUE

# Will the So-Called Arab Spring Benefit the Region?

**YES: Elias D. Mallon,** from "Will Democracy Bloom? A Closer Look at the Arab Spring," *America* (October 10, 2011)

**NO: Elliott Abrams,** from "Dictators Go, Monarchs Stay: American Policy Before and After the Arab Spring," *Commentary* (vol. 134, no. 3, October 2012)

---

## Learning Outcomes

**After reading this issue you should be able to:**

- Define and describe what is meant by the term "Arab Spring."
- Understand the pivotal (if unintended) role played by Muhammad Bouazzi.
- Understand the diversity within Islam.

---

### ISSUE SUMMARY

**YES:** Elias D. Mallon, education and interreligious affairs officer with the Catholic Near East Welfare Association in New York, takes a cautiously optimistic long-term view of the prospects, arguing for the establishment of some form of democracy in the region.

**NO:** Elliott Abrams, deputy national security advisor under the George W. Bush administration, takes a more pessimistic long-term view, citing the choice between monarchy and democracy that faces the region and the uncertainty of the outcome.

The so-called Arab Spring of 2011 caught and held the world's attention for months. What began as peaceful protests led in some cases to the toppling of strongmen who had ruled harshly for decades. Tunisia and Egypt, for example, are now in the process of negotiating a social contract between the state and its citizens. Other countries, particularly Libya and Syria, have seen far-bloodier revolutions. And, the prospect for stability in these nations remains much more in doubt.

Though the intention in all the cases of popular uprisings has been to create more open, pluralistic, democratic societies, special challenges exist in a region that has no recent experience with self-government. As in Europe several hundred years ago, there must be a negotiation between church and state. It took centuries for Europeans to carve out a secular society that could exist alongside the powerful Christian church. In the Middle East, there will have to be an accommodation between Islam and state constitutions. One key question is whether moderate Islamist parties will be able to keep in check the more radical groups, known as Salafists in Egypt.

Once a dictator has fallen, citizens will have to renegotiate a balance of power with whatever state they ultimately create. At least a moderate degree of social and economic stability would be a precondition for this to happen. And, in some parts of this region, the struggle for control of oil revenues is likely to play a significant role. Though oil offers the potential for funding a rebuilding and expansion of infrastructure, who controls and benefits from these resources is likely to remain a contentious question.

There is also much greater diversity in religion, culture, and language than might be immediately apparent. Islam, the dominant religion, is not a monolith. And, beyond the different "schools" within it, are the numerous religious minorities. Local languages can vary significantly, making even basic communication across regions problematic. And, cultural roots that lie very deep and are based in family, clan, and shared history, will have to be at least partially subsumed into some sense of national unity.

This issue offers us an opportunity to consider point of view. Since the "Arab Spring" is at the beginning of its evolution, we do not have the advantage enjoyed by historians who can look back over centuries in assessing how a situation was resolved. What observers several decades in the future might understand remains hidden from us. Given this reality, we must stand within a particular discipline and use its tools of analysis to help us understand what we are seeing.

If we undertake a purely political analysis, there might be considerable cause for optimism. Seemingly overnight, dictators have been toppled and in some cases killed. Armies have refused to fire on citizens; some soldiers have even joined the opposition. Has a spark been ignited that will spread throughout the region? On the other hand, if we take a historical view, there are many more cautions to consider. Though deposed and in prison, dictators such as Hosni Mubarak of Egypt continue to maintain that Arabs must be ruled; they are not capable of self-rule. If we look at the results of the first real democratic elections in Egypt, we find increasing power being assumed by the executive.

Another question is whether to take a short-term or long-term view. During the American Revolution or the Civil War, say, things looked very precarious for the fledgling democracy in the United States. In retrospect, we can see these struggles as, perhaps, a necessary part of our maturing process. The short-term view in the Middle East looks pretty uncertain. Today, it might be hard to imagine how the shattered economies in the region can restructure and the fledgling democracies accommodate diversity. It is much easier to hope that positive trends will continue if we permit ourselves to take a very long view.

The major thesis of Samuel P. Huntington's *The Clash of Civilizations and the Remaking of the World Order* (Simon & Shuster, 1996) is that attachment to religion, rather than to the nation state, predominates in "Islamic Culture," making this culture uniquely inhospitable to liberal ideas such as pluralism, individualism, and democracy. Those who subscribed to the Huntington thesis were stunned to see country after country—Tunisia, Egypt, Libya, Morocco, Oman, Bahrain, Yemen, and Syria—erupts into revolution and many thousands of people put their lives on the line for exactly these values. When the dust finally settles, it will be interesting to examine the world order that has been remade by the so-called Arab Spring.

In his anecdotal, "you are there" book, *Generation Freedom: The Middle East Uprisings and the Remaking of the Modern World* (HarperCollins, 2011), Bruce Feiler appears to be consciously evoking Huntington's provocative title. As the call to evening prayer sounded across central Cairo on the third Friday of the protests in Tahrir Square, Feiler recounts, Muslims unfolded newspapers to serve as makeshift prayer rugs. Suddenly, many Christians locked arms, forming a human chain around the Muslims to create a sacred space for them to pray. And, according to Feiler, not only had Muslims earlier done the same thing for a Christian mass in the same spot; Muslims and Christians together had also formed a human shield in front of Cairo's historic downtown synagogue. Will these early examples of interreligious cooperation survive the pressures of economic strain and state formation?

The YES and NO selections offer exactly these contrasts. In the YES selection from Elias D. Mallon, we see a cautious optimism that looks to history for encouraging precedents. And, the focus is political. The NO selection from Elliott Abrams finds in history equally compelling causes for concern.

# YES ↵

Elias D. Mallon

## Will Democracy Bloom? A Closer Look at the Arab Spring

On Dec. 17, 2010, a Tunisian street vendor named Mohamed Bouazizi set himself on fire to protest police harassment of his efforts to make a living on the street. His self-immolation set off a popular revolution that resulted in the overthrow of Zine el-Abidine Ben Ali, who had been president of that North African nation for 24 years, and then swept across the Arab world. Within weeks the revolution—named the Arab Spring by the media—spread to Egypt, Syria, Yemen, Libya and Bahrain.

The term Arab Spring, which tends to evoke romantic images of gentle weather, daffodils and new life, has proved misleading. The twin revolutions in Tunisia and Egypt were led by nonviolent activists who had been planning together for two years. But the resignations of Mr. Ben Ali of Tunisia on Jan. 14 and Hosni Mubarak of Egypt on Feb. 11 were anything but romantic, and what followed once the aspirations of others had been kindled turned far more violent.

The Arab Spring turned into a sizzling summer. The spectacular "democratic" successes in Tunisia and Egypt have not been replicated elsewhere in the Arab world. Even in Egypt some are beginning to question how successful their own democratic movement has been. Libya is still in turmoil, and Syria's government and military are brutally attacking nonviolent challenges to their authority. Neither Libya's Muammar el-Qaddafi nor Syria's Bashar al-Assad has followed the example of the Egyptian and Tunisian leaders who stepped down from office.

Three words associated with the Arab Spring are often used, but rarely analyzed: Arab, democracy and citizenship. Each is far more complex than common usage seems to recognize, and all three terms merit further consideration.

### Arab or Arabs?

Arabs are those people who speak the Arabic language. Some commentators would incorrectly add that Arabs are Muslims. In fact, while Arabic is spoken from Iraq to Morocco and while modern standard Arabic is the language of the media, the average Arabic speaker uses a local dialect of Arabic. Locals who live less than an hour's drive from one another often speak different dialects, many of which include words from older local languages, like Aramaic, Syriac and Berber.

As a result, native speakers often have difficulty understanding a local dialect other than their own.

Religiously, the Arabic-speaking world is also more diverse than many outsiders realize. While Islam is the religion of the vast majority of Arabic speakers, it is not monolithic. There are four different "schools" within Sunni Islam. And up to 15 percent of the Muslim world follows Shiite Islam, a minority whose adherents often face discrimination. In addition, large, significant groups of Alawites, Christians, Druze, Jews, Mandaeans and Yazidi live in Arabic-speaking countries. From a distance one might speak of an "Arabic culture, language and religion," but up close the reality is more complex.

The countries involved in the Arab Spring are diverse in size, population and ethnicity. The tiny Kingdom of Bahrain in the Persian Gulf is roughly four times the size of Washington, D.C. Its hereditary Sunni monarchy governs slightly more than one million subjects, 70 percent of whom are Shiite Muslims who experience disenfranchisement and discrimination. Libya, by contrast, which is roughly the size of Alaska, has a population of nearly six million people, 90 percent of whom live along its Mediterranean coast. Libya's population consists of Arabs and indigenous North African peoples: Berbers, black Africans and Mediterranean groups. Egypt is the most populous country in the Middle East. Roughly the size of Texas and New Mexico combined, its 80 million people include Arabs, Copts (who sometimes see themselves ethnically as Egyptians, as opposed to Arabs) and Nilotic peoples. While 90 percent Muslim, Egypt has a large, indigenous Christian population that comprises almost 10 percent of the population. Under tremendous pressure and often subject to violence, Coptic Christians nevertheless form a vibrant, educated community amid Egypt's Muslim majority.

While many countries in the Middle East have long and ancient histories, they are relative newcomers to the modern nation state. For hundreds of years many were provinces of the Turkish Ottoman Empire. Few, if any, existed in their present geographic form before the 20th century. Only after World War I did the victorious French and British divide the Ottoman Middle East into "spheres of influence," which resulted in the emergence of new countries on the Middle East map; the straight borders of many show the artificiality of what was done.

Mallon, Elias D. From *America*, vol. 205n no. 10, October 10, 2011, pp. 12. Copyright © 2011 by America Magazine. All rights reserved. Reprinted by permission of America Press. For subscription information, visit www.americamagazine.org

New countries with new names appeared, such as the Hashemite Kingdom of Jordan, while old regions with names like Syria and Lebanon were given new geographic boundaries. In Egypt, Iraq, Jordan, Syria and, to a lesser extent, Saudi Arabia, the colonial powers set up kingdoms. But between the two world wars, Iraqis and Syrians (and in the 1960s Egyptians and others) overthrew their kings and set up fragile democracies. Many forces worked against these new democracies, and most became authoritarian regimes. One sees a pattern of dictatorship: Hafez al-Assad of Syria held office for 30 years (1970–2000) until his death; Hosni Mubarak was president of Egypt for 30 years (1981–2011); Zine el-Abidine Ben Ali was president of Tunisia for 24 years (1987–2011); Muammar el-Qaddafi held office for 42 years (1969–2011); and Ali Abdullah Saleh has been president of Yemen for 33 years, since 1978.

It is important to note that all these regimes had very different political ideologies; that each leader held onto power for a very long time; and that neither in these countries nor in the region's monarchies (like Jordan, Saudi Arabia, Bahrain and the Gulf States) has there been an opportunity to develop functioning, democratic institutions. There is diversity in civic governance. In Kuwait, Bahrain and Saudi Arabia the parliaments or shura have at best advisory functions. In Bahrain the Shiite majority has little or no voice in the government and faces discrimination. Recently King Abdullah of Jordan granted the National Assembly (House of Nobles appointed by the king; House of Representatives elected popularly) greater voice in the government. While an improvement, Jordan still has an authoritarian government.

## Democracy or Democracies?

There is a great deal of talk about democratic movements. Democracy, however, is not a univocal term. While people who live in democracies tend to think their form of democracy is the best and only form, other forms of democracy do exist. Failure to recognize this fact could lead to considerable disappointment if democracies develop in the Middle East. The United States, Canada, the United Kingdom, France, Turkey and Israel all have democratic systems, but they differ significantly. The United States is a pluralistic democracy with separation of church and state. The United Kingdom is a constitutional monarchy with an established church. France is a secular democracy where religion is to play no role; laicisme is the term used to describe the secular character of France's political system. Turkey is also a secular democratic state, but it is not a pluralistic democracy. Israel is a democracy intimately linked with one religion, Judaism, and one ethnic group.

Two questions should be asked about the Arab Spring: Will democracies arise in the countries involved? And if so, what kind of democracies?

One strong bond links all the countries of the Arab Spring—Islam. A word of caution: though tiny Bahrain is mostly Shiite and the other countries are overwhelmingly Sunni, Sunni Islam is no more monolithic than Islam in general. In each of these countries Islam has distinct characteristics that have arisen from the local history and culture. This is to be expected. Roman Catholics in Ireland are different from Roman Catholics in the Philippines, though they are all Roman Catholics. The same situation exists in Islam. It is fairly safe to assume that however democracy develops as a result of the Arab Spring, Islam will play a significant role. It is unlikely that it will play the same role in each country. While extremist Muslim movements are often hostile to democracy, there is no indication that this disdain is shared by a majority of any population in the region. In fact, majorities in the countries of the Arab Spring indicate that they want some form of democracy.

## Islam and Democracy

Are Islam and democracy compatible? Remembering that Islam is not monolithic, it is important to note several things. Democracy does not arise fully developed overnight. Democracy in Western Europe took several centuries to develop in each country; and there were false starts, setbacks and detours. To expect the countries of the Arab Spring to be fully developed, problem-free democracies in five years [are] naive and unfair.

Democracy requires that the population understand the concept of citizenship and take part in it. Citizenship is a crucial element in civic and political development and serves as a barometer of how democracy is evolving. Equal citizenship has been part of the church's vision for the continuing Christian presence in the Middle East since the 1995 Synod for Lebanon. Citizenship was also mentioned often in the documents of the Catholic synod of bishops' Special Assembly for the Middle East, which took place last fall.

Citizenship as understood in modern democracies expresses a relationship of mutual rights and obligations that exist between an individual citizen and the state. That relationship is built not on religion, race, gender, wealth or education but on participation in public life. In contemporary democracies, citizenship has been separated from religious affiliation. One must not lose sight of the fact that the separation of citizenship and religious affiliation has been a long, painful process within most Western democracies.

While Islam has developed the concept of the dhimmi, the protected non-Muslim inhabitant of a state, there is no developed notion of the citizen (muwatin) in classical Islamic political thinking. Although belonging to a "protected minority," the dhimmi in no way enjoys the full rights and obligations of a citizen in a modern democracy. While it is extremely important that all citizens enjoy equal rights and obligations independent of race, gender or religion, it is naive to think that this can be achieved easily or quickly in most countries of the Arab Spring. At the same time, the rights of religious, ethnic or linguistic minorities and the rights of women will be an important gauge of how democracy is evolving.

## Religious Minorities, a Test Case

In recent times the situation of religious minorities, like Christians, Jews, Zoroastrians and Mandaeans, has become increasingly precarious in the Middle East. The increase in violence against Christians in Iraq and Egypt underlines an important issue. In a region where religion plays a major role in the public arena, the treatment of religious minorities provides a benchmark against which the rights of all citizens can be measured. Islam is no more or less compatible with democracy than is Christianity, Judaism or Buddhism. No major religion was founded at a time when democracies were functioning. And while religions have at times developed structures for consultation that have some democratic characteristics, these structures govern only the members of that particular religion.

Few religions ever had to deal with the religious "other" except as an object of proselytization, competition or scorn. No religious tradition on its own has ever developed a way of dealing with the other as equal. Yet that is precisely what citizenship entails: all citizens, regardless of religious affiliation, are equal before the law.

Christianity spent several centuries in conflict and reflection before it found a way of living in societies where members of other religious traditions were equal before the law. The Roman Catholic Church officially committed itself to freedom of religion in the "Declaration on Religious Freedom," approved at the Second Vatican Council on Dec. 7, 1965. It cannot be expected that Islam will reach that position overnight, although the community of nations must keep religious equality before emerging democracies as an important and achievable goal.

Modern Muslim thinkers have been reflecting upon and writing about the relationship of Islam to the modern state since the beginning of the 20th century. In 1925 Ali Abdel Raziq (d. 1966), an Egyptian legal scholar and Shariah judge, first explored the separation of religion and state in a book whose Arabic title can be translated "Islam and the Foundations of Government." The work was very controversial and not generally accepted, but it opened discussion of democratic government among Islamic scholars. More contemporary figures—for example, Mahmoud Muhammad Taha (executed for heresy by the Sudanese government in January 1985), his student Abdullahi Ahmed An-Na'im, the Iranian Shiite scholar Abdolkarim Soroush and others—form part of a growing list of Muslim scholars who are dealing with the challenges contemporary Muslims face as they attempt to develop democratic institutions and governments. The work of these scholars shows clearly that Islam is not inherently incompatible with modern democracy.

The journey toward democracy will be neither easy nor short. The emerging democracies of the Arab Spring need all the help and support they can get. Those who would help, however, must realize that democracy does not mean "just like us." Any attempt to help that lacks sensitivity to the historical, cultural and religious situation of each country is ultimately no help at all and could nip the Arab Spring in the bud.

---

**ELIAS D. MALLON**, of the Franciscan Friars of the Atonement, serves as education and interreligious affairs officer with the Catholic Near East Welfare Association in New York.

Elliott Abrams

 **NO**

# Dictators Go, Monarchs Stay: American Policy Before and After the Arab Spring

Some months after the invasion of Iraq and the toppling of Saddam Hussein, I sat at lunch with the aging Hosni Mubarak. He was then 76 years old and hard of hearing but soon to "run" for the presidency for a fifth time in 2005. The four times previous, there had been no election at all: Parliament chose him and the people expressed their approval (or in theory, their disapproval) in a referendum. In 2005, under American pressure for reform and a political opening, Mubarak changed the rules and allowed something that looked better to take place. Parliament played no role; he ran as the candidate of his National Democratic Party (NDP); and he allowed two people to run against him. A contested election!

To be sure, Mubarak won—with 88.6 percent of the vote. Of course, we will never know the actual percentages, nor the actual turnout. Later that year, in parliamentary elections, a bit of competition was also permitted. A few small parties won seats and the Muslim Brotherhood was permitted by the regime to capture 88 seats of the 454, while Mubarak's NDP claimed "only" 311.

And that was it. Three months later, the man who had been Mubarak's main opponent in the presidential election, Ayman Nour, was sentenced to five years in prison for his effrontery. In the next round of parliamentary elections, more than five years later, Mubarak made it clear he believed the tentative steps toward reform in 2005 had been a mistake. In 2010, the NDP claimed 420 seats and the Brotherhood was pushed down to 53. Understanding full well that the regime was turning back the clock, Egyptians did not go to the polls; turnout was estimated at around 10 percent. Thus ended a brief moment of reform in the Arab Republic of Egypt.

As history has shown, Mubarak's mistake was not the small steps toward reform in 2005; it was reversing them and then baldly stealing the 2010 election. Within two months, he was gone, and when he fell, I thought back to that lunch with him and the comments he made then about Iraq. The Iraq conflict was already quite bloody, with the quick overthrow of Saddam soon followed by civil war. Mubarak scoffed at the elections we in the Bush administration were planning for January 30, 2005. The Iraqis were incapable of democracy, he argued; you don't understand them like I do; they need a general to rule them.

Mubarak's formula for Iraq was his formula for Egypt. He believed, sincerely I think, that Arab societies would fracture into chaos and violence unless they were *ruled*. And when he looked at the Arab world in the decades after he became Egypt's ruler (upon Anwar Sadat's assassination in 1981), he saw a flat landscape: Every single country was *ruled*—by a general (except Muammar Qaddafi, a mere colonel), or a monarch, or a strongman such as Tunisia's Ben Ali.[1]

Today Mubarak sees a different landscape from his prison cell. Free elections have chosen new governments in Iraq, Tunisia, Egypt, and Libya. When it comes, the fall of the Assad regime in Syria will mean elections there, too. The fake republics of the Arab world are going or gone, except for Algeria—where the army rules behind the facade of a "civilian" president. The Algerian military elites are known as *lepouvoir,* the power, in a system that Mubarak would have viewed as perfectly appropriate. There are elections, but everyone understands they are not *sérieux.*

The "Arab Spring" of 2011 was a region-wide effort whose purpose was to make plain that such arrangements are *not* perfectly appropriate for Arabs, and to demand real elections and real democracy instead. The striking fact about Mubarak, Ben Ali, and Qaddafi is that they gave no ground at all to this argument, which seemed to them dangerous and preposterous. Theirs had been "the time of the despots—charisma quit the world of the Arabs," Fouad Ajami wrote. "They banished politics." And thus they were overthrown, as Assad will be.

The usual defense of these men, especially now that the results of the Arab Spring have proven so worrisome, is that they were right at bottom, and the attack on the U.S. embassy in Cairo and the murder of the American ambassador to Libya prove it. We will see chaos and violence and Islamist extremist regimes follow them for many years. Had the rulers permitted genuine reform, they would have let the same genie out of the bottle—and everywhere it seems the genie is a member of the Muslim Brotherhood.

There are two claims here: that slow reform was impossible, and that opening the political system up inevitably leads to Islamist rule. Both are wrong.

THE FUNDAMENTAL problem for the big men in those fake republics was the paucity of their legitimacy. They lacked any religious, monarchical, or democratic claim to rule. And their poor records of economic modernization provided no basis for the claim of "performance legitimacy" that has been asserted for those in power at various times in Chile, Singapore, or China. The rulers of the Arab republics survived solely by force. Every critical journalist or human-rights advocate or blogger or minor dissident politician became an enemy of the state.

Contrast their fates with that of the Arab world's eight monarchs, not one of whom has been swept away by the spreading revolts. Those eight countries differ in many ways but are alike in the essentials. The monarchy, derived from tribal leadership, often predates the state and its colonial borders. The al-Saud founded the first Saudi kingdom in 1744; the al-Sabah have ruled what is now Kuwait since 1718; the Alaoui dynasty has ruled Morocco since 1631, using the title "sultan" rather than "king" until 1957; the sultan of Oman is the 14th in his line, a band which began to rule parts of Oman even before the arrival of Islam. The historical connection to the precolonial past has granted the monarchs far more legitimacy than any claimed by self-appointed strongmen. What is more, the monarchy is often sustained by religious belief. The royal families of Jordan and Morocco are descendants of the Prophet. The king of Morocco is also called "Commander of the Faithful," and it is no accident that in Saudi Arabia the favored title for the ruler is not "king" but "Custodian of the Two Holy Mosques."

While sometimes the royal family monopolizes the affairs of state (Saudi Arabia, the United Arab Emirates), in several cases commoners hold all public offices from prime minister on down and monarchic rule is combined with electoral politics (Jordan, Morocco). Rarely is a monarchy so personalized a form of rule as that of Mubarak, Ben Ali, or Qaddafi. This means that the system is more supple. It allows for the give and take of nondemocratic politics (electoral, tribal, familial, regional), with shock absorbers built in and a certain amount of dissent permitted. Those civilian cabinet ministers are excellent targets for public criticism, and are dispensable. And finally, in the monarchies, succession is rarely a crisis: Son follows father or younger brother follows [elder], through a system legitimized by time. It is striking, by contrast, how much the struggle over whether Mubarak's son Gamal would succeed him or which of Qaddafi's sons would follow him contributed to unhappiness with the regime and to its ultimate instability and downfall.

The monarchies face enormous challenges as well, or at least those not favored by heaven with the combination of tiny populations and enormous oil and gas wealth (as is the case with the United Arab Emirates and Qatar). To get the balance right between royal prerogative and the rising expectations of subjects for a political role is not easy, as England's Charles I found out in 1649 and as France's Louis XVI did in 1793. After all, there was once a shah in Iran and there were kings in Iraq, Libya, and Egypt—all of whom lost their thrones to revolution. Still, the surviving monarchs appear to have more tools at their disposal today than the dictators had, to resist reform slyly or to guide it slowly and carefully.

The despots had and have a much more complex task: How does a wholly illegitimate ruler who holds power through force and fear begin a program of reform even if he is convinced he must? This proved to be a completely hypothetical question in the Arab case, since none of the men who have been overthrown ever saw reform as anything but a threat. Real elections, real political parties, real freedom to criticize the regime were dangerous foreign ideas at variance with Mubarak's "insight" that Arabs must be *ruled*. But it would have been possible had he been persuaded, as some of the men around him were, that reform was necessary. Saying "I stand for order, but things are opening up and will get better" could have been persuasive. I well remember a leading Egyptian liberal saying to me in 2003 that she did not favor free elections right then in Egypt; she favored them in a decade's time if she and others had those 10 years to organize freely. Mubarak could have permitted that. He did not, after all, crush the Muslim Brotherhood; in crafting those election results in 2005 and 2010, he permitted the Brothers to sit in parliament. The parties and people he crushed were the liberals, the Ayman Nours, while the Brotherhood thrived in the mosques.

Suppose Mubarak had, even as late as January 2011, announced that he would be 83 years old at the time of the forthcoming presidential elections and would not run. And suppose he had then added that the speculation about his sons' succeeding him was wrong: They would not run either and were withdrawing from politics. This would have allowed his party to choose a younger and more attractive candidate—someone like Ahmed Shafik, the retired Air Force commander who had served successfully as the minister of aviation and was a Mubarak protégé and confidant. When, under the worst possible circumstances, Shafik did run as the candidate of the old regime in the May 2012 elections, he won 48.27 percent of the vote. Under my hypothetical scenario, Shafik would surely have won a free election. That could have produced a smooth transition away from Mubarak, a precedent for free elections, and a government that was far more legitimate and that could undertake a slow and steady political opening. At the very last minute, such arguments were made to Mubarak, it is said, but it was too late.

Ben Ali, Assad, and Qaddafi also saw no need for reform, even if occasionally they saw the need to fool Westerners into thinking reform was just around the corner. For his part, Mubarak made little effort at fooling us, and I recall George W Bush's reaction when Mubarak would resist any discussion of political reform. He's just too old, Bush would say to his own staff later; he will not change and he will not allow change. But in point of fact, in countries as varied as Chile, Taiwan, and Spain, we have seen dictatorships ruled by old men that give way to or evolve into democratic systems without bloody revolutions. We may be seeing it now in Tunisia, where the regime was brought down almost without violence and democracy appears to have a fighting chance. We might even be seeing a version of it in Libya, where, after eight months of fighting, elections proved to be free and fair and were won by an alliance of moderate, secular parties. The murderous, possibly al-Qaeda-linked, attack on the American consulate in Benghazi may reflect al-Qaeda's continuing strength, but it tells us nothing about whether terrorism has popular support in Libya.

Don't these cases demonstrate that slow and peaceful reform would have been possible had it been allowed? Such change would have given reformers a fighting chance. After all, extremists and conspirators are often skilled at fighting tyrannies because, by definition, they work in the dark, in secret, in hiding; in the Arab world the mosque is their preferred hiding place and organizing tool. The ones who can't organize in that manner are the moderates, since their tools are open debate, a free press, and the ability to set up political parties. So if we see moderate and secular voices gaining ground among the populace even under the worst circumstances in Libya and Tunisia, where they are struggling against terrorist groups and against Islamists who emerge from the dictatorship well organized and with the patina of having fought the regime resolutely, it is reasonable to think they would have done even better in a fair match.

It may turn out that among the worst crimes of the old dictators was that they provided so many advantages to the Islamists in the struggle for power after the fall of the old regime.

**THE QUESTION** now is whether, using those advantages, Islamists will take power, retain power permanently, and produce ever more extreme Islamist republics. This is not inevitable, for the dictators left behind more than the Muslim Brotherhood; they also left behind a real thirst for legitimate, democratic rule. Decades of life in fake republics have produced a widespread desire among Arab populations to live in a real one.

Right now the Islamists are using the tools democracy provides, such as free elections, to take power when they can, but their commitment is to the words of the Prophet, not those of Locke or Jefferson. And so now Arab democrats find themselves understandably worried that the ballot box they sought for so long will become a one-way path to Islamist rule. Thus we may see the tragic irony of a Western-educated, wholly secular industrialist in Egypt reduced to hoping that his country's Army would crush and remove a recently elected Brotherhood government, while a radical Islamist will be singing the praises of free elections. Could the Islamists ditch democracy when they begin to lose popularity, as may well happen to them? Perhaps the Brothers will soon be quoting Turkey's popularly elected Islamist, Recep Tayyip Erdogan, who once said democracy is like a train: When you arrive at your station, you get off.

It won't be that easy. Democratic rules are too widely accepted in the region now to be so swiftly jettisoned. That is a problem for today's secularists in Tunisia and Egypt—but wait a few years and it will probably be a problem for the Islamists there. They have gained power through the ballot box and have no way to resist losing power in the same fashion—except to seize power as the despots did and lose their democratic legitimacy. As Olivier Roy, the French expert on Islam and politics, has written: "Experience has shown that in the Middle East, when people are offered the opportunity to take part in free elections, they show up . . . Islamist movements throughout the region are constrained to operate in a democratic arena that they did not create and that has legitimacy in the eyes of the people."

If majorities conclude that Islam is not the answer and that Islamist parties have no answer to poverty or unemployment, might the Islamists anticipate defeat and simply cancel the next election? That, too, is easier said than done. "To impose an Islamist form of authoritarianism, the Islamists would need either control of the police and army or their own paramilitary forces, none of which they have," Roy writes. "In Egypt and Tunisia, the army remains outside Islamist control (in Egypt, it may be outside anyone's control). Elections will really matter, and their results can be expected to swing back and forth for the next decade or more."

Is this excessive optimism? It may well be, for we saw in August how quickly Egypt's new president, Mohamed Morsi, moved to decapitate the army. Whether that institution, in Egypt or elsewhere, would defend new democratic rules, or new Islamist rulers, remains to be seen. Roy does quote what the speaker of the Egyptian parliament, a Muslim Brother, said in denying a Salafist demand to perform the call to prayer while parliament was in session: "We are all Muslims; if you want to pray, there is a mosque in parliament, but parliament is not a mosque." And Roy believes that once democracy takes hold in these countries, "religion will not dictate what politics should be but will itself be reduced to politics" because there will be "a reformulation of religion's place in the public sphere."

This may be correct, but there is another possibility. As we have seen from Moscow to Caracas, democracy's failure to deliver the benefits people expect can also lead to a desire to turn back the clock. What was once seen as intolerable repression can be transformed by nostalgia into a lost nirvana of law and order, and even comparative plenty, if the new regimes fail. There is an old precedent for this: It wasn't long after the Red Sea split that the Hebrew slaves complained to Moses, "Would to God we had died by the hand of the LORD in the land of Egypt, when we sat by the flesh pots, and when we did eat bread to the full." In the months since Hosni Mubarak was toppled, a million and a half new Egyptians have been born. Does the new Brotherhood government have a way to feed them, and provide jobs and food for their parents? Perhaps the failure of the new regime will lead to its replacement in the next free election, but other alternatives exist. A new strongman or junta may find a path to power if there is real chaos and economic collapse.

And even if this is avoided—if parties can alternate in power and the Islamists can be removed peacefully—the long-term danger is not eliminated. "The next decade or more" is Roy's timeline, and that is a very long time in politics. Even an Islamist regime that is defeated can, in 5 or 10 years of holding power, do enormous damage. Egypt's Muslim Brotherhood government may raise the status of Hamas and lower that of the Palestinian Authority; preside over an exodus of Copts and Christians more generally; or refuse to take the persistent counter-terror actions that are needed to fight jihadis in the Sinai and thereby avoid confrontations with Israel over terrorist attacks on Eilat. If such a government came to power in Syria, it might be good news for Sunnis in Lebanon but a disastrous development for the king of Jordan and his efforts to prevent the Brotherhood from increasing its power in his country. It is easier for us in the West to be long-term optimists than it is for Israelis, Jordanians, Middle Eastern Christians, and others to whom Brotherhood rule is a nearby and near-term threat.

But Roy's comments provide hints at a strategy for those of us who are democrats and *not* Islamists, as do the writings of our own expert on the region, Fouad Ajami. In August Ajami admitted that skeptics see the Islamists as "opportunists who hijacked the democratic process." Yet, he asked, "what choice do we have but to accept the democratic claims of these new Islamists? . . . We have to grant them time." They may get that "next decade or more" to perform, moderate, or fail—but meanwhile we have a role to play.

The first responsibility is to become far more vocal defenders of the democratic process than we were when the strongmen held sway. Then, we issued the occasional statement of distaste; now, we should state very clearly what our standards are and strongly denounce deviations from democratic norms. We should tie our foreign aid to performance—and not only to periodic free elections, but to respect for freedom of speech and press and assembly, protection of the rights of minorities and women, the rule of law—and of course protection of our embassy from further attacks. We should give plenty of useful aid and comfort to the moderate parties seeking to resist Islamist gains—money, training, and most of all any political solidarity they believe will be useful.

If this seems obvious, it is not so to the government of the United States. When Secretary of State Hillary Clinton traveled to Cairo in July, prominent Copts refused to meet with her as a protest for what they view as American favoritism for the Brotherhood and our slighting of liberal and secular groups. Visiting Cairo at the end of July, Secretary of Defense Leon Panetta said, "I was convinced that President Morsi is his own man, and that he is the president of all the Egyptian people," adding that Morsi "is truly committed to implementing democratic reforms." Already in August, Morsi's moves against press freedom in Egypt were eliciting protests from Egyptian journalists and human-rights groups—but near silence from Washington.

Given Morsi's past—a lifetime as a Brotherhood apparatchik and in recent years a member of its Guidance Bureau, and a happy participant in Brotherhood election rallies that included extremist leaders shouting extremist slogans—one may wonder why Panetta was "convinced" so easily. Certainly Egyptian Copts and liberals will wonder, and will wonder if the United States is about to make the kind of pact with the devil we made with Mubarak: Look out for certain interests of ours, stay within certain red lines, and we'll pretty much ignore the domestic situation and the fate of democracy and human rights.

That would be a historic mistake. Recall again that General Shafik won nearly half the vote in Egypt's presidential election, and that the moderate, secularist coalition won a majority in Libya. In Jordan and Morocco, Islamists may win elections, but their ambitions are held in check not only by some opposition within the public but also by the monarchy itself. Each case is different (as Syria's will be), but the pattern suggests that the Brothers are not the automatic and inevitable winners, or at least not the permanent winners. The struggle will last decades.

To say that we should play no role because this is a struggle among Arabs or Muslims would not be "leading from behind" but abandoning the fight. To begin with, there are everywhere non-Muslim and non-Arab minorities who clamor for our—Western and especially American—assistance and protection. Why adopt the policy that we have no role when Muslim and Arab moderates, liberals, and secularists are wrestling with Islamists? When European moderates and liberals were fighting for power against Communist parties, the fact that we ourselves were not European did not make us believe that we had no role. We have interests and principles at stake, and should defend them. And when people who share those principles and whose victories advance our interests seek our help, it is not rueful wisdom that suggests we adopt a position of neutrality in their struggle and a lack of interest in their fate. It is a new version of the belief that American "intervention" in the world is illegitimate, immoral, and likely to be disastrous.

The Middle East's "big men" are nearly gone now: dead, in prison or in exile, or tottering. And while the old dictators claimed to be great bulwarks against the Islamists, when they fell they left behind only one well-organized political force—the very Islamists they claimed to fear most. They wasted decades that were marked by corruption and theft, repression and brutality. With their passing, there are for the moment only two forms of government in the Arab world, monarchies and democracies—each system with a claim to be legitimate, each now to struggle in its own unique way with the political, social, and economic challenges the region faces. Now their countries must discover if indeed, as Mubarak believed, Arabs must be ruled, or can rule themselves.

## Note

1. Lebanon had an elected government, to be sure, but from 1976 to 2005 that government was a cosmetic pretense behind which Syria

occupied and ruled the country. And for most Arabs, Lebanon has always been an anomaly, with its cosmopolitan capital, French cuisine, and significant Catholic presence.

**ELLIOTT ABRAMS** was a deputy national-security adviser in the administration of George W. Bush, where he led the National Security Council's Middle East and democracy directorates.

# EXPLORING THE ISSUE

## Will the So-Called Arab Spring Benefit the Region?

### Critical Thinking and Reflection

1. What is the basis for Elias Mallon's long-term optimism? Critically analyze and discuss.
2. What is the basis for Elliott Abrams's greater concern and caution? Critically analyze and discuss.
3. What does Mallon mean by writing: "Two questions should be asked about the Arab Spring: Will democracies arise in the countries involved? And, if so, what kind of democracies?" Review Mallon's examples of various forms of democracy; then, critically analyze and discuss this statement.
4. Based on your reading, are Islam and democracy compatible? Research, analyze, and critically discuss.
5. Why will treatment of religious minorities represent a "test case"? Analyze and critically discuss.
6. What roles might Islamists, the army, and journalism play in the fate of the "Arab Spring"? Explain, analyze, and critically discuss.
7. Why does Eliot Abrams say that, based on Egypt's President Morsi's early decisions, "Egypt's Copts and liberals will wonder if the United States is about to make the same pact with the devil we made with Mubarak"? Critically analyze and discuss.

### Is There Common Ground?

We are looking at a recent phenomenon from two different points of view—one primarily political and the other primarily historical. In addition, the selections each invite us to take both long-term and short-term views. This gives us an excellent opportunity to notice how differently things can look, depending on the academic discipline used for analysis and on the length of time we are considering. Unlike many of the issues you have been exploring, this one does not offer us the benefit of distance from the events in question. They are unfolding in newspaper headlines and extended commentary. This is what history looks like while it is still evolving. People who lived during the Renaissance probably had no idea they were living during a pivotal period in world history.

*Question:* During this "messy" period of uncertainty, would you be more likely to take a cautiously optimistic or a guardedly pessimistic view? On what basis?

### Create Central

www.mhhe.com/createcentral

### Additional Resources

For a careful look at the conditions necessary for creating political order, see Francis Fukuyama's *The Origins of Political Order: from Pre-human Times to the French Revolution* (Farrar, Straus and Giroux, 2011). The three conditions he deems essential are: a stable state, a stable society, and the rule of law that holds the sovereign accountable. Each of the countries in this region must create institutions for itself—hopefully in years rather than the centuries required when Europe underwent state formation several centuries ago. When the power of a police state to enforce the will of the strongman disappears, who or what will take its place is an open question.

Robin Wright, a foreign correspondent in the region for four decades, has written one of the most hopeful of the recent books to tackle the unprecedented convulsions in the Middle East, *Rock the Casbah: Rage and Rebellion Across the Islamic World* (Simon & Schuster, 2011). Underpinning and accompanying the revolts, Wright finds a counter-jihad unfolding in the Islamic bloc of 57 countries, as well as "among Muslim minorities worldwide." This includes the rejection of both violence itself and the principle of violence to achieve political goals. Wright's greatest strength is in taking us deep into daily life where, she claims, the culture of change "resonates in comedians' jokes and sermons from young satellite sheiks, in playwrights' plots and poetry contests, in underground music clubs and women's self-empowerment sessions, in new comic book superheroes and hip-hop songs."

# *Internet Reference . . .*

### Arab Spring: An Interactive Timeline of Middle East Protests

In December 2010, a man in Tunisia burned himself to death in protest at his treatment by police. What followed was an extraordinary year as pro-democracy rebellions erupted across the Middle East. This interactive timeline traces key events.

**www.guardian.co.uk/world/interactive/2011/mar/22/
middle-east-protest-interactive-timeline**